Praise for *Advanced .NET Debugging*

"While the .NET environment provides a developer with a powerful toolbox to accomplish their goals, it can often be a daunting task to debug some of the issues that inevitably crop up during software development. This book provides the crucial details about how the CLR works internally, which you need to know to diagnose many classes of bugs in your .NET programs, and it provides clear examples of how to solve the same types of issues we see our customers struggle with on a daily basis. This book is required reading for all serious .NET developers."

—Lee Culver, CLR Quick Response Team, Microsoft Corporation

"Have you ever wondered why your .NET application is not responding? Or why it's intermittently consuming high CPU? Or crashing? When things go wrong you need to think low level, using the proper knowledge and tools to investigate the internals of your application. *Advanced .NET Debugging* delivers the knowledge necessary to quickly isolate nasty software problems. Welcome to the debugging world!"

—Roberto A. Farah, Senior Premier Field Engineer, Microsoft Corporation

"Mario Hewardt's *Advanced .NET Debugging* is an excellent resource for both beginner and experienced developers working with .NET. The book is also packed with many debugging tips and discussions of CLR internals that will benefit developers architecting software. I highly recommend Mario's book."

—Jeffrey Richter, consultant, trainer, and author at Wintellect

"Mario has done it again. His *Advanced Windows Debugging* (coauthored with Daniel Pravat) is an invaluable resource for native code debugging, and *Advanced .NET Debugging* achieves the same quality, clarity and breadth to make it just as invaluable for .NET debugging. The detail he provides on how to measure managed heap usage, understand the behavior of the garbage collector, and how to track down synchronization bugs will make you more efficient at finding and fixing bugs in your managed code projects."

—Mark Russinovich, Technical Fellow, Microsoft Corporation

"This book talks about tools such as SOS in the kind of depth that I have not seen elsewhere. It's a definite aid in understanding and debugging managed application behavior."

—Maoni Stephens, GC Developer, Microsoft Corporation

"*Advanced .NET Debugging* is essential reading for someone who wants to get under the covers and obtain an intimate understanding of how the .NET Common Language Runtime works. It clearly identifies the layout of the system and how the assemblies are loaded and organized. I recommend it to anyone who wants to debug more complex issues brought on by synchronization problems and corruption. It also effectively addresses the difficult task of postmortem debugging."

—Pat Styles, Microsoft Corporation

ADVANCED .NET DEBUGGING

The Addison-Wesley
Microsoft Technology Series

✦ Addison-Wesley

Visit **informit.com/mstechseries** for a complete list of available publications.

Books in the **Addison-Wesley Microsoft Technology Series** address the latest Microsoft technologies used by developers, IT professionals, managers, and architects. Titles in this series cover a broad range of topics, from programming languages to servers to advanced developer techniques. The books are written by thought leaders and experts in their respective communities, including many MVPs and RDs. The format of this series was created with ease-of-use in mind, incorporating features that make finding topics simple; visually friendly charts and fonts; and thorough and intuitive indexes.

With trusted authors, rigorous technical reviews, authoritative coverage, and independent viewpoints, the Microsoft Community can rely on Addison-Wesley to deliver the highest quality technical information.

ADVANCED .NET DEBUGGING

Mario Hewardt

✦ Addison-Wesley

Upper Saddle River, NJ • Boston • Indianapolis • San Francisco
New York • Toronto • Montreal • London • Munich • Paris • Madrid
Capetown • Sydney • Tokyo • Singapore • Mexico City

Many of the designations used by manufacturers and sellers to distinguish their products are claimed as trademarks. Where those designations appear in this book, and the publisher was aware of a trademark claim, the designations have been printed with initial capital letters or in all capitals.

The author and publisher have taken care in the preparation of this book, but make no expressed or implied warranty of any kind and assume no responsibility for errors or omissions. No liability is assumed for incidental or consequential damages in connection with or arising out of the use of the information or programs contained herein.

The publisher offers excellent discounts on this book when ordered in quantity for bulk purchases or special sales, which may include electronic versions and/or custom covers and content particular to your business, training goals, marketing focus, and branding interests. For more information, please contact:

U.S. Corporate and Government Sales
(800) 382-3419
corpsales@pearsontechgroup.com

For sales outside the United States, please contact:

International Sales
international@pearson.com

Visit us on the Web: informit.com/aw

Library of Congress Cataloging-in-Publication Data
Hewardt, Mario.
  Advanced .NET debugging / Mario Hewardt.
      p.   cm.
  Includes index.
  ISBN 978-0-321-57889-1 (pbk. : alk. paper) 1. Microsoft .NET. 2. Debugging in computer science.
  I. Title.

  QA76.76.M52H495 2010
  004.2'4—dc22

                                                                  2009035081

ISBN-13: 978-0-321-57889-1
ISBN-10:   0-321-57889-9

Text printed in the United States on recycled paper at RR Donnelley in Crawfordsville, Indiana.
Second printing, March 2011

To my loving wife, Pia, and beautiful baby girl, Gemma.

CONTENTS

LIST OF CODE LISTINGS

FOREWORD

Last year, we celebrated the ten-year anniversary of the CLR group at Microsoft. The purpose of the CLR was to provide a safe and robust environment that also enabled great productivity for developers. Today, the CLR is used in a very wide range of scenarios from big server applications that have extremely high requirements of performance and scalability, to desktop applications for daily uses. The popularity of the CLR also poses challenges for people who build and support software on top of it because their products might have to handle running on very different machine configurations and networks, not to mention the fact that people build much more powerful, more sophisticated software as hardware progresses at a fast speed. All this means that when something is not working as expected, and you are the one responsible for investigating and fixing the problem, knowledge and tools to help you do that efficiently are invaluable.

To allow for increased productivity, the CLR takes over many mechanisms on behalf of developers so they can focus on building their domain logic instead. It is crucial to know some essential concepts that will best help you in analyzing problems with your applications without spending a lot of time understanding all of the CLR internal details. However, it's not an easy task to know what these essential concepts are. Many people acquire this knowledge by trial and error, which is time-consuming and presents the risk of getting inaccurate answers.

Fortunately, Mario's book combines just the right amount of explanation of the runtime to help you understand his thought process and the techniques he uses to solve problems with many practical and clever tricks learned from debugging real-world applications. So if you want to quickly get up to speed debugging your CLR applications, this is definitely the book to read. It covers many aspects of debugging managed applications—in particular, it provides insights into areas that are hard to diagnose, such as thread synchronization problems. The illustration of debugging techniques is largely done with examples, which makes it easy to follow.

One of the debugging tools this book primarily focuses on is the SOS debugger extension, which was written and is maintained by the CLR group. We update SOS with each of our releases to make it more extensive and to give you a deeper look at the new features. It is a powerful tool for finding out what's going on in a managed process. Much of what it can do for you is not obtainable via other debugging tools. For example, you can find out what root is keeping an object on the managed heap live, which is a common issue for managed application developers to address. When you familiarize yourself with this tool, you will find that you have a much better picture of how your application is working. I have yet to see another book that describes it in nearly as much detail as this book does.

With the knowledge from this book, you will be able to get to root causes of issues with much less time and effort. I hope you'll have as much fun reading this book as I did when I was reviewing the manuscript.

Patrick Dussud
Technical Fellow, CLR, .NET FX
Microsoft Corporation

PREFACE

Since the release of *Advanced Windows Debugging* at the end of 2007, I have received many requests regarding an equivalent book focused on .NET. The initial outline for *Advanced Windows Debugging* did contain a chapter on .NET debugging, but that chapter was eventually cut—primarily due to my conviction that spending just one chapter on it was not sufficient coverage and would confuse rather than enlighten readers. Since then, .NET has become a very popular platform choice for developers. Some statistics seem to show that the usage of C# is almost at the same levels as traditional C++. Knowing how to properly navigate some of the challenges involved with .NET development is a key factor in achieving success.

Why is a book on .NET debugging using debuggers such as WinDbg, NTSD, and CDB needed? There are obviously other debuggers available (some more user friendly than others). Although using the native debuggers may seem daunting at first, they pack such an incredible amount of firepower that, when fully realized, they make finding the root cause of the nastiest bugs a less time-consuming task. That is the case partly because when using the native debuggers it's much easier to glean critical internal information about the CLR (the .NET runtime) itself and hence use that information to troubleshoot problems. Examples of such detailed information are the garbage collector, interoperability layer, synchronization primitives, and so on. Not only is this information critical in a lot of debugging scenarios, but it is also quite educational as it provides a deeper look into how the runtime is designed. Finally, there are times (more and more in today's "connected" solutions) when utilizing a ZERO footprint debugger is required. The "friendlier" debuggers typically force an explicit and local install step, which copies the required binaries onto the target machine, stores configuration in various places on the system, and so on. On a live machine where configuration changes are prohibited (such as on a customer or data center machine), the only viable option is to use the native debuggers since no configuration changes are required.

The book you are holding serves to address the gap in the debugging literature and focuses on teaching the power of the native debuggers within the context of the CLR. The book takes a very focused and pragmatic approach and utilizes real-world examples of debugging scenarios to ensure that you get not only an academic understanding but also a complete practical experience. I hope you will enjoy reading this book as much as I enjoyed writing it.

Who Should Read This Book?

Knowing which tools to use during root cause analysis and how to approach different categories of problems can make the difference between shipping a high quality product versus a product that will cost a lot of money to support. Even when every effort has been put into making a product bug free, issues surface on customer machines, and knowing how to troubleshoot a problem in that scenario is key to avoiding customer headaches and downtime. It is the responsibility of *all* software engineers to understand which tools to utilize in order to do root cause analysis in different environments. If you master the art of debugging, the quality of your product will dramatically increase and your reputation for producing quality and reliable software will increase.

Software Developers

Far too often, I see developers struggle with really tough bugs and end up spending several days (sometimes weeks) trying to narrow down the problem and arrive at the root cause. In many of these situations, I ask the developers which tools they used to figure it out. The answer always comes back the same: code reviews and tracing, followed by further code reviews and further tracing. Although code reviews and, more specifically, tracing are important aspects of troubleshooting a bug, they can also be very costly. Let's face it; if we could trace absolutely everything we needed to solve any given problem in our code, there would not be a need for debuggers. The simple truth is that there are scenarios where tracing isn't sufficient and attaching a debugger to a misbehaving process is crucial. Many times after explaining that tool X would have cut down on the time it took to troubleshoot a particular problem, developers are simply amazed that such a tool exists.

This book targets those developers who are tasked with developing code on the .NET platform and resolving complex code issues. Gaining a solid understanding of the tool set available to help developers troubleshoot complex and costly problems is imperative to the success of a product. Knowing which tools to use and which instrumentation to enable throughout the development process is key to achieving success.

Quality Assurance

The quality assurance (QA) job is that of finding problems in code that developers produce. Elaborate test plans and fully automated testing procedures allow QA engineers to, in a very efficient manner, test components inside and out. Much in the same way that it is critical for developers to know about the tools and instrumentation available, so it is for QA engineers. During their testing they may encounter any given problem, and having the right tools available and enabled during testing helps them, as well as the developer, to resolve the problem in a time-efficient manner. Without the right tool set in place while running tests, you may end up having to restart the test (with the tool turned on) only to realize that it is not a systematically reproducible problem. The debuggers and tools examined in this book will make QA engineers more efficient and also help the overall product team achieve faster results.

Product Support Engineers

Product support engineers face very similar challenges as those faced by developers and QA engineers. The key difference is the environment under which they operate. Not only are they faced with resolving customer issues, but they often have to deal with code from multiple sources (i.e., not just product-specific code). Additionally, product support engineers typically work with static snapshots of processes and can't rely on a live process to debug, making it even harder to troubleshoot. Under these conditions, knowing how to utilize the debuggers and associated tools can mean the difference between going back and forth with the customer a number of times (often a costly and frustrating proposition) and being able to resolve the problem right away.

Operations Engineers

As more and more software offerings are moving into the cloud (service-based offerings), more and more code is run in dedicated data centers rather than on customer machines. The group of engineers that makes sure that the services are up and running and in pristine shape are the operations engineers. One of the key challenges for the operations engineers is to resolve all problems that cause the service to run suboptimally. Quite often, this means solving the problem as quickly as possible. If a particular problem cannot be solved by the operations team, the product team gets involved, a process that can be time-consuming since it can involve going back and forth, giving the operations team directions on how to troubleshoot the problem. By utilizing the correct set of tools, the operations team can solve a lot of the problems encountered without escalating the issue to the product team, thereby saving both parties time; and most importantly, the customer will see less downtime.

Prerequisites

Although this book teaches you how to use the native debuggers, the focus is primarily on how to debug .NET code and not on the basic operations of the native debuggers. Topics such as how to attach the debugger to the target process, setting up symbol paths, setting break points, and so on are covered briefly in Chapter 3, "Basic Debugging Tasks," but in-depth details are not covered. Further details on the native debuggers and how they relate to native code debugging can be found in my previous book, written with Daniel Pravat, *Advanced Windows Debugging* (Boston, MA: Addison-Wesley, 2007).

A solid understanding of C# is required as all sample code is written in that language. An excellent book on C# is Mark Michaelis' *Essential C# 3.0* (Boston, MA: Addison-Wesley, 2009), and there is a new edition planned, *Essential C# 4.0*, for publication in January 2010.

Although C# is a prerequisite, intimate knowledge of the CLR is not. This book doesn't just cover how to debug .NET applications. It also gives in-depth explanations of a lot of the core pieces of the .NET platform, a crucial foundation for successful debugging.

Organization

At a high level, this book is organized into three parts: Part I, "Overview," Part II, "Applied Debugging," and Part III, "Advanced Topics." Each of these parts is defined a bit in this section, as are the chapters that make them up.

Part I—Overview

Part I consists of a set of chapters that guides the reader through the basics of .NET debugging using the native debuggers. Topics such as all the tools that are required, introduction to MSIL, basic debugging tasks, and so on are fully examined and illustrated. If you are familiarizing yourself with the debuggers for the first time, I recommend reading these chapters in sequence.

Chapter 1—Introduction to the Tools

Chapter 1 provides a brief introduction to the tools used throughout the book, including basic usage scenarios, download locations, and installation instructions. Among the tools covered are: Debugger Tools for Windows, SOS, SOSEX, CLR Profiler, and more.

Chapter 2—CLR Fundamentals

This chapter discusses the core fundamentals of the .NET runtime. The chapter begins with a high-level overview of the major runtime components and subsequently drills down into the details and covers topics such as assembly loading, runtime metadata, and much more. The native debuggers and tools will be used to illustrate the internal workings of the runtime.

Chapter 3—Basic Debugging Tasks

This chapter introduces the reader to performing the most common debugging tasks when debugging .NET applications using the native debuggers. Tasks related to examining thread-specific data, the garbage collector heap, the .NET exceptions, the basics of postmortem debugging, and much more are covered.

Part II—Applied Debugging

Part II constitutes the meat of the material and examines core CLR components and how to troubleshoot common problems related to those components. Each chapter begins with an overview of the component, utilizing the debuggers to illustrate key concepts. Following the overview is a set of real-world examples of common programming mistakes utilizing that component. The thought process behind tackling these bugs together with illustrative debug sessions is fully shown. The chapters in Part II can be read in any order as they focus on component-specific problems commonly encountered.

Chapter 4—Assembly Loader

The complexity of .NET applications can range from simple command-line applications to complex multiprocess/multimachine server applications with a large number of assemblies living in harmony. To efficiently debug problems in .NET applications, you must be careful to understand the dependencies of .NET assemblies. This chapter takes a look at how the CLR assembly loader does its work and the common problems surrounding that area.

Chapter 5—Managed Heap and Garbage Collection

Although .NET developers can enjoy the luxury of automatic memory management, care must still be taken to avoid costly mistakes. The highly sophisticated CLR garbage collector is an automatic memory manager that enables developers to focus less on memory management and more on application logic. Even though the CLR manages memory for the developer, care must be taken to avoid pitfalls that can wreak havoc in your applications. In this chapter, we look at how the garbage collector works, how to peek into the internals of the garbage collector, and some common programming mistakes related to automatic garbage collection.

Chapter 6—Synchronization

A multithreaded environment enables a great deal of flexibility and efficiency. With this flexibility comes a lot of complexity in the form of thread management. To avoid costly mistakes in your application, care must be taken to ensure that threads perform their work in an orchestrated fashion. This chapter introduces the synchronization primitives available in .NET and discusses how the debuggers and tools can be used to debug common thread synchronization problems. Scenarios such as deadlocks and thread pool problems are discussed.

Chapter 7—Interoperability

.NET relies heavily on underlying Windows components. To invoke the native Windows components, the CLR exposes two primary methods of interoperability:

- Platform invocation
- COM interoperability

Because the .NET and Win32 programming models are often very different, idiosyncrasies often lead to hard-to-track-down problems. In this chapter, we look at some very common mistakes made when working in the Interoperability layer and how to use the debuggers and tools to troubleshoot the problems.

Part III—Advanced Topics

Part III covers topics such as postmortem debugging, power tools, and new and upcoming .NET enhancements.

Chapter 8—Postmortem Debugging

Quite often, it's not feasible to expect full access to a failing machine so that a problem can be debugged. Bugs that surface on production machines on customer sites are rarely available for debugging. This chapter outlines the mechanisms for debugging a problem without access to the physical machine. Topics discussed include the basics of crash dumps, generating crash dumps, analyzing crash dumps, and so on.

Chapter 9—Power Tools

In addition to the "standard" tools available during .NET debugging, there are several other incredibly powerful tools available. This chapter introduces the reader to these power tools such as PowerDBG (debugging via Powershell) and others.

Chapter 10—CLR 4.0

With the imminent release of CLR 4.0, this chapter takes an abbreviated tour of the CLR 4.0 enhancements. The chapter is structured so that each topic in previous chapters of the book is covered from a CLR 4.0 perspective.

Conventions

Code, command-line activity, and syntax descriptions appear in the book in a monospaced font. Many of the examples and walkthroughs in this book show a great deal of what is known as "debug spew." Debug spew simply refers to the output that the debugger displays as a result of some action that the user takes. Typically, this debug spew consists of information shown in a very compact and concise form. To effectively reference bits and pieces of this data and make it easy for you to follow, the boldface and italic types are used. Additionally, anything with the boldface type in the debug spew indicates commands that you will be entering. The following example illustrates the mechanism.

```
0:000> ~*kb
.  0  Id: 924.a18 Suspend: 1 Teb: 7ffdf000 Unfrozen
ChildEBP RetAddr  Args to Child
0007fb1c 7c93edc0 7ffdf000 7ffd4000 00000000 ntdll!DbgBreakPoint
0007fc94 7c921639 0007fd30 7c900000 0007fce0 ntdll!LdrpInitializeProcess+0xffa
0007fd1c 7c90eac7 0007fd30 7c900000 00000000 ntdll!_LdrpInitialize+0x183
00000000 00000000 00000000 00000000 00000000 ntdll!KiUserApcDispatcher+0x7
0:000> dd 0007fd30
0007fd30  00010017 00000000 00000000 00000000
0007fd40  00000000 00000000 00000000 ffffffff
0007fd50  ffffffff f735533e f7368528 ffffffff
0007fd60  f73754c8 804eddf9 8674f020 85252550
0007fd70  86770f38 f73f4459 b2f3fad0 804eddf9
0007fd80  b30dccd1 852526bc b30e81c1 855be944
0007fd90  85252560 85668400 85116538 852526bc
0007fda0  852526bc 00000000 00000000 00000000
```

In this example, you are expected to type in ~***kb** in the debug session. The result of entering that command shows several lines with the most critical piece of information being *0007fd30*. Next, you should enter the *dd 0007fd30* command illustrated to glean more information about the previously highlighted number *0007fd30*.

All tools used in this book are assumed to be launched from their installation folder. For example, if the Windows debuggers are installed in the *C:\Program Files\Debugging Tools for Windows* folder, the command line for launching windbg.exe will be shown as follows:

```
C:\>windbg
```

Required Tools

All of the tools utilized in this book are available for download free of charge. Chapter 1 outlines the tools used in the book and where to download them from.

Sample Code

The most efficient way to demonstrate how to debug problematic .NET code is to use real-world examples. Unfortunately, including full-blown, real-world examples in a book format is unfeasible and would make it hard to follow in a concise fashion. To that extent, the sample problematic code accompanying the book has been reduced to the bare essentials (although never at the expense of completeness). All sample code was written using C# and .NET 2.0. Each of the sample scenarios can be downloaded from the book's Web site located at www.advanceddotnetdebugging.com. Associated with each sample scenario is an MSBuild project file. MSBuild ships with the .NET SDK 2.0 and is a full-fledged, command-line-driven build environment that is compatible with Microsoft Visual Studio. All debug sessions are illustrated using the 32-bit version of the .NET framework.

Support

Even after painstaking effort to make this book error free, errors will undoubtedly be found. You can report errors either on the book's Web site located at www.advanceddotnetdebugging.com or by emailing me directly at marioh@ advanceddotnetdebugging.com. An errata sheet will be kept on the Web site with the corresponding errors and fixes.

Summary

With today's complex software solutions, ranging from standalone command-line applications to highly interconnected systems communicating on a worldwide basis, code issues will without question arise. The difficulty in ensuring that such products are bug free may seem like a daunting task, but with the right set of tools and the knowledge required to use those tools, a software engineer's life can be made much easier. Not only will these tools and the correct mindset help the troubleshooting process become more effective, it will also save the company a ton of money and potential loss of customers. This book was written to enable software engineers to gain the knowledge and expertise needed to avoid devastating pitfalls and make the troubleshooting process more productive and successful.

I welcome you to *Advanced .NET Debugging*.

Mario Hewardt
Redmond, WA
September 2009

ACKNOWLEDGMENTS

Based on my prior experience writing *Advanced Windows Debugging*, I knew first-hand the amount of effort it takes to work a full-time job at Microsoft and also write a book in my spare time. Based on the success of *Advanced Windows Debugging* and the consistent requests for a similar book focused on .NET and the CLR, I decided to again take on the challenge of writing and deliver a book that many readers were asking for. Suffice it to say that the task was easier than the first time around but was still a major undertaking—an undertaking not only on my part, but also on the part of the ton of people who were involved in the overall process of taking a book from an idea to the final product.

First and foremost, I would like express my gratitude to the *familia*. My wife, Pia, not only had to endure a constant barrage of "I have to write this weekend" but also, in the midst of all the schedules and deadlines, delivered our beautiful baby girl Gemma in late December 2008. This book would not have been possible without the patience, support, and encouragement that you both have provided.

To team Addison-Wesley, who has once again shown an incredible amount of accommodation in working with an author who writes in his spare time. My team members constantly had to field requests for changes to schedules, provided excellent editorial processes, and eagerly expedited the production schedule to get the book to the readers as quickly as possible. Special thanks go to Joan Murray for making the overall process extremely smooth, Chris Zahn for carefully dissecting and correcting my, at times, contrived English, and Olivia Basegio for taking over the process while Joan was temporarily out of the office. Also, special thanks go to Curt Johnson who did an excellent job in providing the marketing magic for the book.

As always, no matter how careful an author is, technical inaccuracies will always be present. As such, having a great team of engineers review the material is paramount to a book's success. Throughout this project, I've had the pleasure of working with some great engineers (most of whom work in the .NET division), who provided stellar feedback and suggestions and fielded questions in general. A sincere thank you goes out to Mark Russinovich, Maoni Stephens, Roberto Farah, Tess Ferrandez, Lee Culver, Pat Styles, Eric Eilebrecht, Steve Johnson, and Jon Langdon.

Special thanks go to Patrick Dussud who not only meticulously reviewed the manuscript but also wrote the Foreword. This book would not have been what it is today were it not for his engagement.

I would also like to extend my gratitude to Alexandra H. Anderson of Easy Web Launch (www.easyweblaunch.com) for once again delivering an amazing Web page for the book.

Last, but not least, I want to thank all the readers who have provided me with feedback over the years. Your support is what made this book a reality.

About the Author

© www.BrookeClark.com

Mario Hewardt is the originator and coauthor of *Advanced Windows Debugging* and is a senior development lead with Microsoft. With more than 11 years of experience, he has worked on Windows starting from Windows 98 up to Windows Vista. For the past few years, Mario has worked in the SaaS arena and has delivered the Asset Inventory Service, which is a hosted service that allows customers to track their asset inventory. His current charter involves leading a team of engineers delivering the core platform for the next generation Microsoft online management services.

OVERVIEW

## CHAPTER 1

INTRODUCTION TO THE TOOLS

Quite often, I come across developers trying to investigate a particular problem by using either the wrong tools or no tools at all. Strategies range from relying on additional tracing to performing ad-hoc code reviews. By *ad-hoc*, I mean guessing the general area of the code base where the source of the problem might be. For example, a failure in the transaction service of one system may lead to extensive code reviews of the entire transaction engine even though the problem might lie somewhere else entirely. Sometimes, developers get lucky and the problem is truly located in that piece of code. More often than not, the source and the symptom may be far apart. By utilizing more powerful investigative tools, developers can dramatically reduce the amount of time spent troubleshooting.

There are many extremely powerful tools available to make troubleshooting .NET applications much more efficient. Some of the tools focus on a specific category of problems, whereas others tackle several different problem categories. Knowing when and how to use each tool is critical when analyzing .NET application problems. This chapter outlines the tools that are utilized in this book. The outline is meant to be an introduction to each tool and not an exhaustive description. Each tool outline briefly discusses which problem category the tool applies to, where to download the tool from, installation instructions, and examples of running the tool. It is important to note that all of the tools described are available as free downloads.

Debugging Tools for Windows

Usage scenarios:	Collection of debuggers and tools
Version:	6.8.4.0
Download point:	www.microsoft.com/whdc/devtools/debugging/default.mspx

The Debugging Tools for Windows package is a freely available support package that contains a set of powerful debuggers and tools to help in the software troubleshooting process. The package comes in two flavors: 32-bit and 64-bit depending on which architecture you want to debug. For the purposes of this book, all debugging scenarios will be illustrated using the 32-bit version of the package.

There are three user mode debuggers available in the Debugging Tools for Windows package—NTSD, CDB, and WinDbg—and one kernel mode debugger (kd). Although these debuggers are three separate tools, it is important to understand that they all rely on the same core debugger engine. The most significant difference between the debuggers is that WinDbg has a graphical user interface (GUI) component, making it easier to work with when doing source level debugging. In contrast, NTSD and CDB are purely console-based debuggers. The snippets of debugger conversation that will be outlined in the book are all captured using NTSD.

After choosing the flavor of the debugger (32-bit or 64-bit), the installation process for Debugging Tools for Windows is straightforward and the default installation options are typically sufficient. The default installation path is

```
%programfiles%\Debugging Tools for Windows
```

Please note that at the time of publishing the most recent version was 6.8.4.0. It is quite possible that a new version of Debugging Tools for Windows will be released by the time you read this book. Even so, there should be relatively minor changes in the debugger output, and all the material in the book should still apply and be easily followed. The debugger download URL also keeps a history of prior debugger versions (going back two or three releases) that can be downloaded. If you want to use the exact same version, you can download the Debugging Tools for Windows corresponding to version 6.8.4.0.

.NET 2.0—Redistributable

Usage scenarios:	.NET Runtime
Version:	2.0
Download point:	www.microsoft.com/downloads/details.aspx?familyid=0856eacb-4362-4b0d-8edd-aab15c5e04f5&displaylang=en

The .NET 2.0 Redistributable component constitutes the core of the .NET platform. It contains all the fundamental runtime components that are needed for .NET 2.0 applications to run, including all framework assemblies and the .NET runtime binaries.

Table 1-1 Currently Available Major .NET Versions

.NET Version	Included in Windows	Architecture	Latest SP	Runtime Changes	Framework Changes
1.0	None	X86	3	Initial Version	Initial Version
1.1	Windows Server 2003	X86, x64, IA64	1	No*	Yes
2.0	Windows Server 2003 R2**	X86, x64, IA64	1	Yes	Yes
3.0	Windows Vista	X86, x64, ia64		No*	Yes (notably WPF, WCF, WF)
3.5	Windows Server 2008	X86, x64, ia64		No*	Yes

*Minor changes may have been made to the runtime to accommodate the new framework features but it is not considered a major release of the runtime.
**Ships with Windows Server 2003 R2 but does not install by default.

The distinction between framework assemblies and runtime binaries is important as there has been quite a lot of confusion surrounding the various .NET releases. Not counting service packs, the following releases are currently available: 1.0, 1.1, 2.0, 3.0, and 3.5. Table 1-1 illustrates the main difference between each version.

If you are running on an operating system where the .NET 2.0 redistributable component is not installed, the installation process is straightforward. Simply navigate to the installation URL and select the default installation options.

.NET 2.0—SDK

Usage scenarios:	Development libraries and tools
Version:	2.0
Download point:	www.microsoft.com/downloads/details.aspx? FamilyID=FE6F2099-B7B4-4F47-A244-C96D69C35 DEC&displaylang=en

Although the redistributable package enables .NET applications to run on a computer, the .NET SDK component enables developers to create .NET applications by providing all the necessary tools (compiler, assembler, build tool) and libraries. The .NET SDK does not provide a GUI-based integrated development environment but rather a command-line driven environment.

Prior to installing the .NET 2.0 SDK, ensure that the .NET 2.0 Redistributable package has been installed. To install the .NET 2.0 SDK, navigate to the download URL and launch the setup. You will have a few options as part of the installation process:

- Install quick start samples. Quick start samples are great tools when you want to get started building .NET applications. They include small pieces of sample code in the different .NET areas (such as ADO, interoperability, and networking).
- Tools and Debuggers. This option installs a number of tools and debuggers. The debugger that comes as part of the .NET 2.0 SDK is DbgClr. DbgClr is a source-level GUI debugger with a look and feel similar to that of Visual Studio. If you are familiar with the Visual Studio debugger, using DbgClr will be a very similar experience.
- Product Documentation. It is strongly recommended that you install the product documentation as it contains a ton of information useful when developing .NET applications.

The last step of the installation process is to select the installation location (default is `%programfiles\Microsoft.net\SDK`).

Included with the .NET 2.0 SDK is a build utility called MSBUILD. It is the same build utility that Visual Studio utilizes and works on the basis of defining the build process in XML format. Each of the samples in this book comes with an associated MSBUILD XML file (`build.xml`) that can be used to easily compile each of the samples. An exhaustive description of the MSBUILD utility is out of scope for this book, but understanding how to use it to build the samples accompanied in this book is critical. Listing 1-1 shows an example of an MSBUILD project file for a simple .NET command line application written in C#.

Listing 1-1 MSBUILD project file for simple .NET command-line application

```
<Project DefaultTargets = "Compile"
    xmlns="http://schemas.microsoft.com/developer/msbuild/2003" >

    <!-- Set the application name as a property -->
    <PropertyGroup>
        <appname>Welcome</appname>
    </PropertyGroup>
```

```
<!-- Specify the inputs by type and file name -->
<ItemGroup>
    <CSFile Include = "simple.cs"/>
</ItemGroup>

<Target Name = "Compile">
    <!-- Run the Visual C# compilation using input files of type CSFile -->
    <CSC
        Sources = "@(CSFile)"
        OutputAssembly = "$(appname).exe">
        <!-- Set the OutputAssembly attribute of the CSC task
        to the name of the executable file that is created -->
        <Output
            TaskParameter = "OutputAssembly"
            ItemName = "EXEFile" />
    </CSC>
    <!-- Log the file name of the output file -->
    <Message Text="The output file is @(EXEFile)"/>
</Target>
</Project>
```

To build an MSBUILD project, simply invoke the MSBUILD utility and point it to the project file (located in the same folder as source code):

```
C:\MSBuild>c:\Windows\Microsoft.NET\Framework\v2.0.50727\MSBuild.exe build.xml
Microsoft (R) Build Engine Version 2.0.50727.1434
[Microsoft .NET Framework, Version 2.0.50727.1434]
Copyright (C) Microsoft Corporation 2005. All rights reserved.

Build started 4/7/2008 10:25:36 AM.

Project "C:\MSBuild\build.xml" (default targets):

Target Compile:
    C:\Windows\Microsoft.NET\Framework64\v2.0.50727\Csc.exe
/out:Welcome.exe simple.cs
    The output file is Welcome.exe

Build succeeded.
    0 Warning(s)
    0 Error(s)

Time Elapsed 00:00:00.86
```

SOS

Usage scenarios:	General debugging extension for .NET applications
Version:	1.0, 1.1, 2.0
Download point:	Part of .NET SDK

SOS is a debugger extension that can be used to debug .NET applications using the native debuggers. It provides a truly amazing set of commands that enables developers to delve deep into the CLR and help troubleshoot pesky application bugs. Among other things, there are commands that enable you to see the finalization queues, managed heaps, managed threads, setting managed code breakpoints, seeing exceptions, and much more. Throughout the course of the book, the SOS debugger extension will be used heavily to investigate complex application bugs.

Because SOS provides an abstracted view into the internals of the CLR, it's important to note that when debugging using the SOS debugger extension, care must be taken to use the correct version of SOS. Each of the .NET versions ship with its corresponding version of SOS and can be found in the following location:

```
%windir%\microsoft.net\<architecture>\<version>\sos.dll
```

Architecture can be either Framework (for 32-bit) or Framework64 (for 64-bit), and the version represents the version of the .NET framework you are targeting.

Before the SOS debugger extension can be used, it must be loaded into the debugger by using the .load command. Listing 1-2 illustrates the loading process when running notepad.exe under the debugger.

Listing 1-2 Loading the SOS debugger extension command

```
0:000> .load c:\Windows\Microsoft.NET\Framework\v2.0.50727\SOS.dll
0:000> !help
------------------------------------------------------------------------
SOS is a debugger extension DLL designed to aid in the debugging of managed
programs. Functions are listed by category, then roughly in order of
importance. Shortcut names for popular functions are listed in parenthesis.
Type "!help <functionname>" for detailed info on that function.
```

```
Object Inspection                    Examining code and stacks
-----------------------              ---------------------------
DumpObj (do)                         Threads
DumpArray (da)                       CLRStack
DumpStackObjects (dso)               IP2MD
DumpHeap                             U
DumpVC                               DumpStack
GCRoot                               EEStack
ObjSize                              GCInfo
FinalizeQueue                        EHInfo
PrintException (pe)                  COMState
TraverseHeap                         BPMD


Examining CLR data structures        Diagnostic Utilities
-----------------------              ---------------------------
DumpDomain                           VerifyHeap
EEHeap                               DumpLog
Name2EE                              FindAppDomain
SyncBlk                              SaveModule
DumpMT                               GCHandles
DumpClass                            GCHandleLeaks
DumpMD                               VMMap
Token2EE                             VMStat
EEVersion                            ProcInfo
DumpModule                           StopOnException (soe)
ThreadPool                           MinidumpMode
DumpAssembly
DumpMethodSig                        Other
DumpRuntimeTypes                     ---------------------------
DumpSig                              FAQ
RCWCleanupList
DumpIL
0:000> !Threads
Failed to find runtime DLL (mscorwks.dll), 0x80004005
Extension commands need mscorwks.dll in order to have something to do.
0:000>
```

In Listing 1-2, we started by loading the 2.0 version of the SOS debugger extension. Following a successful load, we issued the `!help` extension command that displayed a list of available commands from the SOS extension. Next, we attempted to use the `!threads` command to display all the managed threads in the process. The net result was an error that stated that `mscorwks.dll` could not be found. When a .NET application is first loaded, the CLR is also loaded and initialized. The primary library responsible for the runtime functionality is `mscorwks.dll`. If the runtime is not found in the process being debugged, SOS returns an error essentially indicating that the process is not a .NET process or that the runtime has not been loaded yet and hence the debugger extension commands will not be available.

To avoid specifying the full path to the SOS debugger extension, the `.loadby` debugger command can be utilized. The syntax of the `.loadby` command is as follows:

```
.loadby <extension DLL> <module name>
```

The `extension DLL` represents the name of the debugger extension we want to load (such as `SOS.DLL`) and the `module name` represents a currently loaded module (such as `mscorwks.dll`). The `.loadby` command then attempts to load the extension DLL from the same path that the module is located in. For example, to load the SOS extension from the same directory in which `mscorwks.dll` is located, the following command can be used:

```
.loadby SOS.dll mscorwks
```

One final note on SOS is that it can be loaded and used in Visual Studio 2008 by using the `.load sos` command in an intermediate window.

The Call for Help?

Contrary to what you might believe, the SOS debugger extension is not named after the distress signal. When the .NET framework was in its 1.0 stage, the Microsoft development team used a debugger extension called STRIKE to figure out complex problems in .NET code. As the .NET framework matured, so did the debugger extension, and it became known as Son of Strike (SOS).

SOSEX

Usage scenarios:	General debugging extension for .NET applications
Version:	1.1
Download point:	www.stevestechspot.com/downloads/sosex_32.zip
	or
	www.stevestechspot.com/downloads/sosex_64.zip

SOSEX is another debugger extension targeted at the native debuggers and managed code debugging. It was developed by Steve Johnson and is available as a free download. SOSEX, not surprisingly, stands for SOS Extended. SOSEX adds a set of powerful debugging commands to your arsenal. Examples of such commands include deadlock detection, generational garbage collection commands, and more powerful breakpoint commands.

The installation of SOSEX comes in the form of a ZIP file. Simply extract the files contained in the ZIP file to a location of choice. I typically place extensions in the folder where the debuggers are installed to avoid having to specify full paths when loading the extension. Once loaded, you can begin using the commands as shown in Listing 1-3.

Listing 1-3 Loading the SOSEX debugger extension command

```
0:000> .load sosex.dll
0:000> !sosex.help
SOSEX - Copyright 2007-2008 by Steve Johnson - http://www.stevestechspot.com/
Quick Ref:
-------------------------------------------------------
dumpgen  <decGenNum> [-stat] [-type <TYPE_NAME>]
gcgen    <hexObjectAddr>
refs     <hexObjectAddr>
bpsc     <strSourceFile> <decLineNum> [decColNum]
bpmo     <strTypeName> <strMethodName> <hexILOffset>
vars     [decFrameNum|-w]
date     <hexDateAddr>
isf      <strTypeName> <strFieldName>
dlk

Use !help <command> for more details about each command.
0:000>
```

We will utilize the SOSEX extension throughout the book to make it easier to debug some of the scenarios that will be illustrated.

CLR Profiler

Usage scenarios:	Memory Allocation Profiler
Version:	2.0
Download point:	www.microsoft.com/downloads/details.aspx?FamilyId=A362781C-3870-43BE-8926-862B40AA0CD0&displaylang=en

The CLR Profiler is an invaluable tool when it comes to troubleshooting memory-related issues in .NET applications. It provides features such as

- Heap statistics (including allocation graphs)
- Garbage Collection Statistics
- Garbage Collector Handle Statistics (including allocation graphs)
- Garbage Collection Generation Sizes
- Profiling Statistics

The installation process for the CLR Profiler is straightforward. The installation package comes in the form of a ZIP file. Simply extract the contents of the ZIP file to a specified folder location (default is `C:\CLRProfiler`). If you extract all the files from the ZIP file, you get both the x86 and x64 version of the tool. To launch CLR Profiler, simply run `CLRProfiler.exe`. The installation of the CLR Profiler is accompanied by the source code making modifications and enhancements readily available.

After the CLR Profiler is launched, a dialog appears that contains a number of options as shown in Figure 1-1.

Clicking the Start Application button brings up a dialog where you can choose the application you want to profile. After an application and profiling action has been chosen, the CLR Profiler launches the application and starts collecting data. The CLR Profiler offers a number of different statistical views of the data collected. Figure 1-2 shows an example of a view when profiling the CLR Profiler itself.

As can be seen in Figure 1-2, the CLR Profiler offers a very detailed view of the allocation history and hierarchical relationships in a given application run. We will look at the specifics of the different CLR Profiler views in upcoming chapters.

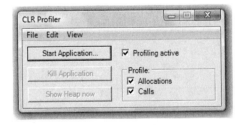

Figure 1-1   CLR Profiler Start dialog

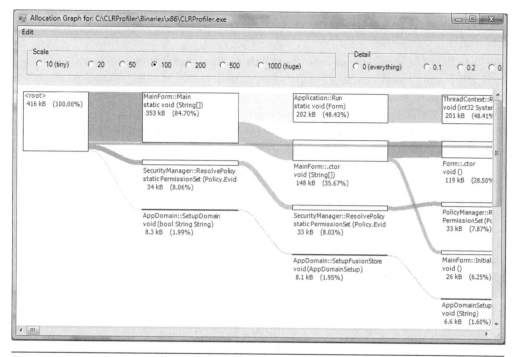

Figure 1-2   Sample View when profiling the CLR Profiler

The data collected is output to a log file that is by default located in %windir%\Temp. The log filename takes the form

```
Pipe_<pid>.log
```

where <pid> is the process identifier of the process being profiled.

The CLR Profiler can also be started and controlled via the command line. Running the CLR Profiler using the /? switch opens a window with all the available options. For example, if I want to profile an application called hello.exe and log all profiling data to a log file named hello.log, I would use the command line

```
clrprofiler -o hello.log -p hello.exe
```

where the -o switch specifies the log filename and the -p switch specifies the executable to be profiled.

In subsequent chapters, we will utilize both the command line and user interface (UI) to illustrate the power of the CLR Profiler.

Performance Counters

Performance counters are an important part of the troubleshooting process. During the .NET framework installation process, a collection of performance counters is installed. These performance counters represent a goldmine of information when analyzing .NET application behavior. To view the performance counters, the Windows Performance Monitor can be used. Table 1-2 lists all the performance counter categories that are part of the .NET runtime.

Throughout the book, the .NET performance counters will be utilized to analyze .NET applications. Figure 1-3 shows an example of a performance counter view when ran on an instance of the CLR Profiler (`CLRProfiler.exe`).

Table 1-2 .NET 2.0 Performance Counters Categories

Performance Counter Category	Description
Exceptions	Performance counters related to exceptions thrown by .NET applications
Interoperability	Performance counters related to a .NET application's relationship to COM, COM+, and external libraries
Just-in-time Compilation	Performance counters related to the Just In Time (JIT) compiler
Loader	Performance counters related to the loading of .NET entities (assemblies, types)
Lock and Thread	Performance counters related to threads and locking behaviors
Memory	Performance counters related to the garbage collector (GC) and memory utilization
Networking	Performance counters related to the data a .NET application sends and receives over the network
Remoting	Performance counters related to the remote objects that a .NET application uses
Security	Performance counters related to the security checks and balances that the .NET framework performs

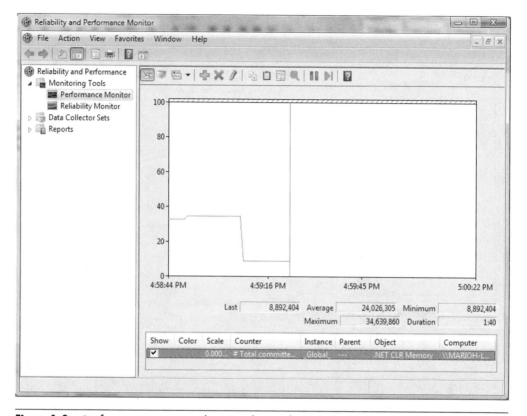

Figure 1-3   Performance counter showing the total committed bytes in the CLR Profiler instance

Reflector for .NET

Usage scenarios: .NET assembly analyzer and disassembler

Version: 5.1

Download point: www.aisto.com/roeder/dotnet/Download.aspx?
File=Reflector

Reflector for .NET is a .NET assembly explorer tool that includes a powerful disassembler that can reproduce the code from the MSIL (Microsoft Intermediate Language) to a higher level language of choice. The language choices are C#, Visual Basic, Delphi, Managed C++, and Chrome. Additionally, it includes an extensibility model in the form of an add-in API. There are many add-ins available ranging from

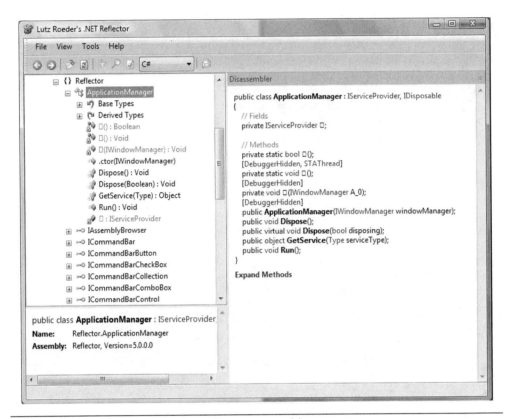

Figure 1-4 Using Reflector on the Reflector executable

a code review add-in to a code metrics add-in. Figure 1-4 shows an example of analyzing the `Reflector.exe` binary itself using Reflector for .NET.

To install the tool, the download location requires that you enter your name, organization, and email address. Once entered, the package (ZIP file) can be downloaded and extracted to a location of choice. To launch Reflector for .NET, run `reflector.exe` from the installation folder.

PowerDbg

Usage scenarios: Debugger tool

Version: 5.0

Download point: www.codeplex.com/powerdbg

PowerDbg is a library developed by Roberto Farah that allows you to control the native debuggers via Powershell (requires 1.0). It is a super useful tool when you want to control the execution of the debuggers using the command line. The PowerDbg script returns information to the user in a neat and easily digestible fashion. The great thing about PowerDbg is that it is easily extensible and enables calling and formatting your favorite commands (or a set of commands in common debug scenarios).

To utilize PowerDbg, the easiest way is to initialize it in the Powershell profile. In my case, I use the following profile path:

```
%windir%\System32\WindowsPowerShell\v1.0\profile.ps1
```

Simply copy the PowerDbg script into that file and reopen a Powershell command window. You can now utilize the PowerDbg commands as illustrated in an example in Figure 1-5.

PowerDbg works on the basis of sending commands to the running WinDbg instance. The first part of any command execution is the opening of a log file, followed by running the actual command and then closing the log file. The logfile is utilized by the PowerDbg script to analyze the results and produce the output. Please note that in order for PowerDbg to find the WinDbg instance, it requires that the title of the window for the WinDbg instance to be named PowerDbg. This can easily be done via the .wtitle command (in WinDbg) as shown here:

```
.wtitle PowerDbg
```

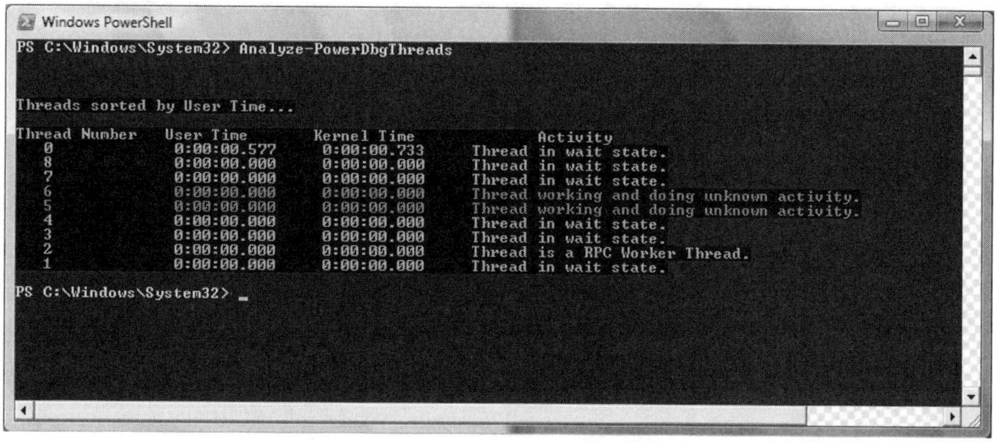

Figure 1-5 Example of PowerDbg running against an instance of WinDbg (perfmon.exe)

If you have configured your WinDbg to automatically configure at startup via a custom initialization script, you can add the `.wtitle` command to the script so that it always executes upon startup.

Managed Debugging Assistants

Usage scenarios:	General CLR Debugging
Version:	2.0
Download point:	Part of the CLR

Managed Debugging Assistants (MDAs) is not a standalone tool per se; rather, it is a component of the CLR that provides invaluable information when running and debugging .NET applications. If you are familiar with Application Verifier for native code, MDAs serve a very similar purpose. Through elaborate instrumentation of the runtime, common programming mistakes can be identified at runtime and subsequently fixed prior to shipping the application. MDAs fall into several categories. Table 1-3 lists each of the categories available with .NET 2.0.

Each of the categories listed in Table 1-3 has a number of different MDAs available to troubleshoot problems within that category. To utilize MDAs, they must first

Table 1-3 Managed Debugging Assistant (MDA) Categories Available in CLR 2.0

MDA Assistant Category	Description
Unmanaged Interop	Debugging assistance related to unmanaged interoperability issues
Unmanaged Interop COM	Debugging assistance related to COM unmanaged interoperability issues
Unmanaged Interop P/Invoke	Debugging assistance related to platform invocation unmanaged interoperability issues
Loader	Debugging issues related to the CLR loader
Threading	Debugging issues related to threading issues
BCL	Debugging issues related to the base class libraries
Miscellaneous	Miscellaneous debugging issues

be enabled (prior to starting the process being debugged). The way to enable the MDAs is via the registry. More specifically, you need to add the following value under the registry key:

```
HKEY_LOCAL_MACHINE\SOFTWARE\Microsoft\.NETFramework\MDA="1"
```

Note that MDA is a string value.

By setting the preceding registry value, you have notified the CLR that MDAs should be utilized. Before you can actually make use of them though, you need to enable specific MDAs on a per application basis. The process of enabling MDAs is done via a configuration file that must be named according to the rule

```
<appname>.exe.dma.config
```

where `appname` is the name of the application that you want to enable MDAs for. The configuration file itself contains all the MDAs that you want enabled. The best way to illustrate this process is to look at an example. We will utilize a sample application that can be found at the following location:

```
Source code: c:\adnd\chapter1\MDASample
Assembly: c:\adndbin\01mdasample.exe
```

The application source code (`01mdasample.cs`) is very straightforward and simply starts a worker thread that spins in an infinite loop while doing a sleep. After the new thread has been started, the main thread simply terminates the worker thread. The big problem observed in this code is the fact that one thread terminates another thread. This may or may not (probably the latter in most cases) work properly due to resource concerns. The question is, "How we can utilize MDAs to notify us about this potential disaster?" As discussed earlier, you need to enable MDAs via the registry. When that is completed, the MDA application configuration file has to be created. Listing 1-4 shows the MDA configuration file for our sample application (`01MDASample.exe.mda.config`).

Listing 1-4 Sample MDA configuration file

```xml
<?xml version="1.0" encoding="UTF-8" ?>
<mdaConfig>
  <assistants>
    <asynchronousThreadAbort />
  </assistants>
</mdaConfig>
```

All MDA configuration files must contain the `mdaConfig` element, which in turn contains the `assistants` element. Under the `assistants` element is a list of MDAs that you want enabled for the application. Please note that the `assistant` elements have to be in alphanumeric order or otherwise the MDAs will not take effect. In the case of our application, we are interested in the `asynchronousThreadAbort` MDA. When the MDA configuration file is placed side by side with the application, the MDA will take effect. Listing 1-5 shows a run of `01MDASample.exe` under the debugger with the MDA configuration file located in the same directory.

Listing 1-5   01MDASample.exe with asynchronousThreadAbort specified in the configuration file

```
...
...
...
0:000> g
ModLoad: 76800000 768bf000   C:\Windows\system32\ADVAPI32.dll
ModLoad: 77b60000 77c23000   C:\Windows\system32\RPCRT4.dll
ModLoad: 76ad0000 76b25000   C:\Windows\system32\SHLWAPI.dll
ModLoad: 762e0000 7632b000   C:\Windows\system32\GDI32.dll
ModLoad: 76e80000 76f1e000   C:\Windows\system32\USER32.dll
ModLoad: 76d50000 76dfa000   C:\Windows\system32\msvcrt.dll
ModLoad: 765b0000 765ce000   C:\Windows\system32\IMM32.DLL
ModLoad: 76730000 767f7000   C:\Windows\system32\MSCTF.dll
ModLoad: 765d0000 765d9000   C:\Windows\system32\LPK.DLL
ModLoad: 76e00000 76e7d000   C:\Windows\system32\USP10.dll
ModLoad: 75340000 754d4000   C:\Windows\WinSxS\x86_microsoft.windows.common-
controls_6595b64144ccf1df_6.0.6000.20533_none_4634c4a0218d65c1\comctl32.dll
ModLoad: 79e70000 7a3ff000   C:\Windows\Microsoft.NET\Framework\v2.0.50727
\mscorwks.dll
ModLoad: 755e0000 7567b000   C:\Windows\WinSxS\x86_microsoft.vc80
.crt_1fc8b3b9a1e18e3b_8.0.50727.762_none_10b2f55f9bffb8f8\MSVCR80.dll
ModLoad: 76f50000 77a1e000   C:\Windows\system32\shell32.dll
ModLoad: 76330000 76474000   C:\Windows\system32\ole32.dll
ModLoad: 790c0000 79bf6000   C:\Windows\assembly\NativeImages_v2.0
.50727_32\mscorlib\32e6f703c114f3a971cbe706586e3655\mscorlib.ni.dll
ModLoad: 79060000 790b6000   C:\Windows\Microsoft.NET\Framework
\v2.0.50727\mscorjit.dll
ModLoad: 60340000 60348000   C:\Windows\Microsoft.NET\Framework
\v2.0.50727\culture.dll
ModLoad: 60340000 60348000   C:\Windows\Microsoft.NET\Framework
\v2.0.50727\culture.dll
<mda:msg xmlns:mda="http://schemas.microsoft.com/CLR/2004/10/mda">
```

```
<!--
    User code running on thread 6332 has attempted to abort thread 8484. This
    may result in a corrupt state or resource leaks if the thread being aborted
    was in the middle of an operation that modifies global state or uses native
    resources. Aborting threads other than the currently running thread is
    strongly discouraged.
-->
<mda:asynchronousThreadAbortMsg break="true">
  <callingThread osId="6332" managedId="1"/>
  <abortedThread osId="8484" managedId="3"/>
</mda:asynchronousThreadAbortMsg>
```

From Listing 1-5, we can see (in bold) that our sample application performed a questionable action (terminating a thread) and that the debuggers stopped execution when this action was encountered. In addition to stopping execution, the MDA also outputted more detailed information such as the thread IDs of the threads that terminated the worker thread and the worker thread itself.

There are many useful MDAs built into the CLR and in subsequent chapters we will showcase scenarios where these MDAs can come in handy when debugging .NET applications.

Summary

If history has taught us anything, it is that software is, without a doubt, gaining in complexity. To make life easier for developers, this complexity is partially mitigated by the introduction of new abstraction layers, unifying the underlying low-level mechanics through a consistent framework and associated runtime. .NET is a great example of an abstraction that provides tremendous benefits to developers. Even though .NET touts this simplicity, you must not forget that the fundamental building blocks should still be understood. For example, .NET has automatic memory management capabilities in the form of a generational garbage collector, yet one of the most common forms of problems encountered are memory "leak" issues. Understanding how the garbage collector works, and even more importantly, which tools to use to analyze application and garbage collector behavior is crucial for the successful development and support of a product. This chapter outlined some of the most useful tools when doing root cause analysis of .NET applications. The discussion of each tool is left intentionally short so as to introduce you to the basic concept of the tool (download, install, usage scenarios). Throughout the remaining portions of the book, we will harness the full power of these tools when performing root cause analysis of real-world problems.

## CHAPTER 2

CLR FUNDAMENTALS

As with any form of troubleshooting, the more you understand the underlying system being debugged the greater success you will have at identifying the root cause. In the .NET world, this translates to understanding how the runtime itself functions. Knowing how the garbage collector works will enable you to more efficiently debug memory "leak" issues. Knowing how the interoperability layer works will enable you to more efficiently debug COM problems. Knowing how synchronization works will enable you to more efficiently debug hangs. And the list goes on and on. Venturing outside of the comfort zone of your own application and digging deep into the runtime will greatly enhance your debugging success. Problems that may have otherwise taken weeks to debug through traditional means can now be solved in a relatively short time span.

In this chapter, we will take a guided tour of the .NET runtime. Some of the core runtime components and concepts useful when debugging .NET applications will be discussed and the debuggers and tools will be used to illustrate the internals of the runtime. This is by no means an exhaustive description of the .NET runtime; the chapter focuses on some of the areas most commonly known to cause problems for developers.

High-Level Overview

At a high level, .NET is a virtual runtime environment that consists of a virtual execution engine, the Common Language Runtime (CLR), and a set of associated framework libraries. Applications written for .NET, at compile time, do not translate into machine code but instead use an intermediary representation that the execution engine translates at runtime (depending on architecture). Although this may seem as if the CLR acts as an interpreter (interpreting the intermediate language), the primary difference between the CLR and an interpreter is that the CLR does not retranslate the intermediate code each and every time. Rather, it takes a one-time hit of translating a chunk of intermediate code into machine code and then reuses the translated machine code in all subsequent invocations. Using a virtual execution engine provides some key benefits to developers. Examples of such benefits include the following:

- Memory management
- Security management
- Code verification

To better understand what components .NET consists of, Figure 2-1 illustrates the 50,000-foot overview of the different entities involved in the .NET world.

At the core of .NET, there is an ECMA standard that states what implementations of the .NET runtime need to adhere to in order to be compliant. This standards document is commonly referred to as the Common Language Infrastructure (CLI). The CLI doesn't just dictate rules for the runtime itself but also includes a set of library classes that are considered crucial and common enough to warrant inclusion. This set of class libraries is called the Base Class Libraries (BCL). The next layer in Figure 2-1 is the Common Language Runtime (CLR). This is an actual component and represents Microsoft's implementation of the CLI. When a .NET redistributable package is installed on a machine, it includes the CLR. On top of the CLR sits the .NET framework. These are all the libraries that are available to developers when creating .NET

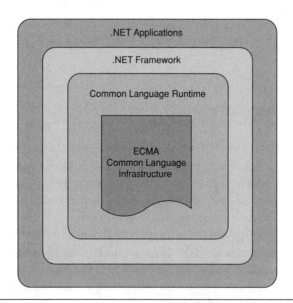

Figure 2-1   High-level overview of the different components in .NET

applications. The .NET framework can be considered a superset of the BCL and includes frameworks such as the Windows Communication Foundation (WCF), Windows Presentation Foundation (WPF), and much more. The libraries that are part of the .NET framework but not the BCL are considered outside of the standards realm, and any applications that make use of them may or may not work on other CLI implementations besides the CLR. At the top level, we have the .NET applications, which run within the confines of the CLR. The key focus of this book is to examine how the CLR functions and how that knowledge is crucial when debugging .NET applications.

Are There Other CLI Compliant Implementations?

Is Microsoft's CLR the only implementation of the CLI out there? Not quite. Because the CLI has become increasingly popular, there are a number of companies/organizations that have produced their own CLI-compliant runtimes. A great example of such an implementation is the Mono project (sponsored by Novell). In addition to being an open source project, the Mono CLI implementation can run on Windows, Linux, Solaris, and Mac OS X.

Additionally, Microsoft has released the Shared Source Common Language Infrastructure (2.0), aka Rotor project, which includes a CLI-compliant implementation of the standard. Because the source code is shared source, this project provides great insights into how a functional implementation works.

Because the CLR is responsible for all aspects of .NET application execution, what does the general execution flow look like? Figure 2-2 illustrates a high-level overview of the execution model starting with the application's source code.

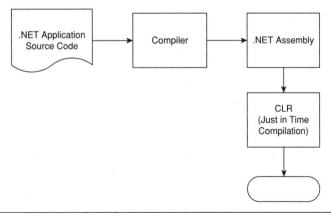

Figure 2-2   High-level view of .NET execution model

Naturally, the starting point is the source code of the .NET application. The source code can be in any of the .NET supported languages such as C#, VB.NET, managed C++, and others. The source code is then fed to the appropriate compiler, which compiles the code into an intermediary language known as the Microsoft Intermediate Language (MSIL). In contrast with a native code application, which during compile and link time is translated into CPU specific instructions, MSIL is a higher-level language that is platform neutral. The net outcome of a compilation is known as an assembly. The notion of an assembly is at the heart of .NET and will be discussed in more detail later in the chapter. For now, you can view the assembly as a self-contained entity that encapsulates everything that needs to be known about the application (including the code, or MSIL for the application). When the .NET assembly is run, the CLR is automatically loaded and begins executing the MSIL. The way that MSIL is executed is by first translating it to instructions native to the platform that the code is executing on. This translation is done at runtime by a component in the CLR known as the Just-In-Time (JIT) compiler.

In the next few chapters, we will take a closer look at the different components (refer to Figure 2-2) that partake in the execution flow of a .NET application. We will utilize the debuggers and associated tools when necessary to illustrate the concepts being discussed.

CLR and the Windows Loader

Applications that are written natively for Windows can be launched via a number of different mechanisms. Windows handles all the work associated with setting up the process address space, loading the executable, and directing the processor to start executing. When the processor starts executing the native instructions, it continues to do so on its own until the process exits. As discussed earlier in the chapter, a .NET application does not contain native instructions. Rather, an intermediate language must be translated to native instructions before the processor can execute them. Even in light of this difference, a .NET application can still be launched in the exact same way as a native application. How is this possible? Does the Windows loader have specific knowledge of .NET applications and automatically bootstrap the CLR? The answer lies in a file format that has been around since the early days and is understood by Windows: the Portable Executable (PE) file format. Figure 2-3 illustrates, at a high level, the general structure of a PE image file.

To support execution of PE images, the PE header includes a field called `AddressOfEntryPoint`. This field indicates the location of the entry point for the PE file. In the case of a .NET assembly, it points to a small piece of stub code located

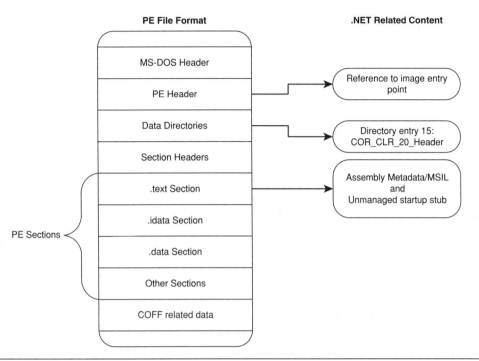

Figure 2-3 High-level overview of the PE file format

in the .text section. The next field of importance is in the data directories. When any given .NET compiler produces an assembly, it adds a data directory entry to the PE file. More specifically, the data directory entry is at index 15 and contains the location and size of the CLR header. The CLR header is then located in the next part of interest in the PE file, namely the .text section. The CLR header consists of a structure named the IMAGE_COR20_HEADER. This structure contains information such as the managed code application entry point, the major and minor version of the target CLR, and the strong name signature of the assembly. You can view this data structure as containing information needed to know which CLR to load and the most basic data about the assembly itself. Other parts of the .text section include the assembly metadata tables, the MSIL, and the unmanaged startup stub. The unmanaged startup stub simply contains the code that will be executed by the Windows loader to bootstrap the execution of the PE file.

In the next few sections, we will take a look at how the Windows loader loads both native images as well as .NET assemblies.

Loading Native Images

To better understand the loading of .NET assemblies, we'll start by looking at how the Windows loader loads native PE images. Let's use good old `notepad.exe` as the example executable (running on Windows Vista Enterprise). Please note that when dealing with PE files there are two important terms used:

- File offset: This is the offset within the PE file of any given location.
- Relative Virtual Address (RVA): This value is applicable only when the PE image has been loaded and is the relative address within the virtual address space of the process. For example, an RVA of `0x200` means `0x200` bytes from the image base address once loaded into memory.

Using your favorite hex editor, go to file offset `0x108` where you will find the `AddressOfEntryPoint` field (remember that this field gives control of execution to this code) with the RVA `0x31F8`. Next, load an instance of `notepad.exe` under the debugger and unassemble the code that is located at <base image address>+`0x31F8` as illustrated in Listing 2-1.

Listing 2-1   Finding the start address of notepad.exe

```
Microsoft (R) Windows Debugger Version 6.8.0004.0 X86
Copyright (c) Microsoft Corporation. All rights reserved.

CommandLine: notepad.exe
Symbol search path is: *** Invalid ***
****************************************************************************
* Symbol loading may be unreliable without a symbol search path.          *
* Use .symfix to have the debugger choose a symbol path.                  *
* After setting your symbol path, use .reload to refresh symbol locations. *
****************************************************************************
Executable search path is:
ModLoad: 000b0000 000d8000   notepad.exe
ModLoad: 773c0000 774de000   ntdll.dll
ModLoad: 77180000 77258000   C:\Windows\system32\kernel32.dll
ModLoad: 770c0000 7717f000   C:\Windows\system32\ADVAPI32.dll
ModLoad: 76cc0000 76d83000   C:\Windows\system32\RPCRT4.dll
ModLoad: 75f20000 75f6b000   C:\Windows\system32\GDI32.dll
ModLoad: 77560000 775fe000   C:\Windows\system32\USER32.dll
ModLoad: 75c80000 75d2a000   C:\Windows\system32\msvcrt.dll
ModLoad: 75dc0000 75e34000   C:\Windows\system32\COMDLG32.dll
ModLoad: 77500000 77555000   C:\Windows\system32\SHLWAPI.dll
```

```
ModLoad: 74ce0000 74e74000   C:\Windows\WinSxS\x86_microsoft.windows.common-
controls_6595b64144ccf1df_6.0.6000.20533_none_4634c4a0218d65c1\COMCTL32.dll
ModLoad: 75f70000 76a3e000   C:\Windows\system32\SHELL32.dll
ModLoad: 6ffc0000 70001000   C:\Windows\system32\WINSPOOL.DRV
ModLoad: 76d90000 76ed4000   C:\Windows\system32\ole32.dll
ModLoad: 77260000 772ec000   C:\Windows\system32\OLEAUT32.dll
(3e28.3808): Break instruction exception - code 80000003 (first chance)
eax=00000000 ebx=00000000 ecx=0012f8c8 edx=77420f34 esi=fffffffe edi=77485d14
eip=77402ea8 esp=0012f8e0 ebp=0012f910 iopl=0         nv up ei pl zr na pe nc
cs=001b  ss=0023  ds=0023  es=0023  fs=003b  gs=0000          efl=00000246
*** ERROR: Symbol file could not be found.  Defaulted to export symbols for ntdll.dll -
ntdll!DbgBreakPoint:
77402ea8 cc              int     3
0:000> .symfix
No downstream store given, using c:\Program Files\Debugging Tools for Windows\sym
0:000> .reload
Reloading current modules
..............
0:000> u 000b0000+0x31F8
notepad!WinMainCRTStartup:
000b31f8 e8f7feffff      call    notepad!__security_init_cookie (000b30f4)
000b31fd 6a58            push    58h
000b31ff 6810330b00      push    offset notepad!WinSqmAddToStream+0x2a (000b3310)
000b3204 e80b090000      call    notepad!_SEH_prolog4 (000b3b14)
000b3209 33db            xor     ebx,ebx
000b320b 895de4          mov     dword ptr [ebp-1Ch],ebx
000b320e 895dfc          mov     dword ptr [ebp-4],ebx
000b3211 8d4598          lea     eax,[ebp-68h]
0:000>
```

From Listing 2-1, you can see that this particular instance of notepad.exe is loaded at address 0x000b0000. When the code located at that address plus the AddressOfEntryPoint RVA (0x31F8) are unassembled, you can see that it corresponds to the WinMainCRTStartup function, which is also the entry point for our application. WinMainCRTStartup is the wrapper function that performs some CRT initialization work prior to calling into the WinMain function of notepad. There is a lot more information located in the PE file that the Windows loader uses during load, but at a high level, the process illustrated is how the entry point of the PE image is found and executed.

Next, we will investigate how .NET assemblies are constructed to enable the Windows Loader to natively support execution of .NET assemblies.

Loading .NET Assemblies

The best way to find out how .NET applications can be launched natively is by looking at a simple .NET command-line application. The source code and assembly can be found here:

- Source code: `c:\adnd\chapter2\simple`
- Assembly: `c:\adndbin\02simple.exe`

If we run the application above, it executes successfully as illustrated by Listing 2-2.

Listing 2-2   Executing 02simple.exe

```
C:\ADNDBin:>02Simple.exe
Welcome to Advanced .NET Debugging!
```

Because .NET applications require the CLR to be loaded, how does Windows know to load and initialize the CLR? One theory is that the Windows loader has been changed to recognize .NET assemblies and launches the CLR automatically when one is detected. Although that theory is partially correct, Windows versions available before .NET was conceived would have to be patched before working. The key to answering this question lies in an extension to the Portable Executable (PE) format. As we mentioned before, the PE format is a file format used by Windows executables to manage the execution of the code contained within the PE file. Executables can be in the form of EXE, DLL, OBJ, SYS, and more files. To support .NET, assembly execution additions were made to the PE file format, which was illustrated in Figure 2-3.

Let us now examine what happens when the Windows loader encounters a .NET application. For this exercise, we will use the `02simple.exe` application located in `C:\ADNDBin`. Please note that the example was run on Windows 2000. The reason for running on an older version of Windows is important as there have been changes that affect how the Windows loader loads .NET assemblies in subsequent versions (examined later in the chapter). To better illustrate the concepts, I have used a utility named `dumpbin.exe` that understands the PE file format and dumps out the contents of a PE file in an easily digestible format. The result of running `dumpbin.exe` on `02simple.exe` can be found here:

```
C:\ADNDBin\02simple.txt
```

The first portion of interest is in the Optional Header Values section as shown in the following:

```
OPTIONAL HEADER VALUES
            10B magic # (PE32)
           8.00 linker version
            600 size of code
            600 size of initialized data
              0 size of uninitialized data
           246E entry point (0040246E)
           2000 base of code
```

The entry point field corresponds to the `AddressOfEntryPoint` field in the PE file and has a value of `0x00402464`. To find what code actually corresponds to the location `0x00402464`, we look into the `.text` section of the PE image and more specifically the `RAW DATA` section as shown in the following listing:

```
00402430:  00 00 00 00 00 00 00 00 00 00 00 00 50 24 00 00  ............P$..
00402440:  00 00 00 00 00 00 00 00 00 00 00 00 00 00 00 00  ................
00402450:  00 00 5F 43 6F 72 45 78 65 4D 61 69 6E 00 6D 73  .._CorExeMain.ms
00402460:  63 6F 72 65 65 2E 64 6C 6C 00 00 00 00 00 FF 25  coree.dll.....ÿ%
00402470:  00 20 40 00                                      . @.
```

The bytes corresponding to the `AddressOfEntryPoint` are shown in bold and, at a high level, translate to the following:

```
JMP 402000
```

The big question here is what does `402000` symbolize? The answer is that `0x402000` references another part of the PE image file, namely the `import` section, which lists all the modules on which the PE file is dependent. At load time, the actual address of the dependent import is fixed and the correct calls can be made. To find out which import `0x402000` refers to, we look at the import section of the PE file and find the following:

```
mscoree.dll
         402000 Import Address Table
         40243C Import Name Table
              0 time date stamp
              0 Index of first forwarder reference

              0 _CorExeMain
```

As you can see, `0x402000` refers to the `mscoree.dll` (Microsoft Object Runtime Execution Engine), which has one export named `_CorExeMain`. The previous JMP instruction can then be translated into the following pseudo code:

```
JMP _CorExeMain
```

As we have seen, `_CorExeMain` is part of `mscoree.dll` and is the first function called when loading a .NET assembly. The primary purpose of `mscoree.dll` (and `_CorExeMain`) is to bootstrap the CLR. For `mscoree.dll` to bootstrap the CLR, a number of tasks have to be performed:

1. Find the CLR version that the .NET assembly is built against by checking the metadata in the PE file.
2. Find the path to the correct version of the CLR on the system.
3. Load and initialize the CLR.

After the CLR has been initialized, the entry point of the assembly (such as `Main()`) is found in the CLR header portion of the PE image. The entry point is JIT compiled and execution begins.

The CLR has so far been referred to as a logical component without mentioning which image actually serves up its functionality. A large part of the CLR is implemented in `mscorwks.dll`. Furthermore, `mscorwks.dll` can have multiple versions present on any given machine. For example, if you have .NET 1.1 and .NET 2.0 installed, you will have the following CLR DLL versions installed on your machine:

- `c:\Windows\Microsoft.NET\Framework\v1.1.4322\mscorwks.dll`
- `c:\Windows\Microsoft.NET\Framework\v2.0.50727\mscorwks.dll`

The basic idea behind multiple installs is that .NET applications target specific versions of the CLR. An application written for the .NET 1.0 CLR will correctly load the 1.0 CLR even in the presence of the .NET 2.0 CLR. This mechanism, in essence, supports the side-by-side execution model present in the .NET world. The job of `mscoree.dll` is to find out which version of the CLR the assembly is targeting by looking at the CLR header in the PE image file. More specifically, `mscoree.dll` looks at the `MajorRuntimeVersion` and `MinorRuntimeVersion` of the header and loads the appropriate version of the CLR.

So far, we have illustrated how a .NET assembly (in the form of an `.EXE`) is launched. Much in the same way that native code Windows applications support the notion of an executable *as well as* a dynamic link library, so does .NET. In the case of a .NET library, as far as the loader is concerned, the only difference is that instead of the PE image importing the `_CorExeMain` imported function, it imports the `_CorDllMain` function.

One interesting question surrounding the loading of `mscoree.dll` is why is the unmanaged stub function that calls `_CorExeMain` required? Because the PE image file contains a .NET header, is it possible for the Windows loader to identify that the PE image is a .NET assembly and automatically load `mscoree.dll`? The answer is yes. In Windows XP and later, the Windows loader was updated to recognize a .NET assembly PE image and automatically load the CLR.

To summarize the .NET assembly loading algorithm, the following occurs:

1. The user executes a .NET assembly.
2. The Windows loader looks at the `AddressOfEntryPoint` field and references the `.text` section of the PE image file.
3. The bytes located at the `AddressOfEntryPoint` location are simply a JMP instruction to an imported function in `mscoree.dll`.
4. Control is transferred to the `_CorExeMain` function in `mscoree.dll` to bootstrap the CLR and transfer execution to the assembly's entry point.

The PE file format is a very versatile format (as can be witnessed by the relative ease of supporting .NET assemblies) and contains a ton of information related to the PE image being loaded and executed. This section focused on how the PE file format was extended to enable native execution of .NET assemblies. Next, we will delve into other critical parts of the CLR starting with the concept of an application domain.

Application Domains

To increase the reliability of code, a code isolation (or separation) layer must exist. This isolation layer needs to guarantee that code running within one isolation boundary cannot adversely affect another piece of code running in a different isolation layer. If this guarantee was not met, one piece of badly behaved code could easily take down either other applications or the entire system. In other words, this isolation layer exists to improve the stability and reliability of the system. Windows implements this isolation mechanism through the notion of a process. All executable code, data, and other resources are self contained within the process with limited access to other processes running on the system (unless enough privileges are held). .NET applications also execute within the confines of a process for the same reason that native code applications do. However, .NET takes it one step further and introduces another *logical*-isolation layer called the application domain. Figure 2-4 shows a high-level overview of the relationship between a process and application domains.

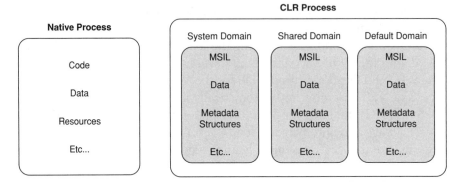

Figure 2-4 Processes and application domains

Any given Windows process that hosts the CLR can have one or more application domains defined that contain the executable code, data, metadata structures, and resources. In addition to the protection guarantees built in by the process, an application domain further introduces the following guarantees:

- Faulty code within an application domain cannot adversely affect code running in a different application domain within the same process.
- Code running within an application domain cannot directly access resources in a different application domain.
- Code-specific configurations can be configured on a per application domain basis. For example, you can configure security-specific settings on a per application domain basis.

Quite often, the notion of an application domain is transparent to the application in the sense that most applications don't explicitly create any application domains. Typically, the creation of new application domains is left to applications that require specific code be hosted within the same process, yet require a level of isolation. To guarantee that the code being hosted doesn't take down other parts of the system, it is loaded into its own application domain. For example, the Internet Information Server (IIS) can host multiple ASP.NET pages, which can be configured to run in individual application domains within the same process. For applications that do not explicitly create any application domains, the CLR (at load time) creates three application domains: system application domain, shared application domain, and the default application domain. In other words, during runtime, the process hosting the CLR will always have at least three application domains (although non-explicitly created by the application itself). We can examine which application domains are present in a CLR-hosted process by using the native debuggers. Let's start an instance of the `02simple.exe` .NET application under the debugger and use the `dumpdomain` command in the SOS debugger extension as illustrated in Listing 2-3.

Listing 2-3 Using the dumpdomain command to show all application domains in 02simple.exe

```
...
...
...
0:001> .loadby sos.dll mscorwks
0:001> !dumpdomain
-----------------------------------------------
System Domain: 7a3bc8b8
LowFrequencyHeap: 7a3bc8dc
HighFrequencyHeap: 7a3bc934
StubHeap: 7a3bc98c
Stage: OPEN
Name: None
-----------------------------------------------
Shared Domain: 7a3bc560
LowFrequencyHeap: 7a3bc584
HighFrequencyHeap: 7a3bc5dc
StubHeap: 7a3bc634
Stage: OPEN
Name: None
Assembly: 004647d0
-----------------------------------------------
Domain 1: 0041fd40
LowFrequencyHeap: 0041fd64
HighFrequencyHeap: 0041fdbc
StubHeap: 0041fe14
Stage: OPEN
Name: 02Simple.exe
Assembly: 004647d0
[C:\Windows\assembly\GAC_32\mscorlib\2.0.0.0__b77a5c561934e089\mscorlib.dll]
ClassLoader: 00464868
SecurityDescriptor: 00458250
  Module Name
790c2000 C:\Windows\assembly\GAC_32\mscorlib\2.0.0.0__b77a5c561934e089\mscorlib.dll

Assembly: 0046d660 [C:\ADNDBin\02Simple.exe]
ClassLoader: 0046d6f8
SecurityDescriptor: 0046d560
  Module Name
003f2c3c C:\ADNDBin\02Simple.exe
```

As we can see from Listing 2-3, there are indeed three application domains in this process: System, Shared, and Domain 1. Domain 1 is the default domain and is named after the image itself (`02simple.exe`). The output for each of the application domains is described in the following list.

- The pointer to the domain. This pointer can be used as input to the `dumpdomain` command and it will limit output for the specified application domain only. For example, if you issue the following command

  ```
  !dumpdomain 7a3bc8b8
  ```

  you would see the output of the system domain only.

- `LowFrequencyHeap`, `HighFrequencyHeap`, and the `StubHeap`. Each application domain typically has code associated with it in the form of MSIL. During the process of JIT compilation, the JIT compiler needs to store data related to the translation process. Examples of such data include the translated machine code and method tables. To that extent, each application domain creates a number of heaps to facilitate this storage. The `LowFrequencyHeap` contains data that is updated and/or accessed less frequently than others, whereas the `HighFrequencyHeap` contains data that is accessed at all times. The last heap is the `StubHeap`, which contains data that aids the CLR when making interoperability calls (such as COM interoperability or platform invocation).

- All assemblies loaded in the application domain. From Listing 2-3, we can see that application domain with the name `02simple.exe` has two assemblies loaded: `mscorlib.dll` and `02simple.exe`. In addition to showing the textual version of the loaded .NET assemblies, it also shows the address to the underlying assembly data structure. For example, the `02simple.exe` assembly has an address of `0x004647d0`. We will utilize this assembly address later in the chapter.

As we can see, the native debuggers can help us glean a lot of information about the isolation boundaries (i.e., application domains) within a .NET process. The last key that is missing is a discussion about the role of each of the three application domains. Remember that even if a .NET application does not explicitly create any application domains, we still always have three: System, Shared, and Default. The role of each of the three application domains is discussed next.

Why Not Use Multiple Processes Instead of Application Domains?

This is a typical question that comes up when discussing application domains. The answer is that constructing and managing a process throughout its lifetime is an expensive proposition. By utilizing the logical notion of application domains, the expense associated with creating and tearing down isolation layers goes down drastically.

The System Application Domain

The primary things done by the system application domain are the following:

1. Creates the two remaining application domains (shared and default)
2. Loads `mscorlib.dll` into the shared application domain (discussed below)
3. Bookkeeping of all other application domains in the process including providing functionality to load and unload application domains
4. Bookkeeping of interned string literals, thereby allowing one copy of any given string literal per process
5. Pre-creation of certain types of exceptions such as the out of memory exception, stack overflow exception, execution engine exception, and so on

The Shared Application Domain

The shared application domain contains domain neutral code. `Mscorlib.dll` is loaded into this application domain (by the system application domain) in addition to the basic types contained in the System namespace (such as `String`, `enum`, `ValueType`, `Array`, and so on). For the most part, non-user code is loaded into the shared application domain, though there are mechanisms available to load user code into the shared application domain. An application hosting the CLR can use loader optimization attributes to inject user code.

The Default Application Domain

Typically, the default application domain is the domain that a .NET application runs in. All the code within the default application domain is valid only in that domain. Because application domains guarantee a logical and reliable boundary, any cross application domain access must be carefully performed using .NET remoting techniques.

Understanding the basics of what an application domain is, which application domains are created automatically, and the fact that application domains can be created dynamically are extremely important when dealing with certain categories of troubleshooting. In Part II, "Applied Debugging," we will see problematic code that is directly related to improper usage of application domains.

Now that we have discussed how a .NET application is loaded, which separation boundaries exist (i.e., application domains), and where different code runs, it's time to take a look at what an assembly actually contains and how the CLR interacts with its content.

Assembly Overview

So far, we have mentioned assemblies without discussing what they are. At a high level, an assembly is the primary building block and deployment unit of .NET applications and can be viewed as a self-describing logical container for other components. When I say *self-describing* I mean that the assembly contains all the necessary information to uniquely identify and describe the assembly. Being able to uniquely identify and describe an assembly is important to ensure that loading and binding of assemblies is performed without conflict and dependencies on other configurable data. By making an assembly self contained, it takes great strides toward eliminating the problem of DLL hell.

There are two different categories of assemblies:

- **Shared assemblies** are assemblies that are intended to be used across different .NET applications. Framework assemblies are good examples of shared assemblies. Because shared assemblies can be used across different .NET applications, it is critical that strong name guarantees are placed on the assembly. Shared assemblies must fully define versioning to allow the CLR to bind to the right version of the assembly. Shared assemblies are typically installed into the Global Assembly Cache (GAC).
- **Private assemblies** are assemblies that are used as part of an application/component but are not suitable to be used by other applications/components. Private assemblies are typically deployed to the same folder (or subfolder) of the application's installation directory. Because the assembly is used in limited scope, the versioning strategy is somewhat more relaxed.

When an assembly is loaded, it is bound to an application domain. From our previous discussion of application domains, we know that a typical .NET application contains three application domains. Besides the system and shared application domain, assemblies are typically loaded in either the default application domain or explicitly created application domains. When an assembly is loaded into an application domain, it stays loaded in that application domain until the application domain is torn down. Because assemblies are bound to an application domain, how can we find out which assemblies are loaded into any given application domain? Earlier in the chapter, we used the `dumpdomain` command of SOS to dump information of all application domains in a given process. As part of the output, the `dumpdomain` command outputs all the assemblies loaded in each application domain. Listing 2-3 showed an example of running the `dumpdomain` extension command during execution of `02simple.exe`. We saw that the default application contained two loaded assemblies: `02simple.exe` and `mscorlib.dll`. In addition, the name of the assemblies is also the address of the assemblies. The address is key when we want more detailed information on each assembly by using the SOS `dumpassembly` command. We can use the `dumpassembly` extension command and pass in the assembly address to get more information, as shown in Listing 2-4.

Listing 2-4 Example of using the dumpassembly command

```
0:000> !dumpassembly 0034db98
Parent Domain: 002ffd38
Name: C:\ADNDBin\02Simple.exe
ClassLoader: 0034e4b8
SecurityDescriptor: 006d7fe8
  Module Name
000e2c3c C:\ADNDBin\02Simple.exe
```

In addition to the name, module name, and security descriptor of the assembly, the parent domain is also displayed. The parent domain address can be used with the SOS `dumpdomain` extension command to output data on the application domain that the assembly is loaded in.

As mentioned earlier, assemblies are self describing. To get a better idea of what it means for an assembly to be self describing, we start by looking at the assembly manifest.

Assembly Manifest

Because an assembly is the fundamental building block of .NET applications and is entirely self describing, where is the descriptive content stored? The answer lies in the metadata section of an assembly, also known as the assembly manifest. An assembly manifest is typically embedded in the assembly PE file but is not required to be. For example, a multimodule assembly can store the manifest in a separate file (i.e., assembly PE file contains manifest only), which then contains the necessary reference data to load and use the dependent modules. Figure 2-5 shows an example of single- and multi-file assemblies.

Even though multi-file assemblies are possible, in practice, most assemblies are single-file assemblies. The next logical question is: what does an assembly manifest actually contain? An assembly manifest typically contains the following pieces of information:

- List of dependent native code modules
- List of dependent assemblies
- Version of the assembly
- Public key token of the assembly (if signed)
- Assembly resources
- Assembly flags such as stack reserve, sub system, and so on

The best way to view the manifest for a given assembly is to use a tool called ILDasm. It is installed as part of the .NET 2.0 SDK and can display very rich assembly information. To view the manifest of an assembly, launch `ildasm.exe` with the name of the assembly from the command line. Let's try it out on our sample application `02simple.exe`. When ILDasm is launched, double-click on the Manifest section, which opens up a new window with all the manifest data. Figure 2-6 illustrates the manifest data when run on `02simple.exe`.

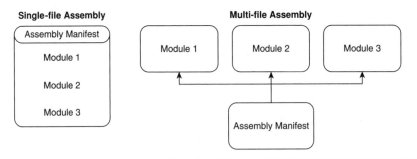

Figure 2-5   Example of single- and multi-file assemblies

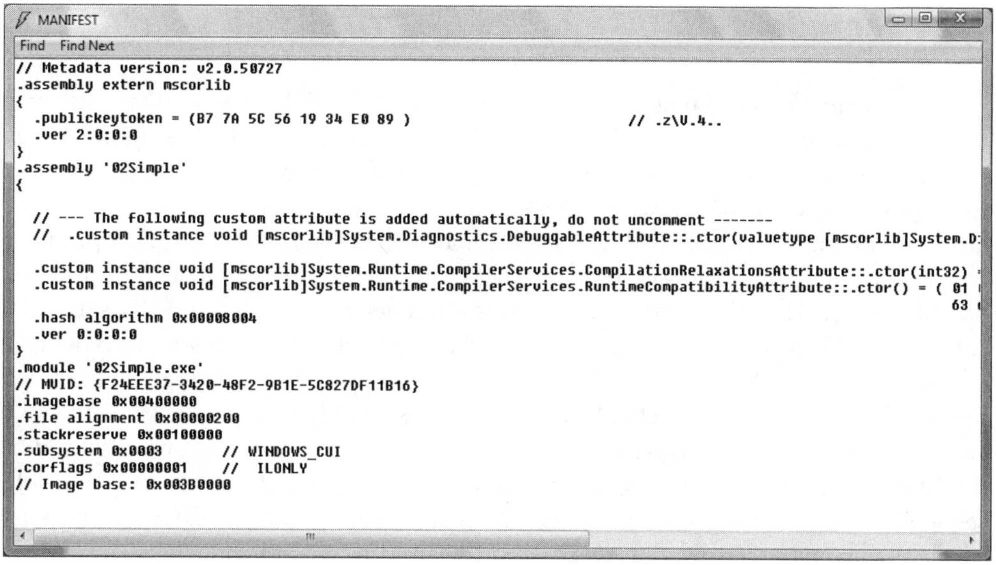

Figure 2-6 Using ILDasm to view assembly manifest data

The first part of the manifest data displayed in Figure 2-6 shows that the 02simple.exe assembly has one external assembly dependency named mscorlib.dll. If the assembly referenced other assemblies as well, they would all be listed in this section. Please note that each external assembly reference contains the public key token for signed assemblies as well as the version of the assembly being referenced. The version is important so that the CLR loader can reference the correct version that the assembly was built against. The next section in the manifest is information about the assembly itself. Information includes the hash algorithm used and the version of the assembly. In our particular example, the version was not specified and is therefore set to 0:0:0:0. The final section contains information about the module (02simple.exe). Even though the assembly manifest for 02simple.exe was relatively trivial, it's easy to understand how the self-descriptive nature of assemblies is implemented. More complicated assemblies contain far more data but follow the general outline illustrated.

Now that we have looked at how a .NET assembly is loaded, the notion of application domains, an overview of assemblies, and the assembly manifest, it's time to take a look at another form of self-describing data, namely the type metadata contained within an assembly.

Type Metadata

A type is the fundamental unit of programmability in .NET. .NET applications work with either custom-defined types or utilize existing types (such as types provided in the framework). Classes, interfaces, and enums are all examples of types available for use. Types can further be broken down into two categories: value types and reference types. Value types are types that are stored on a thread's stack and include enums, structs, and primitive types such as int, bool, char, and so on. Typically, value types are types that are considered relatively small. The other category of types is reference types. Reference types are allocated on the heap and are managed by the garbage collector (GC). Reference types can, of course, contain value types, in which case the value types are located on the heap and managed by the garbage collector. Why was this division of types created? Wouldn't it be easier to simply say that all types are reference types stored on the heap and managed by the GC? The key to this question lies in efficiency. Storing objects on the heap and subsequently managing these objects via the GC is an expensive operation. Objects that are small enough and relatively scoped (i.e., short lived) can more efficiently be stored on a thread's stack. Figure 2-7 shows an example of both a value type and a reference type.

In Figure 2-7, we have an example of a value type (left) and a reference type (right). The value type represents a local variable of type struct declared in a member function of some class. The content of a value type is the address on the stack where the value type instance is stored. In this case, the `localVar` contains a pointer (`0x0028f3c8`) that points to a stack location that in turn contains the value type instance. You can use the regular dump commands (for example, the `dd` command) in the debuggers to dump out the contents. The reference type illustrated in Figure 2-7 contains a pointer (`0x0150588c`) to the instance of the reference type located on the managed heap. The managed heap is fully controlled by the garbage collector (discussed in more detail in Chapter 5, "Managed Heap and Garbage Collection").

To illustrate how the debuggers can be used to look at value and reference types, we use the sample code shown in Listing 2-5.

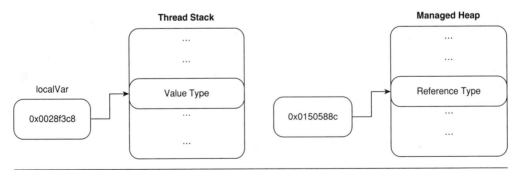

Figure 2-7   Example of a value type and a reference type

Listing 2-5 Example of value and reference types

```
using System;
using System.Text;

namespace Advanced.NET.Debugging.Chapter2
{
    class TypeSample
    {
        TypeSample(int x, int y, int z)
        {
            coordinates.x = x;
            coordinates.y = y;
            coordinates.z = z;
        }

        private struct Coordinates
        {
            public int x;
            public int y;
            public int z;
        }

        private Coordinates coordinates;

        public void AddCoordinates()
        {
            int hashCode = GetHashCode();
            lock (this)
            {
                Coordinates tempCoord;
                tempCoord.x = coordinates.x + 100;
                tempCoord.y = coordinates.y + 50;
                tempCoord.z = coordinates.z + 100;

                System.Console.WriteLine("x={0}, y={1}, z={2}", tempCoord.x,
tempCoord.y, tempCoord.z);
            }
        }

        static void Main(string[] args)
        {
            TypeSample sample = new TypeSample(10,5,10);
            sample.AddCoordinates();
        }
    }
}
```

2. CLR FUNDAMENTALS

The source code and assembly can be found here:

- Source code: `c:\adnd\chapter2\TypeSample\02TypeSample.cs`
- Assembly: `c:\adndbin\02TypeSample.exe`

The source code is relatively straightforward. The `Main` method declares an instance of the reference type `TypeSample` and calls a method called `AddCoordinates`. The `AddCoordinates` function in turn declares a local variable (value type) of type `Coordinates` (struct) and performs some arithmetic and dumps the contents of the value type to the console. Additionally, the `AddCoordinates` function has a lock statement, which will be used later in the chapter to illustrate the notion of sync blocks.

When we run the application, the results are as follows:

```
C:\ADNDBin>02TypeSample.exe
x=110, y=55, z=110
```

Now, let's run the `02TypeSample.exe` application under the debugger and dump out both the local variable `tempCoord` as well as the `sample`. The debugger conversation is illustrated in Listing 2-6.

Listing 2-6   Using the debugger to dump out value and reference types

```
...
...
...
0:000> .symfix
No downstream store given, using c:\Program Files\Debugging Tools for Windows\sym
0:000> .reload
Reloading current modules
....
0:000> .load sosex.dll
0:000> !bpsc 02typesample.cs 34
0:000> g
ModLoad: 76800000 768bf000   C:\Windows\system32\ADVAPI32.dll
ModLoad: 77b60000 77c23000   C:\Windows\system32\RPCRT4.dll
ModLoad: 76ad0000 76b25000   C:\Windows\system32\SHLWAPI.dll
ModLoad: 762e0000 7632b000   C:\Windows\system32\GDI32.dll
ModLoad: 76e80000 76f1e000   C:\Windows\system32\USER32.dll
ModLoad: 76d50000 76dfa000   C:\Windows\system32\msvcrt.dll
ModLoad: 765b0000 765ce000   C:\Windows\system32\IMM32.DLL
ModLoad: 76730000 767f7000   C:\Windows\system32\MSCTF.dll
```

```
ModLoad: 765d0000 765d9000   C:\Windows\system32\LPK.DLL
ModLoad: 76e00000 76e7d000   C:\Windows\system32\USP10.dll
ModLoad: 75340000 754d4000   C:\Windows\WinSxS\x86_microsoft.windows.common-
Controls_6595b64144ccf1df_6.0.6000.20533_none_4634c4a0218d65c1\comctl32.dll
ModLoad: 79e70000 7a3ff000   C:\Windows\Microsoft.NET\Framework\v2.0.50727\mscorwks.dll
ModLoad: 755e0000 7567b000   C:\Windows\WinSxS\x86_microsoft.vc80.crt_1fc8b3b9a1e18e3b
_8.0.50727.762_none_10b2f55f9bffb8f8\MSVCR80.dll
ModLoad: 76f50000 77a1e000   C:\Windows\system32\shell32.dll
ModLoad: 76330000 76474000   C:\Windows\system32\ole32.dll
ModLoad: 790c0000 79bf6000   C:\Windows\assembly\NativeImages_v2.0.50727_32\mscorlib
\32e6f703c114f3a971cbe706586e3655\mscorlib.ni.dll
ModLoad: 79060000 790b6000   C:\Windows\Microsoft.NET\Framework\v2.0.50727\mscorjit.dll
(1fb0.1a64): CLR notification exception - code e0444143 (first chance)
Breakpoint 0 hit
eax=0000006e ebx=0027f1cc ecx=0133588c edx=0000000a esi=0133588c edi=0133588c
eip=00340152 esp=0027f178 ebp=0027f1b0 iopl=0         nv up ei pl nz na po nc
cs=001b  ss=0023  ds=0023  es=0023  fs=003b  gs=0000              efl=00000202
00340152 8b2d40303302    mov    ebp,dword ptr ds:[2333040h] ds:0023:02333040=013358a0
0:000> .loadby sos.dll mscorwks
0:000> !ClrStack -a
OS Thread Id: 0x1a64 (0)
ESP       EIP
0027f178 00340152 Advanced.NET.Debugging.Chapter2.TypeSample.AddCoordinates()
    PARAMETERS:
        this = 0x0133588c
    LOCALS:
        0x0027f178 = 0x0000006e


0027f198 003400b1
Advanced.NET.Debugging.Chapter2.TypeSample.Main(System.String[])
    PARAMETERS:
        args = 0x0133587c
    LOCALS:
        <CLR reg> = 0x0133588c


0027f3b8 79e7c74b [GCFrame: 0027f3b8]
0:000> dd 0x0027f178
0027f178  0000006e 00000037 0000006e 0027f1b0
0027f188  0027f1cc 0133588c 0133588c 003400b1
0027f198  0133587c 00545370 00000000 79e7c74b
0027f1a8  00000000 0027f1d8 0027f230 79e7c6cc
0027f1b8  0027f280 00000000 0027f250 00000000
0027f1c8  002ac030 0027f220 79f07fee 0027f3b8
0027f1d8  df49b45b 0027f404 0027f270 00000000
0027f1e8  0027f3b8 00545370 00000000 00000000
```

(continues)

Listing 2-6 Using the debugger to dump out value and reference types *(continued)*

```
0:000> !dumpobj 0x0133588c
Name: Advanced.NET.Debugging.Chapter2.TypeSample
MethodTable: 002a30b0
EEClass: 002a1234
Size: 20(0x14) bytes
 (C:\ADNDBin\02TypeSample.exe)
Fields:
      MT    Field  Offset              Type VT    Attr     Value Name
002a306c  4000001       4 ...ample+Coordinates  1 instance 01335890 coordinates
0:000>
```

The first thing we do (after setting up the symbols) is to load the `sosex.dll` extension DLL, which enables us to set a breakpoint in the application by using the `bpsc` extension command. The `bpsc` extension command enables you to specify the source filename as well as the line number to which you want the breakpoint to apply. When the breakpoint is set, we continue execution using the g (go) command. When the breakpoint is reached, we load the `sos.dll` extension DLL so that we can utilize the extension commands that enable us to dump out different types of objects (value and reference-type objects). Before we can dump out the objects, we have to find out where the objects are located. To accomplish this, we use the `Clrstack` extension command. The `ClrStack` extension command displays the managed code callstack with a per-frame list of parameters and local variables. As you can see in Listing 2-6, the stack has two frames: `Main` and `AddCoordinates`, respectively. The `AddCoordinates` frame contains a local variable located at address `0x0027f178`. Because we know that the variable in question is a value type (of type `Coordinates`), we can safely use the `dd` command to dump out the raw data corresponding to the contents at address `0x0027f178`. How do you know if a local variable points to a value or reference type? We mentioned earlier that local value parameter types are stored on the stack and, as such, an address of a local value type should be located somewhere within the vicinity of the current stack pointer. The current stack pointer can be easily retrieved using the r (registers) command. The `esp` register displayed as part of the output of the r command gives you a good idea of the source of the address you are looking at. In Listing 2-6, you can see that when dumping the local value type we see the following data: 6e, 37, 62, which correspond to the x,y,z coordinates of the Coordinates type. Next, we look at the Main frame, which contains a local variable (in addition to parameters) located at address `0x0133588c`. Because this local variable refers to a reference type, we cannot simply use the debugger dump commands; rather, we have to utilize an extension command called `dumpobj`. The `dumpobj` extension command takes the address of the reference types and dumps out the object's contents. From Listing 2-6 we can see the following being output:

```
Name: Advanced.NET.Debugging.Chapter2.TypeSample
MethodTable: 002a30b0
EEClass: 002a1234
Size: 20(0x14) bytes
 (C:\ADNDBin\02TypeSample.exe)
Fields:
      MT     Field   Offset                   Type VT    Attr     Value Name
 002a306c  4000001        4 ...ample+Coordinates  1 instance  01335890 coordinates
```

In addition to general information about the type (such as name, size), the type fields with associated offsets are also displayed. In the preceding output, we can see that the type contains a field at offset 4 of type `Coordinates`. Furthermore, the VT column is set to 1, which indicates that this is a value type. The `value` column specifies the address where the field is located. To dump out the fields of a reference object, the `dumpobj` extension command can be utilized again. One caveat exists: If the type is a value type, another extension command, `dumpvc`, must be utilized, as shown in the following:

```
0:000> !dumpvc 002a306c 01335890
Name: Advanced.NET.Debugging.Chapter2.TypeSample+Coordinates
MethodTable 002a306c
EEClass: 002a1298
Size: 20(0x14) bytes
 (C:\ADNDBin\02TypeSample.exe)
Fields:
      MT     Field   Offset              Type VT     Attr    Value Name
 79102290  4000002        0    System.Int32  1 instance       10 x
 79102290  4000003        4    System.Int32  1 instance        5 y
 79102290  4000004        8    System.Int32  1 instance       10 z
```

The `dumpvc` command takes the method table address as well as the value type address as parameters.

So far, we have looked at the two different fundamental types in the CLR, namely value types and reference types. We took a quick look at how the debuggers can be used to interrogate the types. Please note that it is not important to fully understand all of the commands. In Chapter 3, "Basic Debugging Tasks," we will take an in-depth look at how the different commands work.

As we've mentioned before, the essence of .NET is its self-describing nature. We've looked at how assemblies describe themselves via manifests, but so far have not touched on how the type metadata is described. In each assembly PE file, there exists many streams that contain all the type metadata. Table 2-1 provides an overview of the metadata streams.

Table 2-1 Metadata Streams

Stream Name	Description
#Blob	Contains binary data such as method tables
#US	Contains strings in UCS-2 format
#GUID	Contains all the GUIDs used in the assembly
#String	Contains strings in UTF-8 format including names of types and methods
#~	Contains the metadata tables

Before we dive into the details of type metadata, it is important to understand what the memory layout of type instances look like. Figure 2-8 provides a high-level overview of types located on the managed heap.

Each object instance located on the managed heap consists of the following pieces of auxiliary information:

- The **sync block** is a bit mask of auxiliary information or an index into a table maintained by the CLR and contains auxiliary information about the object itself. We will discuss the sync block index later on in this chapter as well as in Chapter 6, "Synchronization."
- The **type handle** is the fundamental unit of the type system in the CLR. It serves as the starting point for fully describing the type located on the managed heap. The type handle is discussed in more detail shortly.
- The **object instance** comes after the sync block index and the type handle and is the actual object data.

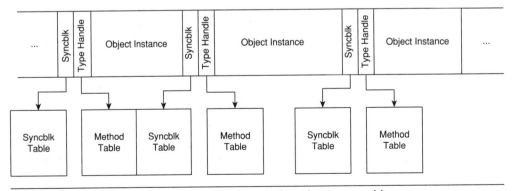

Figure 2-8   High-level overview of objects located on the managed heap

In the next several sections, we will dive deeper into the type handle and sync block index to get an understanding of how the CLR associates type information with the type instance located on the managed heap. Throughout the discussion, we will utilize the sample application `02TypeSample.exe`.

Sync Block Table

Each object that lives on the managed heap is prefixed by what is known as a sync block index into the sync block table that lives in private heaps created by the CLR. The sync block table contains pointers to sync blocks, which in turn contain information such as the object's lock, interoperability data, application domain index, object hash code, and so on. It is possible for an object not to have any sync block data, in which case the sync block index is 0. Please note that the sync block does not always contain a simple index; rather, it can also contain other auxiliary information about the object. In Chapter 6, "Synchronization," we will dissect the sync block to see what types of information can be stored.

An interesting artifact of using an index into a table is that the CLR is free to move/grow the sync block table without having to adjust all sync block object headers.

Let's take a look at what the sync block data look like when viewed in the debuggers. We begin by setting one breakpoint in the `Main` function followed by another breakpoint in the `AddCoordinates` function. The purpose of setting two breakpoints is to illustrate what an object looks like when no locks have been acquired as well as when a lock is taken. Listing 2-7 illustrates the debug conversation when the first breakpoint is hit.

Listing 2-7 Viewing an object's sync block data in the debugger

```
0:000> .symfix
No downstream store given, using c:\Program Files\Debugging Tools for Windows\sym
0:000> .reload
Reloading current modules
....
0:000> .load sosex.dll
0:000> !bpsc 02typesample.cs 34
0:000> !bpsc 02typesample.cs 41
0:000> g
ModLoad: 76680000 7673f000   C:\Windows\system32\ADVAPI32.dll
ModLoad: 763b0000 76473000   C:\Windows\system32\RPCRT4.dll
ModLoad: 76570000 765c5000   C:\Windows\system32\SHLWAPI.dll
ModLoad: 77b90000 77bdb000   C:\Windows\system32\GDI32.dll
ModLoad: 765e0000 7667e000   C:\Windows\system32\USER32.dll
```

(continues)

2. CLR FUNDAMENTALS

Listing 2-7 *Viewing an object's sync block data in the debugger* (continued)

```
ModLoad: 77870000 7791a000   C:\Windows\system32\msvcrt.dll
ModLoad: 76520000 7653e000   C:\Windows\system32\IMM32.DLL
ModLoad: 77710000 777d7000   C:\Windows\system32\MSCTF.dll
ModLoad: 765d0000 765d9000   C:\Windows\system32\LPK.DLL
ModLoad: 76330000 763ad000   C:\Windows\system32\USP10.dll
ModLoad: 75390000 75524000   C:\Windows\WinSxS\x86_microsoft.windows.common-
controls_6595b64144ccf1df_6.0.6000.20533_none_4634c4a0218d65c1\comctl32.dll
ModLoad: 79e70000 7a3ff000   C:\Windows\Microsoft.NET\Framework
\v2.0.50727\mscorwks.dll
ModLoad: 75630000 756cb000   C:\Windows\WinSxS\x86_microsoft
.vc80.crt_1fc8b3b9a1e18e3b_8.0.50727.762_none_10b2f55f9bffb8f8\MSVCR80.dll
ModLoad: 76b90000 7765e000   C:\Windows\system32\shell32.dll
ModLoad: 77920000 77a64000   C:\Windows\system32\ole32.dll
ModLoad: 790c0000 79bf6000   C:\Windows\assembly
\NativeImages_v2.0.50727_32\mscorlib\32e6f703c114f3a971cbe706586e3655\mscorlib.ni.dll
ModLoad: 79060000 790b6000   C:\Windows\Microsoft.NET\Framework
\v2.0.50727\mscorjit.dll
(e98.20fc): CLR notification exception - code e0444143 (first chance)
Breakpoint 0 hit
eax=0000000a ebx=002af46c ecx=0134588c edx=0000000a esi=0134588c edi=0134588c
eip=001900a7 esp=002af438 ebp=002af450 iopl=0         nv up ei pl zr na pe nc
cs=001b  ss=0023  ds=0023  es=0023  fs=003b  gs=0000         efl=00000246
001900a7 8bcf            mov     ecx,edi
0:000> .loadby sos.dll mscorwks
0:000> !ClrStack -a
OS Thread Id: 0x20fc (0)
ESP       EIP
002af438 001900a7
Advanced.NET.Debugging.Chapter2.TypeSample.Main(System.String[])
    PARAMETERS:
        args = 0x0134587c
    LOCALS:
        <CLR reg> = 0x0134588c

002af65c 79e7c74b [GCFrame: 002af65c]
0:000> dd 0x0134588c-0x4
01345888  00000000 000d30b0 0000000a 00000005
01345898  0000000a 00000000 00000000 00000000
013458a8  00000000 00000000 00000000 00000000
013458b8  00000000 00000000 00000000 00000000
013458c8  00000000 00000000 00000000 00000000
013458d8  00000000 00000000 00000000 00000000
013458e8  00000000 00000000 00000000 00000000
013458f8  00000000 00000000 00000000 00000000
0:000>
```

Upon stopping execution on breakpoint 1, we use the `ClrStack` extension command to get the thread-managed code call stack. Each of the frames displays the local variables as well as the parameters passed into the frame. In our case, we have only one frame (`Main`) and the local variable (`0x0134588c`) points to an instance of the `TypeSample` class. The pointer points to the start of the actual object instance, so in order to see the sync block index we have to subtract 4 bytes (`DWORD`) from the object instance pointer. As you can see from Listing 2-7, the dump at location `0x0134588c`-`0x4` yields a content of 0x0, which means that the object does not have a sync block index associated with it. Next, we continue execution until the second breakpoint is hit and once again display the object instance pointer (minus 4 bytes):

```
...
...
...
0:000> g
(e98.20fc): CLR notification exception - code e0444143 (first chance)
Breakpoint 1 hit
eax=0000006e ebx=002af46c ecx=0134588c edx=00000001 esi=0134588c edi=0134588c
eip=00190177 esp=002af3fc ebp=002af430 iopl=0         nv up ei pl nz na po nc
cs=001b  ss=0023  ds=0023  es=0023  fs=003b  gs=0000          efl=00000202
00190177 8b1d40303402    mov     ebx,dword ptr ds:[2343040h]
ds:0023:02343040=013458a0
0:000> !ClrStack -a
OS Thread Id: 0x20fc (0)
ESP        EIP
002af3fc 00190177 Advanced.NET.Debugging.Chapter2.TypeSample.AddCoordinates()
    PARAMETERS:
        this = 0x0134588c
    LOCALS:
        0x002af404 = 0x0000006e
        0x002af3fc = 0x0134588c

002af438 001900b1 Advanced.NET.Debugging.Chapter2.TypeSample.Main(System.String[])
    PARAMETERS:
        args = 0x0134587c
    LOCALS:
        <CLR reg> = 0x0134588c

002af65c 79e7c74b [GCFrame: 002af65c]
0:000> dd 0x0134588c-0x4
01345888 00000001 000d30b0 0000000a 00000005
01345898 0000000a 80000000 790fd8c4 00000014
013458a8 00000013 003d0078 0030007b 002c007d
013458b8 00790020 007b003d 007d0031 0020002c
013458c8 003d007a 0032007b 0000007d 00000000
013458d8 00000000 00000000 00000000 00000000
013458e8 00000000 00000000 00000000 00000000
013458f8 00000000 00000000 00000000 00000000
```

Note that we use the `ClrStack` extension command to get the object instance pointer again. Doing so is critical as the objects that are located on the managed heap can be moved around at the garbage collection's leisure. In this particular run, the object instance pointer is the same (`0x0134588c`), which indicates that the object has not been moved. Next, we once again dump out the contents of the object instance pointer (minus 4 bytes to get to the sync block index), and this time we see that the object in fact has a sync block index of `0x1`. If we look at the source code, we see that the `AddCoordinates` function acquired a lock on the object and caused the CLR to create the sync block index for the object. The next question is how can we take a closer look at the sync block table (more specifically at index 1). Unfortunately, the sync block table is located in the private memory area of the CLR and direct interrogation of the table is not possible. There is, however, an extension command called `syncblk` that is part of the SOS extension DLL that can help shed some light on the sync block table. The sync block extension command can be run with the sync block index of interest or with no arguments, in which case it will dump out all entries in the sync block table. The output of the `syncblk` extension command when run on our sample application (index 1) is shown in the following listing:

```
0:000> !syncblk 1
Index SyncBlock MonitorHeld Recursion Owning Thread Info   SyncBlock Owner
    1 0011fc74           1         1 001051b8  2288   0    0131588c
Advanced.NET.Debugging.Chapter2.TypeSample
-----------------------------
Total           1
CCW             0
RCW             0
ComClassFactory 0
Free            0
0:000>
```

Here, we can see that sync block index 1 refers to a locked monitor owned by thread `0x001051b8`. In Chapter 6, we will take a closer look at synchronization problems and how the sync block can be used to track down the problem. The sync block command focuses primarily on the locking aspects of the sync block and other information (such as an object's hash code) is not displayed.

You might notice that the source code of our sample application has a few strange statements. More specifically, the `AddCoordinates` function includes a call to `GetHashCode` as well as the `lock` statement itself. The reason behind the `GetHashCode` call is to force a sync block entry to be created. When the lock statement is executed, it checks to see if a sync block entry exists for the object and, if so, uses it for the synchronization data. If a sync block does not exist, the CLR utilizes what is known as a thin lock, which is stored outside of the sync block.

This concludes our introduction to the sync block table. In Chapter 6, we will see, in depth, how the sync block information can be utilized to track down synchronization problems.

The next interesting field in Figure 2-8 is the type handle field, which is described next.

Type Handle

All instances of type reference get put on the managed heap controlled by the GC. All instances contain what is known as a type handle. Simply put, the type handle points to what is known as the method table for that particular type. The method table contains metadata that fully describe the particular type. Figure 2-9 illustrates the overall layout of the method table.

The type handle is the glue of the CLR type system and associates the object instance with all of its relevant type data. The type handle of an object instance stored on the managed heap is a pointer to what is known as a method table. The method table contains a lot of information about the type of the object itself, including pointers to other key CLR data structures (such as the EEClass). The very first category of data that the type handle points to contains some miscellaneous information about the type itself. Table 2-2 illustrates the fields in this category.

Table 2-2 Fields in the Miscellaneous Part of the Method Table

Type Handle Offset	Name	Description
+0	Flags	Bitmask that provides information about the type itself. For example, `0x00040000` indicates that the type is a class but not an array.
+4	Base Size	This is the size in bytes of an instance of the type when allocated on the managed heap.
+8	Flags2	Additional type information.
+10	NumMethods	Indicates the total number of methods that the type contains.
+12	NumVirtMethods	Indicates the number of virtual methods that the type contains.
+14	NumInterfaces	Indicates the number of interfaces that the type implements.
+16	Parent	Pointer to the parent method table.

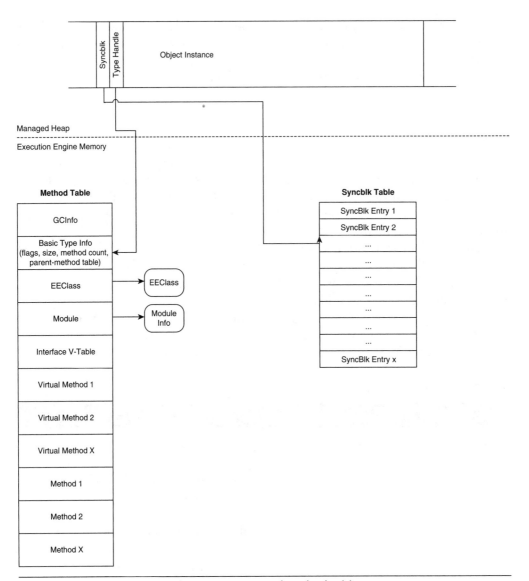

Figure 2-9   Managed heap object instances and method tables

Let's take a look at what a method table looks like in the debugger. We will again use the 02TypeSample.exe sample application. After you've launched the application under the debugger, set a breakpoint at line 41 and continue execution until the breakpoint hits. Listing 2-8 shows the debug conversation.

Listing 2-8 Dumping the method table in the debuggers

```
0:000> .load sosex.dll
0:000> !bpsc 02typesample.cs 41
0:000> g
ModLoad: 76680000 7673f000   C:\Windows\system32\ADVAPI32.dll
ModLoad: 763b0000 76473000   C:\Windows\system32\RPCRT4.dll
ModLoad: 76570000 765c5000   C:\Windows\system32\SHLWAPI.dll
ModLoad: 77b90000 77bdb000   C:\Windows\system32\GDI32.dll
ModLoad: 765e0000 7667e000   C:\Windows\system32\USER32.dll
ModLoad: 77870000 7791a000   C:\Windows\system32\msvcrt.dll
ModLoad: 76520000 7653e000   C:\Windows\system32\IMM32.DLL
ModLoad: 77710000 777d7000   C:\Windows\system32\MSCTF.dll
ModLoad: 765d0000 765d9000   C:\Windows\system32\LPK.DLL
ModLoad: 76330000 763ad000   C:\Windows\system32\USP10.dll
ModLoad: 75390000 75524000   C:\Windows\WinSxS\x86_microsoft.windows.common-
controls_6595b64144ccf1df_6.0.6000.20533_none_4634c4a021
ModLoad: 79e70000 7a3ff000   C:\Windows\Microsoft.NET\Framework
\v2.0.50727\mscorwks.dll
ModLoad: 75630000 756cb000   C:\Windows\WinSxS\x86_microsoft.vc80
.crt_1fc8b3b9a1e18e3b_8.0.50727.762_none_10b2f55f9bffb8f8\MSVCR80.d
ModLoad: 76b90000 7765e000   C:\Windows\system32\shell32.dll
ModLoad: 77920000 77a64000   C:\Windows\system32\ole32.dll
ModLoad: 790c0000 79bf6000   C:\Windows\assembly
\NativeImages_v2.0.50727_32\mscorlib\32e6f703c114f3a971cbe706586e3655\
mscorlib.ni.dl
ModLoad: 79060000 790b6000   C:\Windows\Microsoft.NET\Framework
\v2.0.50727\mscorjit.dll
(2110.2740): CLR notification exception - code e0444143 (first chance)
Breakpoint 0 hit
eax=0000000a ebx=0025f42c ecx=0163588c edx=0000000a esi=0163588c edi=0163588c
eip=003400a7 esp=0025f3f8 ebp=0025f410 iopl=0        nv up ei pl zr na pe nc
cs=001b  ss=0023  ds=0023  es=0023  fs=003b  gs=0000            efl=00000246
003400a7 8bcf            mov     ecx,edi
0:000> .loadby sos.dll mscorwks
0:000> !ClrStack -a
OS Thread Id: 0x2740 (0)
ESP       EIP
0025f3f8 003400a7
Advanced.NET.Debugging.Chapter2.TypeSample.Main(System.String[])
    PARAMETERS:
        args = 0x0163587c
    LOCALS:
        <CLR reg> = 0x0163588c

0025f618 79e7c74b [GCFrame: 0025f618]
```

(continues)

Listing 2-8 Dumping the method table in the debuggers *(continued)*

```
0:000> dd 0x0163588c
0163588c   002930b0 0000000a 00000005 0000000a
0163589c   00000000 00000000 00000000 00000000
016358ac   00000000 00000000 00000000 00000000
016358bc   00000000 00000000 00000000 00000000
016358cc   00000000 00000000 00000000 00000000
016358dc   00000000 00000000 00000000 00000000
016358ec   00000000 00000000 00000000 00000000
016358fc   00000000 00000000 00000000 00000000
0:000> dd 002930b0
002930b0   00040000 00000014 00070402 00000004
002930c0   790fd0f0 00292c3c 002930f8 00291244
002930d0   00000000 00000000 79371278 7936b3b0
002930e0   7936b3d0 793624d0 003400c8 0029c015
002930f0   00340070 00000000 00000080 00000000
00293100   00000000 00000000 00000000 00000000
00293110   00000000 00000000 00000000 00000000
00293120   00000000 00000000 00000000 00000000
0:000>
```

In Listing 2-8, we used the ClrStack extension command to find the local variable on the Main frame. The local variable is a pointer to an instance of type TypeSample located on the managed heap. Next, we dump out the instance and notice that the first field has a value of 0x002930b0, which corresponds to the type handle. To find more information about the type handle (which points to the method table), we dump out the contents of the type handle. The first field displayed (0x00040000) corresponds to the flags field and indicates that the type is a class (non array). The next field indicates the base size of the instance, which in this case is 0x14 bytes (20 decimal). From the source code in Listing 2-5 we can see that the TypeSample class consists of a structure with 4 integers equaling a size of 16 (4*sizeof(DWORD)). The remaining 4 bytes are allocated for the type handle value. The next field of interest is the Flags2 field (WORD) and its value is 0x0402. This bitmask tells the CLR that the type does not need any special class initialization logic as well as the fact that the class does not have any security properties. The next WORD-sized field contains the value 0x0007 and indicates that the class has a total of seven methods. If we look at the source code in Listing 2-5, we can see that the class only has two explicit methods, namely Main and AddCoordinates. What are these other five methods? The first thing to remember is that even though we did not explicitly define any constructors, the C# compiler automatically generated a default constructor for us. The second thing to remember is that all classes are derived from the Object class. The Object class defines four methods that are inherited by all subclasses, namely `ToString`, `Equals`, `GetHashCode`, and `Finalize`. The four inherited methods, the implicit constructor, and our own two methods add up to a total of seven. The next field of interest is the field (of size WORD) indicating the number of virtual methods in the class. In our particular example, the field has a value of `0x0004`, which means that our class has four virtual methods defined. Once again, we look back at the parent Object, which has four virtual methods defined on it (as discussed earlier). The field that states the number of interfaces our class implements is next, which in our case is `0x0000` since we do not implement any interfaces. The final field of interest is the parent method table field, which contains a pointer to the parent object's method table. The pointer in our case is `0x790fd0f0`. Using the same strategy we are employing on our own types method table, you can now dump out the contents of the parent method table and interrogate the contents of that type.

The next part of the method table is a pointer to the module information that the type is associated with. From our dump in Listing 2-8, we can see that the pointer value is `0x00292c3c`. To get extended information on a module, we can use the `DumpModule` extension command and pass in the pointer value:

```
0:000> !DumpModule 00292c3c
Name: C:\ADNDBin\02TypeSample.exe
Attributes: PEFile
Assembly: 0044d8b0
LoaderHeap: 00000000
TypeDefToMethodTableMap: 002900c0
TypeRefToMethodTableMap: 002900cc
MethodDefToDescMap: 002900fc
FieldDefToDescMap: 0029010c
MemberRefToDescMap: 00290120
FileReferencesMap: 00290148
AssemblyReferencesMap: 0029014c
MetaData start address: 00c8214c (1168 bytes)
```

We will take a closer look at Module information later in this chapter.

The next field of interest is the pointer to what is known as an EEClass. We will cover the EEClass data structure later in the chapter.

The next couple of DWORD fields are not used during debugging of .NET applications and can be safely ignored. This constitutes the essence of the method table. The remaining fields contain the virtual method table for the type. Each DWORD field constitutes a pointer to the method itself. In our case, the number of methods fields indicated that we have a total of seven methods. The pointers in the virtual method table are highlighted here:

2. CLR FUNDAMENTALS

```
002930d0   00000000 00000000 79371278 7936b3b0
002930e0   7936b3d0 793624d0 003400c8 0029c015
002930f0   00340070 00000000 00000080 00000000
```

We can use U (unassemble), the extension command, to unassemble each of the method pointers above. For example, if we unassembled the method pointer at address 0x003400c8, we would see the following:

```
0:000> !u 003400c8
Normal JIT generated code
Advanced.NET.Debugging.Chapter2.TypeSample..ctor(Int32, Int32, Int32)
Begin 003400c8, size 35
>>> 003400c8 57               push    edi
003400c9 56               push    esi
003400ca 8bf1             mov     esi,ecx
003400cc 8bfa             mov     edi,edx
003400ce 833d082e290000   cmp     dword ptr ds:[292E08h],0
003400d5 7405             je      003400dc
003400d7 e86b82de79       call    mscorwks!JIT_DbgIsJustMyCode
(7a128347)
003400dc 8bce             mov     ecx,esi
003400de e8d5230279       call    mscorlib_ni+0x2a24b8 (793624b8)
 (System.Object..ctor(), mdToken: 06000001)
003400e3 90               nop
003400e4 90               nop
003400e5 897e04           mov     dword ptr [esi+4],edi
003400e8 8b442410         mov     eax,dword ptr [esp+10h]
003400ec 894608           mov     dword ptr [esi+8],eax
003400ef 8b44240c         mov     eax,dword ptr [esp+0Ch]
003400f3 89460c           mov     dword ptr [esi+0Ch],eax
003400f6 90               nop
003400f7 90               nop
003400f8 5e               pop     esi
003400f9 5f               pop     edi
003400fa c20800           ret     8
0:000>
```

The U command unassembled the code for us, as well as provided additional annotation. For example, we can see that the code we just unassembled is the constructor for the TypeSample class. Please note that some of the method pointers in the method table may point to unmanaged code. For example, the method pointer 0x0029c015 points to an unmanaged code section:

```
0:000> !u 0029c015
Unmanaged code
0029c015 b001             mov     al,1
```

```
0029c017 eb04          jmp      0029c01d
0029c019 b002          mov      al,2
0029c01b eb00          jmp      0029c01d
0029c01d 0fb6c0        movzx    eax,al
0029c020 c1e003        shl      eax,3
0029c023 0530302900    add      eax,293030h
0029c028 e917487600    jmp      00a00844
0029c02d 0000          add      byte ptr [eax],al
0029c02f 00e8          add      al,ch
```

The key to understanding this is to realize that some methods may not have been compiled by the JIT compiler yet. In reality, you are seeing a piece of JIT stub code that kickstarts the compilation process and then transfers control to the newly generated code.

This concludes our discussion of the type handle and method table. Although we have manually taken a look at the contents of the method table, there exists an extension command called DumpMT that will dump out method table information in an easy-to-digest format. What follows is an example of the output of the DumpMT extension command when run on our method table located at 0x002930b0:

```
0:000> !dumpmt 002930b0
EEClass: 00291244
Module: 00292c3c
Name: Advanced.NET.Debugging.Chapter2.TypeSample
mdToken: 02000002   (C:\ADNDBin\02TypeSample.exe)
BaseSize: 0x14
ComponentSize: 0x0
Number of IFaces in IFaceMap: 0
Slots in VTable: 7
```

Even though this extension command exists and makes it much easier to look at the method table contents, it is important to understand how to manually traverse this data structure.

Next, we will take a look at what is known as the method descriptor.

Method Descriptors

In the last section, we discussed the notion of a method table and how the method table described a particular type. Part of the method table includes the virtual method table with pointers to the code behind the type's methods. Because the virtual method table contains raw pointers to code, how are the methods themselves self describing? The answer to that question lies in what is called a method descriptor. A method descriptor contains detailed information about a method such as the textual representation of the method, the module it is contained within, the token, and the code address of the code behind the method.

To find the method descriptor for a given method, we can use the dumpmt extension command with the -md switch. For example, if we run the 02typesample.exe application under the debugger and dump out the method table for the local variable sample we can see the following:

```
0:000> !dumpmt -md 000e30b0
EEClass: 000e1244
Module: 000e2c3c
Name: Advanced.NET.Debugging.Chapter2.TypeSample
mdToken: 02000002  (C:\ADNDBin\02TypeSample.exe)
BaseSize: 0x14
ComponentSize: 0x0
Number of IFaces in IFaceMap: 0
Slots in VTable: 7
-----------------------------------------------
MethodDesc Table
    Entry MethodDesc      JIT Name
79371278  7914b928     PreJIT System.Object.ToString()
7936b3b0  7914b930     PreJIT System.Object.Equals(System.Object)
7936b3d0  7914b948     PreJIT System.Object.GetHashCode()
793624d0  7914b950     PreJIT System.Object.Finalize()
009200c8  000e3030       JIT Advanced.NET.Debugging.Chapter2.TypeSample..ctor(Int32,
Int32, Int32)

000ec015  000e3038     NONE
Advanced.NET.Debugging.Chapter2.TypeSample.AddCoordinates()
00920070  000e3040     JIT
Advanced.NET.Debugging.Chapter2.TypeSample.Main(System.String[])
0:000>
```

The MethodDesc Table portion of the output lists all the method descriptors for the TypeSample type. The Entry column indicates where the code in memory for that method is located, and the MethodDesc column shows the address of the method descriptor. The JIT column indicates the status of the code address and can be one of the following:

- PreJIT indicates that the code located at the Entry address is pre JIT compiled.
- JIT indicates that the code has been JIT compiled.
- NONE indicates that the method has not yet been JIT compiled.

Finally, the Name column gives the textual representation of the method name. To get further information on a given method, we can feed the address shown in the `MethodDesc` column to the `dumpmd` extension command as shown in the following:

```
0:000> !dumpmd 000e3040
Method Name: Advanced.NET.Debugging.Chapter2.TypeSample.Main(System.String[])
Class: 000e1244
MethodTable: 000e30b0
mdToken: 06000003
Module: 000e2c3c
IsJitted: yes
m_CodeOrIL: 00920070
```

The most interesting parts of the output are the `IsJitted` and `m_CodeOrIL` fields, which give clues as to the status (as far as JIT compilation is concerned) of the method. If `IsJitted` is set to `yes`, it means that the method has been JIT compiled and that the `m_CodeOrIL` address contains the actual code. If `IsJitted` is set to `no`, the `m_CodeOrIL` field is set to `0xffffffff`, as shown in the following:

```
0:000> !dumpmd 000e3038
Method Name: Advanced.NET.Debugging.Chapter2.TypeSample.AddCoordinates()
Class: 000e1244
MethodTable: 000e30b0
mdToken: 06000002
Module: 000e2c3c
IsJitted: no
m_CodeOrIL: ffffffff
```

Modules

Previously, we explained that an assembly can be viewed as a logical container for one or more code modules. A module then can be viewed as containing the actual code and/or resources for a given component. When traversing various kinds of CLR data structures (such as method tables, method descriptors, etc.), they all typically contain a pointer to the module where they are defined. For example, dumping out a method descriptor for the `AddCoordinates` function of `02TypeSample.exe` yields the following:

```
0:000> !dumpmd 000e3038
Method Name:
Advanced.NET.Debugging.Chapter2.TypeSample.AddCoordinates()
Class: 000e1244
MethodTable: 000e30b0
mdToken: 06000002
Module: 000e2c3c
IsJitted: no
m_CodeOrIL: ffffffff
```

2. CLR FUNDAMENTALS

The address of the module where the type is located is at address 0x000e2c3c.
In order to get extended information about the module at any given address,
we can use the dumpmodule extension command as illustrated below.

```
0:000> !dumpmodule 000e2c3c
Name: C:\ADNDBin\02TypeSample.exe
Attributes: PEFile
Assembly: 002cd8b8
LoaderHeap: 00000000
TypeDefToMethodTableMap: 000e00c0
TypeRefToMethodTableMap: 000e00cc
MethodDefToDescMap: 000e00fc
FieldDefToDescMap: 000e010c
MemberRefToDescMap: 000e0120
FileReferencesMap: 000e0148
AssemblyReferencesMap: 000e014c
MetaData start address: 000c214c (1168 bytes)
```

In addition to the name, attributes, assembly address where the module is
located, and loader heap fields, there is a set of maps defined. These maps simply
map tokens to the underlying CLR data structures. For example, if we want to map
a method definition token to a method descriptor, we would first dump out the data
located at the `MethodDefToDescMap` address:

```
0:000> dd 000e00fc
000e00fc  00000000 000e3030 000e3038 000e3040
000e010c  00000000 000e3014 000e3048 000e3054
000e011c  000e3060 00000000 00000000 00000000
000e012c  00000000 7914b920 00000000 00000000
000e013c  00000000 00000000 00000000 000e2c3c
000e014c  00000000 790c2000 000e0174 00000400
000e015c  00000002 00000000 00000000 00000000
000e016c  00000000 000e2c3c 00000000 00000000
```

Here, we can see that the method definition tokens at locations one, two, and
three contain addresses to method descriptors. The dumpmd extension can then be
used for each of these addresses to get further information on the method descriptors:

```
0:000> !dumpmd 000e3030
Method Name: Advanced.NET.Debugging.Chapter2.TypeSample..ctor(Int32, Int32, Int32)
Class: 000e1244
MethodTable: 000e30b0
mdToken: 06000001
Module: 000e2c3c
IsJitted: yes
m_CodeOrIL: 009200c8
0:000> !dumpmd 000e3038
```

```
Method Name: Advanced.NET.Debugging.Chapter2.TypeSample.AddCoordinates()
Class: 000e1244
MethodTable: 000e30b0
mdToken: 06000002
Module: 000e2c3c
IsJitted: no
m_CodeOrIL: ffffffff
0:000> !dumppmd 000e3040
Method Name: Advanced.NET.Debugging.Chapter2.TypeSample.Main(System.String[])
Class: 000e1244
MethodTable: 000e30b0
mdToken: 06000003
Module: 000e2c3c
IsJitted: yes
m_CodeOrIL: 00920070
```

In addition to being able to dump out module-specific information, the dump-module extension command can also output a complete list of types that are defined within that module as well as any types that the module references. To get this list of information, we use the -mt switch as illustrated here:

```
0:000> !dumpmodule -mt 000e2c3c
Name: C:\ADNDBin\02TypeSample.exe
Attributes: PEFile
Assembly: 002cd8b8
LoaderHeap: 00000000
TypeDefToMethodTableMap: 000e00c0
TypeRefToMethodTableMap: 000e00cc
MethodDefToDescMap: 000e00fc
FieldDefToDescMap: 000e010c
MemberRefToDescMap: 000e0120
FileReferencesMap: 000e0148
AssemblyReferencesMap: 000e014c
MetaData start address: 000c214c (1168 bytes)
```

Types defined in this module

```
    MT    TypeDef Name
-------------------------------------------------
000e30b0 0x02000002 Advanced.NET.Debugging.Chapter2.TypeSample
000e306c 0x02000003 Advanced.NET.Debugging.Chapter2.TypeSample+Coordinates
```

Types referenced in this module

```
    MT    TypeRef Name
-------------------------------------------------
790fd0f0 0x01000001 System.Object
790fd260 0x01000002 System.ValueType
```

Metadata Tokens

So far, we have seen a number of different runtime constructs such as assemblies, modules, method descriptors, method tables, and so on. All of these constructs exist to support the type system and self-descriptive nature of .NET binaries. The metadata required by the CLR is stored in the runtime engine in the form of tables. There are a lot of different kinds of metadata tables and we won't discuss all of them here, but it is important to highlight how the CLR utilizes the metadata tables and how they are referenced by using what is known as a metadata token. At a high level, a metadata token is represented by 4 bytes, as illustrated in Figure 2-10.

The high-order byte represents the table that the token is referencing. Table 2-3 outlines the different tables available.

A metadata token of value 06000001 can then be interpreted as referencing index 1 (low-order bytes) of the method definition table (high-order byte 0x06). Is there a way to look at the contents of some of these tables? Yes, the output of the DumpModule command we discussed earlier displays a list of common table mappings. What follows is an example of the output of the DumpModule command.

```
0:000> !DumpModule 00292c3c
Name: C:\ADNDBin\03ObjTypes.exe
Attributes: PEFile
Assembly: 0033d2e8
LoaderHeap: 00000000
TypeDefToMethodTableMap: 002900c0
TypeRefToMethodTableMap: 002900d8
MethodDefToDescMap: 00290124
FieldDefToDescMap: 00290150
MemberRefToDescMap: 00290174
FileReferencesMap: 002901b4
AssemblyReferencesMap: 002901b8
MetaData start address: 013d2330 (2424 bytes)
```

Let's take a look at the first map TypeDeftoMethodTableMap located at address 0x002900c0. The TypeDeftoMethodTableMap maps type definitions to their corresponding method tables. If we dump out the map using the dd command, we can see the following:

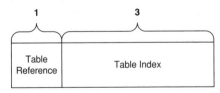

Figure 2-10 Layout of a metadata token

Table 2-3 Metadata Tables

Type	Description
0x00000000	Module
0x01000000	Type reference
0x02000000	Type definition
0x04000000	Field definition
0x06000000	Method definition
0x08000000	Parameter definition
0x09000000	Interface implementation
0x0a000000	Member reference
0x0c000000	Custom attribute
0x0e000000	Permission
0x11000000	Signature
0x14000000	Event
0x17000000	Property
0x1a000000	Module reference
0x1b000000	Type specification
0x20000000	Assembly
0x23000000	Assembly reference
0x26000000	File
0x27000000	Exported type
0x28000000	Manifest resource
0x2a000000	Generic parameter
0x2b000000	Method specification
0x2c000000	Generic parameter constraint

```
0:000> dd 002900c0
002900c0  00000000 00000000 0029313c 002930e8
002900d0  002931c0 002932e8 00000000 790fd0f0
002900e0  790fd260 7911a508 00000000 00000000
002900f0  00000000 00000000 79101118 00000000
00290100  79102290 00000000 00000000 790fea5c
00290110  00000000 00000000 790fd8c4 00000000
00290120  00000000 00000000 00293078 00293080
00290130  00293088 00293090 00293098 002930a0
```

Here, we can see that a method table pointer exists at index 2 (0x0029313c). We can easily verify what we are seeing by using the DumpMT command:

```
0:000> !DumpMT 0029313c
EEClass: 002912e0
Module: 00292c3c
Name: Advanced.NET.Debugging.Chapter3.ObjTypes
mdToken: 02000002   (C:\ADNDBin\03ObjTypes.exe)
BaseSize: 0x1c
ComponentSize: 0x0
Number of IFaces in IFaceMap: 0
Slots in VTable: 10
```

The method table at index 2 corresponds to the method table for the Advanced.NET.Debugging.Chapter3.ObjTypes type with a metadata token of 02000002. The low-order bytes of the token are correct (index 2) and, by consulting Table 2-3, we can verify that the high-order bit (02) refers to a type.

EEClass

We have looked at a number of different CLR data structures by either manually walking them or using the debuggers and extension commands. Several of the debugger conversations have included the notion of an EEClass, which we will describe next. The EEClass data structure is best viewed as the logical equivalent of the method table, and as such can be described as a mechanism to enable the self-descriptive nature of the CLR type system. Internally, the EEClass and method table are two distinct constructs, but logically they represent the same concept, thus begging the question of why the separation was introduced to begin with. The separation occurred based on how frequently type fields were used by the CLR. Fields that are used quite frequently are stored in the method table, whereas fields that are used less frequently are stored in the EEClass data structure.

Figure 2-11 provides an overview of the most key elements of the EEClass data structure.

Please note that Figure 2-11 represents an overview of the fields available in the EEClass structure and is not meant to give an accurate offset-based view.

The hierarchical nature of object-oriented languages such as C# is replicated in the EEClass structure. When the CLR loads types, it creates a similar hierarchy of EEClass nodes with parent and sibling pointers, enabling it to traverse the hierarchy in an efficient manner. For the most part, the fields in the EEClass data structure are straightforward. One field of importance is the MethodDesc chunk field that contains a pointer to the first chunk of method descriptors in the type. This enables you to

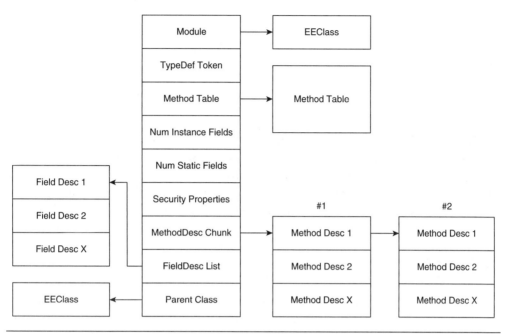

Figure 2-11   EEClass overview

traverse the method descriptors that are part of any given type. Each chunk also contains a pointer to the next chunk in the chain. The easiest (and safest) way to look at the contents of an `EEClass` instance is to use the `dumpclass` extension command as illustrated in the following.

```
0:000> !dumpmt 000e30b0
EEClass: 000e1244
Module: 000e2c3c
Name: Advanced.NET.Debugging.Chapter2.TypeSample
mdToken: 02000002   (C:\ADNDBin\02TypeSample.exe)
BaseSize: 0x14
ComponentSize: 0x0
Number of IFaces in IFaceMap: 0
Slots in VTable: 7
0:000> !dumpclass 000e1244
Class Name: Advanced.NET.Debugging.Chapter2.TypeSample
mdToken: 02000002 (C:\ADNDBin\02TypeSample.exe)
Parent Class: 790fd08c
Module: 000e2c3c
Method Table: 000e30b0
```

```
Vtable Slots: 4
Total Method Slots: 7
Class Attributes: 100000
NumInstanceFields: 1
NumStaticFields: 0
        MT    Field   Offset                  Type VT    Attr     Value Name
000e306c  4000001        4 ...ample+Coordinates  1 instance            coordinates
```

One of the ways in which you can get the EEClass pointer of a type is via its method table. We can use the dumpmt extension command to dump out the method table, grab the EEClass pointer, and feed it to the dumpclass extension command. The output of the dumpclass extension command includes the parent class pointer, module, method table, field counts, and a detailed drill down for each type field.

Summary

In this chapter, we took a look at the basic anatomy of a .NET application by utilizing the debuggers and associated extensions to gain a better understanding of some of the basic building blocks of the CLR. Although we didn't explain each and every debugger command in detail, don't worry; all commands will be explained fully in Chapter 3. There are also several other key components of the CLR that were not discussed, such as the garbage collector and assembly loader. Each of these components will be discussed in detail in Part II of the book where we take a look at some of common pitfalls when utilizing those CLR components.

## CHAPTER 3

BASIC DEBUGGING TASKS

In Chapter 2, "CLR Fundamentals," we looked at some key CLR internals by briefly introducing the debuggers and associated extension commands. In this chapter, we will dig deeper into the debugger and take a look at some of the basic debugging tasks that will be important throughout the remainder of this book. We will start with the basics on how to start a process under the debugger, setting symbol and source paths, controlling the execution of the debugger, object operations, thread operations, code operations, and much more. In addition to a theoretical description of the commands, we will also utilize a number of different .NET applications to illustrate the practical aspects of the commands. Please note that this chapter is not meant to be an exhaustive description of all of the debugger functionality. Rather, it serves to provide the knowledge required throughout the remainder of the book.

The Debugger and the Debugger Target

Two major components are involved when doing any type of debugging: the debugger itself and the debugger target (process being debugged). The debugger represents the engine that enables you to interact with the process that you are debugging. All interactions with the debugger target (such as setting breakpoints, inspecting state, etc.) are presented in the form of commands to the debugger, which subsequently executes the commands in the context of the debugger target. For example, if we want to debug `02simple.exe`, we could launch the `02simple.exe` application under the debugger and use the debugger process to control the execution of the `02simple.exe` process as illustrated in Figure 3-1.

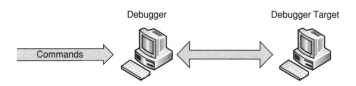

Figure 3-1 Debugger and debugger target during a debug session

As seen in Figure 3-1, the debugger and the debugger target can be located on two different machines providing the convenience of remote debugging when physical access to the debugger target is not possible.

To get a better understanding of how the debugging process works, let's take a look at an example. Let's say that we want to debug the 02simple.exe application using a debugger called ntsd.exe (available in the Debugging Tools for Windows package). To invoke the debugger, we simply launch it from the command prompt using the following command:

```
C:\> ntsd
```

If no arguments are specified, ntsd simply displays a list of available options. To specify an application to debug, we can simply add it as a command-line argument as shown in the following:

```
C:\> ntsd c:\ADNDBin\02simple.exe
```

Next, the debugger itself is launched in a new console window, and it displays a slew of information to the user. Listing 3-1 shows the initial data displayed.

Listing 3-1   Initial launch of the debugger when debugging 02simple.exe

```
Microsoft (R) Windows Debugger Version 6.9.0003.113 X86
Copyright (c) Microsoft Corporation. All rights reserved.

CommandLine: c:\ADNDBin\02simple.exe
Symbol search path is: *** Invalid ***
************************************************************************
* Symbol loading may be unreliable without a symbol search path.      *
* Use .symfix to have the debugger choose a symbol path.              *
* After setting your symbol path, use .reload to refresh symbol locations. *
************************************************************************
Executable search path is:
ModLoad: 00400000 00408000   02simple.exe
ModLoad: 7c900000 7c9af000   ntdll.dll
ModLoad: 79000000 79045000   C:\WINDOWS\system32\mscoree.dll
ModLoad: 7c800000 7c8f6000   C:\WINDOWS\system32\KERNEL32.dll
(1568.1600): Break instruction exception - code 80000003 (first chance)
eax=00251eb4 ebx=7ffdf000 ecx=00000000 edx=00000001 esi=00251f48 edi=00251eb4
eip=7c90120e esp=0013fb20 ebp=0013fc94 iopl=0         nv up ei pl nz na po nc
cs=001b  ss=0023  ds=0023  es=0023  fs=003b  gs=0000            efl=00000202
*** ERROR: Symbol file could not be found.  Defaulted to export symbols for
ntdll.dll -
```

```
ntdll!DbgBreakPoint:
7c90120e cc              int     3
0:000>
```

The first category of information presented relates to something that the debugger refers to as symbols and symbol search path. At the initial launch, the debugger is notifying you that a symbol search path has not been set. We will discuss symbol files in more detail later in the chapter but for now you can think of symbol files as metadata associated with images and libraries that greatly enhance the debugging experience. Next, a set of modules are listed (such as `02simple.exe`, `ntdll.dll`, `mscoree.dll`, etc.). This list signifies all the modules that the application has loaded up until this point. The next valuable piece of information that the debugger displays is the event that caused the debugger to stop execution. In this particular case, we can see that it's due to a *break instruction exception*. Anytime a process is started under the debugger or a debugger attached to a process, the debugger injects a breakpoint instruction causing the execution of the debugger target to halt. The breakpoint instruction is obviously crucial to allow the user a chance to interact with the debugger and debugger target. The next set of data displays the registers as well as register content followed by displaying the instruction that caused the latest event to occur (in our case, the breakpoint instruction `int 3`). Lastly, the debugger displays a prompt and simply sits there waiting for the user to enter commands for the debugger to execute. Please note that the prompt is displayed in the following format:

```
X:Y>
```

The X represents the active target being debugged (in most debug sessions, this will be 0) and Y represents the thread ID that caused the debugger to break execution.

At this point, we have successfully launched an application under the debugger and we are politely being asked by the debugger to start entering our commands. This form of debugging works perfectly when you can launch any given problematic application under the debugger from the start. However, situations exist where an application is already running and it's not always feasible to restart the application under the debugger. In those cases, we prefer a mechanism that enables us to attach the debugger to an already running application. For example, imagine that you have developed a Web service that is hosted in Internet Information Service (IIS). Over time, the Web service process starts exhibiting strange behaviors, and you want to debug the process while it's in this state. In this scenario, you can utilize the -p command-line argument that the debugger supports. The -p argument simply tells the debugger that you are interested in debugging an already running process. The -p argument must be accompanied by the process that you are interested in debugging by specifying the process ID. There are a number of different ways to find the process ID of any given process. One convenient way is to utilize the `tlist.exe` command available as part of the Debugging Tools for Windows package. Simply run `tlist.exe` and it displays a list of all processes and their associated process IDs. To illustrate this scenario, let's say we want to debug an already running instance of `03simple.exe`. First, we launch `03simple.exe` and rather than pressing any key to exit the application, we simply run `tlist.exe` to see what the process ID is for `03simple.exe`. Listing 3-2 illustrates the abbreviated output of `tlist.exe` after `03simple.exe` was launched.

Listing 3-2   tlist.exe output

```
C:\>tlist
    0 System Process
    4 System
  712 smss.exe
  768 csrss.exe
  792 winlogon.exe
  836 services.exe
...

...

...
 5828 wlmail.exe          Inbox - Windows Live Mail
 4288 OSE.EXE
 2424 devenv.exe          03simple.cs - Microsoft Visual Studio
 1540 03Simple.exe
 1320 cmd.exe             C:\WINDOWS\system32\cmd.exe - tlist
 3120 tlist.exe
```

As you can see, `03simple.exe` is shown to have a process ID of `1540`. Now, we have all the information that we need to attach the debugger to the `03simple.exe` process by running the following:

```
C:\> ntsd -p 1540
```

Again, a new debugger window is displayed with an initial set of information as shown in Listing 3-3.

Listing 3-3   Attaching the debugger to an already running instance of 03simple.exe

```
Microsoft (R) Windows Debugger Version 6.9.0003.113 X86
Copyright (c) Microsoft Corporation. All rights reserved.
*** wait with pending attach
Symbol search path is: *** Invalid ***
```

```
**************************************************************************
* Symbol loading may be unreliable without a symbol search path.       *
* Use .symfix to have the debugger choose a symbol path.               *
* After setting your symbol path, use .reload to refresh symbol locations. *
**************************************************************************
Executable search path is:
ModLoad: 00400000 00408000   c:\ADNDBin\03Simple.exe
ModLoad: 7c900000 7c9af000   C:\WINDOWS\system32\ntdll.dll
ModLoad: 79000000 79045000   C:\WINDOWS\system32\mscoree.dll
ModLoad: 7c800000 7c8f6000   C:\WINDOWS\system32\KERNEL32.dll
ModLoad: 77dd0000 77e6b000   C:\WINDOWS\system32\ADVAPI32.dll
ModLoad: 77e70000 77f02000   C:\WINDOWS\system32\RPCRT4.dll
ModLoad: 77fe0000 77ff1000   C:\WINDOWS\system32\Secur32.dll
ModLoad: 77f60000 77fd6000   C:\WINDOWS\system32\SHLWAPI.dll
ModLoad: 77f10000 77f59000   C:\WINDOWS\system32\GDI32.dll
ModLoad: 7e410000 7e4a1000   C:\WINDOWS\system32\USER32.dll
ModLoad: 77c10000 77c68000   C:\WINDOWS\system32\msvcrt.dll
ModLoad: 76390000 763ad000   C:\WINDOWS\system32\IMM32.DLL
ModLoad: 79e70000 7a3d6000   C:\WINDOWS\Microsoft.NET\Framework\v2.0.50727
\mscorwks.dll
ModLoad: 78130000 781cb000   C:\WINDOWS\WinSxS\x86_Microsoft.VC80.CRT
_1fc8b3b9a1e18e3b_8.0.50727.762_x-ww_6b128700\MSVCR80.dll
ModLoad: 7c9c0000 7d1d7000   C:\WINDOWS\system32\shell32.dll
ModLoad: 773d0000 774d3000   C:\WINDOWS\WinSxS\x86_Microsoft.
Windows.Common-Controls_6595b64144ccf1df_6.0.2600.5512_x-ww_35d4ce83\comctl32.dll
ModLoad: 5d090000 5d12a000   C:\WINDOWS\system32\comctl32.dll
ModLoad: 790c0000 79b90000   C:\WINDOWS\assembly\NativeImages_v2.0
.50727_32\mscorlib\1519aecdfda7ccb6075750b4429d2834\mscorlib.ni.dll
ModLoad: 774e0000 7761d000   C:\WINDOWS\system32\ole32.dll
ModLoad: 79060000 790b3000   C:\WINDOWS\Microsoft.NET\Framework
\v2.0.50727\mscorjit.dll
(604.168c): Break instruction exception - code 80000003 (first chance)
eax=7ffd4000 ebx=00000001 ecx=00000002 edx=00000003 esi=00000004 edi=00000005
eip=7c90120e esp=00c8ffcc ebp=00c8fff4 iopl=0         nv up ei pl zr na pe nc
cs=001b  ss=0023  ds=0023  es=0023  fs=0038  gs=0000            efl=00000246
*** ERROR: Symbol file could not be found.  Defaulted to export symbols for
C:\WINDOWS\system32\ntdll.dll -
ntdll!DbgBreakPoint:
7c90120e cc              int     3
0:003>
```

As you can see, much of the information that is displayed is similar in nature to Listing 3-1, with the exception of the loaded module list, which has far more modules. This is to be expected because the number of modules typically goes up as the application executes over time and there certainly will be far more than during the initial break-in.

Noninvasive Debugging

So far, we have discussed two different ways of debugging a target. One is by launching the target application under the debugger and the other is to attach the debugger to an already running instance of the application. Both actions forcefully stop the execution of the application and enable the user to interact with the target via the debugger. There is a third option known as noninvasive debugging. If you noninvasively attach the debugger to a target, the debugger does not break the execution of the target; rather, it suspends all threads running in the target and enables you to inspect the state of the target. Please keep in mind that due to the way noninvasive debugging works, commands that would normally allow you to control the execution of the target (such as the g and bp command) are disabled.

At this point, we have successfully started a debug session and interpreted some of the initial information displayed by the debugger. What are the next steps? How do we actually go about debugging the target? Earlier, I mentioned that the debugger was complaining about symbols and the symbol search path not being set. I also mentioned that symbols can be viewed as metadata making debugging a far more feasible prospect. In the next section, we'll dive into the details of symbols and how we can make best use of them in the debugger.

Symbols

Before we dive into the details of how to utilize symbols and sources in the debuggers, let's step back and quickly define what a symbol file is. A symbol file is nothing more than an auxiliary data source that annotates your application code with additional information that can be useful during debugging. Imagine for a second that this auxiliary data did not exist and that only your application's binary was present. Debugging only the application binary would be a painful effort as you would not be able to see, for example, function names, data structure names, and much more. This is where the symbol files come in. A symbol file "annotates" the application binary with additional information making it much easier to debug your code. All of this annotation comes in the form of a symbol file. Symbol files nowadays typically have the extension pdb and are fully understood by the debuggers to make life easier for the engineer debugging the problem.

In the native world, symbol files play a key role in determining the success of a debug session. In the managed world, even though .NET binaries are far more self descriptive than native binaries, symbol files are equally important. Having symbols available will greatly increase your debugging success. Examples of information that is crucial are line numbers and local variable names.

There are two different types of symbol files: private and public. Private symbols files are what most developers are used to working with. They contain all the symbolic information that is needed during a debug session. Public symbols, on the other hand, only contain select symbolic information making debugging slightly harder. A great example of public symbols files are the symbols stored on the Microsoft symbol server. Every time you point your debugger to the Microsoft symbols servers, the public symbols are pulled down and used during the debug session. One question you might be asking yourself is, why was the separation of private and public symbol files introduced? If private symbols contain far more information and make it much easier to debug, why not just make the private symbols available? The answer lies in protecting intellectual property. Private symbols expose a ton of information about the underlying technology making it easier to reverse engineer aspects of the technology. To better protect IP, public symbols still allow customers to debug the technology without gaining access to the in-depth information otherwise provided with private symbols.

To use symbols in the debuggers, we must first tell the debugger where the symbols are located. If they are located in the same directory as the application or in certain well-known locations, the debuggers will automatically pick them up. If not, the debuggers offer a set of commands that you can use to set what is known as a symbol path. When the symbol path has been set, the debuggers try to load the symbols from the well-known locations as well as the symbol path that you added. First, we will take a look at the `sympath` meta-command. If you execute the `sympath` command without any parameters, the debugger displays the currently set symbol path as shown in the following:

```
0:000> .sympath
Symbol search path is: <empty>
```

Initially, the symbol path is set to empty and the debuggers use the well-known symbol paths to load the symbols. Let's say that you have an application that, once installed, is located in the following folder:

```
C:\program files\My application
```

Furthermore, let's say you need to debug an instance of that application and that your symbol files are stored in the following folder:

```
C:\MySymbols
```

To use the symbols, you have to run the following command:

```
0:000> .sympath c:\mysymbols
Symbol search path is: c:\mysymbols
```

At this point, the debugger has recorded the new symbol path but has not yet loaded any symbols that are applicable from that path. To tell the debugger to load the symbols, we can use the `reload` meta-command, which enumerates all the loaded modules in the process address space and attempts to find the associated symbol files associated with each module.

```
0:000> .reload
Reloading current modules
....
*** ERROR: Symbol file could not be found.  Defaulted to export symbols for
ntdll.dll -
```

If the debugger fails to find a symbol file, it displays an error as shown previously. In this particular case, it successfully loaded all the symbols except for the `ntdll.dll` module, which was not found. `Ntdll.dll` is a module that is part of Windows and as such we would like to download the symbols for this module from the Microsoft public symbol server. There is a simple meta-command called `symfix` that automatically sets the symbol path to the public Microsoft symbol server as illustrated in the following:

```
0:000> .symfix
No downstream store given, using c:\Program Files\Debugging Tools for
Windows (x86)\sym
```

The message stating that no downstream store was given simply implies that no local path was given to cache the symbols that end up being downloaded. Rather than redownloading the same symbols each and every time, you can specify a path to the `symfix` command that will store the downloaded symbols locally so that next time the debugger picks any existing symbol files from the local cache. By default, if no local path (downstream store) was specified, the debuggers will use the `sym` folder under the installation path of the debugging package.

At this point, we know how to set the symbol path for our own symbols (using `sympath`) as well as how to set the symbol path to point to the public Microsoft symbol servers. Another interesting variation of the `sympath` and `symfix` commands are the `sympath+` and `symfix+` commands. These commands do not overwrite the existing symbol path but rather append another path to the existing symbol path already set. For example, let's say that we have set our symbol path to `c:\mysym` using the `sympath` command. If we want to append another symbol path, we could use the following command:

```
0:000> .sympath c:\adndbin
Symbol search path is: c:\adndbin
0:000> .sympath+ c:\mysym
Symbol search path is: c:\adndbin;c:\mysym
0:000>
```

This concludes the abbreviated tour of how to set up the debugger to access the correct symbols. Without proper symbols, debugging can quickly become an insurmountable obstacle, and knowing how to point the debuggers to the correct symbols is key to any debug session.

Controlling Execution

During any debugging session, it is useful to be able to control the execution of the target. We may want to set a few breakpoints, resume execution until a breakpoint hits, look at the state of the target, step into functions, resume execution again, and so on. The native debuggers provide a set of commands that enable you to control this execution. In the next few sections, I will discuss the commands most commonly used to control execution.

Breaking Execution

There are a number of different ways that the debugger can break execution depending on how the debugger has been configured. In the most basic case, you may find that you want to manually break execution (such as in the case of a deadlock) to do some troubleshooting. To manually break execution, you use the key sequence CTRL-C. This causes the debugger to inject a thread into the target process and issue a breakpoint statement. Other ways in which the debugger can break execution includes setting breakpoints, which is discussed in more detail later in the chapter. Setting breakpoints provides a convenient way to choose at what point in the execution flow you want the debugger to break execution. Finally, another common occurrence that causes the debugger to break execution is when an exception occurs (first or second chance). Exceptions are also discussed in more detail later in the chapter.

Resuming Execution

Whenever the debugger breaks execution (due to a breakpoint or other event), you are presented with a debugger prompt and allowed to interact with the debugger target. Typically, you use this opportunity to investigate some state on the debugger target or set up additional breakpoints that you want to be notified about in the future. When you are satisfied with the investigation at the current break-in, you may want to resume execution until another debugger event occurs. To resume execution, you can use the g (go) debugger command. In its most basic form, the g command simply resumes execution until the next debugger event occurs. A very common example of this is when you start a process under the debugger. Let's start the 03breakpoint.exe application under the debugger using the following command line:

```
C:\ADNDBin\ntsd 03Breakpoint.exe
```

Upon execution of the previous command line, the debugger automatically breaks into the debugger as soon as it is launched, as shown in Listing 3-4.

Listing 3-4   Initial breakpoint when starting a process under the debugger

```
Microsoft (R) Windows Debugger Version 6.9.0003.113 X86
Copyright (c) Microsoft Corporation. All rights reserved.

CommandLine: 03Breakpoint.exe
Symbol search path is: *** Invalid ***
***************************************************************************
* Symbol loading may be unreliable without a symbol search path.          *
* Use .symfix to have the debugger choose a symbol path.                  *
* After setting your symbol path, use .reload to refresh symbol locations. *
***************************************************************************
Executable search path is:
ModLoad: 00400000 00408000   03Breakpoint.exe
ModLoad: 7c900000 7c9af000   ntdll.dll
ModLoad: 79000000 79045000   C:\WINDOWS\system32\mscoree.dll
ModLoad: 7c800000 7c8f6000   C:\WINDOWS\system32\KERNEL32.dll
(dbc.a98): Break instruction exception - code 80000003 (first chance)
eax=00251eb4 ebx=7ffd5000 ecx=00000000 edx=00000001 esi=00251f48 edi=00251eb4
eip=7c90120e esp=0013fb20 ebp=0013fc94 iopl=0         nv up ei pl nz na po nc
cs=001b  ss=0023  ds=0023  es=0023  fs=003b  gs=0000          efl=00000202
*** ERROR: Symbol file could not be found.  Defaulted to export symbols for
ntdll.dll -
```

```
ntdll!DbgBreakPoint:
7c90120e cc              int     3
0:000>
```

The initial breakpoint that occurred is the default behavior for the debugger as it presents the earliest opportunity for the engineer debugging to start investigating the application. Remember that at this point, the target has stopped execution and is awaiting your commands. When you have completed all the commands you want to run (setting up symbol paths, etc.), you can simply resume execution using the g command, as shown in the following:

```
0:000> .symfix
No downstream store given, using c:\Program Files\Debugging Tools for Windows\sym
0:000> .reload
Reloading current modules
....
0:000> g
ModLoad: 5cb70000 5cb96000   C:\WINDOWS\system32\ShimEng.dll
ModLoad: 77dd0000 77e6b000   C:\WINDOWS\system32\ADVAPI32.dll
ModLoad: 77e70000 77f02000   C:\WINDOWS\system32\RPCRT4.dll
ModLoad: 77fe0000 77ff1000   C:\WINDOWS\system32\Secur32.dll
ModLoad: 77f60000 77fd6000   C:\WINDOWS\system32\SHLWAPI.dll
ModLoad: 77f10000 77f59000   C:\WINDOWS\system32\GDI32.dll
ModLoad: 7e410000 7e4a1000   C:\WINDOWS\system32\USER32.dll
ModLoad: 77c10000 77c68000   C:\WINDOWS\system32\msvcrt.dll
ModLoad: 76390000 763ad000   C:\WINDOWS\system32\IMM32.DLL
ModLoad: 79e70000 7a3d6000   C:\WINDOWS\Microsoft.NET\Framework
\v2.0.50727\mscorwks.dll
ModLoad: 78130000 781cb000   C:\WINDOWS\WinSxS\x86_Microsoft
.VC80.CRT_1fc8b3b9a1e18e3b_8.0.50727.762_x-ww_6b128700\MSVCR80.dll
ModLoad: 7c9c0000 7d1d7000   C:\WINDOWS\system32\shell32.dll
ModLoad: 773d0000 774d3000   C:\WINDOWS\WinSxS\x86_Microsoft.Windows.Common-
Controls_6595b64144ccf1df_6.0.2600.5512_x-ww_35d4ce83\comctl32.dll
ModLoad: 5d090000 5d12a000   C:\WINDOWS\system32\comctl32.dll
ModLoad: 60340000 60348000   C:\WINDOWS\Microsoft.NET\Framework\v2.0.50727
\culture.dll
ModLoad: 790c0000 79b90000   C:\WINDOWS\assembly\NativeImages
_v2.0.50727_32\mscorlib\1519aecdfda7ccb6075750b4429d2834\mscorlib.ni.dll
ModLoad: 774e0000 7761d000   C:\WINDOWS\system32\ole32.dll
ModLoad: 79060000 790b3000   C:\WINDOWS\Microsoft.NET\Framework
\v2.0.50727\mscorjit.dll
Press any key to call an instance function
```

When the g command is executed, the debugger instructs the target to resume execution until another debug event occurs. In our previous example, the target application is waiting for input from the user.

AVOID THE INITIAL AND EXIT BREAKPOINTS If you do not want the debugger to initially stop execution when launched, you can use the −g switch when starting the debugger. For example, using the same sample application as before, we can launch it using

```
ntsd -g 03Breakpoint.exe
```

Using the −g switch causes the debugger to launch but does not stop execution on the initial launch. Similarly, any time the target is about to exit, the debugger stops execution. This can also be controlled by using the −G (note the upper case) switch, which avoids the final breakpoint during process termination.

Stepping Through Code

Often, it is necessary to step through the code that we are investigating in the debugger. Remember: Using the native debuggers while debugging managed code, we are typically stepping through the machine code generated by the JIT compiler. Less frequently, we may be stepping through regular native code when needing to investigate something in the CLR itself. The two primary commands we will be using to step through code are the p (step) and t (trace) commands. Let's use an application called 03breakpoint.exe to illustrate how these commands can be used. Start the 03breakpoint.exe application under the debugger and resume execution until the application prompts you to press any key. Press any key to continue execution, at which point you are asked again to press any key. At that point, press CTRL-C to break execution in the Main function. Listing 3-5 shows the commands we execute to get the machine code that the JIT compiler generates for AddAndPrint function as well as how we go about setting a breakpoint on this function.

Listing 3-5 Setting a breakpoint in the AddAndPrint function

```
Microsoft (R) Windows Debugger Version 6.9.0003.113 X86
Copyright (c) Microsoft Corporation. All rights reserved.

CommandLine: 03Breakpoint.exe
...
```

...

...

```
0:000> .symfix
```
No downstream store given, using c:\Program Files\Debugging Tools for Windows
(x86)\sym
```
0:000> .reload
```
Reloading current modules

....

```
0:000> g
```
ModLoad: 763c0000 76486000   C:\Windows\system32\ADVAPI32.dll
ModLoad: 77260000 77323000   C:\Windows\system32\RPCRT4.dll
ModLoad: 77980000 779d8000   C:\Windows\system32\SHLWAPI.dll
ModLoad: 76570000 765bb000   C:\Windows\system32\GDI32.dll

...

...

...

ModLoad: 790c0000 79bf6000   C:\Windows\assembly\NativeImages_v2.0.50727_32\
mscorlib\5b3e3b0551bcaa722c27dbb089c431e4\mscorlib.ni.dll
ModLoad: 79060000 790b6000   C:\Windows\Microsoft.NET\Framework
\v2.0.50727\mscorjit.dll
Press any key (1st instance function)
 Adding 10+5=15
Press any key (2nd instance function)
(1a48.1e70): Break instruction exception - code 80000003 (first chance)
eax=7ffda000 ebx=00000000 ecx=00000000 edx=77bcd094 esi=00000000 edi=00000000
eip=77b87dfe esp=01d7faa4 ebp=01d7fad0 iopl=0   nv up ei pl zr na pe nc
cs=001b ss=0023 ds=0023 es=0023 fs=003b gs=0000   efl=00000246
ntdll!DbgBreakPoint:
77b87dfe cc   int   3
```
```
0:004> .loadby sos.dll mscorwks
```
```
0:004> !name2ee 03breakpoint.exe
```
**Advanced.NET.Debugging.Chapter3.Breakpoint.AddAndPrint**
Module: 000c2d8c (03Breakpoint.exe)
Token: 0x06000002
MethodDesc: 000c3178
Name: Advanced.NET.Debugging.Chapter3.Breakpoint.AddAndPrint(Int32, Int32)
JITTED Code Address: *002a0178*
```
0:004> bp 002a0178
```
```
0:004> g
```
(1a48.1e58): Control-C exception - code 40010005 (first chance)
First chance exceptions are reported before any exception handling.
This exception may be expected and handled.
eax=01c4fcbc ebx=00000000 ecx=00000000 edx=77b99a94 esi=00000000 edi=00000002
eip=77886da1 esp=01c4fcac ebp=01c4fd30 iopl=0         nv up ei pl zr na pe nc
cs=001b  ds=0023  ds=0023  es=0023  fs=003b  gs=0000          efl=00000246

*(continues)*
```

Listing 3-5 Setting a breakpoint in the AddAndPrint function *(continued)*

```
KERNEL32!CtrlRoutine+0xbf:
77886da1 c745fcfeffffff   mov      dword ptr [ebp-4],0FFFFFFFEh
ss:0023:01c4fd2c=00000000
0:003> g
gBreakpoint 0 hit
eax=01ee4344 ebx=001cf33c ecx=01ee4344 edx=00000064 esi=01ee4344 edi=01ee4344
eip=002a0178 esp=001cf2dc ebp=001cf320 iopl=0         nv up ei ng nz ac po cy
cs=001b  ss=0023  ds=0023  es=0023  fs=003b  gs=0000            efl=00000293
002a0178 57                push     edi
0:000>
```

In Listing 3-5, you can see that we started by setting up the proper symbol path, followed by setting a breakpoint on AddAndPrint function. When we resumed execution, we immediately hit the breakpoint, and we are now located at the beginning of the AddAndPrint function itself. Don't worry about the details of the bp command we used to get to this point, as they will be discussed in more detail later in this chapter. How do we know where we are currently in the code? The answer lies in the instruction pointer (eip register on x86 systems). If we want to see what the next few instructions look like, we can use the u command as shown in the following:

```
0:000> u
002a0178 57                push     edi
002a0179 56                push     esi
002a017a 53                push     ebx
002a017b 55                push     ebp
002a017c 83ec08            sub      esp,8
002a017f 890c24            mov      dword ptr [esp],ecx
002a0182 8bfa              mov      edi,edx
002a0184 833d582f0c0000    cmp      dword ptr ds:[0C2F58h],0
```

As with most functions, the first few instructions contain what is known as the function prolog, which sets up the current stack frame. Let's use the p command to step through a few of the first instructions:

```
0:000> p
eax=01ee4344 ebx=001cf33c ecx=01ee4344 edx=00000064 esi=01ee4344 edi=01ee4344
eip=002a0179 esp=001cf2d8 ebp=001cf320 iopl=0         nv up ei ng nz ac po cy
cs=001b  ss=0023  ds=0023  es=0023  fs=003b  gs=0000            efl=00000293
```

```
002a0179 56                 push    esi
0:000>
eax=01ee4344 ebx=001cf33c ecx=01ee4344 edx=00000064 esi=01ee4344 edi=01ee4344
eip=002a017a esp=001cf2d4 ebp=001cf320 iopl=0         nv up ei ng nz ac po cy
cs=001b  ss=0023  ds=0023  es=0023  fs=003b  gs=0000          efl=00000293
002a017a 53                 push    ebx
0:000>
eax=01ee4344 ebx=001cf33c ecx=01ee4344 edx=00000064 esi=01ee4344 edi=01ee4344
eip=002a017b esp=001cf2d0 ebp=001cf320 iopl=0         nv up ei ng nz ac po cy
cs=001b  ss=0023  ds=0023  es=0023  fs=003b  gs=0000          efl=00000293
002a017b 55                 push    ebp
0:000>
eax=01ee4344 ebx=001cf33c ecx=01ee4344 edx=00000064 esi=01ee4344 edi=01ee4344
eip=002a017c esp=001cf2cc ebp=001cf320 iopl=0         nv up ei ng nz ac po cy
cs=001b  ss=0023  ds=0023  es=0023  fs=003b  gs=0000          efl=00000293
002a017c 83ec08             sub     esp,8
```

As you can see in this listing, the p command executes a single instruction and displays the resulting values of all registers. You may be wondering about the empty command input in the example. This is another nifty feature of the debuggers. If you don't type any command and simply press Enter, the last executed command executes again (in this case, p). Another variant of the p command is the pc command, which steps over all instructions until the next call instruction is encountered. It is shown in the following listing. Let's try it in the debugger session we have open.

```
0:000> pc
eax=00000096 ebx=01ee3dac ecx=79102290 edx=00000000 esi=01ee4344 edi=00000064
eip=002a01ae esp=001cf2c4 ebp=001cf320 iopl=0         nv up ei pl nz na pe nc
cs=001b  ss=0023  ds=0023  es=0023  fs=003b  gs=0000          efl=00000206
002a01ae e8691ee1ff         call    000b201c
```

We can see that the pc command steps over a number of instructions until it reaches the call 00b201c instruction. What happens if we use the p command to step over the call instruction? The p command executes the call instruction in its entirety and returns to the next instruction after the call instruction:

```
0:000> p
eax=01ee4350 ebx=01ee3dac ecx=79102290 edx=003160f0 esi=01ee4344 edi=00000064
eip=002a01b3 esp=001cf2c4 ebp=001cf320 iopl=0         nv up ei pl nz na pe nc
cs=001b  ss=0023  ds=0023  es=0023  fs=003b  gs=0000          efl=00000206
002a01b3 8bf0               mov     esi,eax
```

It is possible to step into the call instruction using the t command, which we will look at in a moment. The final variant of the p command is the pt command, which simply executes instructions until it reaches a ret instruction:

```
0:000> pt
Adding 100+50=150
eax=00000001 ebx=001cf33c ecx=01ee3d1c edx=00000000 esi=01ee4344 edi=01ee4344
eip=002a01f5 esp=001cf2dc ebp=001cf320 iopl=0         nv up ei pl nz na pe nc
cs=001b  ss=0023  ds=0023  es=0023  fs=003b  gs=0000          efl=00000206
002a01f5 c20400          ret     4
```

When executed, we can see that the AddAndPrint function has finished its work (by outputting the result of the addition) and the debugger stops at the ret instruction, which transfers control back to the calling function (Main).

Now let's turn our attention to the t (trace) command. Much like the p command, the t command executes a single instruction and displays the resulting values of all registers. The key difference is that when a call instruction or an interrupt is encountered the t command executes each of those instructions. Let's restart the sample application 03breakpoint.exe and use the same commands as in Listing 3-5 to position ourselves at the beginning of the AddAndPrint function. We would like to step our way to the call instruction and trace into the code behind the call instruction, as shown in the following:

```
0:003> g
gBreakpoint 0 hit
eax=01d44344 ebx=0028f1ac ecx=01d44344 edx=00000064 esi=01d44344 edi=01d44344
eip=009f0178 esp=0028f14c ebp=0028f190 iopl=0         nv up ei ng nz ac po cy
cs=001b  ss=0023  ds=0023  es=0023  fs=003b  gs=0000          efl=00000293
009f0178 57             push    edi
0:000> pc
eax=00000096 ebx=01d43dac ecx=79102290 edx=00000000 esi=01d44344 edi=00000064
eip=009f01ae esp=0028f134 ebp=0028f190 iopl=0         nv up ei pl nz na pe nc
cs=001b  ss=0023  ds=0023  es=0023  fs=003b  gs=0000          efl=00000206
009f01ae e8691e8aff     call    0029201c
0:000> t
eax=00000096 ebx=01d43dac ecx=79102290 edx=00000000 esi=01d44344 edi=00000064
eip=0029201c esp=0028f130 ebp=0028f190 iopl=0         nv up ei pl nz na pe nc
cs=001b  ss=0023  ds=0023  es=0023  fs=003b  gs=0000          efl=00000206
0029201c 8b4104         mov     eax,dword ptr [ecx+4] ds:0023:79102294=0000000c
0:000>
```

By using the pc command, we can quickly step to the next call instruction (call 0029201c) followed by executing the t command, which steps into the code located at address 0029201c.

There are a number of variants of the t command including the following:

- `ta <address>`: Traces until the specified address is reached and displays each step including any called functions.
- `tc`: Traces until it reaches the next call instruction and displays each step including any called functions.
- `tt`: Traces until it reaches the next `ret` instructions and displays each step including any called functions.

Exiting a Debugging Session

After you have completed a debug session, there are a couple of different ways to exit the debug session. If you want to end the debug session and terminate the target, the q (quit) command can be used. Often, it's desirable to end the debug session and let the target continue running. In these cases, the qd (quit and detach) command can be used as the debugger detaches from the target application but does not terminate it. The qd command is only available on Windows XP and later.

Loading Managed Code Extensions

There are two different types of commands that can be used in the native debuggers. The first type is called meta-commands. Meta-commands are commands that can be considered built into the debugging engine itself. Examples of such commands are `help`, `sympath`, and `cls`. When executing meta-commands, all commands must be prefixed by a ".". For example, to set the symbol path, we can use the `sympath` meta-command as shown in the following:

```
0:000> .sympath c:\adndbin
Symbol search path is: c:\adndbin
```

To get a complete list of the meta-commands available, please use the `help` command. The other type of command is known as the extension command. Extension commands are implemented outside of the debugger engine in separate DLLs known as debugger extensions. The native debuggers ship with quite a few debugger extension DLLs that have been developed by various technology groups at Microsoft to aid in debugging issues within each respective technology. In addition to the extension DLLs that ship with the debugging tools, it is possible to develop your own extension DLLs by using the debugger SDK (software development kit). (Please see the debugger documentation or Chapter 11 of *Advanced Windows Debugging*.) All extension commands are executed by prefixing the command with a "!". For example, to invoke the htrace extension command, we would use the following:

```
0:000> !htrace -enable
Handle tracing enabled.
Handle tracing information snapshot successfully taken.
```

In addition to the plethora of extension DLLs shipped with Debugging Tools for Windows, there is a number of other extension DLLs. Two are of particular interest when debugging managed code using the debuggers. The two extension DLLs are called SOS and SOSEX.

Before we can use these extension DLLs, the debugger must first be notified of their presence by using the load meta-command. The load meta-command takes the path to the extension DLL that you want to load. For example, to load an extension DLL called myext.dll located under c:\adndbin, we would use the following command:

```
.load c:\adndbin\myext.dll
```

Let's take a look at how we can load the SOS and SOSEX extension DLLs using the load meta-command.

Loading the SOS Extension DLL

The SOS extension DLL (sos.dll) is specific to the version of the CLR that the application is using. As such, each major CLR version revision ships with a new version of the SOS extension DLL to ensure that the extension DLL can take advantage of the new capabilities of that version of the CLR. The SOS extension DLL is shipped as part of the runtime and can be located in the following path:

```
%systemroot%\Microsoft.NET\Framework\<framework version>\sos.dll
```

We can simply take the previous path, specify which framework version we are interested in, and pass it to the debugger using the load meta-command. For example, on my system, I would use the following debugger command to load the SOS extension command corresponding to version 2.0 of the CLR:

```
.load c:\windows\Microsoft.NET\Framework\v2.0.50727\sos.dll
```

WHY MULTIPLE VERSIONS? Why do we need multiple versions of the SOS extension DLL? Because the SOS extension DLL is aware of the internals of the CLR; anytime changes or enhancements are made to the CLR, a new version of SOS must be made available.

The approach just presented can be somewhat cumbersome due to having to find the correct version of the CLR the application is targeting as well as having to type in long paths. To get around this problem, we can use another meta-command called `loadby`. The general syntax of the `loadby` meta-command is shown in the following:

```
.loadby DLLName ModuleName
```

The `loadby` meta-command attempts to find the path of the `ModuleName` specified (by looking at the list of modules loaded into the process) and uses that path to load the `DLLName` (extension DLL) specified. Because we already said that the SOS extension DLL is CLR version specific, if we can find a module that guarantees us a path where the SOS extension DLL is located, we can easily use the `loadby` command to load the SOS extension DLL. It turns out that the module we are looking for is called `mscorwks`, which is one of the workhorse engines of the CLR. Simply issue the following command

```
.loadby sos.dll mscorwks
```

and the debugger engine loads the proper version of the SOS extension command.

In situations where the `mscorwks` module has not yet been loaded, the `loadby` meta-command fails with the following error:

```
0:000> .loadby sos.dll mscorwks
Unable to find module 'mscorwks'
```

If you need to load the SOS extension DLL as soon as the `mscorwks` module has been loaded, the `sxe` command can be used. The `sxe` command controls the behavior of exceptions that occur in the target application. I'm not going to describe each and every option for the `sxe` command but one of the useful options is the `sxe ld` option, which allows you to break in the debugger as soon as a particular module has been loaded. We can use the `sxe ld` command to tell the debugger to break when

3. BASIC DEBUGGING TASKS

mscorwks has been loaded and then load the SOS extension DLL subsequent to that, as shown in Listing 3-6.

Listing 3-6 Loading the SOS extension command as soon as mscorwks.dll is loaded

```
Microsoft (R) Windows Debugger Version 6.9.0003.113 X86
Copyright (c) Microsoft Corporation. All rights reserved.

CommandLine: 01MDASample.exe
Symbol search path is: *** Invalid ***
...

...

...

(1ff0.1d6c): Break instruction exception - code 80000003 (first chance)
eax=00000000 ebx=00000000 ecx=002ff964 edx=77b99a94 esi=fffffffe edi=77b9b6f8
eip=77b87dfe esp=002ff97c ebp=002ff9ac iopl=0         nv up ei pl zr na pe nc
cs=001b  ss=0023  ds=0023  es=0023  fs=003b  gs=0000             efl=00000246
*** ERROR: Symbol file could not be found.  Defaulted to export symbols for
ntdll.dll -
ntdll!DbgBreakPoint:
77b87dfe cc              int     3
0:000> .symfix
No downstream store given, using c:\Program Files\Debugging Tools for Windows
(x86)\sym
0:000> .reload
Reloading current modules
....
0:000> sxe ld mscorwks.dll
0:000> g
ModLoad: 79e70000 7a3ff000   C:\Windows\Microsoft.NET\Framework
\v2.0.50727\mscorwks.dll
eax=00000000 ebx=00000000 ecx=00000000 edx=4000001e esi=7ffdf000 edi=20000000
eip=77b99a94 esp=002fefd4 ebp=002ff018 iopl=0         nv up ei pl zr na pe nc
cs=001b  ss=0023  ds=0023  es=0023  fs=003b  gs=0000             efl=00000246
ntdll!KiFastSystemCallRet:
77b99a94 c3              ret
0:000> .loadby sos.dll mscorwks
0:000>
```

As you can see from Listing 3-6, the debugger breaks execution when mscorwks is loaded, which enables us to use the loadby meta-command to load the SOS extension DLL.

SOS and Silverlight

Silverlight introduces its own, slimmed down version of the CLR housed in `coreclr.dll`. To debug Silverlight applications using the native debuggers, the proper version of the SOS extension DLL must be downloaded. SOS for Silverlight is part of the Silverlight Developer Runtime and can be downloaded from www.microsoft.com/silverlight/resources/tools.aspx

When installed, the SOS for Silverlight extension DLL is placed in the Silverlight installation folder. For example, on my machine, it is located here:

```
c:\Program Files\Microsoft Silverlight\2.0.31005.0\sos.dll
```

Loading the SOSEX Extension DLL

SOSEX is an extension DLL for managed code debugging developed by Steve Johnson. It is available as a free download (see Chapter 1, "Introduction to the Tools," for location and installation instructions). SOSEX enhances the capabilities of SOS by making certain types of debugging tasks far more efficient. We will discuss the details of the SOSEX commands later in this chapter, but for now I will show you how to properly load the SOSEX extension DLL under the debugger.

When you have successfully downloaded and installed the extension DLL into a folder of choice, you can use the `load` meta-command to load it under the debugger. As mentioned earlier, please make sure to specify the full path to the SOSEX extension DLL. Alternatively, you can simply copy the SOSEX extension DLL into the debugger installation path to avoid typing full paths. In the following example, I installed the SOSEX extension DLL into `c:\myexts` folder and can use the following command to load it:

```
.load c:\myexts\sosex.dll
```

Please note that even though the SOSEX debugger extension loads without `mscorwks.dll` being loaded, the commands themselves do not work and generate the following error:

```
Unable to initialize .NET interface. The CLR may not yet be loaded in the target
process.
```

If you need to use any of the SOSEX debugger commands as soon as the `mscorwks.dll` module is loaded, you can use the same technique as describer earlier by using `sxe ld mscorwks.dll`.

Controlling CLR Debugging

During debugging of a .NET application, the debuggers may load an auxiliary .NET debugging DLL named `mscordacwks.dll`, which is used to display the various pieces of information that managed code debugging entails (such as the output of SOS commands). The path from where `mscordacwks.dll` is loaded depends on the location of `mscorwks.dll` that is loaded into the process. During live debugging, this typically does not present a problem because we always want to load the version of `mscordacwks.dll` that corresponds to the version of `mscorwks.dll` we have loaded; but in cases where we are doing postmortem debugging (crash dump debugging), they may be different. To control the debugging behavior, we can utilize the `cordll` meta-command and tell the debuggers the exact location where to load `mscordacwks.dll` from. For example, if we want to specify a new path, we can use the following command:

```
.cordll -lp c:\x\y\z
```

This instructs the debugger to load `mscordacwks.dll` from `c:\x\y\z` folder. If you want to unload the `mscordacwks.dll`, the –u switch can be used.

In Chapter 8, "Postmortem Debugging," we will see the criticality of this command when debugging crash dumps.

Setting Breakpoints

Setting breakpoints is a way to instruct a target application to stop execution at the point where the breakpoint is defined. Breakpoints enable developers to inspect the state of the application during the execution flow and makes for easier root cause analysis. During native code debugging, breakpoints are fairly easy to set because (most of the time) we know the location of code that we are interested in. The command that enables us to set breakpoints is the `bp` (breakpoint) command. The `bp` command in its simplest form takes a parameter that specifies the location where the breakpoint should be set. Let's look at a simple example of setting a breakpoint in native code. Listing 3-7 shows the steps necessary to set a breakpoint on the `SaveFile` function in an instance of `notepad.exe`.

Listing 3-7   Setting a breakpoint in notepad.exe

```
Microsoft (R) Windows Debugger Version 6.9.0003.113 X86
Copyright (c) Microsoft Corporation. All rights reserved.
```

```
CommandLine: notepad.exe
...

...

...

ntdll!DbgBreakPoint:
7c90120e cc                  int     3
0:000> .symfix
No downstream store given, using c:\Program Files\Debugging Tools for Windows\sym
0:000> .reload
Reloading current modules
..............
0:000> X notepad!*Save*
01001a28 notepad!NpSaveDialogHookProc = <no type information>
0100270f notepad!CheckSave = <no type information>
0100a528 notepad!g_ftSaveAs = <no type information>
01003a39 notepad!SaveGlobals = <no type information>
010012e4 notepad!_imp__GetSaveFileNameW = <no type information>
0100a540 notepad!szSaveFilterSpec = <no type information>
01004eae notepad!SaveFile = <no type information>
01009854 notepad!fInSaveAsDlg = <no type information>
0100136c notepad!s_SaveAsHelpIDs = <no type information>
01009090 notepad!szSaveCaption = <no type information>
0:000> bp notepad!SaveFile
0:000> g
ModLoad: 5cb70000 5cb96000   C:\WINDOWS\system32\ShimEng.dll
ModLoad: 6f880000 6fa4a000   C:\WINDOWS\AppPatch\AcGenral.DLL
ModLoad: 76b40000 76b6d000   C:\WINDOWS\system32\WINMM.dll
ModLoad: 774e0000 7761d000   C:\WINDOWS\system32\ole32.dll
...

...

...

ModLoad: 01790000 01a55000   C:\WINDOWS\system32\xpsp2res.dll
ModLoad: 73ba0000 73bb3000   C:\WINDOWS\system32\sti.dll
ModLoad: 74ae0000 74ae7000   C:\WINDOWS\system32\CFGMGR32.dll
Breakpoint 0 hit
eax=0007fbb0 ebx=00000104 ecx=00002bd2 edx=7c90e4f4 esi=00000000 edi=7c80ba7f
eip=01004eae esp=0007fb40 ebp=0007fdbc iopl=0         nv up ei pl nz na po nc
cs=001b  ss=0023  ds=0023  es=0023  fs=003b  gs=0000          efl=00000202
notepad!SaveFile:
01004eae 8bff                mov     edi,edi
0:000>
```

After setting up and reloading the symbols, we utilize the X (examine symbols) command to display all symbols that contain "SaveFile". It turns out that one of the symbols matches perfectly and also happens to be a function. Then, we use the bp command to set the breakpoint on that function (alternatively, we could have used the

3. BASIC DEBUGGING TASKS

actual address 0x01004eae). When we resume execution and go to the notepad File menu, followed by the Save option, the debugger breaks execution on the SaveFile function. In its simplest form, that is all it takes to set a breakpoint in a native code application: Find the address of the function you are interested in and use the bp command.

With managed code, things get a little trickier. In Chapter 2, we talked about how Just In Time compilation allows the CLR, at runtime, to translate the intermediate language (IL) of a particular function to machine code. The CLR is free to place this machine code anywhere it sees fit. The question then becomes, if we know we want to set a breakpoint in function X, how do we know where the machine code of function X is located so we can accurately set the breakpoint? The answer lies in understanding how to properly ask the CLR for the function address after it has been compiled and then use the breakpoint commands to actually set the breakpoint. Please note that there are variants of the approach depending on whether the function has been compiled. We will utilize a small application shown in Listing 3-8 to illustrate the act of setting managed code breakpoints.

Listing 3-8 Sample breakpoint application

```
using System;
using System.Text;

namespace Advanced.NET.Debugging.Chapter3
{
    class Breakpoint
    {
        static void Main(string[] args)
        {
            //
            // Calling instance function once
            //
            Console.WriteLine("Press any key (1st instance function)");
            Console.ReadKey();
            Breakpoint bp = new Breakpoint();
            bp.AddAndPrint(10, 5);

            //
            // Calling instance function twice
            //
            Console.WriteLine("Press any key (2nd instance function)");
            Console.ReadKey();
```

```
        bp = new Breakpoint();
        bp.AddAndPrint(100, 50);
    }

    public void AddAndPrint(int a, int b)
    {
        int res = a + b;
        Console.WriteLine("Adding {0}+{1}={2}", a, b, res);
    }
    }
}
```

The source code and binary for Listing 3-8 can be found in the following folders:

- Source code: `C:\ADND\Chapter3\Breakpoint`
- Binary: `C:\ADNDBin\03breakpoint.exe`

Setting Breakpoints on JIT Compiled Functions

As discussed earlier, a function is compiled by the just in time compiler and placed in memory. If we knew the address of where the JIT compiler places the machine code, we can use the debugger's `bp` command to set a breakpoint. Let's use the `03breakpoint.exe` application discussed previously and see if we can set a breakpoint on the `AddAndPrint` function. More specifically, we'd like to set a breakpoint on the second invocation of the function to investigate a potential bug in it. Begin by starting `03breakpoint.exe` under the debugger and resume execution until the first prompt is shown asking you to press any key. Press any key and wait until the second prompt to press any key. At this point, break into the debugger using CTRL-C. This is the starting point of setting a breakpoint in the second `AddAndPrint` function. The first task is to figure out whether the function has been compiled by the JIT compiler. The key to finding this out is to use the SOS command called `name2ee`. The `name2ee` command takes the following form:

```
!name2ee <module name> <type or method name>
```

The `module name` parameter is the module of interest and the `type or method` name (fully qualified) is the name of the type or method that you want to get information about. In our case, the module name is `03breakpoint.exe` and the type name is `Advanced.NET.Debugging.Chapter3.Breakpoint.AddAndPrint`.

```
0:004> !name2ee 03breakpoint.exe
Advanced.NET.Debugging.Chapter3.Breakpoint.AddAndPrint
Module: 00112d8c (03Breakpoint.exe)
Token: 0x06000002
MethodDesc: 00113178
Name: Advanced.NET.Debugging.Chapter3.Breakpoint.AddAndPrint(Int32, Int32)
JITTED Code Address: 003e0178
0:004>
```

As you can see, the last line of the output states that the method has been JIT-TED (another term for just in time compiled) and that the address of the compiled code is 003e0178. We can do a brief sanity check on this code by using the U command (discussed in more detail later), as shown in Listing 3-9.

Listing 3-9   Sanity checking the JIT address by disassembling the JIT generated code

```
0:004> !U 003e0178
Normal JIT generated code
Advanced.NET.Debugging.Chapter3.Breakpoint.AddAndPrint(Int32, Int32)
Begin 003e0178, size 80
>>> 003e0178 57                  push    edi
003e0179 56             push     esi
003e017a 53             push     ebx
003e017b 55             push     ebp
003e017c 83ec08         sub      esp,8
003e017f 890c24         mov      dword ptr [esp],ecx
003e0182 8bfa           mov      edi,edx
003e0184 833d582f110000 cmp      dword ptr ds:[112F58h],0
003e018b 7405           je       003e0192
003e018d e8b581d479     call     mscorwks!JIT_DbgIsJustMyCode (7a128347)
003e0192 33d2           xor      edx,edx
003e0194 89542404       mov      dword ptr [esp+4],edx
003e0198 90             nop
003e0199 8b44241c       mov      eax,dword ptr [esp+1Ch]
003e019d 03c7           add      eax,edi
003e019f 89442404       mov      dword ptr [esp+4],eax
003e01a3 8b1d4c30c602   mov      ebx,dword ptr ds:[2C6304Ch]  ("Adding {0}+{1}={2}")
...
...
...
003e01e2 8bd5           mov      edx,ebp
003e01e4 8bcb           mov      ecx,ebx
003e01e6 e8359c0079     call     mscorlib_ni+0x329e20 (793e9e20)
(System.Console.WriteLine
(System.String, System.Object, System.Object, System.Object), mdToken: 060007c8)
003e01eb 90             nop
003e01ec 90             nop
```

```
003e01ed 90              nop
003e01ee 83c408          add     esp,8
003e01f1 5d              pop     ebp
003e01f2 5b              pop     ebx
003e01f3 5e              pop     esi
003e01f4 5f              pop     edi
003e01f5 c20400          ret     4
0:004>
```

The first part of the disassembly gives a good indication of the correctness of the address passed in to the U command. We can see that the U command tells us that the code located on that address is `Normal JIT generated code`. In addition, the next line also tells us the full name of the method that the code corresponds to (in our case, `Advanced.NET.Debugging.Chapter3.Breakpoint.AddAndPrint`). Finally, the third line tells us the starting address (`003e0178`) and the size of the generated code (`80`). After the initial set of information, the disassembled instructions are shown. We have now located the proper address for the dynamically generated code and set a breakpoint on it. If we resume execution (don't forget to press a key to start the second call), we very quickly hit the breakpoint, as shown in the following:

```
0:003> g
Breakpoint 0 hit
eax=01cdbed8 ebx=0025f0fc ecx=01cdbed8 edx=00000064 esi=01cdbed8 edi=01cdbed8
eip=003f0178 esp=0025f09c ebp=0025f0e0 iopl=0         nv up ei ng nz ac pe cy
cs=001b  ss=0023  ds=0023  es=0023  fs=003b  gs=0000             efl=00000297
003f0178 57              push    edi
0:000> !ClrStack
OS Thread Id: 0xf7c (0)
ESP       EIP
0025f09c 003f0178 Advanced.NET.Debugging.Chapter3.Breakpoint.AddAndPrint(Int32,
Int32)
0025f0a4 003f0105 Advanced.NET.Debugging.Chapter3.Breakpoint.Main(System.String[])
0025f2f0 79e7c74b [GCFrame: 0025f2f0]
```

After the breakpoint hits, we use the `ClrStack` command to ensure that we have hit the correct code location.

Initially, we said we wanted to set a breakpoint on the second invocation of `AddAndPrint` due to a potential bug related to that particular invocation. I'm sure by now you've figured out that the reason for setting a breakpoint on the second invocation is due to the easy nature of setting a breakpoint on a function that has already been JIT compiled (prior invocation of the same function caused it to be JIT compiled). Simply use the `name2ee` command to find out the address of the JIT compiled code and use the `bp` command.

There is an alternative approach that can be used when setting breakpoints. The SOS debugger extension includes a command called `bpmd` that simplifies life dramatically by finding the correct JIT compiled address automatically and setting the breakpoint based only on the fully qualified method name.

Next, we will take a look at how we can set a breakpoint on a function that has yet to be JIT compiled. After all, we don't always have the luxury of setting breakpoints on JIT compiled functions. Sometimes, it is necessary to set a breakpoint on first invocation where the function may not be compiled yet.

Setting Breakpoints on Functions Not Yet JIT Compiled

In the previous section, we discussed two mechanisms to set breakpoints on code that has already been JIT compiled. The first approach involved finding the address of the JIT compiled code and subsequently using the `bp` command to set a breakpoint. This works well if the code has already been JIT compiled but breaks down if the JIT compiler has not had a chance to compile the IL yet. A common occurrence of this is when you want to set a breakpoint on the very first execution of a function. Because we can't rely on finding the address of the compiled code, how do we set the breakpoint? Fortunately, the `bpmd` command can handle the setting of breakpoints on code that has not been JIT compiled. It does this by setting what is known as deferred breakpoints. A deferred breakpoint is nothing more than a breakpoint that cannot be fully resolved at the point of setting the breakpoint but rather relies on some future event to occur before the breakpoint is actually set. Bpmd does this seeming magic by registering for internal CLR JIT compilation notifications. When it receives a JIT compilation notification, it checks to see if it is related to any of the existing deferred breakpoints, and if so, the breakpoint becomes active before the function has had a chance to run. Furthermore, the `bpmd` command also receives module load notifications, which in essence means that the assembly that you are setting a breakpoint in doesn't even have to be loaded at the point of setting the breakpoint. When the assembly is loaded, the command is once again notified and checks to see if any of the deferred breakpoints are located within that module and activates any breakpoints that can be resolved.

BPMD AND MODULE LOAD NOTIFICATIONS At the time of writing, the module load notification mechanism in the bpmd command suffered from a bug that did not properly receive notifications and, as such, the deferred breakpoint became orphaned and never triggered. The alternative strategy is to use SOSEX, which is discussed later in the chapter.

Let's begin by seeing how we can set a breakpoint using the bpmd command on a function that has not yet been compiled (AddAndPrint) using our sample 03breakpoint.exe application. Begin by starting the application under the debugger and resume execution until asked to Press any key (1st instance function). Next, use CTRL-C to break execution. The first task we will perform is to prove to ourselves that the AddAndPrint method has not yet been compiled. The process is illustrated in the following by utilizing the name2ee command discussed earlier.

```
0:000> !name2ee
03breakpoint.exeAdvanced.NET.Debugging.Chapter3.Breakpoint.AddAndPrint
Module: 00912c24 (03Breakpoint.exe)
Token: 0x06000002
MethodDesc: 00912ff0
Name: Advanced.NET.Debugging.Chapter3.Breakpoint.AddAndPrint(Int32, Int32)
Not JITTED yet. Use !bpmd -md 00912ff0 to break on run.
```

The output of the command clearly tells us that the method AddAndPrint has not yet been compiled and that we can use the bpmd command with the method descriptor switch to set a breakpoint. If we set a breakpoint using the command stated, we will see the following:

```
0:000> !bpmd -md 00912ff0
MethodDesc = 00912ff0
Adding pending breakpoints...
```

Here, the bpmd command is clearly telling us that it is setting what is known as a pending (deferred) breakpoint. If we resume execution, we can see that the debugger receives a notification and breaks execution on the method when called:

```
0:003> g
 (8d8.b0): CLR notification exception - code e0444143 (first chance)
JITTED 03Breakpoint!Advanced.NET.Debugging.Chapter3.Breakpoint.AddAndPrint(Int32,
Int32)
Setting breakpoint: bp 00CB0138
[Advanced.NET.Debugging.Chapter3.Breakpoint.AddAndPrint(Int32, Int32)]
Breakpoint 0 hit
eax=00912ff0 ebx=0013f4ac ecx=01282e08 edx=0000000a esi=01282e08 edi=01282e08
eip=00cb0138 esp=0013f458 ebp=0013f490 iopl=0         nv up ei pl nz ac po nc
cs=001b  ss=0023  ds=0023  es=0023  fs=003b  gs=0000           efl=00000212
00cb0138 57              push    edi
```

The interesting part is the notification output where we can see that the debugger received a CLR notification exception (0xe0444143). Furthermore, we can see that the notification occurred due to the JIT compiler compiling the `AddAndPrint` method, at which point a breakpoint was set using the `bp` command with a code address of `0x00cb0138`. If we were to unassemble this address, we could quickly verify that it corresponds to the `AddAndPrint` method. The final event that occurs is that the breakpoint is actually hit and the debugger breaks execution. One final note on `bpmd`: If the method name that is specified is overloaded, `bpmd` will set a breakpoint on all overloaded methods.

---

bp and Previous CLR Versions

In prior versions of the CLR (1.0 and 1.1), it was possible to set a breakpoint on a not yet JIT compiled method using the `bp` command. In essence, we would find where the JIT compiler stores the address of the compiled code, set a break on write breakpoint, and resume execution until the JIT compiler finished the compilation process and stored the address. At that point, the breakpoint would be hit and you could use the address placed there by the JIT compiler to set a breakpoint on it. This was a rather long and arduous process and fortunately the `bpmd` command was introduced in CLR 2.0 to make life much easier when setting breakpoints.

Setting Breakpoints in Precompiled Assemblies

Much like any other piece of code, .NET code executes in the context of a process. The JIT compiler is invoked to translate the IL contained within the assembly into machine code. Anytime .NET code accesses the same piece of code, the CLR first checks to see if it has already been compiled and, if so, reuses the compiled code. When the process dies, all the work that the JIT compiler has already done in translating IL to machine code goes away with it. The next time the assembly needs to be invoked, the JIT compiler goes back to work and translates the same piece of code again. To avoid having to redo the compilation, the CLR has the capability to work with what is known as precompiled (or NGEN'd) assemblies. A precompiled assembly is nothing more than a native image of the corresponding assembly with all the code already translated into machine code. If the CLR needs to execute a piece of code contained within an assembly that also has a native image on the machine, the JIT compilation step is skipped altogether and the machine code is simply loaded from the native image. Even though this may seem like a huge performance booster, you may be wondering if some of the benefits of runtime JIT compilation are lost. The answer is that, generally speaking, those benefits still remain because the step of creating the precompiled assembly occurs during installation time and not compile time. Thus, we can still reap the benefits of running the JIT compiler on the architecture it was meant to run on. The key difference is that the JIT compiler persists the output of the compilation into a native image rather than memory.

In light of native images, how does it relate to debugging .NET code? There really is not much difference debugging .NET code that has native images. As a matter of fact, at times, it can make it easier because you do not have to worry about whether a function has been JIT compiled. There are a couple of caveats to be aware of though. When a native image is loaded, you will see another module loaded into the address space of the process. This module is loaded from the native image cache. The native image cache is a collection of all precompiled assemblies that exist on a system and can be found in the following location:

```
%windir%\assembly\NativeImages_v2.0.50727_<architecture>
```

The architecture is either 32 or 64 depending on the bitness of the machine. Any time a native image is generated, it is placed into this location.

NGEN Sometimes, you may hear others refer to precompiled assemblies as NGEN'd assemblies. The reason for this is that the tool to generate native images is called `ngen.exe` (located under the .NET redistribution folder `%windir%\microsoft.net\framework\v2.0.50727`). `Ngen.exe` takes care of generating and placing the generated native images in the native image cache.

In the previous section, we looked at an example where the method we wanted to set a breakpoint on was not yet JIT compiled. Let's take a look at the same example, but this time we will precompile the assembly first and see what differences we can see. The application we will use is called `03ObjTypes.exe` (refer to Listing 3-10). Before we can use it for this exercise, we first need to go through the process of precompiling it:

```
%windir%\microsoft.net\framework\v2.0.50727\ngen install 03ObjTypes.exe
```

After it has been precompiled, we go ahead and launch the application under the debugger. The initial debugger spew looks like the following:

```
Microsoft (R) Windows Debugger Version 6.9.0003.113 X86
Copyright (c) Microsoft Corporation. All rights reserved.

CommandLine: 03ObjTypes.exe
```

```
Symbol search path is: *** Invalid ***
****************************************************************************
* Symbol loading may be unreliable without a symbol search path.          *
* Use .symfix to have the debugger choose a symbol path.                  *
* After setting your symbol path, use .reload to refresh symbol locations. *
****************************************************************************
Executable search path is:
ModLoad: 010b0000 010b8000    03ObjTypes.exe
ModLoad: 77890000 779b7000    ntdll.dll
ModLoad: 79000000 79046000    C:\Windows\system32\mscoree.dll
ModLoad: 77700000 777db000    C:\Windows\system32\KERNEL32.dll
(858.1138): Break instruction exception - code 80000003 (first chance)
eax=00000000 ebx=00000000 ecx=0020f594 edx=778e9a94 esi=fffffffe edi=778eb6f8
eip=778d7dfe esp=0020f5ac ebp=0020f5dc iopl=0         nv up ei pl zr na pe nc
cs=001b  ss=0023  ds=0023  es=0023  fs=003b  gs=0000              efl=00000246
*** ERROR: Symbol file could not be found.  Defaulted to export symbols for
ntdll.dll -
ntdll!DbgBreakPoint:
778d7dfe cc              int     3
```

So far, nothing looks out of the ordinary. The `03ObjTypes.exe` assembly is loaded together with the standard Windows system DLLs. If we resume execution, we can see the following:

```
0:000> g
ModLoad: 76160000 76226000    C:\Windows\system32\ADVAPI32.dll
ModLoad: 774e0000 775a3000    C:\Windows\system32\RPCRT4.dll
ModLoad: 77330000 77388000    C:\Windows\system32\SHLWAPI.dll
ModLoad: 76110000 7615b000    C:\Windows\system32\GDI32.dll
ModLoad: 76450000 764ed000    C:\Windows\system32\USER32.dll
ModLoad: 777e0000 7788a000    C:\Windows\system32\msvcrt.dll
ModLoad: 77a10000 77a2e000    C:\Windows\system32\IMM32.DLL
ModLoad: 77260000 77328000    C:\Windows\system32\MSCTF.dll
ModLoad: 771b0000 771b9000    C:\Windows\system32\LPK.DLL
ModLoad: 77460000 774dd000    C:\Windows\system32\USP10.dll
ModLoad: 75110000 752ae000    C:\Windows\WinSxS\x86_microsoft.windows.common-
controls_6595b64144ccf1df_6.0.6001.18000_none_5cdbaa5a083979cc\comctl32.dll
ModLoad: 79e70000 7a3ff000    C:\Windows\Microsoft.NET\Framework\v2.0.50727
\mscorwks.dll
ModLoad: 753b0000 7544b000    C:\Windows\WinSxS\x86_microsoft
.vc80.crt_1fc8b3b9a1e18e3b_8.0.50727.1434_none_d08b6002442c891f\MSVCR80.dll
ModLoad: 766a0000 771af000    C:\Windows\system32\shell32.dll
ModLoad: 775b0000 776f4000    C:\Windows\system32\ole32.dll
ModLoad: 790c0000 79bf6000    C:\Windows\assembly\NativeImages_v2.0.50727_32
\mscorlib\5b3e3b0551bcaa722c27dbb089c431e4\mscorlib.ni.dll
```

```
ModLoad: 30000000 30012000   C:\Windows\assembly
\NativeImages_v2.0.50727_32\03ObjTypes.exe\
f322c1140e18febc7214db75604eca91\03ObjTypes.exe.ni.exe
```

As per expectation, a whole bunch of modules were loaded, including the CLR modules; less expected is the last module loaded: 03ObjTypes.ni.exe. This is the native image corresponding to our 03ObjTypes.exe application (the ni stands for native image). The address range that was loaded in is 0x30000000-0x30012000. At this point, the native image has been loaded and we are presented with the familiar "Press any key to continue (AddCoordinate)" prompt. Let's manually break execution and see what happens when we try to figure out if the AddCoordinate method has been compiled yet. Remember that in the previous exercise the AddCoordinate method had not yet been compiled.

```
0:004> !name2ee 03ObjTypes.exe
Advanced.NET.Debugging.Chapter3.ObjTypes.AddCoordinate
Module: 30004000 (03ObjTypes.exe)
Token: 0x06000002
MethodDesc: 30004820
Name: Advanced.NET.Debugging.Chapter3.ObjTypes.AddCoordinate(Coordinate)
JITTED Code Address: 300025f8
```

This time, we can see that the AddCoordinate method is, in fact, already compiled (as we would expect since the assembly was precompiled) and that the code is located at address 0x300025f8. This address falls within the module range of the precompiled assembly (0x30000000-0x30012000).

Setting Breakpoints on Generic Methods

Generics is a mechanism introduced into V2 of the CLR that enables developers to add generality into their classes. Prior to generics, one way to achieve generality was to simply treat all types as Objects (base class for all classes in .NET) and use casting when necessary. Although this approach did the job, there were several drawbacks associated with it. One of the drawbacks was the treatment of all the different types as the base Object and performing casting to specialize the type. In these situations, you lose a lot of the compile time type safety that is otherwise offered. In addition, performance can suffer if value types are used because boxing and unboxing is performed each time a value type is cast to an Object (reference) type. Generics offer developers a way of achieving generality without compromising on type safety and performance. In this part of the chapter, we will look at how generic types are treated differently when debugging and, more specifically, when setting breakpoints on generic types and methods. We will utilize 03ObjTypes.exe to illustrate how to set breakpoints on generic types using the bpmd command.

Let's begin by running 03ObjTypes.exe under the debugger until you see the following prompt:

```
Press any key to continue (Generics)
```

At this point, manually break into the debugger, load the SOS extension DLL, and use the bpmd command to set a breakpoint on the GreaterThan method (part of the Comparer generic type). The debug session is illustrated in the following:

```
Press any key to continue (Generics)
(a54.1fa4): Break instruction exception - code 80000003 (first chance)
eax=7ffdb000 ebx=00000000 ecx=00000000 edx=7791d094 esi=00000000 edi=00000000
eip=778d7dfe esp=040ef894 ebp=040ef8c0 iopl=0         nv up ei pl zr na pe nc
cs=001b  ss=0023  ds=0023  es=0023  fs=003b  gs=0000              efl=00000246
ntdll!DbgBreakPoint:
778d7dfe cc              int     3
0:004> .loadby sos mscorwks
0:004> !bpmd 03ObjTypes.exe Advanced.NET.Debugging.Chapter3.Comparer`1.GreaterThan
Found 1 methods...
MethodDesc = 001a3188
Adding pending breakpoints...
```

As you can see, the process is very similar to setting breakpoints on nongeneric types with one notable exception: the addition of `1 as part of the fully qualified method name. To set a breakpoint on generic types using bpmd, the bpmd command needs to know the particular type on which you are interested in setting the breakpoint. More specifically, it needs to know the number of generic items that the generic type is declared to have. This is very important when you have more than one generic type with the same name but with a different number of generic types associated with it. In our particular case, the Comparer generic type has the following class declaration:

```
public class Comparer<T> where T: IComparable
{
    ...
}
```

We can see that it takes one generic type to instantiate an instance of the `Comparer` class. If there was another generic class called `Comparer` that took two generic types to instantiate, we would instead use the following command to set a breakpoint:

```
!bpmd 03ObjTypes.exe Advanced.NET.Debugging.Chapter3.Comparer`2.GreaterThan
```

Object Inspection

During most debugging sessions, one of the first tasks that we need to perform is analyzing the state of the application to convince ourselves that the application failure is due to some invalid state. Often, we don't have the luxury of restarting the application and stepping through the repro of the problem a line at a time, making it very difficult to infer the root cause. After we have convinced ourselves that the application is in some invalid state, we can begin theorizing on how the application could have gotten into that state. This part of the chapter describes the different commands we have at our disposal to investigate the state of the application. We begin by detailing the most commonly used commands available in the native debuggers followed by the managed code commands available in the SOS debugger extension. We will once again utilize the `03ObjTypes.exe` as shown in Listing 3-10.

Listing 3-10   Sample application used to illustrate object inspection techniques

```csharp
using System;
using System.Text;

namespace Advanced.NET.Debugging.Chapter3
{
    public class ObjTypes
    {
        public struct Coordinate
        {
            public int xCord;
            public int yCord;
            public int zCord;

            public Coordinate(int x, int y, int z)
            {
                xCord = x;
                yCord = y;
                zCord = z;
            }
        }
    }
```

(continues)

Listing 3-10   Sample application used to illustrate object inspection techniques *(continued)*

```
private Coordinate coordinate;

int[] intArray = new int[] { 1, 2, 3, 4, 5 };
string[] strArray = new string[] {"Welcome",
                                  "to",
                                  "Advanced",
                                  ".NET",
                                  "Debugging"};

static void Main(string[] args)
{
    Coordinate point= new Coordinate(100, 100, 100);
    Console.WriteLine("Press any key to continue (AddCoordinate)");
    Console.ReadKey();
    ObjTypes ob = new ObjTypes();
    ob.AddCoordinate(point);

    Console.WriteLine("Press any key to continue (Arrays)");
    Console.ReadKey();
    ob.PrintArrays();

    Console.WriteLine("Press any key to continue (Generics)");
    Console.ReadKey();
    Comparer<int> c = new Comparer<int>();
    Console.WriteLine("Greater {0}", c.GreaterThan(5, 10));

    Console.WriteLine("Press any key to continue (Exception)");
    Console.ReadKey();
    ob.ThrowException(null);
}

public void AddCoordinate(Coordinate coord)
{
    coordinate.xCord += coord.xCord;
    coordinate.yCord += coord.yCord;
    coordinate.zCord += coord.zCord;

    Console.WriteLine("x:{0}, y:{1}, z:{2}",
                      coordinate.xCord,
                      coordinate.yCord,
                      coordinate.xCord);
}
```

```csharp
        public void PrintArrays()
        {
            foreach (int i in intArray)
            {
                Console.WriteLine("Int: {0}", i);
            }
            foreach (string s in strArray)
            {
                Console.WriteLine("Str: {0}", s);
            }
        }

        public void ThrowException(ObjTypes obj)
        {
            if (obj == null)
            {
                throw new System.ArgumentException("Obj cannot be null");
            }
        }
    }

    public class Comparer<T> where T: IComparable
    {
        public T GreaterThan(T d, T d2)
        {
            int ret = d.CompareTo(d2);
            if (ret > 0)
                return d;
            else
                return d2;
        }

        public T LessThan(T d, T d2)
        {
            int ret = d.CompareTo(d2);
            if (ret < 0)
                return d;
            else
                return d2;
        }
    }
}
```

The source code and binary for Listing 3-10 can be found in the following folders:

- Source code: `C:\ADND\Chapter3\ObjTypes`
- Binary: `C:\ADNDBin\03ObjTypes.exe`

Dumping Raw Memory

There are a number of commands available to dump out raw memory in the debuggers. The most commonly used command is the `d` (display memory) command. In its simplest form, the `d` command takes a parameter that indicates the address of the memory you would like to display. The output of the `d` command is a neatly formatted display of the memory in question, as shown in the following:

```
0:000> dd 0x01e06bec
01e06bec  001c30b0 00000000 00000000 00000000
01e06bfc  80000000 790fd8c4 00000014 00000013
01e06c0c  003a0078 0030007b 002c007d 00790020
01e06c1c  007b003a 007d0031 0020002c 003a007a
01e06c2c  0032007b 0000007d 00000000 00000000
01e06c3c  00000000 00000000 00000000 00000000
01e06c4c  00000000 00000000 00000000 00000000
01e06c5c  00000000 00000000 00000000 00000000
```

The leftmost column shows the beginning address of the memory displayed on that line followed by the memory contents itself. There are a number of different variations of the `d` command depending on the data type that you want to dump. For example, `du` treats the memory being dumped as Unicode characters:

```
0:000> du 7ffdfc00
7ffdfc00  "ADVAPI32.dll"
```

Other variations include the following:

- `da`: Treats memory being dumped as ASCII characters.
- `dw`: Treats memory being dumped as word values.
- `db`: Treats memory being dumped as byte values and ASCII characters.
- `dq`: Treats memory being dumped as quad word values.

Although it's sometimes useful to dump raw memory, when dealing with managed code debugging, it is far more useful to dump the CLR objects in a more structured and easy-to-digest form. For example, if we use the d command to dump out the following raw memory, we get the following:

```
0:000> dd 0x01c56bec
01c56bec  002130b0 00000000 00000000 00000000
01c56bfc  80000000 790fd8c4 00000014 00000013
01c56c0c  003a0078 0030007b 002c007d 00790020
01c56c1c  007b003a 007d0031 0020002c 003a007a
01c56c2c  0032007b 0000007d 00000000 00000000
01c56c3c  00000000 00000000 00000000 00000000
01c56c4c  00000000 00000000 00000000 00000000
01c56c5c  00000000 00000000 00000000 00000000
```

It's quite difficult to infer what the underlying memory actually represents. Now consider the following more informative memory dump of the same address:

```
0:000> !dumpobj 0x01c56bec
Name: Advanced.NET.Debugging.Chapter3.ObjTypes
MethodTable: 002130b0
EEClass: 00211240
Size: 20(0x14) bytes
 (C:\ADNDBin\03ObjTypes.exe)
Fields:
      MT    Field   Offset                 Type VT     Attr     Value Name
0021306c  4000001        4 ...jTypes+Coordinate  1 instance 01c56bf0 coordinate
```

This time, the output is far more informative as it tells us that the address represents a CLR type instance corresponding to the type Advanced.NET. Debugging.Chapter3.ObjTypes. In addition, it gives us some basic information on the type instance as well as the fields contained within the instance. Throughout the book, we will use a combination of the raw memory dump techniques as well as the friendlier dump commands.

Before we delve into the dump commands available for .NET types, we must first discuss the different types available in the CLR type system. The two basic forms of types available are value types and reference types. A value type is a type that derives from System.ValueType and is typically allocated on the stack. If a value type is part of a reference type (for example, a class), the value type will be allocated on the managed heap as part of the aggregating type. In C#, an example of a value type is a struct type. Reference types, on the other hand, are any types that are derived (directly or indirectly) from System.Object but not from System.ValueType and are always allocated on the managed heap. Why was the choice made to have two different forms of types? The answer lies in performance. Allocating small objects on the stack is far more efficient than allocating them on the managed heap. (I will discuss the managed heap in detail in Chapter 5, "Managed Heap and Garbage Collection.")

As we know, all objects derive from the parent of all types in .NET—System.Object—including value types. This means that we have a unified type system where all objects are rooted from the same top-level parent. This unification, for example, enables us to write code like the following:

```
int i = 10;
object o = i;              // implicit boxing
object oo = (object)i;     // explicit boxing
int ii = (int) oo;         // explicit unboxing
```

In this code, we assign the value type i to a reference type o as well as a reference type oo. We already discussed that value types are defined on the stack, whereas reference types are defined on the managed heap. So, how is it possible to assign a stack-based entity to something that should be allocated on the managed heap? The answer lies in what is known as boxing. Transparent to the developer, the CLR automatically performs the following tasks when value types are assigned to reference types:

1. Allocates memory on the managed heap.
2. Copies the memory of the value type (from the stack) to the newly allocated reference type on the managed heap.

The reciprocal of boxing is unboxing, where a reference type is assigned to a value type. Unboxing does not, strictly speaking, incur the same cost as a boxing operation. More specifically, when an unboxing operation is performed, the CLR does not copy the contents of the boxed value type. Rather, it simply returns a managed pointer to the value type instance contained within the reference type. Often, however, an assignment is also associated with an unboxing operation, which does incur the cost of copying the boxed value type contents onto the stack.

Even though this happens transparently, it is important to know because it can have implications for your debugging session (and also performance if a lot of boxing and unboxing is occurring).

Let's begin our discussion of dumping types by examining value types.

Dumping Value Types

Before we discuss the commands that can be used to dump value types, we first have to understand how to recognize the difference between a value type and a reference type. Let's say we had an address of an object at 0x00846710. How do we know if this address represents a value type or a reference type? The best way to figure out if a pointer points to a value type is trying to use the DumpObj command, which works with reference types only. The DumpObj command takes a pointer to a reference type and displays the contents of that reference type. If the pointer specified is instead pointing to a value type, the DumpObj command will show the following error:

```
0:000> !DumpObj 0x002bf0b4
<Note: this object has an invalid CLASS field>
Invalid object
```

As we mentioned earlier, if a value type is not aggregated as part of a reference type (such as declaring a local variable primitive or value type in a function), it is allocated on the stack, and we can use the d commands discussed earlier to dump out the contents of the value type. Let's use the 03ObjTypes.exe application as an example. Run the application under the debugger and manually break execution when prompted to press any key, as shown in Listing 3-11.

Listing 3-11   Breaking into the 03ObjTypes.exe instance

```
0:000> .symfix
No downstream store given, using c:\Program Files\Debugging Tools for Windows
(x86)\sym
0:000> .reload
Reloading current modules
....
0:000> g
ModLoad: 763c0000 76486000   C:\Windows\system32\ADVAPI32.dll
ModLoad: 77260000 77323000   C:\Windows\system32\RPCRT4.dll
ModLoad: 77980000 779d8000   C:\Windows\system32\SHLWAPI.dll
ModLoad: 76570000 765bb000   C:\Windows\system32\GDI32.dll
ModLoad: 764d0000 7656d000   C:\Windows\system32\USER32.dll
ModLoad: 77330000 773da000   C:\Windows\system32\msvcrt.dll
ModLoad: 764a0000 764be000   C:\Windows\system32\IMM32.DLL
ModLoad: 77cd0000 77d98000   C:\Windows\system32\MSCTF.dll
ModLoad: 76490000 76499000   C:\Windows\system32\LPK.DLL
ModLoad: 779e0000 77a5d000   C:\Windows\system32\USP10.dll
ModLoad: 753d0000 7556e000   C:\Windows\WinSxS\x86_microsoft.windows.common-
controls_6595b64144ccf1df_6.0.6001.18000_none_5cdbaa5a083979cc\comctl32.dll
ModLoad: 79e70000 7a3ff000   C:\Windows\Microsoft.NET\Framework\v2.0.50727
\mscorwks.dll
ModLoad: 75670000 7570b000   C:\Windows\WinSxS\x86_microsoft
```

(continues)

Listing 3-11 Breaking into the 03ObjTypes.exe instance *(continued)*

```
.vc80.crt_1fc8b3b9a1e18e3b_8.0.50727.1434_none_d08b6002442c891f\MSVCR80.dll
ModLoad: 76750000 7725f000   C:\Windows\system32\shell32.dll
ModLoad: 775f0000 77734000   C:\Windows\system32\ole32.dll
ModLoad: 790c0000 79bf6000   C:\Windows\assembly\NativeImages_v2.0.50727_32
\mscorlib\5b3e3b0551bcaa722c27dbb089c431e4\mscorlib.ni.dll
ModLoad: 79060000 790b6000   C:\Windows\Microsoft.NET\Framework\v2.0.50727
\mscorjit.dll
Press any key to continue
(1758.12b4): Break instruction exception - code 80000003 (first chance)
eax=7ffda000 ebx=00000000 ecx=00000000 edx=77bcd094 esi=00000000 edi=00000000
eip=77b87dfe esp=0419fed0 ebp=0419fefc iopl=0         nv up ei pl zr na pe nc
cs=001b  ss=0023  ds=0023  es=0023  fs=003b  gs=0000            efl=00000246
ntdll!DbgBreakPoint:
77b87dfe cc              int     3
0:004> .loadby sos mscorwks
```

First, we would like to show the managed call stack and associated local variables. We can use the `ClrStack` command to get this information, as shown in the following:

```
0:004> !ClrStack -a
OS Thread Id: 0x12b4 (4)
Unable to walk the managed stack. The current thread is likely not a
managed thread. You can run !threads to get a list of managed threads in the process
0:004>
```

The `ClrStack` command displays an error stating that the current thread context is not a valid managed thread. Because we manually broke execution, the thread context of the debugger is on the debugger thread, which is a native thread, and we are forced to first switch to the managed thread context before running the `ClrStack` command. Let's use the `~` command to switch the context to thread 0 and try the `ClrStack` command again:

```
0:004> ~0s
eax=0012ed24 ebx=0012ed1c ecx=792274ec edx=79ec9058 esi=0012eb78 edi=00000000
eip=77b99a94 esp=0012eb28 ebp=0012eb48 iopl=0         nv up ei pl zr na pe nc
cs=001b  ss=0023  ds=0023  es=0023  fs=003b  gs=0000            efl=00000246
ntdll!KiFastSystemCallRet:
77b99a94 c3              ret
0:000> !ClrStack -a
OS Thread Id: 0x10b4 (0)
ESP        EIP
```

```
0012ecf4 77b99a94 [NDirectMethodFrameSlim: 0012ecf4]
Microsoft.Win32.Win32Native.ReadConsoleInput
(IntPtr, InputRecord ByRef, Int32, Int32 ByRef)
0012ed0c 793e8f28 System.Console.ReadKey(Boolean)
     PARAMETERS:
          intercept = 0x00000000
     LOCALS:
          <no data>
          0x0012ed1c = 0x00000001
          <no data>
          <no data>
          <no data>
          <no data>
          <no data>
          <no data>
          <no data>
          <no data>

0012ed4c 793e8e33 System.Console.ReadKey()
0012ed50 002c00c1 Advanced.NET.Debugging.Chapter3.ObjTypes.Main(System.String[])
     PARAMETERS:
          args = 0x01b958ac
     LOCALS:
          0x0012ed54 = 0x00000064
          <CLR reg> = 0x00000000

0012ef94 79e7c74b [GCFrame: 0012ef94]
```

This time, the ClrStack command displayed the stack trace for our managed thread including the local variables and parameters associated with each frame. The frame of interest in the call stack is the Main frame and more specifically the local variable at address 0x0012ed54. Because we don't know whether the local variable points to a reference type or simply a value type on the stack, we can use the DumpObj command to see if it properly identifies the address as a reference to a managed heap object:

```
0:000> !DumpObj 0x0012ed54
<Note: this object has an invalid CLASS field>
Invalid object
```

The result of DumpObj clearly indicates that the address does not correspond to a reference type and we are left to assume that the address is, in fact, a value type. To further convince ourselves that that is the case, we can glance at the address itself.

Remember that value types are stored on the stack and, as such, any address that is located around the current stack pointer would be a good indication that we are dealing with a value type. If we dump out the registers using the r command, we can take a look at the esp register (which is the current stack pointer):

```
0:000> r
eax=0012ed24 ebx=0012ed1c ecx=792274ec edx=79ec9058 esi=0012eb78 edi=00000000
eip=77b99a94 esp=0012eb28 ebp=0012eb48 iopl=0         nv up ei pl zr na pe nc
cs=001b  ss=0023  ds=0023  es=0023  fs=003b  gs=0000              efl=00000246
ntdll!KiFastSystemCallRet:
77b99a94 c3              ret
```

The esp register contains the value 0x0012eb28, which is in close proximity to the address we were investigating: 0x0012ed54. At this point, we can safely conclude that the address we are looking at is, in fact, a stack-based address and more than likely a value type. Now, we can use the dd command to display the raw memory associated with the value type:

```
0:000> dd 0x0012ed54
0012ed54  00000064 00000064 00000064 0012ed9c
0012ed64  0012ed80 79e73560 00505408 00000000
0012ed74  79e7c74b 00000003 0012ed84 0012ee00
0012ed84  79e7c6cc 0012ee50 00000000 0012ee20
0012ed94  00000000 0022c040 0012edf0 79f07fee
0012eda4  0012ef94 7cc80b79 0012efe0 0012ee40
0012edb4  00000000 0012ef94 00505408 00000000
0012edc4  00000000 00000000 00000000 00000001
```

The first three values in the raw memory dump are 0x64 (100) and correspond to each of the fields in our value type named Coordinate.

So far, we have looked at a simple example of displaying the contents of a value type instance declared in a function. It is also common for value types to be embedded in a reference type that is stored on the managed heap. In these cases, we cannot simply use the raw memory dump commands; rather, we have to rely on some helper commands to dump out the value type. The first step in the process is to dump out the contents of the reference type itself by utilizing the DumpObj command. Let's again turn to our 03ObjTypes.exe example. Start by running the application under the debugger, followed by manually breaking execution when prompted to press any key. Load the SOS debugger extension, set a breakpoint on the AddCoordinate function, and resume execution until the breakpoint triggers. The process is illustrated in Listing 3-12.

Listing 3-12   Breakpoint hit in AddCoordinates function of 03ObjTypes.exe example

```
0:004> .loadby sos mscorwks
0:000> !bpmd 03ObjTypes.exe Advanced.NET.Debugging.Chapter3.ObjTypes.AddCoordinate
Found 1 methods...
MethodDesc = 000d3038
Adding pending breakpoints...
0:000> g
(232c.1d08): Control-C exception - code 40010005 (first chance)
First chance exceptions are reported before any exception handling.
This exception may be expected and handled.
eax=040dfdd4 ebx=00000000 ecx=00000000 edx=77b99a94 esi=00000000 edi=00000002
eip=77886da1 esp=040dfdc4 ebp=040dfe48 iopl=0         nv up ei pl zr na pe nc
cs=001b  ss=0023  ds=0023  es=0023  fs=003b  gs=0000         efl=00000246
KERNEL32!CtrlRoutine+0xbf:
77886da1 c745fcfeffffff  mov     dword ptr [ebp-4],0FFFFFFFEh
ss:0023:040dfe44=00000000
0:003>
0:003> g
g(232c.209c): CLR notification exception - code e0444143 (first chance)
JITTED 03ObjTypes.exe!Advanced.NET.Debugging.Chapter3.
ObjTypes.AddCoordinate(Coordinate)
Setting breakpoint: bp 002A0180
[Advanced.NET.Debugging.Chapter3.ObjTypes.AddCoordinate(Coordinate)]
Breakpoint 0 hit
eax=000d3038 ebx=0040ef9c ecx=01de6bec edx=001b5408 esi=01de6bec edi=01de6bec
eip=002a0180 esp=0040ef40 ebp=0040ef80 iopl=0         nv up ei pl nz na pe nc
cs=001b  ss=0023  ds=0023  es=0023  fs=003b  gs=0000         efl=00000206
002a0180 57              push    edi
0:000> !ClrStack -a
OS Thread Id: 0x209c (0)
ESP        EIP
0040ef40 002a0180
Advanced.NET.Debugging.Chapter3.ObjTypes.AddCoordinate(Coordinate)
    PARAMETERS:
        this = 0x01de6bec
        coord = 0x00000064

0040ef50 002a00f5 Advanced.NET.Debugging.Chapter3.ObjTypes.Main(System.String[])
    PARAMETERS:
        args = 0x01de58ac
    LOCALS:
        0x0040ef54 = 0x00000064
        <CLR reg> = 0x01de6bec

0040f18c 79e7c74b [GCFrame: 0040f18c]
```

In the `ClrStack` output, the `AddCoordinate` frame displays a parameter called the `this` parameter. The `this` pointer points to the current object instance similarly to how the current instance pointer is passed to a function of a class in native code. We can now use the `DumpObj` command on the `this` pointer to display the contents of the `ObjTypes` class:

```
0:000> !DumpObj 0x01de6bec
Name: Advanced.NET.Debugging.Chapter3.ObjTypes
MethodTable: 000d30d0
EEClass: 000d1244
Size: 20(0x14) bytes
 (C:\ADNDBin\03ObjTypes.exe)
Fields:
      MT    Field   Offset               Type VT    Attr    Value Name
000d3088  4000001       4 ...jTypes+Coordinate  1 instance 01de6bf0 coordinate
```

We will discuss the output of `DumpObj` in more detail in the next section. For now, the most important part is the `Fields` section, which contains the member data of the object. As we can see, we only have one field available in this object type. Table 3-1 details the meaning of each of the columns in the field's output.

Table 3-1 DumpObj Field Details

MT	The method table of the field.
Field	The field metadata token of the field. The high order bits (4) indicates that it is a field and lower order bits (1) is the offset into the field metadata table.
Offset	Offset of the field in the memory layout of the reference type instance.
Type	The truncated name of the type.
VT	If set to 1, indicates that this is a value type and if set to 0, it's a reference.
Attr	Specifies the attributes of the object. In the example earlier, we can see that the object is an instance.
Value	The value of the field.
Name	Name of the field (in our case, the name of the member field coordinate).

If we want to display the content of the field itself, we have two options. One is to use the `dd` command of the reference type object address (`0x01de6bec`) plus the offset (`0x4`) to dump out the contents of the value type:

```
0:000> dd 0x01de6bec+0x4
01de6bf0   00000000 00000000 00000000 80000000
01de6c00   790fd8c4 00000014 00000013 003a0078
01de6c10   0030007b 002c007d 00790020 007b003a
01de6c20   007d0031 0020002c 003a007a 0032007b
01de6c30   0000007d 00000000 00000000 00000000
01de6c40   00000000 00000000 00000000 00000000
01de6c50   00000000 00000000 00000000 00000000
01de6c60   00000000 00000000 00000000 00000000
```

Here, you can clearly see the value type contents where each of the axes is set to 0. A different and more esthetically pleasing way to dump value types that are part of a reference type is to use the DumpVC command. The DumpVC command exists for the sole purpose of displaying value types and takes the following form:

```
!DumpVC <MethodTable address> <Address>
```

The method table address and address options can easily be retrieved from the output of the DumpObj command. In the prior debug output, the method table (MT) is set to 0x000d3088 and the address is 0x01de6bf0 (corresponds to the Value column in the Fields output from the DumpObj command). The output of the DumpVC command is shown in the following:

```
0:000> !DumpVC 0x000d3088  0x01de6bf0
Name: Advanced.NET.Debugging.Chapter3.ObjTypes+Coordinate
MethodTable 000d3088
EEClass: 000d12a8
Size: 20(0x14) bytes
 (C:\ADNDBin\03ObjTypes.exe)
Fields:
      MT    Field   Offset              Type VT     Attr    Value Name
79102290  4000002        0       System.Int32  1 instance       0 xCord
79102290  4000003        4       System.Int32  1 instance       0 yCord
79102290  4000004        8       System.Int32  1 instance       0 zCord
```

As you can see, the output gives far more detailed information in comparison with the equivalent raw memory dump using the dd command. In addition to displaying all the members of the value type (with associated information), it also gives some initial basic information such as the name of the value type and the size. The most interesting part is the Fields section, which, much like DumpObj, lists all the attributes of each individual field of the value type. We can see that all three of the fields are themselves value types (as one would expect because they are all of type Int32). We could again use the DumpVC command to dump out the contents of each of the fields.

This concludes our discussion of how to dump out the contents of value types. We discussed how to dump out "standalone" instances of value types as well as how to dump out value types that are part of other reference types. Next, we turn our attention to dumping out the contents of reference types.

Dumping Basic Reference Types

In the previous section, we already saw that the DumpObj command can be used to dump reference types. The DumpObj takes the general form

```
!DumpObj [-nofields] <object address>
```

where the object address is the address of the object you want to dump. By default, DumpObj dumps out general information of the type as well as its associated fields. If you are interested in the general information only, you can use the -nofields option, which excludes the field information.

Let's take a closer look at the output of a DumpObj command execution.

```
0:000> !DumpObj 0x01de6bec
Name: Advanced.NET.Debugging.Chapter3.ObjTypes
MethodTable: 000d30d0
EEClass: 000d1244
Size: 20(0x14) bytes
  (C:\ADNDBin\03ObjTypes.exe)
Fields:
      MT    Field   Offset                 Type VT    Attr     Value Name
000d3088  4000001       4 ...jTypes+Coordinate  1 instance 01de6bf0 coordinate
```

The first piece of information that the DumpObj command presents is the Name of the type, which in our case is the ObjTypes type. Next, it displays the types MethodTable and EEClass pointers and finally the Size and Assembly that the type is defined in. Following the general section is a list of Fields that the type contains. Table 3-1 discussed the meaning of each of the columns in the field's row. Because each of the fields can, in turn, be references to other reference type instances, DumpObj can be subsequently used to display information about the contained fields.

As a final note, the DumpObj command can be invoked using the shorthand form do.

Dumping Arrays

The CLR treats arrays as first class reference types (all arrays derive from the System.Array type) and, as such, dumping the contents of an array can be

accomplished by using the DumpObj command. Again, let's turn to our
03ObjTypes.exe application to illustrate the process of dumping out arrays. Start
by running 03ObjTypes.exe under the debugger and continue execution until
asked to Press any key to continue (Arrays). At this point, manually break
execution and issue the ClrStack -a command, which serves as our starting point
for this discussion:

```
0:000> !ClrStack -a
OS Thread Id: 0xff8 (0)
ESP        EIP
001af3a8 77b99a94 [NDirectMethodFrameSlim: 001af3a8]
Microsoft.Win32.Win32Native.ReadConsoleInput(IntPtr, InputRecord ByRef, Int32, Int32
ByRef)
001af3c0 793e8f28 System.Console.ReadKey(Boolean)
    PARAMETERS:
        intercept = 0x00000000
    LOCALS:
        <no data>
        0x001af3d0 = 0x00000001
        <no data>
        <no data>
        <no data>
        <no data>
        <no data>
        <no data>
        <no data>

001af400 793e8e33 System.Console.ReadKey()
001af404 0097010c Advanced.NET.Debugging.Chapter3.ObjTypes.Main(System.String[])
    PARAMETERS:
        args = 0x01c758ac
    LOCALS:
        0x001af408 = 0x00000064
        <CLR reg> = 0x01c76c84

001af64c 79e7c74b [GCFrame: 001af64c]
0:000>
```

The primary frame of interest is the Main function frame, which lists a <CLR
reg> pointer value of 0x01c76c84. If we run the DumpObj on this pointer (as shown
in Listing 3-13), we quickly see that it corresponds to an instance of type ObjTypes,
which also happens to be a type that has two array fields defined.

Listing 3-13   Dumping out the ObjTypes type

```
0:000> !DumpObj 0x01c76c84
Name: Advanced.NET.Debugging.Chapter3.ObjTypes
MethodTable: 002a3114
EEClass: 002a129c
Size: 28(0x1c) bytes
 (C:\ADNDBin\03ObjTypes.exe)
Fields:
      MT    Field   Offset                 Type VT     Attr    Value Name
002a30c0  4000001        c ...jTypes+Coordinate  1 instance 01c76c90 coordinate
7912d7c0  4000002        4       System.Int32[]   0 instance 01c76d3c intArray
7912d8f8  4000003        8      System.Object[]   0 instance 01c76d5c strArray
```

From the output, we can see that the first array field (intArray) is of type System.Int32[] and the second (strArray) is of type System.Object[]. In essence, the first is an array of integers and the second is an array of objects. From our previous discussion on dumping basic reference types, we know we can continue using the DumpObj command on each of the reference type fields (such as our array fields) to get further information on each field. Running the DumpObj command on the integer array yields the following:

```
0:000> !DumpObj 01c76d3c
Name: System.Int32[]
MethodTable: 7912d7c0
EEClass: 7912d878
Size: 32(0x20) bytes
Array: Rank 1, Number of elements 5, Type Int32
Element Type: System.Int32
Fields:
None
```

Although the output of the DumpObj command yields some useful information such as the array rank, number of elements, and the type of each element, it does not tell us what each of the array slots actually contains. To get that information, we can use the raw memory dump commands, such as dd, on the array pointer itself, as illustrated in Listing 3-14.

Listing 3-14   Raw memory dump of a value type array

```
0:000> dd 01c76d3c
01c76d3c  7912d7c0 00000005 00000001 00000002
01c76d4c  00000003 00000004 00000005 00000000
```

```
01c76d5c   7912d8f8 00000005 790fd8c4 01c76ca0
01c76d6c   01c76cc0 01c76cd8 01c76cfc 01c76d18
01c76d7c   80000000 790fd8c4 00000014 00000013
01c76d8c   003a0078 0030007b 002c007d 00790020
01c76d9c   007b003a 007d0031 0020002c 003a007a
01c76dac   0032007b 0000007d 00000000 79102290
```

The first value in the memory output of any array is the method table of the array type itself. Passing this method table pointer to the DumpMT command displays more information about the type, as shown in the following:

```
0:000> !DumpMT 7912d7c0
EEClass: 7912d878
Module: 790c2000
Name: System.Int32[]
mdToken: 02000000   (C:\Windows\assembly\GAC_32\mscorlib\2.0.0.0__
b77a5c561934e089\mscorlib.dll)
BaseSize: 0xc
ComponentSize: 0x4
Number of IFaces in IFaceMap: 4
```

The output tells us that the type itself is an integer array (Int32) but still doesn't display the individual elements of the array. The next value of interest from Listing 3-14 is what follows the method table pointer, namely the size of the array itself. In Listing 3-14, we can see that the size of the array is 5. Following the array size are the elements (1, 2, 3, 4, 5). That sums up how we can go about displaying arrays of value types. The key is the memory layout for an array of value types, shown in Figure 3-2.

What about arrays of reference types? Can we use the same method? Absolutely. The key difference in the memory layout, however, is that in addition to the method table for the array itself, there will also be a method table pointer corresponding to the type of element that the array contains. Figure 3-3 illustrates the memory layout of an array of reference types.

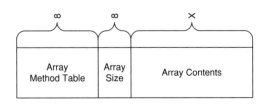

Figure 3-2 Memory layout for an array of value types

3. BASIC DEBUGGING TASKS

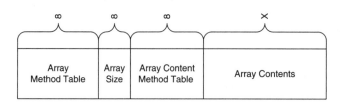

Figure 3-3 Memory layout for an array of reference types

Let's continue the debug session we started earlier and see how we can dump out the contents of the string array field that is part of the ObjTypes class. From Listing 3-14, we can see that the pointer to the string array is 0x01c76d5c. Using the dd command on that pointer yields the following output:

```
0:000> dd 01c76d5c
01c76d5c   7912d8f8 00000005 790fd8c4 01c76ca0
01c76d6c   01c76cc0 01c76cd8 01c76cfc 01c76d18
01c76d7c   80000000 790fd8c4 00000014 00000013
01c76d8c   003a0078 0030007b 002c007d 00790020
01c76d9c   007b003a 007d0031 0020002c 003a007a
01c76dac   0032007b 0000007d 00000000 79102290
01c76dbc   00000064 00000000 79102290 00000064
01c76dcc   00000000 79102290 00000064 00000000
```

We already know that the first value (0x7912d8f8) corresponds to the method descriptor for System.Object[] and that the second value is the number of elements in the array (5). The third value is new and corresponds to the method descriptor for the elements within the array itself. If we use the DumpMT command, we can see the following:

```
0:000> !DumpMT 790fd8c4
EEClass: 790fd824
Module: 790c2000
Name: System.String
mdToken: 02000024   (C:\Windows\assembly\GAC_32\mscorlib\2.0.0.0__
b77a5c561934e089\mscorlib.dll)
BaseSize: 0x10
ComponentSize: 0x2
Number of IFaces in IFaceMap: 7
Slots in VTable: 194
```

Here, we can clearly confirm that the array we are looking at is, in fact, an array of strings. The remaining 5 values are the references to each string contained within the array and we can use the DumpObj command on each reference to find out the string value:

```
0:000> !DumpObj -nofields 01c76ca0
Name: System.String
MethodTable: 790fd8c4
EEClass: 790fd824
Size: 32(0x20) bytes
  (C:\Windows\assembly\GAC_32\mscorlib\2.0.0.0__b77a5c561934e089\mscorlib.dll)
String: Welcome
0:000> !DumpObj -nofields 01c76cc0
Name: System.String
MethodTable: 790fd8c4
EEClass: 790fd824
Size: 22(0x16) bytes
  (C:\Windows\assembly\GAC_32\mscorlib\2.0.0.0__b77a5c561934e089\mscorlib.dll)
String: to
...

...
```

Note that since we are only interested in the string value itself, we use the -nofields option to eliminate displaying all the fields that are part of the string type.

At this point, we have illustrated how to dump out the contents of both value type arrays as well as reference type arrays. For each type of array, it's a somewhat mundane process of dumping out the raw memory and using DumpObj on each of the references (in the case of a reference array). Fortunately, there is a command that automates the process of dumping out arrays: DumpArray. The DumpArray command takes the following general form:

```
!DumpArray
        [-start <startIndex>]
        [-length <length>]
        [-details]
        [-nofields]
        <array object address>
```

The -start option enables you to control which index in the array you want to start at and the -length option enables you to control how many elements to display from the array. For example, if you want to dump out the first three elements of an array at address X starting at index 2, you could use the following command line:

```
!DumpArray -start 2 -length 3 X
```

Adding the -details option results in more verbose output by the DumpArray command, applying the DumpObj and DumpVC commands to each element in the array. Finally, the -nofields option causes DumpArray to exclude the fields output when used with the -details option.

Again, we will use the same debug session we already started and use the DumpArray on each of the arrays listed in Listing 3-13, starting with the integer array at address 0x01c76d3c.

```
0:000> !DumpArray -details 01c76d3c
Name: System.Int32[]
MethodTable: 7912d7c0
EEClass: 7912d878
Size: 32(0x20) bytes
Array: Rank 1, Number of elements 5, Type Int32
Element Methodtable: 79102290
[0] 01c76d44
    Name: System.Int32
    MethodTable 79102290
    EEClass: 79102218
    Size: 12(0xc) bytes
      (C:\Windows\assembly\GAC_32\mscorlib\2.0.0.0__b77a5c561934e089\mscorlib.dll)
    Fields:
          MT    Field   Offset                 Type VT     Attr     Value Name
    79102290  40003e9        0        System.Int32  1 instance         1 m_value
[1] 01c76d48
    Name: System.Int32
    MethodTable 79102290
    EEClass: 79102218
    Size: 12(0xc) bytes
      (C:\Windows\assembly\GAC_32\mscorlib\2.0.0.0__b77a5c561934e089\mscorlib.dll)
    Fields:
          MT    Field   Offset                 Type VT     Attr     Value Name
    79102290  40003e9        0        System.Int32  1 instance         2 m_value
[2] 01c76d4c
    Name: System.Int32
    MethodTable 79102290
    EEClass: 79102218
    Size: 12(0xc) bytes
      (C:\Windows\assembly\GAC_32\mscorlib\2.0.0.0__b77a5c561934e089\mscorlib.dll)
    Fields:
          MT    Field   Offset                 Type VT     Attr     Value Name
    79102290  40003e9        0        System.Int32  1 instance         3 m_value
[3] 01c76d50
    Name: System.Int32
    MethodTable 79102290
    EEClass: 79102218
    Size: 12(0xc) bytes
      (C:\Windows\assembly\GAC_32\mscorlib\2.0.0.0__b77a5c561934e089\mscorlib.dll)
    Fields:
```

```
        MT     Field   Offset                  Type VT     Attr     Value Name
    79102290  40003e9      0          System.Int32  1 instance         4 m_value
[4] 01c76d54
    Name: System.Int32
    MethodTable 79102290
    EEClass: 79102218
    Size: 12(0xc) bytes
      (C:\Windows\assembly\GAC_32\mscorlib\2.0.0.0__b77a5c561934e089\mscorlib.dll)
    Fields:
        MT     Field   Offset                  Type VT     Attr     Value Name
    79102290  40003e9      0          System.Int32  1 instance         5 m_value
```

The DumpArray command conveniently displayed each of the elements of the array with the corresponding values (1, 2, 3, 4, 5). As you can see, using DumpArray is far more convenient than manually inspecting the array. For the sake of brevity, we will leave it as an exercise to you to use the DumpArray command on the string array from Listing 3-13. Note that the DumpArray automatically recognizes whether it is dealing with a value type or reference type.

Dumping Stack Objects

Each managed thread running in the context of the CLR has an associated set of data. In addition to the bookkeeping data that the CLR maintains, each thread contains some basic information that enables the CLR to maintain the integrity of the stack as well as any parameters and local variables. Most of the time, we can use the ClrStack command to find out the parameters and local variables for each frame, but sometimes a more in-depth investigation of the stack is needed. SOS contains a command called DumpStackObjects that does an in-depth stack walk and displays all the managed objects that can be found on that thread stack. The syntax for DumpStackObjects is as follows:

```
!DumpStackObjects [-verify] [top stack [bottom stack]]
```

If no arguments are specified, DumpStackObjects displays all the managed objects for the current thread. If you want to limit the output of the command, you can specify a range (top and bottom stack). The verify option performs a verification on each of the managed objects that it finds and can be useful for detecting corrupt objects.

Let's take a look at an example of DumpStackObjects. Start by running 03ObjTypes.exe under the debugger and continue execution until you see the following prompt:

```
Press any key to continue (Generics)
```

Manually break into the debugger and switch the thread context to thread 0 using ~0s. After the thread context has been switched, load the sos extension and run the DumpStackObjects command as shown in the following:

```
0:003> ~0s
eax=00000422 ebx=002df18c ecx=7918b1dc edx=00000000 esi=002defe8 edi=00000000
eip=778e9a94 esp=002def98 ebp=002defb8 iopl=0         nv up ei pl zr na pe nc
cs=001b  ss=0023  ds=0023  es=0023  fs=003b  gs=0000             efl=00000246
ntdll!KiFastSystemCallRet:
778e9a94 c3              ret
0:000> .loadby sos mscorwks
0:000> !DumpStackObjects
OS Thread Id: 0x10dc (0)
ESP/REG  Object    Name
002df0e4 01e25a80 Microsoft.Win32.SafeHandles.SafeFileHandle
002df1ac 01e26d64 Advanced.NET.Debugging.Chapter3.ObjTypes
002df1b0 01e26d64 Advanced.NET.Debugging.Chapter3.ObjTypes
002df1c0 01e258ac System.Object[]     (System.String[])
002df1ec 01e258ac System.Object[]     (System.String[])
002df2c4 01e258ac System.Object[]     (System.String[])
002df46c 01e258ac System.Object[]     (System.String[])
002df494 01e258ac System.Object[]     (System.String[])
```

There are three main columns in the output of DumpStackObjects:

- ESP/REG. This column indicates the location of the stack where the managed object is located.
- Object. The object column is the address of the managed object. We can feed this address to the DumpObj command to get more detailed information about the object. For example, feeding object address 0x01e26d64 from the previous listing to the DumpObj command yields the following:

```
0:000> !DumpObj 01e26d64
Name: Advanced.NET.Debugging.Chapter3.ObjTypes
MethodTable: 002e3124
EEClass: 002e12d8
Size: 28(0x1c) bytes
 (C:\ADNDBin\03ObjTypes.exe)
Fields:
      MT    Field   Offset                 Type VT     Attr    Value Name
002e30d0 4000001        c ...jTypes+Coordinate  1 instance 01e26d70 coordinate
7912d7c0 4000002        4        System.Int32[]  0 instance 01e26e1c intArray
7912d8f8 4000003        8       System.Object[]  0 instance 01e26e3c strArray
```

As you can see from the output of `DumpStackObjects`, several of the rows have the same object address. This is expected because objects may end up getting passed from one function (frame) to the other where each frame contains its own reference to the same managed object.

- Name. The name column gives the textual representation of the type that the managed object corresponds to.

DUMPSTACKOBJECTS SHORTCUT Because the `DumpStackObjects` command is a rather long command to type each time you want to use it, there is a shorthand form: `dso>`.

Finding Object Sizes

The size of any given object represents the amount of memory that the particular type occupies. We have already seen a number of ways to get the size of an object, such as using the `DumpObj` command. An example of the `DumpObj` command is shown in the following:

```
0:000> !DumpObj 01de1198
Name: System.SharedStatics
MethodTable: 790feba4
EEClass: 790feaf8
Size: 28(0x1c) bytes
  (C:\Windows\assembly\GAC_32\mscorlib\2.0.0.0__b77a5c561934e089\mscorlib.dll)
Fields:
      MT    Field   Offset                 Type VT     Attr     Value Name
790fd8c4  4000512        c        System.String  0 instance 00000000
_Remoting_Identity_IDGuid
79119d38  4000513       10  ...nizer+StringMaker  0 instance 01de25cc _maker
79102290  4000514       14        System.Int32   1 instance        0
_Remoting_Identity_IDSeqNum
790ffcc8  4000515        4        System.Int64   1 instance 0
_memFailPointReservedMemory
790feba4  4000511      120 System.SharedStatics  0    shared    static _sharedStatics
    >> Domain:Value  0017fd30:01de1198 <<
```

In this example, `DumpObj` reports the size of the object to be `28` (`0x1c`) bytes. This is useful information when you want to find out the exact size of a single object. Often, the object itself references other objects, which may reference other objects, and so forth. Knowing the total size of an object (including traversing the sizes of type fields) can at times shed some light on objects that may be exceptionally large and troublesome. Using the same reference as previously, we can use the `ObjSize` command to dump out the total size of the object as shown in the following:

```
0:000> !ObjSize 01de1198
sizeof(01de1198) =         9624 (       0x2598) bytes (System.SharedStatics)
```

The total size reported is `9624` bytes, which is substantially larger than the originally reported size of `28` bytes. If you run the `ObjSize` command without specifying an address, the command will list the size for all objects on all managed threads in the process.

Dumping Exceptions

The idea behind an exception model has been around for some time, and one of the ways in which Windows implements its version of the exception model is known as Structured Exception Handling (SEH). Similarly, the .NET exception model builds on top of the Windows SEH to provide a richer object-based exception model enabling far more detailed exception information to be propagated. The additional information that the CLR carries with each exception is stored on the managed heap. As a matter of fact, an exception in the eyes of the CLR is a first class reference type, and we can utilize any of the techniques discussed earlier to dump out the details of an exception. All CLR exceptions are surfaced as SEH exceptions with an error code of `0xe0434f4d`, which means that any time an exception is thrown the debugger will report the exception as in the following:

```
(a98.cd0): CLR exception - code e0434f4d (first chance)
(a98.cd0): CLR exception - code e0434f4d (!!! second chance !!!)
```

After the exception is reported in the debugger (assuming it is not handled), the execution stops, enabling you to investigate the source of the exception. Because all exceptions are reported with an error code of `0xe0434f4d`, how can we distinguish different .NET exceptions? The answer lies in figuring out where the extended exception information is stored. The following listing illustrates a typical (abbreviated) native stack trace when a .NET exception is thrown:

```
ChildEBP RetAddr  Args to Child
0013f304 79f55b05 e0434f4d 00000001 00000001 KERNEL32!RaiseException+0x53
0013f364 7a0904d5 01283cac 00000000 00000000 mscorwks!
RaiseTheExceptionInternalOnly+0x226
0013f428 00cb0472 01282e54 01283cac 01282e54 mscorwks!JIT_Throw+0xfc
WARNING: Frame IP not in any known module. Following frames may be wrong.
```

```
0013f480  79e7be1b  0013f4cc  00000000  0013f510  0xcb0472
0013f490  79e7bd9b  0013f560  00000000  0013f530  mscorwks!CallDescrWorker+0x33
...
...
0013ff18  79edae8b  00400000  00000000  8ba1dfa4  mscorwks!
SystemDomain::ExecuteMainMethod+0x398
0013ff68  79edadf3  00400000  8ba1df7c  7c911440  mscorwks!ExecuteEXE+0x59
0013ffb0  79004044  0007f4cc  79e70000  0013fff0  mscorwks!_CorExeMain+0x11b
0013ffc0  7c817067  7c911440  0007f4cc  7ffdf000  mscoree!_CorExeMain+0x2c
0013fff0  00000000  79004010  00000000  78746341  KERNEL32!BaseProcessStart+0x23
```

At the top of the stack are a couple of frames that are responsible for surfacing the exception. The frame of most interest is RaiseTheExceptionInternalOnly in the mscorwks module. More specifically, the first argument (0x01283cac) to that function is the address of the managed exception. We can utilize the DumpObj command to display all the properties of the managed exception. Let's try it by running 03ObjTypes.exe under the debugger and continue execution until a CLR exception is thrown (remember that all CLR exceptions are surfaced with an exception code of 0xe0434f4d). When execution has stopped, use the kb command to display the call stack:

```
0:000> kb
ChildEBP RetAddr  Args to Child
0013f304  79f55b05  e0434f4d  00000001  00000001  KERNEL32!RaiseException+0x53
0013f364  7a0904d5  01283cac  00000000  00000000  mscorwks!
RaiseTheExceptionInternalOnly+0x226
0013f428  00cb0483  01282e54  01283cac  01282e54  mscorwks!JIT_Throw+0xfc
WARNING: Frame IP not in any known module. Following frames may be wrong.
0013f480  79e7be1b  0013f4cc  00000000  0013f510  0xcb0483
0013f490  79e7bd9b  0013f560  00000000  0013f530  mscorwks!CallDescrWorker+0x33
0013f510  79e7bce8  0013f560  00000000  0013f530  mscorwks!
CallDescrWorkerWithHandler+0xa3
0013f650  79e7bbd0  00913178  0013f72c  0013f6e0  mscorwks!MethodDesc::CallDescr+0x19c
0013f668  79e802f4  00913178  0013f72c  0013f6e0  mscorwks!
MethodDesc::CallTargetWorker+0x20
0013f67c  79edb56e  0013f6e0  47284667  00000000
mscorwks!MethodDescCallSite::CallWithValueTypes_RetArgSlot+0x18
0013f7e0  79edb367  00913030  00000001  0013f81c  mscorwks!ClassLoader::RunMain+0x220
0013fa48  79edb23c  00000000  47284bb7  00000000
mscorwks!Assembly::ExecuteMainMethod+0xa6
0013ff18  79edae8b  00400000  00000000  47284e2b
mscorwks!SystemDomain::ExecuteMainMethod+0x398
0013ff68  79edadf3  00400000  47284ef3  7c911440  mscorwks!ExecuteEXE+0x59
0013ffb0  79004044  0007f4cc  79e70000  0013fff0  mscorwks!_CorExeMain+0x11b
0013ffc0  7c817067  7c911440  0007f4cc  7ffde000  mscoree!_CorExeMain+0x2c
0013fff0  00000000  79004010  00000000  78746341  KERNEL32!BaseProcessStart+0x23
```

Next, we pick out the first argument to the `RaiseTheExceptionInternalOnly` function (`0x01283cac`) and use the `DumpObj` command with that address to display the managed exception:

```
0:000> !DumpObj 01283cac
Name: System.ArgumentException
MethodTable: 7910139c
EEClass: 79101324
Size: 76(0x4c) bytes
 (C:\WINDOWS\assembly\GAC_32\mscorlib\2.0.0.0__b77a5c561934e089\mscorlib.dll)
Fields:
      MT    Field   Offset                 Type VT     Attr    Value Name
790f9244  40000b5        4        System.String  0 instance 00000000 _className
79107d4c  40000b6        8   ...ection.MethodBase  0 instance 00000000
_exceptionMethod
790f9244  40000b7        c        System.String  0 instance 00000000
_exceptionMethodString
790f9244  40000b8       10        System.String  0 instance 01283cf8 _message
79112734  40000b9       14   ...tions.IDictionary  0 instance 00000000 _data
790f984c  40000ba       18     System.Exception  0 instance 00000000 _innerException
790f9244  40000bb       1c        System.String  0 instance 00000000 _helpURL
790f8a7c  40000bc       20        System.Object  0 instance 01283d54 _stackTrace
790f9244  40000bd       24        System.String  0 instance 00000000
_stackTraceString
790f9244  40000be       28        System.String  0 instance 00000000
_remoteStackTraceString
790fdb60  40000bf       34        System.Int32  0 instance        0
_remoteStackIndex
790f8a7c  40000c0       2c        System.Object  0 instance 00000000 _dynamicMethods
790fdb60  40000c1       38        System.Int32  0 instance -2147024809 _HResult
790f9244  40000c2       30        System.String  0 instance 00000000 _source
790fcfa4  40000c3       3c        System.IntPtr  0 instance        0 _xptrs
790fdb60  40000c4       40        System.Int32  0 instance -532459699 _xcode
790f9244  40001e5       44        System.String  0 instance 00000000 m_paramName
```

From the output of `DumpObj`, we can get all the information we need about the managed code exception including the type of exception (`ArgumentException`) and all the fields associated with the exception (stack trace, message, HRESULT, parameter name, etc.). We can further use the `DumpObj` command on the message field to find out the exception message:

```
0:000> !DumpObj -nofields 01283cf8
Name: System.String
MethodTable: 790f9244
```

```
EEClass: 790f91a4
Size: 54(0x36) bytes
  (C:\WINDOWS\assembly\GAC_32\mscorlib\2.0.0.0__b77a5c561934e089\mscorlib.dll)
String: Obj cannot be null
```

Although dumping exceptions using the `DumpObj` command is a feasible approach, the `DumpObj` command can be a bit noisy. Most of the time, all we want to display about an exception is the type of the exception, the stack traces (including the internal stack trace), and the message. Fortunately, the SOS debugger extension includes a command called `PrintException`. The `PrintException` command takes the address to the managed exception and prints out the exception information in a more digestible fashion. If we were to use the same exception address as previously used (`0x01283cac`), the `PrintException` command would display the following:

```
0:000> !PrintException 01283cac
Exception object: 01283cac
Exception type: System.ArgumentException
Message: Obj cannot be null
InnerException: <none>
StackTrace (generated):
    SP       IP       Function
    0013F430 00CB0483 Advanced.NET.Debugging.Chapter3.
ObjTypes.ThrowException(Advanced.NET.Debugging.Chapter3.ObjTypes)
    0013F444 00CB0133
Advanced.NET.Debugging.Chapter3.ObjTypes.Main(System.String[])

StackTraceString: <none>
HResult: 80070057
```

Another command that is useful when investigating exceptions is the `Threads` command, which displays information about each managed thread in the system including the last exception that was thrown by that thread. If we ran the `Threads` command in the previous debug session, we would see the following:

```
0:000> !Threads
ThreadCount: 2
UnstartedThread: 0
BackgroundThread: 1
PendingThread: 0
DeadThread: 0
Hosted Runtime: no
                                    PreEmptive  GC Alloc       Lock
      ID OSID ThreadOBJ    State    GC          Context        Domain    Count APT
Exception
```

```
   0    1  a0c 00190d50       a020 Enabled  00000000:00000000 0015bf28    0 MTA
System.ArgumentException (01283cac)
   2    2  580 0019aa88       b220 Enabled  00000000:00000000 0015bf28    0 MTA
(Finalizer)
```

Here, we can see that the managed thread with an ID of 1 threw a `System.ArgumentException`.

The last exception command of interest is the `StopOnException` command. Although it is not strictly speaking related to dumping out information about a specific exception, it lets you set a "breakpoint" when a specific exception is thrown. The syntax for the `StopOnException` is shown in the following:

```
!StopOnException [-derived]
                 [-create | -create2]
                 <Exception>
                 [<Pseudo-register number>]
```

The `create` and `create2` switches control whether you want the breakpoint to hit on a first or second chance occurrence of the specified exception. The derived option increases the scope of the breakpoint to include not only the exception specified but also any of the exceptions that are derived from the specified exception. The pseudo-register is optional and indicates which pseudo register the command will use to set the breakpoint. If no pseudo register is specified, it will default to `$t1`. Let's look at some examples. If we want to set a breakpoint when a first chance `System.ArgumentException` is thrown, we can use the following command:

```
!StopOnException -create System.ArgumentException
```

However, if we want to set a breakpoint for any exceptions derived from `System.Exception`, we could use the following command:

```
!StopOnException -derived System.Exception
```

Why Doesn't the Debugger Break on CLR Exceptions?

All the examples so far assume that the debugger has been configured properly to break on all first and second chance managed exceptions. Depending on the debugger configuration, this may or may not be the case for your particular configuration. To re-enable breaking on all managed exceptions, we can use the sxe command. The sxe command enables you to control the action that the debugger will take when an exception occurs. Adding the `clr` switch to the `sxe` command tells the debugger to always stop on all managed exceptions:

```
sxe clr
```

Thread Operations

During native code debugging, all thread-related debugger commands work on the basis of native Windows threads. Managed code debugging presents a new twist, however, because managed code threads employ their own thread "structure," and walking the stacks becomes a task that the debuggers are natively unable to do. We already know that the CLR translates calls into managed code on-the-fly and that the JIT compiler is free to place the generated code anywhere it sees fit. The native debuggers do not have any knowledge of the JIT compiler nor where it places the generated code, and hence they are unable to properly display the stack trace. Let's look at an example. Run `03simple.exe` under the debugger and when asked to press any key to exit the application, break the execution in the debugger using CTRL-C. Next, we dump out thread 0 to see what a managed code call stack looks like in the native debugger, as illustrated in Listing 3-15.

Listing 3-15 Example of managed code call stack using the kn command

```
0:000> kn
 # ChildEBP RetAddr
00 0013f24c 7c90dacc ntdll!KiFastSystemCallRet
01 0013f250 7c912dc8 ntdll!NtRequestWaitReplyPort+0xc
02 0013f270 7c8743e8 ntdll!CsrClientCallServer+0x8c
03 0013f358 7c87450d KERNEL32!GetConsoleInput+0xdd
04 0013f378 0090a61c KERNEL32!ReadConsoleInputA+0x1a
WARNING: Frame IP not in any known module. Following frames may be wrong.
05 0013f400 793b8138 0x90a61c
06 0013f468 793b8043 mscorlib_ni+0x2f8138
07 0013f490 79e7bd9b mscorlib_ni+0x2f8043
08 0013f510 79e7bce8 mscorwks!CallDescrWorkerWithHandler+0xa3
09 0013f650 79e7bbd0 mscorwks!MethodDesc::CallDescr+0x19c
0a 0013f668 79e802f4 mscorwks!MethodDesc::CallTargetWorker+0x20
0b 0013f67c 79edb56e mscorwks!MethodDescCallSite::CallWithValueTypes_RetArgSlot+0x18
0c 0013f7e0 79edb367 mscorwks!ClassLoader::RunMain+0x220
0d 0013fa48 79edb23c mscorwks!Assembly::ExecuteMainMethod+0xa6
0e 0013ff18 79edae8b mscorwks!SystemDomain::ExecuteMainMethod+0x398
0f 0013ff68 79edadf3 mscorwks!ExecuteEXE+0x59
```

(continues)

Listing 3-15 Example of managed code call stack using the kn command *(continued)*

```
10 0013ffb0 79004044 mscorwks!_CorExeMain+0x11b
11 0013ffc0 7c817067 mscoree!_CorExeMain+0x2c
12 0013fff0 00000000 KERNEL32!BaseProcessStart+0x23
```

All of the frames in the call stack are executing code in the `mscorwks` and `mscorlib` modules, which are responsible for making the function calls to the actual managed code (wherever it may be located in memory). Frames `0xc` through `0x11` indicate that the `Main` function in the application is being called (as can be seen by the `ExecuteMainMethod` function). Frames `0x8` through `0xa` then deal with the act of interpreting the `Main` function metadata and subsequently make the call. The managed code frame itself (`0x5`) is clearly identified with no associated symbol files and the following warning:

```
WARNING: Frame IP not in any known module. Following frames may be wrong.
```

The debugger tries to interpret the code at location `0x90a61c` but fails to associate it with any existing module information and displays the warning. This is as per expectations because managed code is managed by the CLR itself and is outside of the realm of the native call stack. Clearly, this call stack is not very useful when debugging managed code. It would be far better if we had a real managed code call stack. Fortunately, the SOS debugger extension has intimate knowledge of managed code call stacks and offers a number of thread commands, which we will discuss next.

ClrStack

The `ClrStack` command can be used to get a managed code call stack as shown in Listing 3-16.

Listing 3-16 Displaying the managed code call stack using the ClrStack command

```
0:000> !ClrStack
OS Thread Id: 0xb70 (0)
ESP       EIP
0013f418 7c90e4f4 [NDirectMethodFrameSlim: 0013f418] Microsoft.Win32.Win32Native.
ReadConsoleInput(IntPtr, InputRecord ByRef, Int32, Int32 ByRef)
0013f430 793b8138 System.Console.ReadKey(Boolean)
0013f470 793b8043 System.Console.ReadKey()
0013f474 00cb00a6 Advanced.NET.Debugging.Chapter2.Simple.Main(System.String[])
0013f69c 79e7be1b [GCFrame: 0013f69c]
0:000>
```

The first piece of information that the ClrStack command displays is the thread ID of the thread being displayed. This is the underlying operating system thread ID. Next, it displays all the frames of the managed call stack. This time, we can more clearly see what functions are being called. First, the Main function is called, followed by a call to ReadKey, which in turn translates to a number of frames with the topmost frame being annotated with NDirectMethodFrameSlim. This is an indication that a transition between managed code and native code is taking place (discussed in more detail in Chapter 7, "Interoperability." Each of the frames also shows the type of the argument each frame expects.

The ClrStack extension command also has a couple of switches that enable various additional pieces of information to be displayed.

ClrStack -l can be used to show local variable information (minus the names) as shown in the following:

```
0:000> !ClrStack -l
OS Thread Id: 0x10ac (0)
ESP        EIP
0013f410 7c90e4f4 [NDirectMethodFrameSlim: 0013f410] Microsoft.Win32.Win32Native.
ReadConsoleInput(IntPtr, InputRecord ByRef, Int32, Int32 ByRef)
0013f428 793b8138 System.Console.ReadKey(Boolean)
    LOCALS:
        <no data>
        0x0013f438 = 0x00000001
        <no data>
        <no data>
        <no data>
        <no data>
        <no data>
        <no data>
        <no data>
        <no data>

0013f468 793b8043 System.Console.ReadKey()
0013f46c 00cb00c1 Advanced.NET.Debugging.Chapter3.Simple.Main(System.String[])
    LOCALS:
        <CLR reg> = 0x01281bac
```

As we can see, the Main function frame has a local variable with the address 0x01281bac. We can now use the !DumpObj command to get extended information about this local variable:

```
0:000> !DumpObj 0x01281bac
Name: System.Text.StringBuilder
```

```
MethodTable: 790f9664
EEClass: 790f95d0
Size: 20(0x14) bytes
  (C:\WINDOWS\assembly\GAC_32\mscorlib\2.0.0.0__b77a5c561934e089\mscorlib.dll)
Fields:
        MT    Field   Offset               Type VT     Attr     Value Name
790fcfa4   40000b1        8    System.IntPtr  0 instance         0 m_currentThread
790fdb60   40000b2        c    System.Int32   0 instance 2147483647 m_MaxCapacity
790f9244   40000b3        4    System.String  0 instance  01281bc0 m_StringValue
```

The local variable is of type StringBuilder and the last field of the object is named m_StringValue with a value of 0x01281bc0. We can again use the DumpObj command to get the actual string value:

```
0:000> !DumpObj 01281bc0
Name: System.String
MethodTable: 790f9244
EEClass: 790f91a4
Size: 146(0x92) bytes
  (C:\WINDOWS\assembly\GAC_32\mscorlib\2.0.0.0__b77a5c561934e089\mscorlib.dll)
String: Welcome to Advanced .NET Debugging!
Fields:
        MT    Field   Offset               Type VT     Attr    Value Name
790fdb60   4000096        4     System.Int32  0 instance        65 m_arrayLength
790fdb60   4000097        8     System.Int32  0 instance        35 m_stringLength
790fad38   4000098        c     System.Char   0 instance        57 m_firstChar
790f9244   4000099       10    System.String  0   shared   static Empty
    >> Domain:Value  0015bf38:790d57b4 <<
79122994   400009a       14   System.Char[]  0   shared   static WhitespaceChars
    >> Domain:Value  0015bf38:012816c8 <<
```

This time, the type of object is shown to be string and the actual string value is also shown:

```
Welcome to Advanced .NET Debugging
```

The next switch we will discuss is the –p switch to the ClrStack command. The –p switch shows all the arguments to each managed code frame on the call stack, as shown in the following:

```
0:000> !ClrStack -p
OS Thread Id: 0x10ac (0)
ESP       EIP
```

```
0013f410 7c90e4f4 [NDirectMethodFrameSlim: 0013f410] Microsoft.Win32.Win32Native.
ReadConsoleInput(IntPtr, InputRecord ByRef, Int32, Int32 ByRef)
0013f428 793b8138 System.Console.ReadKey(Boolean)
    PARAMETERS:
        intercept = 0x00000000

0013f468 793b8043 System.Console.ReadKey()
0013f46c 00cb00c1 Advanced.NET.Debugging.Chapter3.Simple.Main(System.String[])
    PARAMETERS:
        args = 0x01281b08

0013f69c 79e7be1b [GCFrame: 0013f69c]
```

In the output, we can see that the `Main` frame has an `args` value of `0x01281b08`. From the frame itself, we can also see that the `Main` function takes a `String []`. If we dump the object at the address, we can see the following:

```
0:000> !DumpObj 0x01281b08
Name: System.Object[]
MethodTable: 7912254c
EEClass: 79122ac0
Size: 16(0x10) bytes
Array: Rank 1, Number of elements 0, Type CLASS
Element Type: System.String
Fields:
None
```

The last switch to `ClrStack` is the `-a` switch, which is simply a combination of `-l` and `-p`.

Please note that if the `ClrStack` command is run in the context of a nonmanaged code thread, it displays an error as shown in the following:

```
0:001> !ClrStack
OS Thread Id: 0x1608 (1)
Unable to walk the managed stack. The current thread is likely not a
managed thread. You can run !threads to get a list of managed threads in
the process.
```

As you can see, `ClrStack` tells you that the thread is most likely not a managed code thread and that the threads command can be used to get a list of all managed threads in the process.

Threads

The `Threads` command tells the SOS extension to enumerate all managed code threads running in the process. Using the same `03simple.exe` application, we can see that the following managed code threads are active in the process:

```
0:001> !Threads
ThreadCount: 2
UnstartedThread: 0
BackgroundThread: 1
PendingThread: 0
DeadThread: 0
Hosted Runtime: no
                                 PreEmptive   GC Alloc          Lock
       ID OSID ThreadOBJ   State   GC         Context     Domain  Count APT
Exception
   0    1 10ac 00190d88    a020 Enabled  00000000:00000000 0015bf38      0 MTA
   2    2 10b0 0019aaf8    b220 Enabled  00000000:00000000 0015bf38      0 MTA
(Finalizer)
```

The first part of the output for the `Threads` command is a summary of all thread activity in the process including the number of threads. The next part is the more interesting part and contains the following pieces of information:

- The first (and unnamed) column is the debugger thread ID. In the sample output previously, the first thread has an ID of `0` and the second an ID of `2`.
- The `ID` column is the CLR thread ID for the managed thread.
- The `OSID` column is the operating system thread ID.
- The `ThreadObj` is a pointer to the underlying CLR thread data structure.

Unfortunately, the public symbols for `mscorwks.dll` do not contain the thread data structure. However, we can still glean some insight into the internals of the thread data structure by looking at the SSCLI source code. More specifically, the data structure that the CLR uses to represent a thread is located in the following location:

```
rotor\sscli20\clr\src\vm\threads.h
```

We won't go into all the details of the threads class, but suffice it to say that there exists a data member called `m_ExposedObject` located right after the `m_OSThreadId` member in the memory layout. Because we already know the OS thread ID by the output from the `Threads` command (`10ac` and `10b0`), we can easily dump the contents of the `ThreadObj` pointer until we see either of the OS thread IDs. The `m_ExposedObject` follows the thread ID, which is shown in the following.

Listing 3-17 shows an example of finding the managed code thread object from the `ThreadObj` (Threads output) pointer of value `00190d88`.

Listing 3-17   Finding the managed thread data structure from thread object pointer

```
0:001> dd 00190d88
00190d88   79f04514 0000a020 00000000 0013f410
00190d98   00000000 00000000 00000000 00000001
00190da8   00000000 00190db0 00190db0 00190db0
00190db8   00000000 00000000 baad0000 0015d110
00190dc8   00000000 00000000 00000000 00000000
00190dd8   00000000 00000000 00000000 baadf00d
00190de8   001688f0 001a0050 001a0168 000000f0
00190df8   001a0050 00000000 00000000 00000100
0:001> dd
00190e08   00000000 00000000 00000000 00000000
00190e18   00000000 00000000 00000000 dfca504a
00190e28   00000000 00000000 00000000 00000000
00190e38   00000000 baadf00d ffffffff ffffffff
00190e48   ffffffff ffffffff 00000000 00000000
00190e58   00000000 00000000 00191158 00000000
00190e68   0019abd8 00000000 00140000 00040000
00190e78   baadf00d baadf00d baadf00d baadf00d
0:001>
00190e88   baadf00d 00000000 00000764 00000000
00190e98   00000760 00000000 0000075c 00000000
00190ea8   00000758 00000000 baadf00d baadf00d
00190eb8   baadf00d 00000000 00000000 baadf00d
00190ec8   00000768 ffffffff ffffffff 00000001
00190ed8   000010ac 008f12fc 008f11f8 80000000
00190ee8   00000002 00000000 00000000 baadf00d
00190ef8   00000000 00000001 00000000 00000000
0:001> dd 008f12fc
008f12fc   01282ed4 00000000 00000000 00000000
008f130c   00000000 00000000 00000000 00000000
008f131c   00000000 00000000 00000000 00000000
008f132c   00000000 00000000 00000000 00000000
008f133c   00000000 00000000 00000000 00000000
008f134c   00000000 00000000 00000000 00000000
008f135c   00000000 00000000 00000000 00000000
008f136c   00000000 00000000 00000000 00000000
0:001> !do 01282ed4
Name: System.Threading.Thread
MethodTable: 790fa000
```

(continues)

Listing 3-17 Finding the managed thread data structure from thread object pointer (*continued*)

```
EEClass: 790f9f90
Size: 52(0x34) bytes
 (C:\WINDOWS\assembly\GAC_32\mscorlib\2.0.0.0__b77a5c561934e089\mscorlib.dll)
Fields:
      MT    Field   Offset              Type VT    Attr     Value Name
791020b8  4000627        4 ....Contexts.Context  0 instance  00000000 m_Context
7910bdcc  4000628        8 ....ExecutionContext  0 instance  00000000
m_ExecutionContext
790f9244  4000629        c        System.String  0 instance  00000000 m_Name
790f9cac  400062a       10      System.Delegate  0 instance  00000000 m_Delegate
79122b40  400062b       14   System.Object[][]  0 instance  00000000
m_ThreadStaticsBuckets
79122414  400062c       18        System.Int32[]  0 instance  00000000
m_ThreadStaticsBits
790fe2e4  400062d       1c ...ation.CultureInfo  0 instance  00000000
m_CurrentCulture
790fe2e4  400062e       20 ...ation.CultureInfo  0 instance  00000000
m_CurrentUICulture
790f8a7c  400062f       24        System.Object  0 instance  00000000
m_ThreadStartArg
790fcfa4  4000630       28        System.IntPtr  0 instance   1641864
DONT_USE_InternalThread
790fdb60  4000631       2c         System.Int32  0 instance         2 m_Priority
79102238  4000632      160 ...LocalDataStoreMgr  0   shared    static
s_LocalDataStoreMgr
      >> Domain:Value  0015bf38:00000000 <<
790f8a7c  4000633      164        System.Object  0   shared    static s_SyncObject
      >> Domain:Value  0015bf38:01282ec8 <<
```

The `State` field of the `Threads` output shows the current state of the thread. For the two thread states listed (`a020` and `b220`), we can use the following bit masks as defined in the Rotor source code (`sscli20\clr\src\vm\threads.h`):

```
TS_LegalToJoin = 0x00000020,    // Is it now legal to attempt a Join()?

TS_Background = 0x00000200,    // Thread is a background thread
```

The `Preemptive GC` field indicates whether the thread can be preempted due to a garbage collection activity.

The `GC Alloc Context` field will be discussed in Chapter 5, Managed Heap and Garbage Collection.

The `Domain` field tells us which application domain the thread is running in. We can use the `DumpDomain` command on the pointers to get extended information application domain information.

The `LockCount` field indicates whether the thread has taken a managed lock.

Finally, the `APT` field stands for Apartment and tells us which COM apartment mode the thread is in.

There are a couple of switches available to the `Threads` command. More specifically, the `-live` switch limits the output of the `Threads` command to only threads that are considered alive and active. The `-special` switch displays all the "special" threads of the process such as the garbage collection thread, debugger threads, threads pool timer threads, and so on.

DumpStack

The `ClrStack` command shows only the managed code call stack, whereas the `k` family of commands only shows the native call stack. To dump the managed code and native code call stacks, the `DumpStack` command can be used. To illustrate the output of the `DumpStack` command, we use the same debug session we investigated before (breaking into the debugger when `03simple.exe` prompts for pressing any key). Listing 3-18 shows the output of the `DumpStack` command in abbreviated form.

Listing 3-18 *Output of DumpStack command*

```
0:000> !DumpStack
OS Thread Id: 0x10ac (0)
Current frame: ntdll!KiFastSystemCallRet
ChildEBP RetAddr  Caller,Callee
0013f244 7c90dacc ntdll!NtRequestWaitReplyPort+0xc
0013f248 7c912dc8 ntdll!CsrClientCallServer+0x8c,
 calling ntdll!ZwRequestWaitReplyPort
0013f268 7c8743e8 KERNEL32!GetConsoleInput+0xdd, calling ntdll!CsrClientCallServer
0013f2dc 79e85194 mscorwks!Thread::HandleThreadAbort+0x9c, calling
ntdll!RtlRestoreLastWin32Error
0013f2e0 79e85199 mscorwks!Thread::HandleThreadAbort+0xa1, calling
mscorwks!_EH_epilog3
0013f300 79e7b7f3 mscorwks!Module::IsJumpTargetTableEntry+0x26, calling
mscorwks!X86JumpTargetTable::ComputeSize
0013f314 79e84cf7 mscorwks!NDirectSlimStubWorker1+0xa9, calling mscorwks!RunML
0013f320 79e77d92 mscorwks!Thread::EnablePreemptiveGC+0xf, calling
mscorwks!Thread::CatchAtSafePoint
0013f350 7c87450d KERNEL32!ReadConsoleInputA+0x1a, calling KERNEL32!GetConsoleInput
```

(continues)

Listing 3-18 Output of DumpStack command *(continued)*

```
0013f370 0090a61c 0090a61c
...
...

...
0013fba4 7c91003d ntdll!RtlFreeHeap+0x647, calling ntdll!_SEH_epilog
0013fbd4 7c91003d ntdll!RtlFreeHeap+0x647, calling ntdll!_SEH_epilog
0013fbd8 7c911432 ntdll!RtlpFreeDebugInfo+0x5c, calling ntdll!RtlFreeHeap
0013fbdc 7c911463 ntdll!RtlpFreeDebugInfo+0x77, calling
ntdll!RtlLeaveCriticalSection
0013fbe4 7c911440 ntdll!RtlpFreeDebugInfo+0x6a, calling ntdll!_SEH_epilog
0013fbfc 79e739ea mscorwks!UnsafeEELeaveCriticalSection+0x1d, calling  (JitHelp:
CORINFO_HELP_GET_THREAD)
0013fc04 79e739d7 mscorwks!UnsafeEELeaveCriticalSection+0xa, calling
ntdll!RtlLeaveCriticalSection
0013fc08 79e739ea mscorwks!UnsafeEELeaveCriticalSection+0x1d, calling  (JitHelp:
CORINFO_HELP_GET_THREAD)
0013fc0c 79e739af mscorwks!CrstBase::Leave+0x77, calling
mscorwks!UnsafeEELeaveCriticalSection
0013fc10 79e739cc mscorwks!CrstBase::Leave+0x96, calling mscorwks!_EH_epilog3
0013fc50 79e75877 mscorwks!EEHeapAlloc+0x12d, calling ntdll!RtlAllocateHeap
0013fc64 7c91003d ntdll!RtlFreeHeap+0x647, calling ntdll!_SEH_epilog
0013fc68 79e75923 mscorwks!EEHeapFree+0x83, calling ntdll!RtlFreeHeap
0013fc74 79e7593f mscorwks!EEHeapFree+0xa5, calling mscorwks!_EH_epilog3
0013fc88 79e75896 mscorwks!EEHeapAlloc+0x163, calling mscorwks!_EH_epilog3
0013fc8c 79e75848 mscorwks!EEHeapAllocInProcessHeap+0x51, calling
mscorwks!EEHeapAlloc
0013fc9c 79e7593f mscorwks!EEHeapFree+0xa5, calling mscorwks!_EH_epilog3
0013fca0 79e758f6 mscorwks!EEHeapFreeInProcessHeap+0x21, calling mscorwks!EEHeapFree
0013fcb0 79e737aa mscorwks!SaveLastErrorHolder::~SaveLastErrorHolder+0x14, calling
ntdll!RtlGetLastWin32Error
0013fcb8 79e758da mscorwks!operator delete[]+0x41, calling mscorwks!_EH_epilog3
0013fce0 79e758da mscorwks!operator delete[]+0x41, calling mscorwks!_EH_epilog3
0013fce4 79e7fe39
mscorwks!SArray<CORBBTPROF_TOKEN_LIST_ENTRY,1>::~SArray<CORBBTPROF_TOKEN_LIST_ENTRY,
1>+0x21, calling mscorwks!operator delete
0013fce8 79e7fdeb
mscorwks!SArray<CORBBTPROF_TOKEN_LIST_ENTRY,1>::~SArray<CORBBTPROF_TOKEN_LIST_ENTRY,
1>+0x27, calling mscorwks!_EH_epilog3
0013fdb0 79e7b29b mscorwks!HardCodedMetaSig::GetBinarySig+0x146, calling
mscorwks!_EH_epilog3
0013fdb4 79e7ce70 mscorwks!Binder::FetchMethod+0x5a, calling
mscorwks!HardCodedMetaSig::GetBinarySig
```

```
0013fdcc 79e7c4bb mscorwks!Binder::CheckInit+0xb, calling
mscorwks!MethodTable::IsClassInited
0013fdd4 79e7ce07 mscorwks!Binder::GetMethod+0x63, calling
mscorwks!Binder::CheckInit
0013fdd8 79e7ce1b mscorwks!Binder::GetMethod+0x79, calling mscorwks!_EH_epilog3
0013fddc 79ede7a0 mscorwks!EEPolicy::GetActionOnFailure+0x8f, calling
mscorwks!_EH_epilog3
0013fe00 79e75a3a mscorwks!CLRException::HandlerState::CleanupTry+0x13, calling
mscorwks!GetCurrentSEHRecord
0013fe10 79ed32ec mscorwks!EEStartupHelper+0x7d5, calling
mscorwks!CLRException::HandlerState::CleanupTry
0013fe28 79ed3333 mscorwks!EEStartupHelper+0x904, calling
mscorwks!__security_check_cookie
0013fe4c 79f11b6a mscorwks!REGUTIL::InitOptionalConfigCache+0x186, calling
mscorwks!SString::CaseCompareHelper
0013feb8 7c9101bb ntdll!RtlAllocateHeap+0xeac, calling ntdll!_SEH_epilog
0013febc 79e75877 mscorwks!EEHeapAlloc+0x12d, calling ntdll!RtlAllocateHeap
0013feec 79ed3477 mscorwks!EEStartup+0x50, calling mscorwks!EEStartupHelper
0013fef0 79ed3496 mscorwks!EEStartup+0x75, calling mscorwks!_SEH_epilog4
0013ff18 79edae8b mscorwks!ExecuteEXE+0x59, calling
mscorwks!SystemDomain::ExecuteMainMethod
0013ff68 79edadf3 mscorwks!_CorExeMain+0x11b, calling mscorwks!ExecuteEXE
0013ff74 7c911440 ntdll!RtlpFreeDebugInfo+0x6a, calling ntdll!_SEH_epilog
0013ffb0 79004044 mscoree!_CorExeMain+0x2c
0013ffc0 7c817067 KERNEL32!BaseProcessStart+0x23
0013ffc4 7c911440 ntdll!RtlpFreeDebugInfo+0x6a, calling ntdll!_SEH_epilog
0:000>
```

As you can see, the output from `DumpStack` is quite elaborate but can be very valuable when an aggregate call stack view is required.

Using the `-EE` switch to the `DumpStack` command results in only managed functions being displayed. The net result is essentially the same as using the `ClrStack` command with the exception of displaying the method descriptor pointers.

It is also possible to specify a stack range that you want `DumpStack` to work on. This can help reduce the amount of information that the command displays.

EEStack

Sometimes, it is important to get the call stacks for all the managed threads in a process, and rather than using the `Threads` command followed by `DumpStack` for each and every thread in the `Threads` command output, the `EEStack` command can be used. The EEStack command simply calls DumpStack for each active thread in the process. The two switches available to the EEStack command are

- -short, which narrows down the output to only threads considered "interesting." In this case, interesting is defined by the following:

  The thread has taken a lock.

  The thread has been hijacked to perform a garbage collection.

  The thread is currently executing in managed code.

- -EE, which is simply passed directly to DumpStack to display managed code call stacks only.

COMState

When working with the COM subsystem, it is important to be aware of the different apartment models that COM offers. There are two primary apartment models available. The first apartment model is called the single threaded apartments (STA) and the second multi threaded apartments (MTA). Any time a thread wants to use any COM objects, it must also tell the COM subsystem which apartment model it is interested in utilizing. The notion of a thread being initialized for a specific apartment model is crucial when working with the .NET interoperability layer (discussed in more detail in Chapter 7), and being able to find out a thread's apartment model while debugging COM interoperability problems is even more important. The SOS debugger extension provides the COMState command that can be used to find out the apartment model for each thread in the system. An example of the output of the COMState command is shown in the following:

```
0:000> !COMState
    ID      TEB    APT   APTId CallerTID Context
 0  ff8  7ffdf000 MTA      0         0 00398fd8
 1 1554  7ffde000 Ukn
 2 2260  7ffdd000 MTA      0         0 00398fd8
 3 1eb8  7ffdc000 Ukn
 4 23a0  7ffda000 Ukn
```

The ID column represents the thread ID. The TEB column indicates the thread environment block for each thread. The teb command can be used with the TEB pointer to get extended information about the thread (such as last error value, stack limits, etc.). The APT column indicates for which apartment model the thread is initialized. MTA corresponds to the multi threaded apartment and STA the single threaded apartment model. Ukn typically indicates that the thread has not initialized COM at that point in time.

Code Inspection

The key to any debugging session is having the capability to investigate the state of a system and make inferences about the sequence of code that could have led to the observed state. As such, it is also critically important to be able to investigate what code is executed and follow the flow of execution throughout any given system. In this part of the chapter, we will take a look at the commands available to us when doing code inspections. By code inspection, I mean being able to take a raw code byte stream and infer what the piece of code is doing. Note that this will serve as an introduction to the commands; we will see them in action in more detail in subsequent chapters in the book.

Unassembling Code

When debugging native code, a very common command used is the u (unassemble) command and its associated variations. The u command essentially unassembles the raw code byte stream into assembly level instructions, making it much easier to deduce what the code did or is about to do. In the managed code world, we can still use the u command to unassemble code addresses (assuming we know the address of where the code is located). However, what makes life a little trickier is the fact that the u command is inherently unaware of managed code per se and treats all code as plain old machine code. The following is an example of using the u command on a managed function:

```
002c035d b990221079     mov     ecx,offset mscorlib_ni+0x42290 (79102290)
002c0362 e8b51ce5ff     call    0011201c
002c0367 8bf8           mov     edi,eax
002c0369 8b460c         mov     eax,dword ptr [esi+0Ch]
002c036c 894704         mov     dword ptr [edi+4],eax
002c036f 57             push    edi
0:000>
002c0370 8bd5           mov     edx,ebp
002c0372 8bcb           mov     ecx,ebx
002c0374 e8a79a1279     call    mscorlib_ni+0x329e20 (793e9e20)
```

As you can see, there are a couple of call instructions. One call instruction calls into an address of 0x0011201c and the other call statement calls into the mscorlib_ni (precompiled version of mscorlib) module at offset 0x329e20. This type of unassembly doesn't really tell us a whole lot. What code is located at address 0x0011201c and what function is being called in mscorlib_ni?

Fortunately, the SOS debugger extension contains a more useful version of the u command very innovatively called the U command. Because the SOS extension has more intimate knowledge of the CLR, the U command annotates the unassembly, making it much easier to understand the code flow. If we use the U command on the same code shown previously, we can see the following:

```
0:000> !U eip
002c0362 e8b51ce5ff      call      0011201c (JitHelp: CORINFO_HELP_NEWSFAST)
002c0367 8bf8             mov       edi,eax
002c0369 8b460c           mov       eax,dword ptr [esi+0Ch]
002c036c 894704           mov       dword ptr [edi+4],eax
002c036f 57               push      edi
002c0370 8bd5             mov       edx,ebp
002c0372 8bcb             mov       ecx,ebx
002c0374 e8a79a1279       call      mscorlib_ni+0x329e20 (793e9e20)
(System.Console.WriteLine(System.String, System.Object, System.Object,
System.Object), mdToken: 060007c8)
```

Here, we can see that the call instructions we had a hard time understanding before have been annotated with the actual textual representation of the function itself. The first call instruction calls into a function referred to as CORINFO_ HELP_NEWSFAST. The second call instruction into the mscorlib_ni module has now been annotated to show that we are calling the System.Console.WriteLine function.

U COMMAND AND METHOD DESCRIPTORS In addition to specifying a code address when using the U command, you can also specify a method descriptor.

Getting a Method Descriptor from a Code Address

In the previous example, we saw how the native u command can be used to unassemble code. We also saw how the u command is unable to deal with managed code; hence the U command was used to get a better and annotated view of the unassembled code. One example of an instruction that was fairly unusable from the u command output was the following:

```
call    mscorlib_ni+0x329e20 (793e9e20)
```

There exists a mechanism by which you can translate any managed code address into a method descriptor and subsequently use the DumpMD command to get further information. The command is called IP2MD (instruction pointer to method descriptor) and has the following syntax:

```
!IP2MD <Code address>
```

If we were to use it on the address of the previous call instruction (0x793e9e20), we would see the following:

```
0:000> !ip2md 0x793e9e20
MethodDesc: 79259d40
Method Name: System.Console.WriteLine
(System.String, System.Object, System.Object, System.Object)
Class: 79101018
MethodTable: 79101118
mdToken: 060007c8
Module: 790c2000
IsJitted: yes
m_CodeOrIL: 793e9e20
```

In addition to the method name, it displays information such as the method descriptor address, method table, JIT status, and code address. The IP2MD command comes in handy when you want to quickly figure out which function the corresponding assembly code is located in.

Showing the Intermediate Language Instructions

Although it's useful to see the unassembled code, it is also sometimes useful to correlate the unassembled code to the corresponding IL instructions. The DumpIL command can be used for this purpose. For example, the machine code located at address 0x793e9e20 corresponds to the WriteLine function and we can use the DumpIL command to see the corresponding IL instructions, as shown in the following:

```
0:000> !IP2MD 0x793e9e20
MethodDesc: 79259d40
Method Name: System.Console.WriteLine
(System.String, System.Object, System.Object, System.Object)
```

```
Class: 79101018
MethodTable: 79101118
mdToken: 060007c8
Module: 790c2000
IsJitted: yes
m_CodeOrIL: 793e9e20
0:000> !DumpIL 79259d40
ilAddr = 79b28110
IL_0000: call System.Console::get_Out
IL_0005: ldarg.0
IL_0006: ldarg.1
IL_0007: ldarg.2
IL_0008: ldarg.3
IL_0009: callvirt System.IO.TextWriter::WriteLine
IL_000e: ret
```

As you can see, the DumpIL command expects the method descriptor address as a parameter. To find the method descriptor for the code located at 0x793e9e20, we use the IP2MD command, take the resulting method descriptor, and pass it to the DumpIL command, which in turn outputs the resulting IL.

CLR Internals Commands

Throughout this chapter, we have already seen several commands that enable you to gain a deeper insight into the various objects that the CLR utilizes to effectively execute managed code. In this part of the chapter, we will take a look at some auxiliary commands that help us understand the internal workings of the CLR.

Throughout our discussion of the CLR internals commands, we will use the 03ObjTypes.exe sample application, running under the debugger and broken into when the following prompt is shown:

```
Press any key to continue (AddCoordinate)
```

Getting the CLR Version

To quickly find out which version of the CLR is currently being used in any given debug session, the EEVersion command can be used. Additionally, it provides the version of SOS being utilized as well as the mode in which the CLR is running (server or workstation).

```
0:000> !EEVersion
2.0.50727.1434 retail
Workstation mode
SOS Version: 2.0.50727.1434 retail build
```

Finding the Method Descriptor from a Name

Many of the commands in the SOS debugger extension work on the basis of method descriptors. Several different ways exist to find the method descriptor for any given method. One of the most useful ways to find the method descriptor for a method given the name of the method is the `Name2ee` command. The `Name2ee` command takes the name of the module and a fully qualified method name and outputs information regarding the method including the method descriptor. Let's take a look at how the `Name2ee` command can be used on a method in our `03ObjTypes.exe` sample application. Issue the `Name2ee` command as shown in the following:

```
0:004> .loadby sos mscorwks
0:004> !Name2ee 03ObjTypes.exe Advanced.NET.Debugging.Chapter3.
ObjTypes.AddCoordinate
Module: 001e2c3c (03ObjTypes.exe)
Token: 0x06000002
MethodDesc: 001e3070
Name: Advanced.NET.Debugging.Chapter3.ObjTypes.AddCoordinate(Coordinate)
Not JITTED yet. Use !bpmd -md 001e3070 to break on run.
```

The result of running the `Name2ee` command is information about the method including the method descriptor address (`0x001e3070`), which can be used in any SOS command that requires the method descriptor to be specified.

The `Name2ee` command can also be used to get the more detailed information on a particular type. The only difference is that we would specify a fully qualified type name rather than a method name. Using the same debug session as previously, we can, for example, find out more detailed information about the `ObjTypes` type:

```
0:004> !Name2ee 03ObjTypes.exe Advanced.NET.Debugging.Chapter3.ObjTypes
Module: 001e2c3c (03ObjTypes.exe)
Token: 0x02000002
MethodTable: 001e3124
EEClass: 001e12d8
Name: Advanced.NET.Debugging.Chapter3.ObjTypes
```

Dumping the Sync Block of an Object

Every CLR managed type has an associated synchronization block used for synchronization purposes (as briefly discussed in Chapter 2). The `SyncBlk` command can be used to get information on the details of this synchronization block and is quite useful when investigating deadlock problems.

In Chapter 6, "Synchronization," we take a look at some very common synchronization problems and how this command can be used to track down the root cause.

Dumping the Method Table of an Object

Each managed object has an associated method table that contains information about the object (see Chapter 2 for a detailed discussion of method tables). The `DumpMT` command can be used to display information about the method table given a method table address. Using the same debug session as before, we can dump the method table information of type `ObjTypes` as shown in the following:

```
0:000> !Name2ee 03ObjTypes.exe Advanced.NET.Debugging.Chapter3.ObjTypes
Module: 001e2c3c (03ObjTypes.exe)
Token: 0x02000002
MethodTable: 001e3124
EEClass: 001e12d8
Name: Advanced.NET.Debugging.Chapter3.ObjTypes
0:000> !DumpMT 001e3124
EEClass: 001e12d8
Module: 001e2c3c
Name: Advanced.NET.Debugging.Chapter3.ObjTypes
mdToken: 02000002   (C:\ADNDBin\03ObjTypes.exe)
BaseSize: 0x1c
ComponentSize: 0x0
Number of IFaces in IFaceMap: 0
Slots in VTable: 9
```

Dumping Information About the Managed Heap and Garbage Collector

The CLR garbage collector is a highly efficient automatic memory manager that takes care of ensuring that memory is optimally laid out and managed. To efficiently debug .NET applications, we must have the capability to investigate the internal state of the garbage collector. The SOS debugger extension has quite a few commands that help us with this task. Table 3-2 lists some of the available commands and their associated descriptions.

Table 3-2   Examples of SOS Managed Heap and Garbage Collector Commands

Command	Description
DumpHeap	Traverses the managed heap and collects and outputs detailed information about the heap itself and the objects located on the heap.
GCRoot	Displays information about the references (roots) to a specific object. This can be very useful information when trying to figure out why an object has not yet been garbage collected.
TraverseHeap	Traverses the managed heap and outputs the results in a file that is understood by the CLR profiler tool.
VerifyHeap	As with any heap, the managed heap can also get corrupted. This command verifies the integrity of the managed heap.

I'll defer the in-depth discussion of each of the commands in Table 3-2 until Chapter 5, where we will take a look at some common real-world examples of bugs that can surface when misusing the managed heap and garbage collector.

Diagnostics Commands

In addition to all the great inspection commands so far discussed, the SOS debugger contains some very useful diagnostics commands that provide auxiliary information during a debug session. In this part of the chapter, we will take a look at some of the more useful diagnostics commands and examples on how to use them.

Finding the Application Domain of an Object

In Chapter 2, we discussed the notion of an application domain and how .NET object instances are (most of the time) tied to a specific application domain. To find out in which application domain a particular object instance lives, the `FindAppDomain` command can be used as shown in the following:

```
0:000> !DumpStackObjects
OS Thread Id: 0x1964 (0)
ESP/REG  Object    Name
001aef54 01b85a80 Microsoft.Win32.SafeHandles.SafeFileHandle
001af01c 01b86d64 Advanced.NET.Debugging.Chapter3.ObjTypes
```

```
001af020 01b86d64 Advanced.NET.Debugging.Chapter3.ObjTypes
001af030 01b858ac System.Object[]     (System.String[])
001af05c 01b858ac System.Object[]     (System.String[])
001af134 01b858ac System.Object[]     (System.String[])
001af2e4 01b858ac System.Object[]     (System.String[])
001af30c 01b858ac System.Object[]     (System.String[])
0:000> !FindAppDomain 01b86d64
AppDomain: 0022fd30
Name: 03ObjTypes.exe
ID: 1
```

After the application domain of an object is known, you can use the `DumpDomain` command to get further information on the application domain. Knowing the application domain of a given object instance can give you clues as to the origin of the object itself.

Process Information

During debug sessions, it is sometimes useful to get more information about the process being debugged. Examples of useful data include memory usage, environment variables, and process times. To dump this information while debugging, the `ProcInfo` command can be used. The `ProcInfo` command has the syntax

```
!ProcInfo [-env] [-time] [-mem]
```

where the –env, -time, -mem switches control which piece of information about the process that should be displayed. If no switch is specified, it simply displays all three categories of information. Here is an example of `ProcInfo` run on the `03ObjTypes.exe` sample application:

```
0:000> !ProcInfo
-----------------------------------------------
Environment
=C:=C:\ADNDBin
=ExitCode=E0434F4D
ALLUSERSPROFILE=C:\ProgramData
APPDATA=C:\Users\marioh\AppData\Roaming
AVENGINE=C:\PROGRA~1\CA\SHARED~1\SCANEN~1
...
...
...
USERDOMAIN=REDMOND
USERNAME=marioh
```

```
USERPROFILE=C:\Users\marioh.REDMOND
VS90COMNTOOLS=c:\Program Files\Microsoft Visual Studio 9.0\Common7\Tools\
windir=C:\Windows
----------------------------------------------
Process Times
Process Started at: 2008 Dec  3 6:42:5.00
Kernel CPU time   : 0 days 00:00:00.03
User   CPU time   : 0 days 00:00:00.03
Total  CPU time   : 0 days 00:00:00.06
----------------------------------------------
Process Memory
WorkingSetSize:      7528 KB      PeakWorkingSetSize:      8504 KB
VirtualSize:       103004 KB      PeakVirtualSize:       103004 KB
PagefileUsage:       7716 KB      PeakPagefileUsage:       7720 KB
----------------------------------------------
72 percent of memory is in use.

Memory Availability (Numbers in MB)

                    Total       Avail
Physical Memory      3061         839
Page File            4095        3495
Virtual Memory       2047        1914
```

SOSEX Extension Commands

We have seen numerous examples of managed code extension commands available in the SOS extension that make life easier when debugging managed code. There exists another extension called SOSEX, which brings much needed and missing functionality to light for managed code debugging. In the next few sections, we will take a look at the extension commands available in SOSEX.

Extended Breakpoint Support

SOSEX introduces a set of new breakpoint commands that enable you to manage the list of breakpoints (enabled and disabled state) as well as set breakpoints on any given source code location.

Breakpoint List

SOSEX keeps a list of all the managed code breakpoints that have been set using the SOSEX breakpoint commands. It features a number of commands that allow you to manage the breakpoint list. The first command is the `mbl` command, which displays all the breakpoints. For example, if we had set on breakpoint using the SOSEX commands, the `mbl` command would output the following:

```
0:000> !mbl
0 e : 03simple.cs, line 10: pass=1 oneshot=false thread=ANY
   03Simple!Advanced.NET.Debugging.Chapter3.Simple.Main(string[])+0x1(IL)
      0 e 00ac0085
```

You can also manage the state of the breakpoints in the list by using one of the following commands:

- `mbc` clears the specified breakpoint from the list or alternatively clears all breakpoints.
- `mbd` disables the specified breakpoint from the list or alternatively disables all breakpoints.
- `mbe` enables the specified breakpoint from the list or alternatively enables all breakpoints.

Setting Breakpoints

SOSEX introduces a new command called mbp that enables you to set a breakpoint on any given source code location. For example, let's say that we want to set a breakpoint in `03sample.cs` on line 10 prior to printing out the `Welcome to Advanced .NET Debugging` string to the console. To accomplish this, launch the debugger specifying the `03sample.exe` application as a command-line argument, as shown in Listing 3-19.

Listing 3-19   Using the SOSEX bpsc command

```
Microsoft (R) Windows Debugger Version 6.9.0003.113 X86
Copyright (c) Microsoft Corporation. All rights reserved.

CommandLine: c:\ADNDBin\03Simple.exe
...
...
...
0:000> .symfix
No downstream store given, using c:\Program Files\Debugging Tools for Windows\sym
0:000> .reload
Reloading current modules
....
```

```
0:000> .load sosex.dll
0:000> !mbp 03simple.cs 10
0:000>
```

After we set up the proper symbol path, we use the `.load` command to load the SOSEX extension. Subsequently, we use the `mbp` command to set a breakpoint in the `03simple.cs` source file on line 10. Listing 3-20 shows the output when we issue the `g` command to resume execution.

Listing 3-20   Breakpoint hit using the bpsc command

```
0:000> g
ModLoad: 5cb70000 5cb96000    C:\WINDOWS\system32\ShimEng.dll
ModLoad: 77dd0000 77e6b000    C:\WINDOWS\system32\ADVAPI32.dll
ModLoad: 77e70000 77f02000    C:\WINDOWS\system32\RPCRT4.dll
ModLoad: 77fe0000 77ff1000    C:\WINDOWS\system32\Secur32.dll
ModLoad: 77f60000 77fd6000    C:\WINDOWS\system32\SHLWAPI.dll
ModLoad: 77f10000 77f59000    C:\WINDOWS\system32\GDI32.dll
ModLoad: 7e410000 7e4a1000    C:\WINDOWS\system32\USER32.dll
ModLoad: 77c10000 77c68000    C:\WINDOWS\system32\msvcrt.dll
ModLoad: 76390000 763ad000    C:\WINDOWS\system32\IMM32.DLL
ModLoad: 79e70000 7a3d6000    C:\WINDOWS\Microsoft.NET\Framework
\v2.0.50727\mscorwks.dll
ModLoad: 78130000 781cb000    C:\WINDOWS\WinSxS\x86_Microsoft.VC80.CRT
_1fc8b3b9a1e18e3b_8.0.50727.762_x-ww_6b128700\MSVCR80.dll
...
...
...
(cfc.126c): CLR notification exception - code e0444143 (first chance)
Breakpoint 0 hit
eax=00912fe8 ebx=0013f4ac ecx=012819f4 edx=00000000 esi=00190de8 edi=00000000
eip=00cc0085 esp=0013f474 ebp=0013f490 iopl=0         nv up ei pl zr na pe nc
cs=001b  ss=0023  ds=0023  es=0023  fs=003b  gs=0000              efl=00000246
00cc0085 8b0d3c302802    mov     ecx,dword ptr ds:[228303Ch]
ds:0023:0228303c=01281a04
0:000> .loadby sos.dll mscorwks
0:000> !ClrStack
OS Thread Id: 0x126c (0)
ESP        EIP
0013f474 00cc0085 Advanced.NET.Debugging.Chapter3.Simple.Main(System.String[])
0013f69c 79e7be1b [GCFrame: 0013f69c]
0:000>
```

As soon as we issue the g command, the debugger breaks and displays the Breakpoint 0 hit message. To convince ourselves that we have in fact hit the correct breakpoint, we load the SOS extension and use the ClrStack extension command to display the stack trace of where we are currently. It should come as no surprise that the stack trace shows that we are in the Main function of our very simple type.

In addition to mbp, SOSEX also includes another great breakpoint command named mbm. The mbm command allows you to set a breakpoint on a particular IL offset in a particular type. This command can come in handy when source code isn't readily available, such as when working with code generation (Reflection.Emit). To see how mbm can be used, we will utilize the same 03simple.exe application. Rather than using the mbp as previously illustrated, we will use the mbm command to set a breakpoint at the beginning of the Main method (at offset 0). Listing 3-21 illustrates the debugger conversation.

Listing 3-21 Using the mbpm extension command

```
Microsoft (R) Windows Debugger Version 6.9.0003.113 X86
Copyright (c) Microsoft Corporation. All rights reserved.

CommandLine: 03Simple.exe
Symbol search path is: *** Invalid ***
...

...

...

0:000> .load sosex.dll
0:000> !mbm *!Advanced.NET.Debugging.Chapter3.Simple.Main 0
The CLR has not yet been initialized in the process.
Breakpoint resolution will be attempted when the CLR is initialized.
0:000> g
ModLoad: 76160000 76226000   C:\Windows\system32\ADVAPI32.dll
ModLoad: 774e0000 775a3000   C:\Windows\system32\RPCRT4.dll
ModLoad: 77330000 77388000   C:\Windows\system32\SHLWAPI.dll
ModLoad: 76110000 7615b000   C:\Windows\system32\GDI32.dll
...

...

...

Breakpoint: CLR initialized. Attempting to resolve managed breakpoints.
ModLoad: 766a0000 771af000   C:\Windows\system32\shell32.dll
ModLoad: 775b0000 776f4000   C:\Windows\system32\ole32.dll
ModLoad: 790c0000 79bf6000   C:\Windows\assembly\NativeImages_v2.0.50727_32
\mscorlib\5b3e3b0551bcaa722c27dbb089c431e4\mscorlib.ni.dll
(1798.1ba8): CLR notification exception - code e0444143 (first chance)
```

```
(1798.1ba8): CLR notification exception - code e0444143 (first chance)
Breakpoint: Matching method Advanced.NET.Debugging.Chapter3.Simple.Main resolved,
but not yet jitted. Setting JIT notification...
ModLoad: 79060000 790b6000   C:\Windows\Microsoft.NET\Framework\v2.0.50727
\mscorjit.dll
(1798.1ba8): CLR notification exception - code e0444143 (first chance)
Breakpoint: JIT notification received for method
Advanced.NET.Debugging.Chapter3.Simple.Main(System.String[]).
Breakpoint set at Advanced.NET.Debugging
.Chapter3.Simple.Main(System.String[]).
Breakpoint 0 hit
eax=00113020 ebx=0024eddc ecx=01cd5890 edx=00000005 esi=004a5148 edi=00000000
eip=00380084 esp=0024eda4 ebp=0024edc0 iopl=0         nv up ei pl zr na pe nc
cs=001b  ss=0023  ds=0023  es=0023  fs=003b  gs=0000              efl=00000246
00380084 90              nop
0:000> .loadby sos.dll mscorwks
0:000> !ClrStack
OS Thread Id: 0x1da8 (0)
ESP       EIP
002af174 002c0084 Advanced.NET.Debugging.Chapter3.
Simple.Main(System.String[])
002af3a4 79e7c74b [GCFrame: 002af3a4]
0:000>
```

After the SOSEX extension DLL is loaded, we use the mpm extension command to set a breakpoint on the `Main` method in the `Advanced.NET.Debugging.Chapter3.Simple` type at offset 0. When we resumed execution, a breakpoint was hit, and using the SOS `ClrStack` extension command we can see that execution stopped at the beginning of the `Main` method. The mbm command also gives you a few configurable options

```
!mbm <strTypeAndMethodFilter> <intILOffset> [Options]
```

where the `Options` switch can be one of the following:

- `/1`. Only trigger this breakpoint once.
- `/p:<passcount>`. Indicates which iteration of the breakpoint should result in execution stopping.
- `/t: <threadid>`. Breakpoint is only triggered when a thread with the specified thread ID hits the breakpoint.

The mbm command also supports wild cards in the `strTypeAndMethodFilter`.

Both of the breakpoint extension commands that SOSEX offers are very useful and make life a lot simpler when setting breakpoints at the source code level.

Managed Metadata

To effectively debug .NET applications using the native debuggers, we need to be able to quickly find metadata such as type names and method names. To facilitate this requirement, the mx command can be used and has the general syntax

```
!mx <Filter String>
```

where the `Filter String` argument represents a wild card search string for the metadata of interest. For example, if we ran `03simple.exe` under the debugger and want to find out all the methods available on the `Simple` type, we can run the following command:

```
0:000> !mx 03simple!*Simple*
03Simple!Advanced.NET.Debugging.Chapter3.Simple
03Simple!Advanced.NET.Debugging.Chapter3.Simple.
Advanced.NET.Debugging.Chapter3.Simple.Main(System.String[])
03Simple!Advanced.NET.Debugging.Chapter3.Simple.
Advanced.NET.Debugging.Chapter3.Simple..ctor()
```

Another command that is very useful is the mln command, which takes an address and identifies the managed code related content of that address. At this point, it accurately identifies JIT compiled code, heap, and stack objects. For example, let's say we have an address X and we want to know what that address represents (from the CLR's perspective). We could employ a number of manual techniques by using the various commands such as DumpObj (to see if it's an object) or U to unassemble the address to see if it contains code. It would be far easier if we had an automated way of identifying the content of the address. For example, if while debugging `03ObjTypes.exe` we were presented with the address `0x01eb6d64`, we could run the mln command on that address to identify the contents of that address:

```
0:000> !mln 0x01eb6d64
Heap Object: 01eb6d64[Advanced.NET.Debugging.Chapter3.ObjTypes]
```

As we can see, the address `0x01eb6d64` corresponds to a managed heap object of type `Advanced.NET.Debugging.Chapter3.ObjTypes`.

Stack Traces

So far, we have seen different ways of displaying the call stack for a managed code thread. We utilized the native debugger kb command, which displays the raw native code call stack (not terribly useful for managed code debugging) as well as the ClrStack command, which displays the managed code call stack. When it is desirable to display a combination of managed code and native code call stacks, the SOSEX mk command can be used. In addition to displaying both managed code and native code frames, it displays the frame number. The following is an example of the output of mk when run while breaking into the debugger of the 03simple.exe application:

```
0:000> !mk
*** WARNING: Unable to verify checksum for
C:\Windows\assembly\NativeImages_v2.0.50727_32\mscorlib
\5b3e3b0551bcaa722c27dbb089c431e4\mscorlib.ni.dll
00:U 0028ea68 778e8d94 ntdll!KiFastSystemCallRet+0x0
01:U 0028ea6c 778f9522 ntdll!NtRequestWaitReplyPort+0xc
02:U 0028ea8c 777a7e05 ntdll!CsrClientCallServer+0xc2
03:U 0028eb78 777a7f35 KERNEL32!GetConsoleInput+0xd2
04:U 0028eb98 003aa61c KERNEL32!ReadConsoleInputA+0x1a
05:U 0028ec20 793e8f28 0x003aa61c
06:M 0028ec88 793e8e33 mscorlib!System.Console.
ReadKey(Boolean)(+0x50 IL)(+0x6d Native)
07:M 0028ecb0 79e7c6cc mscorlib!System.Console.
ReadKey()(+0x0 IL)(+0x7 Native)
08:M 0028ecb0 79e7c6cc
03Simple!Advanced.NET.Debugging.Chapter3.Simple.Main(System.String[])(+0x17
IL)(+0x22 Native) [c:\Publishing\ADND\Code\Chapter3\Simple\03simple.cs, @ 12,13]
09:U 0028ed30 79e7c8e1 mscorwks!CallDescrWorkerWithHandler+0xa3
0a:U 0028ee74 79e7c783 mscorwks!MethodDesc::CallDescr+0x19c
0b:U 0028ee90 79e7c90d mscorwks!MethodDesc::CallTargetWorker+0x1f
0c:U 0028eea4 79eefb9e mscorwks!MethodDescCallSite::Call+0x18
0d:U 0028f008 79eef830 mscorwks!ClassLoader::RunMain+0x263
0e:U 0028f270 79ef01da mscorwks!Assembly::ExecuteMainMethod+0xa6
0f:U 0028f740 79fb9793 mscorwks!SystemDomain::ExecuteMainMethod+0x43f
10:U 0028f790 79fb96df mscorwks!ExecuteEXE+0x59
11:U 0028f7d8 7900b1b3 mscorwks!_CorExeMain+0x15c
12:U 0028f7e8 77744911 mscoree!_CorExeMain+0x2c
13:U 0028f7f4 778ce4b6 KERNEL32!BaseThreadInitThunk+0xe
14:U 0028f834 778ce489 ntdll!__RtlUserThreadStart+0x23
15:U 0028f84c 00000000 ntdll!_RtlUserThreadStart+0x1b
```

Each frame of the output is prefixed by xx: where xx specifies the frame number on the call stack. The importance of the frame number in the output of the mk command becomes crucial in the next command that we will be discussing, which is the mdv command. The mdv command outputs the local variables of any given frame. By default, it outputs the variables of the topmost frame. If we continue our example from earlier, running the mdv command, which displays the variables of the topmost frame (ntdll!KiFastSystemCallRet+0x0), yields the following:

```
0:000> !mdv
Frame 0x0: <Unmanaged Frame>
```

The output makes perfect sense because the topmost frame is not a managed code frame. The mdv command also takes the optional frame number as the parameter enabling us to narrow in on the managed frame of any given call stack output by the mk command. For example, if we were interested in the variables of frame 8 (Main method of our .NET application), we could use the following command:

```
0:000> !mdv 8
Frame 0x8: (Advanced.NET.Debugging.Chapter3.Simple.Main(System.String[])):
[P0]:args:0x1d75890 (System.String[])
```

The output of the command shows that the only variable available to us is the parameter to the Main method (located at address 0x1d75890). The mdv command also exposes the -w switch, which walks the entire call stack and dumps out all the arguments and local variables.

The final command is the mframe command, which allows you to set the current managed frame to be used by the mdt and mdv commands.

The mk, mdv, and mframe commands are an incredibly powerful trio to interrogate managed code call stacks and their respective states.

Object Inspection

A super useful command in native code debugging is the dt command. The dt command can display information about a local, global variable or a data type. The SOSEX debugger extension introduces a similar command called the mdt command. The mdt command has the syntax

```
!mdt [typename | paramname | localname | MT] [ADDR] [-r]
```

where the typename, paramname, and localname indicates the name of the type of interest (or alternatively the method table of the type) and the ADDR specifies the address of the object in question. The -r option means that the mdt command executes recursively, which can come in handy when an object encapsulates another object, which in turn encapsulates another object, and so on. Rather than having to continuously issue the mdt command for each of the embedded objects, the -r switch can be used. The following is an example of using the mdt command on an address that corresponds to an instance of the ObjTypes type defined in 03ObjTypes.exe:

```
0:000> !mdt 0x1b06d64
01b06d64 (Advanced.NET.Debugging.Chapter3.ObjTypes)
    coordinate:01b06d70 (Advanced.NET.Debugging.Chapter3.ObjTypes+Coordinate)
    intArray:01b06e1c (System.Int32[], Elements: 5)
    strArray:01b06e3c (System.String[], Elements: 5)
```

Here, we can see that the type instance contains a coordinate, an integer array, and a string array. We already know that the coordinate member contains x, y, and z members. To have the mdt command output those values as well, we can use the -r switch:

```
0:000> !mdt 0x1b06d64 -r
01b06d64 (Advanced.NET.Debugging.Chapter3.ObjTypes)
    coordinate:01b06d70 (Advanced.NET.Debugging.Chapter3.ObjTypes+Coordinate)
        xCord:0x64 (System.Int32)
        yCord:0x64 (System.Int32)
        zCord:0x80000000 (System.Int32)
    intArray:01b06e1c (System.Int32[], Elements: 5)
    strArray:01b06e3c (System.String[], Elements: 5)
```

Now we can clearly see the values of the coordinate member of the ObjTypes type.

Automated Deadlock Detection

A deadlock is a very common problem when dealing with multithreaded applications. A high-level definition of a deadlock is when two threads fail to make any progress due to holding one synchronization primitive while waiting on a synchronization primitive to be released by the other thread. The key to analysis deadlock scenarios is to correctly identify the threads involved as well as the synchronization primitives held by each thread. A brute force and manual approach when identifying deadlocks is to dump out each thread in the process, analyze the call stack to see if it is stuck waiting for a lock, and record the information about the lock. For each of the threads that is waiting for a lock, you would then find out which thread owns that particular lock and continue your investigation on that thread. Eventually, you arrive at the problematic threads and their corresponding locks. Although this approach eventually gets you the answer to what holds which lock, it is a relatively painful process as manually dumping all the threads in a process is time-consuming and error prone. Fortunately, both the SOS and SOSEX debugger extensions contain commands to make this process easier.

As discussed in Chapter 2, each object contains what is known as a SyncBlk (synchronization block). The synchronization block contains (among other things) information on the lock status of the object. By using the syncblk command, we can display information about all the locks held in a process and the threads that own each of the locks. When we know which threads are waiting on a lock and which threads are holding the locks, we can use the ClrStack command to get further information on each of the threads and find the reason why the threads are not releasing the locks that they own. The following is an example of the output of syncblk when run on a process that is deadlocked:

```
0:005> !syncblk
Index SyncBlock MonitorHeld Recursion Owning Thread Info   SyncBlock Owner
    1 001c999c          3          1 001a5130 1af4  0    01ffab84 System.Object
    3 001c99fc          3          1 001c9380 2370  3    01ffab90 System.Object
-----------------------------
Total             3
CCW               0
RCW               0
ComClassFactory   0
Free              0
```

The output of the syncblk command shown previously shows that two objects are in a locked state as well as the information about the threads that currently hold the locks. Based on the information presented, we can now use the ClrStack command to get the call stacks for each of the owning threads and figure out where the potential deadlock is by using code inspection. I defer to Chapter 6, where we discuss the output of the synblk command in more detail.

The output of the syncblk command gives us the capability to narrow down our search for deadlocks in a process, but it still involves a lot of manual work to figure out which threads are waiting on which specific locks. The SOSEX debugger extension takes the notion of deadlock detection one step further and introduces the dlk command, which automates the task of figuring out which threads may be deadlocked. Using the same example as previously, the output of dlk looks like the following:

```
0:005> !dlk
Deadlock detected:
CLR thread 1 holds sync block 001c999c OBJ:01ffab84[System.Object]
          waits sync block 001c99fc OBJ:01ffab90[System.Object]
CLR thread 3 holds sync block 001c99fc OBJ:01ffab90[System.Object]
          waits sync block 001c999c OBJ:01ffab84[System.Object]
CLR Thread 1 is waiting at DeadLock!DeadLock.Program.Run()(+0x59 IL)(+0x87 Native)
CLR Thread 3 is waiting at DeadLock!DeadLock.
Program.DoWork()(+0x1d IL)(+0x25 Native)

1 deadlock detected.
```

Here, we can clearly see detailed information on each thread owning a lock as well as which lock the thread is waiting for to become available. In this case, thread 1 holds a lock on object 0x01ffab84 and is waiting to acquire a lock on object 0x01ffab90. Thread 3, in turn, is holding a lock on object 0x01ffab90 (which thread 1 is waiting on) and is waiting on object 0x01ffab84 (which is owned by thread 1). In addition, the dlk command also outputs the stack frame of where each of the threads is waiting for a lock to be released. The final piece of information displayed is that dlk tells us that a deadlock has been detected. As you can see, the dlk command automates much of the manual work involved in dealing with deadlock scenarios and should be used extensively whenever a deadlock is being investigated.

In this section, we briefly discussed some of the commands that are available when looking at synchronization problems. More specifically, we illustrated a simple deadlock and how the syncblk and dlk commands can be used to get more detailed information about the threads and locks in a process. In Chapter 6, we will use and explain these commands in more detail when we take a look at some common real-world synchronization problems.

Managed Heap and Garbage Collector Commands

The SOSEX debugger extension augments the managed heap functionality in SOS by providing additional powerful commands that can make it easier to troubleshoot issues related to the managed heap and garbage collector. We will only take a brief look at the commands in this section and use them more extensively in Chapter 5, so if some of the concepts mentioned here do not make sense, don't worry. They will all be explained thoroughly later.

The first command we will discuss is the gcgen command. The gcgen command takes an address of an object located on the managed heap and displays the generation that the object belongs to. For example, the generation of the object located at address `0x01ffab64` can be found by using the following command:

```
0:000> !gcgen 0x01ffab64
Gen 0
```

The output of the command simply shows that the object belongs to generation 0. This command can come in handy when trying to figure out how long an object has been alive (or how many garbage collection attempts it has survived).

The next command is related to the gcgen command and is called dumpgen. The dumpgen command displays all the objects that belong to any given generation. For example, running dumpgen 0 gives the following output (abbreviated):

```
0:000> !dumpgen 0
01fa1018              12 **** FREE ****
01fa1024              72 System.OutOfMemoryException
01fa106c              72 System.StackOverflowException
01fa10b4              72 System.ExecutionEngineException
01fa10fc              72 System.Threading.ThreadAbortException
01fa1144              72 System.Threading.ThreadAbortException
01fa118c              12 System.Object
01fa1198              28 System.SharedStatics
01fa11b4              34 System.String     STRVAL=c:\Zone\
01fa11d8              64 System.String     STRVAL=c:\Zone\DeadLock.config
01fa1218             100 System.AppDomain
TRVAL=file:///c:\Zone\DeadLock.exe
01fa1644              20 System.Security.Policy.Evidence
01fa1658              16 System.Security.Policy.Zone
01fa1668              24 System.Collections.ArrayList
01fa1680              16 System.Object[]
01fa1690              32 System.Collections.ArrayList+SyncArrayList
01fa16b0              12 System.Object
01fa16bc              32 System.Object[]
01fa16dc              12 System.Security.Policy.Url
01fa16e8              52 System.Security.Util.URLString
01fa171c              20 System.RuntimeType
01fa1730              64 System.IO.UnmanagedMemoryStream
01fa1770              36 System.Int64[]
01fa1794              12 System.Object
01fa17a0              32 Microsoft.Win32.Win32Native+OSVERSIONINFO
01fa17c0              46 System.String     STRVAL=Service Pack 1
01fa17f0              40 Microsoft.Win32.Win32Native+OSVERSIONINFOEX
01fa1818              46 System.String     STRVAL=Service Pack 1
```

The output of the dumpgen command shows the address, size, and textual representation of each object of the specified generation.

The last command we will discuss is the `strings` command. The `strings` command enables you to search for any string located on the managed heap. The search supports wild cards as well as specific generations to search in and minimum and maximum lengths. The following is an example of running the `strings` command searching for the string `Debug`:

```
0:000> !strings -m:Debug
Address        Gen     Value
---------------------------
01fd0b04       0       System.Diagnostics.DebuggableAttribute+DebuggingModes
01fd11f8       0       DebuggingFlags
01fd15dc       0       m_debuggingModes
01fd1754       0       System.Diagnostics.DebuggableAttribute+DebuggingModes
790edba0       2       debug
790f0490       2       InvalidOperation_NotADebugModule
---------------------------
6 matching strings
```

The output of the `strings` command shows the address of each string found as well as the generation it belongs to and the value of the string. To search in a specific generation only, the `-g` switch can be used; and to specify minimum and maximum lengths, use the `-n` and `-x` switches.

Crash Dump Files

So far, we have looked at what are commonly known as live debug sessions—*live* meaning that we are debugging an actual physical process with access to all process states and the capability to control the execution of the process we are debugging. At times, live debug sessions are not always feasible because access to the machines is prohibited or not realistic. Examples of such environments include production-level machines that are often housed in locked down data centers with very limited access. Another example involves customers who are not willing to let engineers attach debuggers to their processes because it could lead to costly downtime as well as potentially scare off any footprints being left on the machines. In these scenarios, we have to employ what is known as postmortem debugging. Postmortem debugging works on the basis of taking snapshots of a given process and debugging that snapshot offline. The snapshot is simply a binary file that contains the state of the process at which the snapshot was taken. After the snapshot has been taken, it can be shared out to the engineer slated to do the debugging. The same native debuggers we've utilized so far can be used to debug snapshots, with the exception that some of the commands may not work due to not working with a live and active target.

Let's take a look at an example of how to generate and debug a snapshot. In this particular example, we will use the debuggers themselves to create the snapshot. Plenty of other powerful tools exist that can also be used to take snapshots, and we will discuss those tools in more detail in Chapter 8. Let's start by launching 03ObjTypes.exe under the debugger and resume execution until the debugger breaks with a CLR exception. At this point, we can use the dump command to generate a dump file as shown in the following:

```
Press any key to continue (Exception)
 (2088.177c): CLR exception - code e0434f4d (first chance)
 (2088.177c): CLR exception - code e0434f4d (!!! second chance !!!)
eax=0030f070 ebx=e0434f4d ecx=00000001 edx=00000000 esi=0030f0f8 edi=00135408
eip=777442eb esp=0030f070 ebp=0030f0c0 iopl=0         nv up ei pl nz ac po nc
cs=001b  ss=0023  ds=0023  es=0023  fs=003b  gs=0000          efl=00000212
*** ERROR: Symbol file could not be found.
Defaulted to export symbols for C:\Windows\system32\KERNEL32.dll -
KERNEL32!RaiseException+0x58:
777442eb c9              leave
0:000> .dump /ma c:\dump.dmp
Creating c:\dump.dmp - mini user dump
Dump successfully written
0:000>
```

The dump command takes a filename as a parameter and indicates the filename where the dump will be stored. The dump command can also, optionally, take a number of different switches that control how much of the process state should be stored in the dump file. It should come as no surprise that the more process state is stored the greater the success when debugging. We will take a look at the options in Chapter 8. Now that we have a dump file, we can debug it using the same debugger. To debug the dump file, we need to tell the debugger that we are interested in debugging a snapshot. We can use the -z debugger switch followed by the path to the dump file, as shown in the following:

```
ntsd -z c:\dump.dmp
```

This causes the debugger to read the dump file and then present the all-familiar debug prompt, as shown in the following:

```
Microsoft (R) Windows Debugger Version 6.9.0003.113 X86
Copyright (c) Microsoft Corporation. All rights reserved.


Loading Dump File [c:\dump.dmp]
User Mini Dump File: Only registers, stack and portions of memory are available
```

```
Symbol search path is: *** Invalid ***
Executable search path is:
Windows Server 2008 Version 6001 (Service Pack 1) MP (2 procs) Free x86 compatible
Product: WinNt, suite: SingleUserTS
Debug session time: Mon Dec  8 16:49:17.000 2008 (GMT-8)
System Uptime: not available
Process Uptime: 0 days 0:00:58.000
....................
```
This dump file has an exception of interest stored in it.
The stored exception information can be accessed via .ecxr.
```
(2088.177c): CLR exception - code e0434f4d (first/second chance not available)
eax=0030f070 ebx=e0434f4d ecx=00000001 edx=00000000 esi=0030f0f8 edi=00135408
eip=777442eb esp=0030f070 ebp=0030f0c0 iopl=0         nv up ei pl nz ac po nc
cs=001b  ss=0023  ds=0023  es=0023  fs=003b  gs=0000            efl=00000212
*** ERROR: Symbol file could not be found.
Defaulted to export symbols for kernel32.dll -
kernel32!RaiseException+0x58:
777442eb c9              leave
0:000>
```

The first part of the debugger output from the previous listing states that the debugger loaded a dump file and that the type of the dump file is a mini dump file. Mini dump is just one of the many forms of dump files that can be generated, and it contains limited process state information. The next important piece of information the debugger tells us is that the dump file has an exception contained within it and that the exception information can be retrieved using the ecxr command. If you issue the ecxr command, you will see the information relevant to the exception, such as the register content at the point of the exception, which in turn enables you to get thread stack information.

We will take a look at postmortem debugging in more detail in Chapter 8, where we will take a look at some powerful tools that can make it easier to generate dump files to debug problems offline.

Summary

We've covered a lot of ground in this chapter by introducing the most basic and common debugging tasks and commands. This introduction covered the basic functionality of the native debuggers, the managed code debugger extensions (SOS and SOSEX), as well as a brief discussion of postmortem debugging. This chapter serves as an introduction to the myriad of commands that exist. We will utilize most of the commands in much greater depth in subsequent chapters where we will look at real-world bugs and how to use the commands briefly discussed to arrive at a root cause analysis of each of the bugs.

3. BASIC DEBUGGING TASKS

APPLIED DEBUGGING

## CHAPTER 4

ASSEMBLY LOADER

So far, much of our discussion about the CLR has revolved around assemblies, the basic building blocks of .NET. We looked at the internals of assemblies in both Chapter 2, "CLR Fundamentals," and Chapter 3, "Basic Debugging Tasks," but so far we have omitted the details on how .NET assemblies are loaded into an application domain. One of the goals of the .NET platform is to eliminate what is commonly referred to as DLL (or dependency) hell where the proper binaries are overwritten or simply not available as a result of upgrades and/or downgrades. These problems manifest themselves in the form of application startup failures or sometimes, more subtly, where applications simply misbehave. To avoid the DLL hell problem, the CLR defines strict rules concerning how assemblies are loaded and managed. In this chapter, we will take a tour of the CLR loader (codenamed Fusion) and how it achieves the goal of avoiding DLL hell as well as common pitfalls associated with the CLR loader. Throughout this tour, we will use the debuggers and tools to arrive at the root cause of problems related to incorrectly using the CLR loader.

CLR Loader Overview

The CLR offers a highly sophisticated mechanism for loading .NET assemblies. At a high level, a .NET assembly can either be shared or private. A shared .NET assembly is an assembly that is typically used by two or more applications located on the same machine. The benefits of having a shared assembly are pretty clear; rather than each application maintaining the assembly in a local path, it can be shared and therefore managed and maintained in one place. Shared assemblies are typically located in the Global Assembly Cache (GAC). A private assembly, on the other hand, is an assembly that is private to one particular application and is typically stored in the same folder (or predefined subfolders) as the application itself (although it is not a requirement). In light of the different types of assemblies, how does the CLR loader determine which location to load the assembly from? The answer lies in what is known as load contexts. Figure 4-1 illustrates the high-level CLR assembly load process.

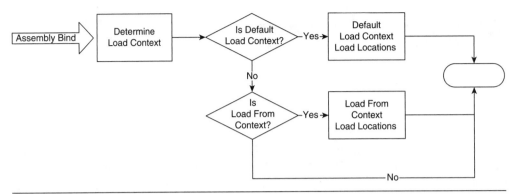

Figure 4-1 High-level overview of the CLR loader

At a high level, when an assembly load is requested, the CLR loader determines the load context (how the load request was issued) and uses different algorithms depending on the context to determine the location of the assembly. Before we discuss each of the load contexts in more detail, the notion of an assembly identity is important to understand and will be discussed next.

Assembly Identity

An assembly's identity defines the uniqueness of any given assembly as seen by the CLR. The identity is crucial when determining which assembly gets loaded during bind time as well as when determining if two or more loaded assemblies are equal. Consider an assembly, quite generically, named `workflow.dll`. Due to the generic nature of the assembly name, it's quite possible that there could be multiple assemblies with the same name on any given system. Furthermore, imagine that you have multiple assemblies that reference the various instances of the `workflow.dll`. How does the application specify the correct instance of the `workflow.dll` that gets loaded; or rather, how does the CLR choose which assembly to load? A lot of factors play into the answer but one key ingredient is the assembly identity. An assembly's identity is comprised of the following key components:

- Assembly name
- Culture
- Version
- Public key
- Processor architecture

The assembly name represents the simple name of the assembly and is quite commonly the file name of the assembly (minus the extension .exe or .dll). An assembly's culture represents the locale that the assembly is targeting (for example, the neutral culture). The version attribute represents the version of the assembly and takes on the following syntax: <major>.<minor>.<build>.<revision>. The public key attribute is used for strong name assemblies and contains the 64-bit hash of the public key corresponding to the private key used to sign the assembly. Finally, the processor architecture attribute introduced in CLR 2.0 specifies the target processor architecture of the assembly. Together, these five attributes constitute an assembly identity. Assembly identity is heavily used by the CLR to determine the correct assembly to load. If all five attributes have been specified and the assembly is loaded using the default load context, there is no ambiguity concerning which assembly the CLR should load.

Interestingly enough, the path of the assembly is, as far as identity is concerned, not something that the CLR concerns itself with when it comes to loading the correct assembly. Two identical assemblies, located in different paths, can be loaded into the same application domain (albeit using different load contexts). Even though the assemblies are identical, they are treated as two very distinct assemblies; as such, the types contained within the assembly are also considered different. This can lead to a lot of headaches and strange casting exceptions. Let's take a look at an example. The application used to illustrate this behavior is shown in Listing 4-1.

Listing 4-1 Application using two identical types

```
namespace Advanced.NET.Debugging.Chapter4
{
    class SimpleType
    {
        private int field1;
        private int field2;

        public int Field1
        {
            get { return field1; }
        }

        public int Field2
        {
            get { return field2; }
        }
```

(continues)

Listing 4-1   Application using two identical types *(continued)*

```
    public SimpleType()
    {
        field1 = 10;
        field2 = 5;
    }
}

class TypeCast
{
    static void Main(string[] args)
    {
        Assembly asmLoadFromContext = null;

        Console.WriteLine("Press any key to load into load from context");
        Console.ReadKey();

        asmLoadFromContext = Assembly.LoadFrom("04assembly.dll");

        SimpleType s = (SimpleType)asmLoadFromContext.CreateInstance(
                    "Advanced.NET.Debugging.Chapter4.SimpleType");

        Console.WriteLine("Press any key to exit");
        Console.ReadKey();
    }
}
}
```

The source code and binary for Listing 4-1 can be found in the following folders:

- Source code: `C:\ADND\Chapter4\TypeCast`
- Binary: `C:\ADNDBin\04TypeCast.exe`

The source code in Listing 4-1 is relatively straightforward. The first part of the code defines a very simple type called `SimpleType`. `SimpleType` only has a constructor that initializes two simple fields. The next section of the code defines a type called `TypeCast` that has a `Main` method. The `Main` method loads an assembly called `04assembly.dll` using the load-from context (discussed later in the chapter). The code for the `04assembly.dll` is shown in Listing 4-2.

Listing 4-2   Source code for the 04assembly.dll

```
using System;
using System.Text;
```

```
namespace Advanced.NET.Debugging.Chapter4
{
    class SimpleType
    {
        private int field1;
        private int field2;

        public int Field1
        {
            get { return field1; }
        }

        public int Field2
        {
            get { return field2; }
        }

        public SimpleType()
        {
            field1 = 10;
            field2 = 5;
        }
    }
}
```

The source code and binary for Listing 4-2 can be found in the following folders:

- Source code: `C:\ADND\Chapter4\TypeCast`
- Binary: `C:\ADNDBin\04assembly.dll`

As you can see, the code in Listing 4-2 also defines a type called `SimpleType` (in the same namespace as Listing 4-1). As a matter of fact, the two types are identical in nature with a constructor and two simple fields. If we go back to Listing 4-1 and its `Main` method, we can see that the next statement is that of creating an instance of the `SimpleType` defined in Listing 4-2. The resulting instance is then assigned to a reference variable of type `SimpleType` (defined in Listing 4-1). Because the two types are identical, this cast should work without a problem. Now, let's run the application and see what happens:

```
C:\ADNDBin>04TypeCast.exe
Press any key to load into load from context

Unhandled Exception: System.InvalidCastException: Unable to cast object of type
'Advanced.NET.Debugging.Chapter4.SimpleType' to type
'Advanced.NET.Debugging.Chapter4.SimpleType'.
```

```
    at Advanced.NET.Debugging.Chapter4.TypeCast.Main(String[] args) in
c:\Publishing\ADND\Code\Chapter4\TypeCast\04TypeCast.cs:line 41
```

Interestingly enough, the application exits with an `InvalidCastException`. More specifically, it states that a cast from `Advanced.NET.Debugging.Chapter4.SimpleType` to `Advanced.NET.Debugging.Chapter4.SimpleType` is invalid. Even though the two types were identical, the CLR appears to treat them as separate type definitions. This is one example of the dangers of mixing different load contexts. In our example, we had a type defined in `04TypeCast.exe` and an identical type defined in `04assembly.dll`. Furthermore, we loaded `04assembly.dll` by using the `Assembly.LoadFrom` API, which implies that the assembly is loaded in the load-from context, essentially allowing two different assemblies with identical types to be loaded in the same application domain but with each of the types being treated as separate entities.

As you can see, understanding assembly identities and how they are loaded by the CLR is crucial to avoiding costly cross context load problems. Before we move on and discuss the different load contexts in more detail, we need to understand the shared assembly mechanism that the CLR introduces, also known as the Global Assembly Cache (GAC).

Global Assembly Cache

Earlier, we introduced the notion of the Global Assembly Cache (GAC) without defining it in detail. The GAC is a common location where all shared assemblies are stored. The contents of the GAC can be found under

```
%windir%\assembly
```

Under the GAC folder are a number of subfolders:

- `GAC`. The GAC folder contains assemblies from .NET versions 1.x.
- `GAC_32`. Contains all 32-bit assemblies.
- `GAC_64`. Contains all 64-bit assemblies. Note that you do not have this folder if you are running a 32-bit version of Windows. If, however, you are running a 64-bit version of Windows, you will have both the `GAC_64` and `GAC_32` folders.
- `GAC_MSIL`. Architecture neutral assemblies.
- `NativeImages_<version>_<architecture>`. This folder contains pre-compiled shared assemblies.

The most important subfolders are the `GAC*` folders, which contain all the shared assemblies present. Each shared assembly has its own subfolder hierarchy as shown in Figure 4-2.

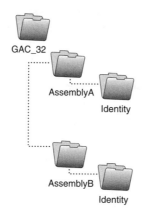

Figure 4-2 GAC subfolder hierarchy

Each folder under the GAC* folder is named after the shared assembly. For example, on my machine, I have a folder called System.Data under the GAC folder. It is under this folder that all the different versions of the given shared assembly reside. How does the GAC distinguish between multiple versions of a shared assembly? You guessed it: by its identity. Under each of the assembly subfolders is another subfolder named after the identity of the assembly in question. The identity takes on a form similar to what we discussed earlier in the "Assembly Identity" section:

```
<version>__<public key>
```

The actual assembly can be found under the identity folder. In a nutshell, this is how the CLR controls versioning of shared assemblies. Each assembly, together with its identity, lives in the common GAC folder. Note that this also implies that each shared assembly must be strongly named and have unique version numbers.

During a shared assembly load (in the default load context), the CLR loader first checks the GAC to see if the assembly is present before resorting to private (albeit predefined) load paths. You can easily check from where an assembly was loaded in the debugger by using the lm f (list modules) command. The lm f command shows all the loaded modules in the target process and their associated load paths:

```
0:004> lm f
start    end       module name
00710000 008c8000  mmc      C:\Windows\system32\mmc.exe
...
...
...
```

```
07030000 075b8000    System_Xml_ni C:\Windows\assembly\NativeImages_v2.0.50727_32\
System.Xml\02cf61328d59df9b3ec09544f449a781\System.Xml.ni.dll
...
...

...
4f400000 4f49c000    Microsoft_ManagementConsole_ni
C:\Windows\assembly\NativeImages_v2.0.50727_32\
Microsoft.Managemen#\b059345a9c2a126e320e17c2090dd354\Microsoft
.ManagementConsole.ni
.dll
...
...

...
C:\Windows\assembly\NativeImages_v2.0.50727_32\System.ServiceProce#\
80a3d0416c6660b86e245bd1f6b66fd8\System.ServiceProcess.ni.dll
```

Here, we can see several assemblies being loaded from the native image folder in the GAC.

BROWSING THE GAC USING WINDOWS EXPLORER You can also view the contents of the GAC using Windows Explorer. When using Windows Explorer, you see a customized view of the GAC implemented by the shell extension `shfusion.dll`.

When it comes to dependent assemblies, the identity of the dependent assembly is stored in the primary assembly manifest, which the CLR uses to find the appropriate assembly to load. For example, part of the `04TypeCast.exe` assembly manifest (which defines dependent assemblies) looks like the following (output produced using ILDAMS):

```
.assembly extern mscorlib
{
  .publickeytoken = (B7 7A 5C 56 19 34 E0 89 )                    // .z\V.4..
  .ver 2:0:0:0
}
```

We can see that `04TypeCast.exe` takes a dependency on the `mscorlib` assembly and that the identity of the assembly should be that of the specified public key token and version.

Please note that even though dependent assemblies are identified via assembly identity, policy can be used to redirect dependent assemblies to other versions with different identities.

Let's now move on to the different load contexts and see in more detail which load algorithm the CLR utilizes to bind to a given assembly.

Default Load Context

Most assemblies fall into the default load context, which is also, usually, the safest option to avoid incorrect versions of assemblies being loaded and creating complications. An assembly that falls into the default load context is usually loaded using one of the variations of the `Assembly.Load` API. What does it mean for it to be the safest way of loading assemblies? In the default load context, the CLR uses all its probing logic (see Figure 4-3) to ensure that the correct version of the assembly is used. Furthermore, dependent assemblies can also be automatically found in this context as well as the load-from context. This is in contrast to the load-from or load-without context where the caller more explicitly chooses the assembly, thereby running the

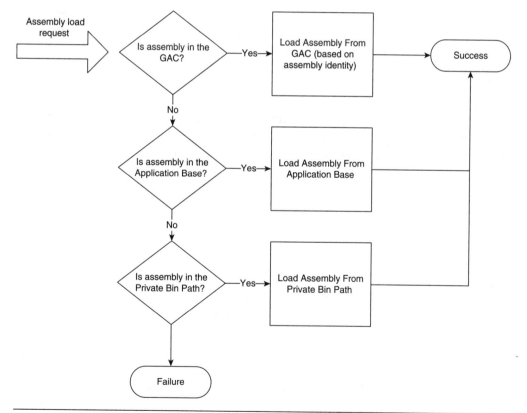

Figure 4-3 Default load context probing logic

risk of picking up an incorrect version. The CLR's probing logic during default load context is shown in Figure 4-3.

From Figure 4-3, we can see that when an assembly load request comes into the default load context, the CLR loader first checks to see if the assembly is in the GAC. If so, the CLR loader proceeds to load the correct version based on the assembly identity requested. If the assembly does not reside in the GAC, the CLR loader then probes a couple of additional paths including the application base path and the private binaries path. If the assembly is found in either of the two locations, the CLR loader attempts the load from there.

Load-from Context

When an assembly is loaded into the load-from context, typically by using one of the `Assembly.LoadFrom`, `AppDomain.CreateInstanceFrom`, `AppDomain.ExecuteAssembly`, API variants, the CLR's probing logic is avoided altogether putting the responsibility of assembly conflict squarely into the caller's hands. All assembly dependencies are also loaded from the same path. Additionally, dependent assemblies in the default load context can be used by an assembly loaded into the load-from context. Figure 4-4 highlights some of the interesting aspects of the load-from context.

In Figure 4-4, we can see that assemblies with the same identity but with different paths are treated as one and the same assembly, causing a reference to the already loaded assembly to be returned. Furthermore, if an assembly has been loaded into the load-from context and another attempt is made to load the same assembly into the default load context, this results in a failure.

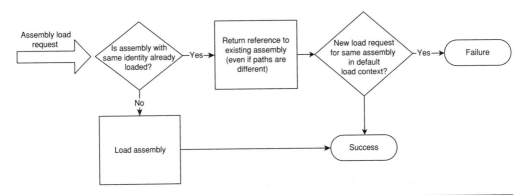

Figure 4-4   Interesting caveats when using the load-from context

Load-without Context

The last load context we will discuss is the load without a context. This context is reserved for assemblies that, generally speaking, do not have a load context period. Examples of such assemblies are those assemblies generated using the `Reflection` namespace and `Emit` APIs. In these cases, the CLR does not do any type of probing. The exception to the rule is when applying identity to a generated assembly using policy. In this case, if an assembly is located in the GAC, it will be used.

At this point, we have discussed assembly identity, the Global Assembly Cache, and the different load contexts that are available. Many subtle and interesting problems can occur when loading assemblies (especially when mixing load contexts). In the remaining part of this chapter, we will take a look at some real-world examples of problems and how the available tools, instrumentation, and debuggers can be used to get to the bottom of the problem.

Simple Assembly Load Failure

Let's begin by looking at a simple assembly load failure and examine the techniques available to us when troubleshooting assembly load failures. We will use the same application as shown in Listings 4-1 and 4-2 where the primary assembly (`04TypeCast.exe`) simply loads another assembly called `04Assembly.dll`. Both files are located under the `c:\adndbin` directory. Before running the application though, please rename the `04assembly.dll` to `04assembly.old`. When the rename is complete, we can proceed and execute the `04TypeCast.exe` assembly:

```
C:\ADNDBin>04TypeCast.exe
Press any key to load into load from context

Unhandled Exception: System.IO.FileNotFoundException: Could not load file or
assembly
'file:///C:\ADNDBin\04assembly.dll' or one of its dependencies.
The system cannot find the file specified.
File name: 'file:///C:\ADNDBin\04assembly.dll'
   at System.Reflection.Assembly._nLoad
(AssemblyName fileName, String codeBase, Evidence assemblySecurity, Assembly
locationHint,
StackCrawlMark& stackMark, Boolean throwOnFileNotFound, Boolean forIntrospection)
   at System.Reflection.Assembly.nLoad(AssemblyName fileName, String codeBase,
Evidence assemblySecurity, Assembly locationHint, StackCrawlMark& stackMark, Boolean
throwOnFileNotFound, Boolean forIntrospection)
   at System.Reflection.Assembly.InternalLoad(AssemblyName assemblyRef, Evidence
assemblySecurity, StackCrawlMark& stackMark, Boolean forIntrospection)
   at System.Reflection.Assembly.InternalLoadFrom(String assemblyFile, Evidence
```

securityEvidence, Byte[] hashValue, AssemblyHashAlgorithm hashAlgorithm, Boolean
forIntrospection, StackCrawlMark& stackMark)
   at System.Reflection.Assembly.LoadFrom(String assemblyFile)
   at Advanced.NET.Debugging.Chapter4.TypeCast.Main(String[] args) in
c:\Publishing\ADND\Code\Chapter4\TypeCast\04TypeCast.cs:line 39

WRN: Assembly binding logging is turned OFF.
To enable assembly bind failure logging, set the registry value
[HKLM\Software\Microsoft\Fusion!EnableLog] (DWORD) to 1.
Note: There is some performance penalty associated with assembly bind failure
logging.
To turn this feature off, remove the registry value
[HKLM\Software\Microsoft\Fusion!EnableLog].

In the output of the command, we see, not unexpectedly, that we get a
FileNotFoundException. Although the information displayed is useful, it's always
best to see if we can glean some more information about the failure in the debugger
rather than just rely on a stack trace. Let's rerun the application under the debugger
making sure we use the sxe 0xe0434f4d to stop on all CLR exceptions. Listing
4-3 illustrates the debugger session.

Listing 4-3   Debugging the FileNotFoundException

```
...
...
...
0:000> sxe 0xe0434f4d
0:000> g
ModLoad: 75e70000 75f36000    C:\Windows\system32\ADVAPI32.dll
ModLoad: 76330000 763f3000    C:\Windows\system32\RPCRT4.dll
...
...
...
ModLoad: 79060000 790b6000    C:\Windows\Microsoft.NET\Framework\v2.0.50727
\mscorjit.dll
Press any key to load into load from context
 ModLoad: 60340000 60348000    C:\Windows\Microsoft.NET\Framework\
v2.0.50727\culture.dll
(d1c.126c): C++ EH exception - code e06d7363 (first chance)
(d1c.126c): C++ EH exception - code e06d7363 (first chance)
(d1c.126c): C++ EH exception - code e06d7363 (first chance)
(d1c.126c): CLR exception - code e0434f4d (first chance)
First chance exceptions are reported before any exception handling.
This exception may be expected and handled.
```

4. ASSEMBLY LOADER

```
eax=0023efdc ebx=e0434f4d ecx=00000001 edx=00000000 esi=0023f064 edi=00345408
eip=773e42eb esp=0023efdc ebp=0023f02c iopl=0         nv up ei pl nz na po nc
cs=001b  ss=0023  ds=0023  es=0023  fs=003b  gs=0000          efl=00000202
KERNEL32!RaiseException+0x58:
773e42eb c9              leave
0:000> kb
ChildEBP RetAddr  Args to Child
0023f02c 79f071ac e0434f4d 00000001 00000001 KERNEL32!RaiseException+0x58
0023f08c 79f9293a 01c978f8 00000000 00000000
mscorwks!RaiseTheExceptionInternalOnly+0x2a8
0023f0c4 79f933b6 0023f180 0035f260 82cf8ddc
mscorwks!UnwindAndContinueRethrowHelperAfterCatch+0x70
*** WARNING: Unable to verify checksum for
C:\Windows\assembly\NativeImages_v2.0.50727_32\mscorlib\5b3e3b0551bcaa722c27dbb089c4
31e4\mscorlib.ni.dll
0023f1fc 7937dd77 00000000 00000001 0023f284 mscorwks!AssemblyNative::Load+0x2d0
0023f2b0 79e7c74b 00000000 0023f2e8 0023f340 mscorlib_ni+0x2bdd77
0023f2c0 79e7c6cc 0023f390 00000000 0023f360 mscorwks!CallDescrWorker+0x33
0023f340 79e7c8e1 0023f390 00000000 0023f360
mscorwks!CallDescrWorkerWithHandler+0xa3
0023f478 79e7c783 002cc028 0023f540 0023f50c mscorwks!MethodDesc::CallDescr+0x19c
0023f494 79e7c90d 002cc028 0023f540 0023f50c
mscorwks!MethodDesc::CallTargetWorker+0x1f
0023f4a8 79eefb9e 0023f50c 82cf8a2c 00000000 mscorwks!MethodDescCallSite::Call+0x18
0023f60c 79eef830 002c3028 00000001 0023f648 mscorwks!ClassLoader::RunMain+0x263
0023f874 79ef01da 00000000 82cf8164 00000001
mscorwks!Assembly::ExecuteMainMethod+0xa6
0023fd44 79fb9793 00290000 00000000 82cf81b4
mscorwks!SystemDomain::ExecuteMainMethod+0x43f
0023fd94 79fb96df 00290000 82cf81fc 00000000 mscorwks!ExecuteEXE+0x59
0023fddc 7900b1b3 00000000 79e70000 0023fdf8 mscorwks!_CorExeMain+0x15c
0023fdec 773e4911 7ffd7000 0023fe38 7725e4b6 mscoree!_CorExeMain+0x2c
0023fdf8 7725e4b6 7ffd7000 7a3b7683 00000000 KERNEL32!BaseThreadInitThunk+0xe
0023fe38 7725e489 7900b183 7ffd7000 00000000 ntdll!__RtlUserThreadStart+0x23
0023fe50 00000000 7900b183 7ffd7000 00000000 ntdll!_RtlUserThreadStart+0x1b
0:000> .loadby sos mscorwks
0:000> !PrintException 01c978f8
Exception object: 01c978f8
Exception type: System.IO.FileNotFoundException
Message: Could not load file or assembly 'file:///C:\ADNDBin\04assembly.dll'
or one of its dependencies. The system cannot find the file specified.
InnerException: <none>
StackTrace (generated):
<none>
StackTraceString: <none>
HResult: 80070002
```

From Listing 4-3, we can see that we first resume execution of the application until the exception stops execution. When it is stopped, we dump out the call stack to find the address of the managed exception from the first parameter to the second stack frame (`mscorwks!RaiseTheExceptionInternalOnly`). We then feed the address into the `PrintException` command to get further information. Interestingly enough, the exception tells us some basic information about the failure (such as which assembly failed to load and the corresponding HRESULT).

HOW DO I GET EXTENDED INFORMATION ON HRESULT VALUES? The debuggers include a command called `error` that can be used to get a textual representation of an HRESULT. Simply pass the HRESULT to the error command and it displays the information:

```
0:000> !error 80070002
Error code: (HRESULT) 0x80070002 (2147942402) - The system cannot find the
file specified.
```

The more interesting information is where the loader actually attempts to load the assembly from. We already know one of the paths (`c:\adndbin\04assembly.dll`) but it is possible that the assembly could be located where we expected the CLR to be able to load it from. The question then becomes, can we ask the CLR loader to tell us the different probing paths it used while looking for the assembly? The answer is yes and it comes in the form of what is known as assembly binding logging, which is a feature of the CLR that enables extensive tracing during the binding phase. The binding logging feature is by default turned off and needs to be enabled. The easiest way to enable the logging feature is to run the `fuslogvw.exe` tool that comes with the .NET 2.0 SDK. It is located in the installation folder under the bin directory. For example, on my machine, the tool is located under

```
c:\Program Files\Microsoft Visual Studio 8\SDK\v2.0\Bin
```

Figure 4-5 shows the main screen after the tool is launched.

The main screen is divided into two parts. The first part contains the actual log entries and has three corresponding columns:

1. Application. The Application column shows which application that the particular log entry came from.
2. Description. The Description column shows the abbreviated form of the log entry.
3. Date/Time. The Date/Time column shows the timestamp of the log entry.

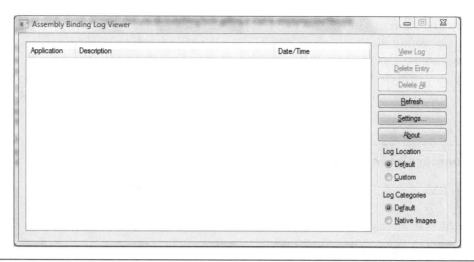

Figure 4-5   Main screen of fuslogvw.exe tool

The right side of the main screen contains a set of buttons that controls the log entries already in existence as well as options for how the logging is performed. The Settings button controls the *how* and *when* aspects of how logging should be performed, as shown in Figure 4-6.

There are a number of options to control the logging. By default, logging is disabled but can be set to any of the following behaviors:

- Log in Exception Text. When this option is selected, assembly binds are logged in exceptions.
- Log Bind Failures to Disk. When this option is selected, only failure cases are logged to disk.

Figure 4-6   Fuslogvw.exe options

- Log All Binds to Disk. When this option is selected, all binding operations are logged to disk.
- Enable Custom Log Path. Enables you to change the path to where the logs are written. If you change the log path, you must also select the Custom Log Location button on the main screen.

Automatically Enable Bind Logging

The settings in `fuslogvw.exe` are controlled via the registry under the following registry key:

`HKLM\Software\Microsoft\Fusion`

The following registry values are legal under the path:

- `LogPath` [SZ]. Controls the log path option.
- `ForceLog` [DWORD=1]. Logs all bind activity.
- `LogFailures` [DWORD=1]. Logs only failed bind activity.
- `LogResourceBinds` [DWORD=1]. Log bind failures to satellite assemblies.

Creating the appropriate registry values provides a programmatic way of controlling the binding logging feature.

Let's see an example of the bind logging feature by enabling the Log Bind Failures to Disk setting. When set, run `04typecast.exe` again until the exception is thrown. Go back to the `fuslogvw.exe` tool and click the Refresh button. One log entry should now appear in the main part of the `fuslogvw.exe` window:

`04TypeCast.exe file:///C:/ADNDBIN/04Assembly.dll 1/1/2009/@1:32:08 PM`

This entry corresponds to the failed load attempt of `04Assembly.dll`. So far, we've been told very little information about the failure itself. To get extended failure information, double-click the log entry, which brings up the default browser with detailed error information. Figure 4-7 shows an example of the error information displayed using Internet Explorer.

The output is structured into three main sections. The first section contains general information about the log entry such as the operation status (failed in our case), the HRESULT (including textual representation), the path of the CLR loader component (`mscorwks.dll`), and the executable path.

```
*** Assembly Binder Log Entry  (1/1/2009 @ 1:32:08 PM) ***

The operation failed.
Bind result: hr = 0x80070002. The system cannot find the file specified.

Assembly manager loaded from:  C:\Windows\Microsoft.NET\Framework\v2.0.50727\mscorwks.dll
Running under executable  C:\ADNDBin\04TypeCast.exe
--- A detailed error log follows.

=== Pre-bind state information ===
LOG: User =          marioh
LOG: Where-ref bind. Location = C:\ADNDBin\04assembly.dll
LOG: Appbase = file:///C:/ADNDBin/
LOG: Initial PrivatePath = NULL
LOG: Dynamic Base = NULL
LOG: Cache Base = NULL
LOG: AppName = 04TypeCast.exe
Calling assembly : (Unknown).
===
LOG: This bind starts in LoadFrom load context.
WRN: Native image will not be probed in LoadFrom context. Native image will only be probed in default load context, like
LOG: No application configuration file found.
LOG: Using machine configuration file from C:\Windows\Microsoft.NET\Framework\v2.0.50727\config\machine.config.
LOG: Attempting download of new URL file:///C:/ADNDBin/04assembly.dll.
LOG: All probing URLs attempted and failed.
```

Figure 4-7   Detailed bind logging error information

The next section contains the prebind information and gets a little more interesting. In addition to the user name that the application was run under, it gives the path of where the assembly was attempted to be loaded from. Also included in this section are the other paths that may be probed during load such as the application base, private path, dynamic base, and cache base. All of these different paths listed represent probing points that the CLR uses when trying to bind to 04Assembly.dll.

The last part of the output is the actual probing log. The output tells us that we are in the load-from context (because we use the LoadFrom API). It also tells us that no application configuration file was found and that it uses the machine wide configuration file instead. The last couple of lines simply state that it attempted to load the assembly from the application base directory and failed. Had we specified a private path, we would have seen the CLR loader probing that path as well.

This concludes our investigation of a very simple assembly load failure. We started off by getting some basic diagnostics information from the output of the application at the point of failure, followed by running the problematic application under the debugger and looking at the exception being thrown, and finally by turning on assembly bind logging to figure out where the CLR loader was looking for the requested assembly (in our case only in the application base path).

Load Context Failure

In this section, we will take another look at a problematic application that fails to load a dependent assembly. Listing 4-4 shows the source code of the failing application.

Please note that some portions of the source code have been omitted for the sake of maintaining focus on the debugging aspects rather than code reviews.

Listing 4-4   Assembly load failure application

```
using System;
using System.Text;
using System.Runtime.Remoting;

namespace Advanced.NET.Debugging.Chapter4
{
    [Serializable]
    class Entity
    {
        public int a;
    }

    [Serializable]
    class EntityUtil
    {
        public void Dump(Entity t)
        {
            Console.WriteLine(t.a);
        }
    }


    class Program
    {
        static void Main(string[] args)
        {
            Program p = new Program();
            p.Run();
        }

        public void Run()
        {
            while (true)
            {
                Console.WriteLine("1. Run in default app domain");
                Console.WriteLine("2. Run in dedicated app domain");
                Console.WriteLine("Q. To quit");
                Console.Write("> ");
                ConsoleKeyInfo k=Console.ReadKey();
                Console.WriteLine();
```

```
            if (k.KeyChar == '1')
            {
                RunInDefault();
            }
            else if (k.KeyChar == '2')
            {
                RunInDedicated();
            }
            else if (k.KeyChar == 'q' || k.KeyChar == 'Q')
                break;
        }

    }

    public AppDomain CreateDomain()
    {
        AppDomainSetup domaininfo = new AppDomainSetup();
        return AppDomain.CreateDomain("MyDomain",
                                      null,
                                      domaininfo);

    }

    public void RunInDefault()
    {
        EntityUtil t2 = new EntityUtil();

        Entity t = new Entity();
        t.a = 10;

        t2.Dump(t);
    }

    public void RunInDedicated()
    {
        AppDomain domain = CreateDomain();
        ObjectHandle h = domain.CreateInstance(
                    "04AppDomain",
                    "Advanced.NET.Debugging.Chapter4.EntityUtil");
        EntityUtil t2 = (EntityUtil)h.Unwrap();

        Entity t = new Entity();
        t.a = 10;

        t2.Dump(t);
    }
    }
}
```

The source code and binary for Listing 4-4 can be found in the following folders:

- Source code: `C:\ADND\Chapter4\AppDomain`
- Binary: `C:\ADNDBin\04AppDomain.exe`

The application is relatively straightforward and consists of two supporting classes named `Entity` and `EntityUtil`. The `Entity` class contains one public field named a and the `EntityUtil` class contains a method named `Dump` that simply takes an argument of type `Entity` and prints out the public field. When the application is run, it displays a menu that enables running using the default application domain or running in a dedicated application domain. The idea behind the application is to exercise the `Entity` and `EntityUtil` classes. If run in the default application domain, all instances of the classes are instantiated in the default application domain, whereas running in a dedicated application domain causes the `EntityUtil` instance to be created in a new application domain and the Entity instance (passed to `EntityUtil`) to be created in the default application domain. Due to application domains providing an isolation layer between code loaded into different application domains, objects passed in-between application domains must be marshaled. In our case, we do simple marshaling by value where a copy of the object is made in the target application domain. Let's run the application and see what happens:

```
C:\ADNDBin>04AppDomain.exe
1. Run in default app domain
2. Run in dedicated app domain
Q. To quit
> 1
10
1. Run in default app domain
2. Run in dedicated app domain
Q. To quit
> 2

Unhandled Exception: System.IO.FileNotFoundException:
Could not load file or assembly '04AppDomain' or one of its dependencies.
The system cannot find the file specified.
File name: '04AppDomain'
   at System.Reflection.Assembly._nLoad
(AssemblyName fileName, String codeBase,
Evidence assemblySecurity, Assembly locationHint,
StackCrawlMark& stackMark, Boolean throwOnFileNotFound,
Boolean forIntrospection)
   at System.Reflection.Assembly.nLoad
(AssemblyName fileName, String codeBase,
Evidence assemblySecurity, Assembly locationHint,
```

```
StackCrawlMark& stackMark, Boolean throwOnFileNotFound,
Boolean forIntrospection)
   at System.Reflection.Assembly.InternalLoad
(AssemblyName assemblyRef, Evidence assemblySecurity,
StackCrawlMark& stackMark, Boolean forIntrospection)
   at System.Reflection.Assembly.InternalLoad
(String assemblyString, Evidence assemblySecurity,
StackCrawlMark& stackMark, Boolean forIntrospection)
   at System.Activator.CreateInstance
(String assemblyName, String typeName, Boolean ignoreCase,
 BindingFlags bindingAttr, Binder binder,
Object[] args, CultureInfo culture, Object[] activationAttributes,
 Evidence securityInfo, StackCrawlMark& stackMark)
   at System.Activator.CreateInstance
(String assemblyName, String typeName)
   at System.AppDomain.CreateInstance
(String assemblyName, String typeName)
   at System.AppDomain.CreateInstance
(String assemblyName, String typeName)
   at Advanced.NET.Debugging.Chapter4.Program.RunInDedicated() in
c:\Publishing\ADND\Code\Chapter4\AppDomain\04AppDomain.cs:line 77
   at Advanced.NET.Debugging.Chapter4.Program.Run() in
c:\Publishing\ADND\Code\Chapter4\AppDomain\04AppDomain.cs:line 48
   at Advanced.NET.Debugging.Chapter4.Program.Main(String[] args) in
c:\Publishing\ADND\Code\Chapter4\AppDomain\04AppDomain.cs:line 28

WRN: Assembly binding logging is turned OFF.
To enable assembly bind failure logging, set the registry value
[HKLM\Software\Microsoft\Fusion!EnableLog] (DWORD) to 1.
Note: There is some performance penalty associated with assembly bind failure
logging.
To turn this feature off, remove the registry value
[HKLM\Software\Microsoft\Fusion!EnableLog].
```

We can see that as long as we run the application in the default application domain, the application executes successfully. However, if we run the application in a dedicated application domain (option 2), a FileNotFoundException is thrown. How is it possible that running in the default application domain works but running in a dedicated application domain does not? As always, we start by looking at the stack trace presented to us. The exception seems to originate from our RunInDedicated function, which in turn calls the CreateInstance function to create an instance of the EntityType class. So far, nothing seems to be out of the ordinary with the code itself. The next step is to run the application under a debugger and look at the exception:

```
0:000> !pe 01cb5dcc
Exception object: 01cb5dcc
```

Exception type: System.IO.FileNotFoundException
Message: Could not load file or assembly '04AppDomain' or one of its dependencies.
The system cannot find the file specified.
InnerException: <none>
StackTrace (generated):
    SP   IP   Function
    0017EE80 008A026C 04AppDomain!Advanced.NET.Debugging.Chapter4.
Program.RunInDedicated()+0x4c
    0017EE9C 008A01BC 04AppDomain!Advanced.NET.Debugging.Chapter4.Program.Run()+0xcc
    0017EEC8 008A00A7
04AppDomain!Advanced.NET.Debugging.Chapter4.Program.Main(System.String[])+0x37

StackTraceString: <none>
HResult: 80070002

The exception raised and printed in the debugger doesn't yield many more clues as to the origin of the problem (it simply restates that an assembly failed to load). We know from the previous section that we can also use the `fuslogvw.exe` tool to figure out in more detail where the CLR is trying to find the assembly. Figure 4-8 shows the results of running `fuslogvw.exe` on our faulty application.

From the CLR loader log in Figure 4-8, we can see that the CLR loader is attempting to load the `04AppDomain.exe` assembly from the `C:\Windows\System32` path. Why is it choosing that particular path? The answer lies in remembering that when an object is marshaled across application domains the object gets serialized, which means that the target application domain must also have access to the assembly where the type is defined. Without the assembly, the deserialization fails. It is also important to note that application domains can control certain parts of the assembly probing paths. More specifically, from Figure 4-8, we can see that the `AppBase` is set to `C:\Windows\System32`. If we take a closer look at the `RunInDedicated` method in our source code (intentionally removed from Listing 4-4), we see the following lines:

```
AppDomainSetup domaininfo = new AppDomainSetup();
domaininfo.ApplicationBase = "C:\\Windows\\System32";
return AppDomain.CreateDomain("MyDomain", null, domaininfo);
```

It turns out that during the creation of the dedicated application domain we set the application base path to be `C:\Windows\System32`, which in turn means that the CLR cannot load any dependent assemblies unless they are also located in this path. Although this may not seem to be the "best" approach for an application

```
*** Assembly Binder Log Entry  (1/3/2009 @ 12:54:43 PM) ***

The operation failed.
Bind result: hr = 0x80070002. The system cannot find the file specified.

Assembly manager loaded from:  C:\Windows\Microsoft.NET\Framework\v2.0.50727\mscorwks.dll
Running under executable  C:\ADNDBin\04AppDomain.exe
--- A detailed error log follows.

=== Pre-bind state information ===
LOG: User =         marioh
LOG: DisplayName = 04AppDomain
 (Partial)
LOG: Appbase = file:///C:/Windows/System32
LOG: Initial PrivatePath = NULL
LOG: Dynamic Base = NULL
LOG: Cache Base = NULL
LOG: AppName = 04AppDomain.exe
Calling assembly : (Unknown).
===
LOG: This bind starts in default load context.
LOG: Download of application configuration file was attempted from file:///C:/Windows/System32/04AppDomain.exe.config.
LOG: Configuration file C:\Windows\System32\04AppDomain.exe.config does not exist.
LOG: No application configuration file found.
LOG: Using machine configuration file from C:\Windows\Microsoft.NET\Framework\v2.0.50727\config\machine.config.
LOG: Policy not being applied to reference at this time (private, custom, partial, or location-based assembly bind).
LOG: Attempting download of new URL file:///C:/Windows/System32/04AppDomain.DLL.
LOG: Attempting download of new URL file:///C:/Windows/System32/04AppDomain/04AppDomain.DLL.
LOG: Attempting download of new URL file:///C:/Windows/System32/04AppDomain.EXE.
LOG: Attempting download of new URL file:///C:/Windows/System32/04AppDomain/04AppDomain.EXE.
LOG: All probing URLs attempted and failed.
```

Figure 4-8 AppBase is set to C:\Windows\System32. CLR loader log for 04AppDomain.exe

domain, it serves to illustrate a common problem that applications experience on a daily basis—that is the problem of the CLR loader picking up incorrect assemblies (or it fails to load an assembly, period).

FileNotFoundException and the FusionLog Property

When the assembly binding logging feature is turned on, you may have noticed that a property named `FusionLog` is set to the log entry data that is collected, in essence propagating the failure via the exception mechanism. Here is an example of a `FileNotFoundException` and its `FusionLog` property when the logging feature is turned on:

```
0:000> !do 01d863e0
Name: System.IO.FileNotFoundException
MethodTable: 791222c4
EEClass: 79122244
Size: 84(0x54) bytes
 (C:\Windows\assembly\GAC_32\mscorlib\2.0.0.0__b77a5c561934e089\mscorlib.dll)
```

```
Fields:
      MT    Field   Offset              Type VT    Attr    Value Name
790fd8c4  40000b5       4         System.String  0 instance 01d6e1f8
_className
7910ebc8  40000b6       8  ...ection.MethodBase  0 instance 00000000
_exceptionMethod
...
...
...
790fd8c4  4001bb5      4c         System.String  0 instance 01d6d18c
_fusionLog
0:000> !do 01d6d18c
Name: System.String
MethodTable: 790fd8c4
EEClass: 790fd824
Size: 2346(0x92a) bytes
  (C:\Windows\assembly\GAC_32\mscorlib\2.0.0.0__b77a5c561934e089\
mscorlib.dll)
String: Assembly manager loaded from:
C:\Windows\Microsoft.NET\Framework\v2.0.50727\mscorwks.dll
Running under executable  C:\ADNDBin\04AppDomain.exe
--- A detailed error log follows.

=== Pre-bind state information ===
LOG: User = REDMOND\marioh
LOG: DisplayName = 04AppDomain
  (Partial)
LOG: Appbase = file:///C:/Windows/System32
LOG: Initial PrivatePath = NULL
Calling assembly : (Unknown).
===
LOG: This bind starts in default load context.
LOG: Configuration file C:\Windows\System32\04AppDomain.exe.config does not
exist.
LOG: No application configuration file found.
LOG: Using machine configuration file from
C:\Windows\Microsoft.NET\Framework\v2.0.50727\config\machine.config.
LOG: Policy not being applied to reference at this time
(private, custom, partial, or location-based assembly bind).
LOG: Attempting download of new URL
file:///C:/Windows/System32/04AppDomain.DLL.
LOG: Attempting download of new URL
file:///C:/Windows/System32/04AppDomain/04AppDomain.DLL.
LOG: Attempting download of new URL
file:///C:/Windows/System32/04AppDomain.EXE.
```

```
LOG: Attempting download of new URL
file:///C:/Windows/System32/04AppDomain/04AppDomain.EXE.

...
...
...
```

One other tool that is useful when it comes to loader problems is that of utilizing the Managed Debugging Assistants (MDAs). Chapter 1, "Introduction to the Tools," presented an overview of what MDAs are and how they can be enabled. For the purposes of the CLR loader, there is an MDA called the binding Failure MDA that can be used when trying to troubleshoot CLR loader issues. To enable the MDA, we save the following XML in a file called 04AppDomain.exe.mda.config:

```
<mdaConfig>
  <assistants>
    <bindingFailure />
  </assistants>
</mdaConfig>
```

This XML simply enables the bindingFailure MDA for the 04AppDomain.exe application. If we rerun 04AppDomain.exe under the debugger and reproduce the problem (by choosing option 2), we can see the following augmented information being presented:

```
> 2
ModLoad: 74e40000 74e7b000    C:\Windows\system32\rsaenh.dll
ModLoad: 60340000 60348000    C:\Windows\Microsoft.NET\Framework\v2.0.50727
\culture.dll
(1c60.18c0): C++ EH exception - code e06d7363 (first chance)
(1c60.18c0): C++ EH exception - code e06d7363 (first chance)
ModLoad: 60340000 60348000    C:\Windows\Microsoft.NET\Framework\v2.0.50727
\culture.dll
<mda:msg xmlns:mda="http://schemas.microsoft.com/CLR/2004/10/mda">
  <!--
      The assembly with display name '04AppDomain' failed to load in the
'LoadFrom'
      binding context of the AppDomain with ID 2. The cause of the failure was:
      System.IO.FileNotFoundException: Could not load file or assembly
'04AppDomain'
      or one of its dependencies. The system cannot find the file specified.
      File name: '04AppDomain'
```

```
WRN: Assembly binding logging is turned OFF.
To enable assembly bind failure logging, set the registry value
[HKLM\Software\Microsoft\Fusion!EnableLog] (DWORD) to 1.
Note: There is some performance penalty associated with assembly bind
failure
logging.
To turn this feature off, remove the registry value
[HKLM\Software\Microsoft\Fusion!EnableLog].


 -->
 <mda:bindingFailureMsg break="true">
  <assemblyInfo appDomainId="2" displayName="04AppDomain" codeBase="" hResult="-
2147024894" bindingContextId="1"/>
 </mda:bindingFailureMsg>
</mda:msg>
(1c60.18c0): Break instruction exception - code 80000003 (first chance)
eax=00000000 ebx=00000000 ecx=7728861f edx=000d0c30 esi=0029b0a4 edi=00000200
eip=7a0c8c7c esp=0029a328 ebp=0029a7ac iopl=0         nv up ei pl nz na po nc
cs=001b  ss=0023  ds=0023  es=0023  fs=003b  gs=0000          efl=00000202
mscorwks!MdaXmlMessage::SendDebugEvent+0x1e6:
7a0c8c7c cc              int     3
```

As soon as the debugger breaks execution due to the exception being thrown, we can see some additional information in XML form. Most of the information we have already found out by looking at the exception itself in an earlier exercise, but the MDA output also gives some additional useful information such as the application domain ID. We can use the DumpDomain command to get more detailed information about the application domain in question:

```
0:000> !DumpDomain
...
...
...
--------------------
Domain 2: 000bfcb8
LowFrequencyHeap: 000bfcdc
HighFrequencyHeap: 000bfd34
StubHeap: 000bfd8c
Stage: OPEN
SecurityDescriptor: 000c1f00
Name: MyDomain
Assembly: 000b45d8
[C:\Windows\assembly\GAC_32\mscorlib\2.0.0.0__b77a5c561934e089\mscorlib.dll]
ClassLoader: 000b4670
```

```
SecurityDescriptor: 000c3150
  Module Name
790c2000 C:\Windows\assembly\GAC_32\mscorlib\2.0.0.0__b77a5c561934e089\mscorlib.dll
0077239c C:\Windows\assembly\GAC_32\mscorlib\2.0.0.0__b77a5c561934e089\sortkey.nlp
00772010 C:\Windows\assembly\GAC_32\mscorlib\2.0.0.0__b77a5c561934e089\sorttbls.nlp
```

ARE THERE OTHER USEFUL LOADER MDAS? Yes, the `loadFromContext` MDA can be activated to alert you when the load-from context is being used. Often, the Load-From context is inadvertently used and can cause some serious headaches. This MDA ensures that notifications are sent whenever an assembly is loaded into the Load-From context.

Interoperability and DllNotFoundException

The CLR provides a very extensive interoperability layer that enables .NET code to interact with the underlying native code modules. Providing this capability is key to taking advantage of legacy native code that is to be exposed via managed code. A couple of different interoperability mechanisms exist depending on the type of native code you are working with. The first one, known as Platform Invocation (P/Invoke), enables the developer to call exported functions in native code modules (or DLLs). To accomplish this, the managed code equivalent method signature must be defined and attributed with the `DllImport` attribute to indicate that it is meant to be a P/Invoke method. The second form of interoperability is known as COM interoperability, and it enables managed code to work with native COM objects. In this part of the chapter, we will take a look at what it means to do interoperability as far as the loader is concerned. We already discussed the intricacies of different load contexts used by the CLR when loading assemblies, but how does that apply to native code platform interoperability? To guide us through this discussion, we will be using a simple application shown in Listing 4-5.

Listing 4-5 Simple example of P/Invoke

```
using System;
using System.Text;
using System.Runtime.InteropServices;

namespace Advanced.NET.Debugging.Chapter4
```

(continues)

Listing 4-5 Simple example of P/Invoke *(continued)*

```
{
    class Interop
    {
        static void Main(string[] args)
        {
          Console.WriteLine("Press any key to P/Invoke");
          Console.ReadKey();
            Console.WriteLine();
            PrintMsg("Printed via P/Invoke");
        }

        [DllImport("04Native.dll", CharSet = CharSet.Auto)]
        internal static extern void PrintMsg(string message);
    }
}
```

The source code and binary for Listing 4-5 can be found in the following folders:

- Source code: `C:\ADND\Chapter4\Interop`
- Binary: `C:\ADNDBin\04Interop.exe and 04Native.dll`

The source code is relatively straightforward. The `Main` method simply calls a P/Invoke method named `PrintMsg` that thunks down to the native code equivalent, which essentially does nothing more than print the string that was passed to the function. If we run this application, we can see that it successfully executes:

```
C:\ADNDBin>04Interop.exe
Press any key to P/Invoke

Printed via P/Invoke
```

For the sake of illustrating the behavior of the CLR when a native DLL cannot be found, let's rename `04Native.dll` in the `C:\ADNDBIN` folder to `04Native.old` and run the application again:

```
C:\ADNDBin>04Interop.exe
Press any key to P/Invoke

Unhandled Exception: System.DllNotFoundException:
Unable to load DLL '04Native.dll': The specified module could not
```

be found. (Exception from HRESULT: 0x8007007E)
```
   at Advanced.NET.Debugging.Chapter4.Interop.PrintMsg(String message)
   at Advanced.NET.Debugging.Chapter4.Interop.Main(String[] args) in
c:\Publishing\ADND\Code\Chapter4\Interop\04Interop.cs:line 14
```

This time, we can see that a `DllNotFoundException` is thrown. In previous parts of the chapter, we discussed the elaborate assembly loading mechanism that the CLR employs to bind to the correct assembly. Does the same logic apply to native DLLs? The short answer is no. Any native DLLs that are used during P/Invoke calls are loaded by the underlying `kernel32!LoadLibrary` API and as such uses the same probing logic that Windows uses when loading libraries in general. For a detailed discussion on how this loading logic works, please see the MSDN documentation for `LoadLibrary`. As a matter of fact, the highly useful `fuslogvw.exe` tool we used extensively earlier to troubleshoot loading issues will not help at all in the case of P/Invoke load issues.

WHAT ABOUT COM INTEROPERABILITY? Much in the same way that P/Invoke relies on the Windows loading logic, the COM interoperability layer depends on the COM loader. COM objects must be properly registered in the registry before they can be accessed by managed code and follow the same loading logic that the COM subsystem employs.

Debugging Light Weight Code Generation

The CLR provides a very convenient and efficient mechanism to generate code on-the-fly (also known as CodeGen). Prior to CLR 2.0, all the necessary APIs to dynamically generate code were housed in the `System.Reflection.Emit` namespace. As part of the code generation exercise, the developer had to maintain the structural integrity of any piece of code running on the CLR. For example, if we wanted to define a simple method called Add that took two integers and returned the sum, we had to define the method itself (including the IL), the type on which the method was defined, the module that the type was defined in, as well as the assembly that housed the module. Although this form of code generation afforded features such as injecting debug information, it was quite elaborate to develop against, especially if you had some smaller simpler methods you wanted to generate. To alleviate the pain, CLR 2.0 introduced what is known as light weight code generation (LCG).

With LCG, it is no longer necessary to define all the different aspects (module, type, assembly, etc.) of a small piece of code; rather, just define the code itself and invoke it via the delegate mechanism. Because code generation is used heavily in many different systems, it is important to understand how we go about debugging dynamically generated code. After all, the code is not generated at compile time with the luxury of associated debug information. It might come as a surprise that debugging dynamically generated code using the native debuggers isn't more difficult. To get a better feel for the process, let's take a look at a simple example. Listing 4-6 shows a very simple application that dynamically generates the code that adds two integers and returns the result.

Listing 4-6   Simple example of LCG generated code

```
using System;
using System.Text;
using System.Reflection.Emit;

namespace Advanced.NET.Debugging.Chapter4
{
    class CodeGen
    {
        private delegate int Add(int a, int b);

        public static void Main()
        {
            Type[] args={typeof(int), typeof(int)};
            DynamicMethod dyn = new
                DynamicMethod("Add",
                              typeof(int),
                              new Type[] { typeof(int), typeof(int) },
                              typeof(CodeGen),
                              true);
            ILGenerator gen = dyn.GetILGenerator();
            gen.Emit(OpCodes.Ldarg_1);
            gen.Emit(OpCodes.Ldarg_2);
            gen.Emit(OpCodes.Add);
            gen.Emit(OpCodes.Ret);

            Add a= (Add) dyn.CreateDelegate(typeof(Add));
            int ret = a(1, 2);
            Console.WriteLine("1+2={0}", ret);
        }
    }
}
```

The source code and binary for Listing 4-6 can be found in the following folders:

- Source code: `C:\ADND\Chapter4\CodeGen`
- Binary: `C:\ADNDBin\04CodeGen.exe`

As you can see, the code is pretty straightforward. We define a delegate (`Add`) that takes two integers and returns the sum. We then go ahead and create an instance of the `DynamicMethod` class and use the `ILGenerator` to emit the IL instructions for our `Add` method. Finally, we declare a delegate instance to the generated code and invoke it. If we run the application, we can see the following output as per expectations:

```
C:\ADNDBin>04CodeGen.exe
1+2=3
```

The question now becomes, if we want to debug this application to see the dynamically generated code in action, how would we do that? For example, if we want to set a breakpoint on the `Add` method, can we use the usual breakpoint commands that exist in the SOS and SOSEX debugger extensions? The answer is Yes, we can! but it requires some additional work to get it done. To use the `bpmd` command, we need to first find the method descriptor of the method we want to set the breakpoint on. Normally, this isn't a problem because we can use a number of different commands to find it. With LCG code, however, we need to do some manual work. More specifically, we need to know the appropriate function in the JIT component from where we can extrapolate the method descriptor. The function in question is called `CILJit::compileMethod`. If we set a native breakpoint on this function (using the `bp` command), we can extrapolate the method descriptor from the third argument passed to the function. Let's rerun `04CodeGen.exe` under the debugger and when prompted to press any key manually break into the debugger, as shown in the following:

```
0:000> .symfix
...

...

...

(1b54.1df8): Break instruction exception - code 80000003 (first chance)
eax=7ffda000 ebx=00000000 ecx=00000000 edx=772ad094 esi=00000000 edi=00000000
eip=77267dfe esp=0441ff58 ebp=0441ff84 iopl=0         nv up ei pl zr na pe nc
cs=001b  ss=0023  ds=0023  es=0023  fs=003b  gs=0000          efl=00000246
ntdll!DbgBreakPoint:
77267dfe cc              int     3
0:004> .loadby sos mscorwks
0:004> bp mscorjit!CILJit::compileMethod
```

```
0:004> g
Breakpoint 0 hit
eax=790b22a0 ebx=0031e80c ecx=790a60a0 edx=77279a94 esi=00555160 edi=00000000
eip=7906114f esp=0031e6c8 ebp=0031e730 iopl=0         nv up ei pl nz na pe nc
cs=001b  ss=0023  ds=0023  es=0023  fs=003b  gs=0000          efl=00000206
mscorjit!CILJit::compileMethod:
7906114f 55              push    ebp
0:000> kb
ChildEBP RetAddr  Args to Child
0031e6c4 79f0f9cf 790b22a0 0031e80c 0031e898 mscorjit!CILJit::compileMethod
0031e730 79f0f945 0056e7a8 0031e80c 0031e898 mscorwks!invokeCompileMethodHelper+0x72
0031e774 79f0f8da 0056e7a8 0031e80c 0031e898 mscorwks!invokeCompileMethod+0x31
0031e7cc 79f0ea33 0056e7a8 0031e80c 00000000
mscorwks!CallCompileMethodWithSEHWrapper+0x84
0031eb84 79f0e795 001e3250 00000000 00107214 mscorwks!UnsafeJitFunction+0x230
0031ec28 79e87f52 00000000 00000000 60f1701d
mscorwks!MethodDesc::MakeJitWorker+0x1c1
0031ec80 79e8809e 00000000 60f1704d 0031ef8c mscorwks!MethodDesc::DoPrestub+0x486
0031ecd0 00190876 0031ed00 725139c9 00000002 mscorwks!PreStubWorker+0xeb
WARNING: Frame IP not in any known module. Following frames may be wrong.
0031ed70 79e7c74b 0031edbc 00000000 0031ee00 0x190876
0031ed80 79e7c6cc 0031ee50 00000000 0031ee20 mscorwks!CallDescrWorker+0x33
0031ee00 79e7c8e1 0031ee50 00000000 0031ee20
mscorwks!CallDescrWorkerWithHandler+0xa3
0031ef3c 79e7c783 001ec028 0031f004 0031efd0 mscorwks!MethodDesc::CallDescr+0x19c
0031ef58 79e7c90d 001ec028 0031f004 0031efd0
 mscorwks!MethodDesc::CallTargetWorker+0x1f
0031ef6c 79eefb9e 0031efd0 60f16c4d 00000000 mscorwks!MethodDescCallSite::Call+0x18
0031f0d0 79eef830 001e3028 00000001 0031f10c mscorwks!ClassLoader::RunMain+0x263
0031f338 79ef01da 00000000 60f16495 00000001
 mscorwks!Assembly::ExecuteMainMethod+0xa6
0031f808 79fb9793 010f0000 00000000 60f164c5
 mscorwks!SystemDomain::ExecuteMainMethod+0x43f
0031f858 79fb96df 010f0000 60f1643d 00000000 mscorwks!ExecuteEXE+0x59
0031f8a0 7900b1b3 00000000 79e70000 0031f8bc mscorwks!_CorExeMain+0x15c
0031f8b0 773e4911 7ffdf000 0031f8fc 7725e4b6 mscoree!_CorExeMain+0x2c
0:000> dd 0031e898
0031e898  001e3250 001e3a31 00571528 00000004
0031e8a8  00000002 00000010 00000000 00000000
0031e8b8  00000000 00020008 00000000 00000000
0031e8c8  00000000 00000000 0056f7eb 0056f7e8
0031e8d8  001e3a31 00000000 00000000 00000000
0031e8e8  00000000 00000101 00000000 00000000
0031e8f8  00000000 00000000 005773aa 005773a8
0031e908  001e3a31 00000000 00000000 0000003c
0:000> !DumpMD 001e3250
```

```
Method Name: DynamicClass.Add(Int32, Int32)
Class: 001e319c
MethodTable: 001e3200
mdToken: 06000000
Module: 001e2c3c
IsJitted: no
m_CodeOrIL: ffffffff
```

To find the method descriptor, we have to dump the third parameter to the CILJit::compileMethod, wherein the first DWORD contains the actual method descriptor, which can be fed to the DumpMD command. After we have the method descriptor, we can use any of the commands that operate on them. For example, if we run the DumpIL command on the method descriptor, we can see the IL behind our Add method:

```
0:000> !DumpIL 001e3250
This is dynamic IL. Exception info is not reported at this time.
If a token is unresolved, run "!do <addr>" on the addr given
in parenthesis. You can also look at the token table yourself, by
running "!DumpArray 01e58738".

IL_0000: ldarg.1
IL_0001: ldarg.2
IL_0002: add
IL_0003: ret
```

With the method descriptor, we can now also set a breakpoint on the dynamic Add method by using the bpmd command, as shown in the following:

```
0:000> !bpmd -md 001e3250
MethodDesc = 001e3250
This DynamicMethodDesc is not yet JITTED. Placing memory breakpoint at 001ec45c
0:000> g
Breakpoint 2 hit
eax=001e3250 ebx=01e583cc ecx=00000001 edx=00000002 esi=01e587c8 edi=01e58038
eip=00aa00a8 esp=0031ed0c ebp=0031ed70 iopl=0         nv up ei pl nz na po nc
cs=001b  ss=0023  ds=0023  es=0023  fs=003b  gs=0000             efl=00000202
00aa00a8 56              push    esi
0:000> !ClrStack -a
OS Thread Id: 0x1e60 (0)
ESP       EIP
0031ed0c 00aa00a8 DynamicClass.Add(Int32, Int32)
    PARAMETERS:
        <no data>
        <no data>
```

```
0031ed10 00a702b9 Advanced.NET.Debugging.Chapter4.CodeGen.Main()
    LOCALS:
        0x0031ed40 = 0x01e5800c
        0x0031ed3c = 0x01e58064
        <CLR reg> = 0x01e583cc
        0x0031ed38 = 0x01e587c8
        0x0031ed60 = 0x00000000
        <CLR reg> = 0x01e58038

0031ef8c 79e7c74b [GCFrame: 0031ef8c]
```

This concludes the discussion of how to debug the LCG mechanism in the CLR. Quite a few components make use of dynamically generated code, and knowing how to debug these systems is key.

Summary

In this chapter, we looked at the intricacies of the CLR loader and how to identify some common pitfalls as well as the tools available to troubleshoot those pitfalls. We looked at an overview of the CLR loader, the different load contexts available, as well as the probing logic used by the CLR in each of the contexts. Additionally, a number of examples of common mistakes were shown and investigated by using the debuggers, the fuslogvw.exe tool, and the loader applicable MDAs. Great care must be taken when dealing with the CLR loader, and particular attention has to be paid to which load context is used during assembly load to avoid a myriad of loader issues that can occur.

## CHAPTER 5

Managed Heap and Garbage Collection

Manual memory management is a very common source of errors in applications today. As a matter of fact, several online studies indicate that the most common errors are related to manual memory management. Examples of such problems include

- Dangling pointers
- Double free
- Memory leaks

Automatic memory management serves to remove the tedious and error-prone process of managing memory manually. Even though automatic memory management has gained more attention with the advent of Java and the .NET platform, the concept and implementation have been around for some time. Invented by John McCarthy in 1959 to solve the problems of manual memory management in LISP, other languages have implemented their own automatic memory management schemes as well. The implementation of an automatic memory management component has become almost universally known as a garbage collector (GC). The .NET platform also works on the basis of automatic memory management and implements its own highly performing and reliable GC. Although using a GC makes life a lot simpler for developers and enables them to focus on more of the business logic, having a solid understanding of how the GC operates is key to avoiding a set of problems that can occur when working in a garbage collected environment. In this chapter, we take a look at the internals of the CLR heap manager and the GC and some common pitfalls that can wreak havoc in your application. We utilize the debuggers and a set of other tools to illustrate how we can get to the bottom of the problems.

Windows Memory Architecture Overview

Before we delve into the details of the CLR heap manager and GC, it is useful to review the overall memory architecture of Windows. Figure 5-1 shows a high-level overview of the various pieces commonly involved in a process.

As you can see from Figure 5-1, processes that run in user mode typically use one or more heap managers. The most common heap managers are the Windows heap manager, which is used extensively in most user mode applications, and the CLR heap manager, which is used exclusively by .NET applications. The Windows heap manager is responsible for satisfying most memory allocation/deallocation requests by allocating memory, in larger chunks known as segments, from the Windows virtual memory manager and maintaining bookkeeping data (such as look aside and free lists) that enable it to efficiently break up the larger chunks into smaller-sized allocations requested by the process. The CLR heap manager takes on similar responsibilities by being the one-stop shop for all memory allocations in a managed process. Similar to the Windows heap manager, it also uses the Windows virtual memory manager to allocate larger chunks of memory, also known as segments, and satisfies any memory allocation/deallocation requests from those segments. They key difference between the two heap managers is how the bookkeeping data is structured to maintain the integrity of the heap. Figure 5-2 shows a high-level overview of the CLR heap manager.

From Figure 5-2, you can see how the CLR heap manager uses carefully managed larger chunks (segments) to satisfy the memory requests. Also interesting to note from Figure 5-2 is the mode in which the CLR heap manager can operate.

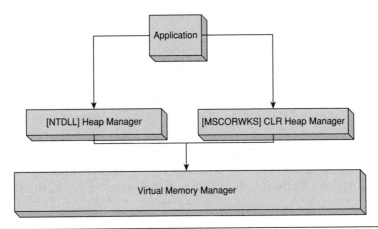

Figure 5-1 High-level overview of Windows memory architecture

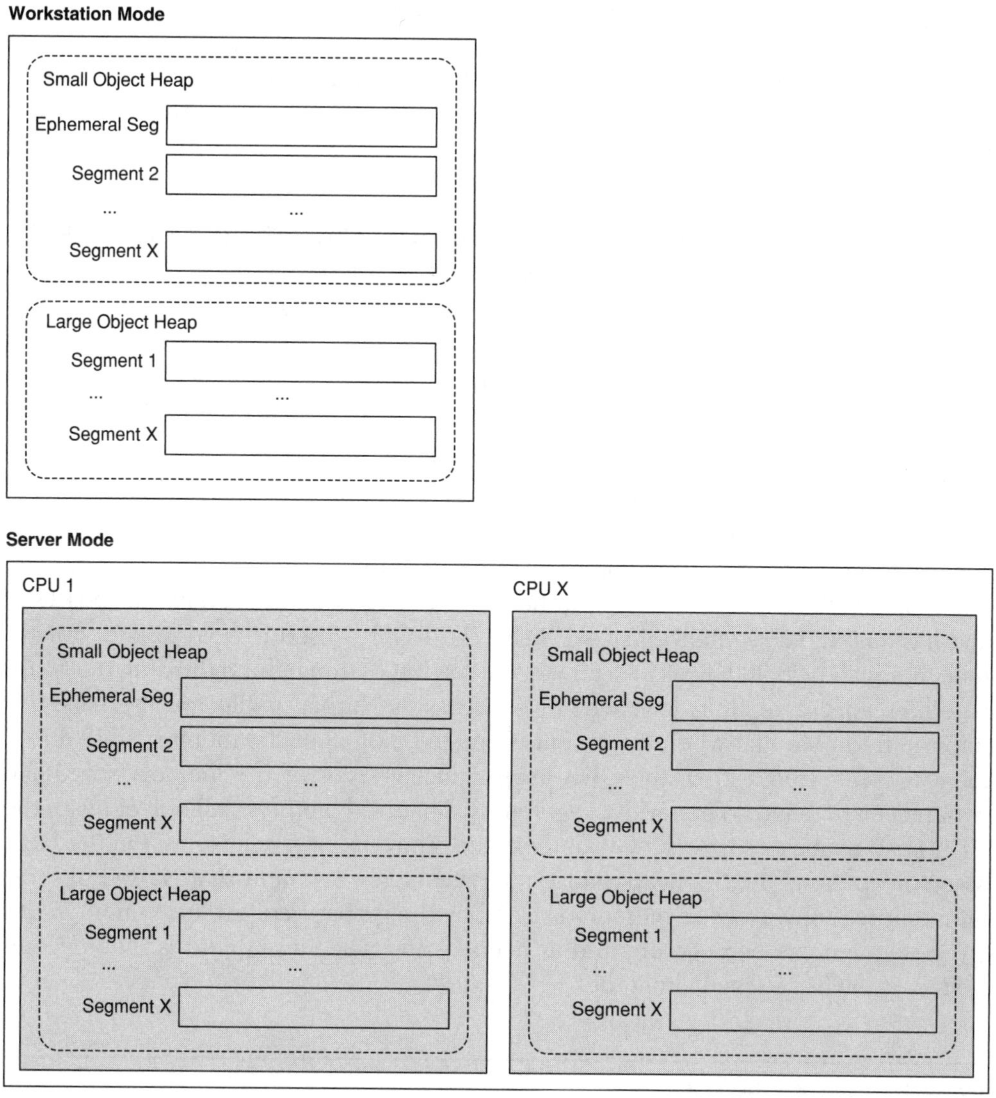

Workstation Mode

Small Object Heap

Ephemeral Seg

Segment 2

...   ...

Segment X

Large Object Heap

Segment 1

...   ...

Segment X

Server Mode

CPU 1

Small Object Heap

Ephemeral Seg

Segment 2

...   ...

Segment X

Large Object Heap

Segment 1

...   ...

Segment X

CPU X

Small Object Heap

Ephemeral Seg

Segment 2

...   ...

Segment X

Large Object Heap

Segment 1

...   ...

Segment X

Figure 5-2 High-level overview of the CLR heap manager

There are two modes of operation: workstation and server. As far as the *CLR heap manager* is concerned, the primary difference is that rather than having just one heap, there is now one heap per processor, where the size of the heap segments is typically larger than that of the workstation heap (although this is an implementation detail that should not be relied upon). From the GC's perspective, there are other fundamental differences between workstation and server primarily in the area of GC threading models, where the server flavor of the GC has a dedicated thread for all GC activity versus the workstation GC, which runs the GC process on the thread that performed the memory allocation.

ARE THE IMPLEMENTATIONS FOR WORKSTATION AND SERVER IN DIFFERENT BINARIES? Prior to version 2.0, the workstation GC was implemented in `mscorwks.dll` and the server GC was implemented in `mscorsvr.dll`. In version 2.0, the implementations were folded into one and the same binary (`mscorwks.dll`). Please note that this is purely a merge at the binary level.

Each managed process starts out with two heaps with their own respective segments that are initialized when the CLR is loaded. The first heap is known as the small object heap and has one initial segment of size 16MB on workstations (the server version is bigger). The small object heap is used to hold objects that are less than 85,000 bytes in size. The second heap is known as the large object heap (LOH) and has one initial segment of size 16MB. The LOH is used to hold objects greater than or equal to 85,000 bytes in size. We will see the reason behind dividing the heaps based on object size limits later when we discuss the garbage collector internals. It is important to note that when a segment is created, not all of the memory in that segment is committed; rather, the CLR heap manager reserves the memory space and commits on demand. Whenever a segment is exhausted on the small object heap, the CLR heap manager triggers a GC and expands the heap if space is low. On the large object heap, however, the heap manager creates a new segment that is used to serve up memory. Conversely, as memory is freed by the garbage collector, memory in any given segment can be decommitted as needed, and when a segment is fully decommitted, it might be freed altogether.

What's in an Address?

Given an address, is there a way to find out the state of that memory? That is, is the memory reserved? Is the memory committed? Is it writable or just readable? The `address` command is an excellent command to answer those questions. Without any arguments, the `address` command gives a detailed view of the memory activity in the process as well as a summary. If an address is specified, the `address` command attempts to find information about that particular address. For example, assume we have an object on the managed heap at address `0x01d96c58`. If we run the `address` command on this address, it shows the following:

```
0:000> !address 0x01d96c58
 ProcessParameters 004d1668 in range 004d0000 0050b000
 Environment 004d0808 in range 004d0000 0050b000
    01d90000 : 01d90000 - 00012000
                      Type      00020000 MEM_PRIVATE
                      Protect   00000004 PAGE_READWRITE
                      State     00001000 MEM_COMMIT
                      Usage     RegionUsageIsVAD
```

The address in question is an allocated and accessible memory location that is read/write enabled and committed.

As briefly mentioned in Chapter 2, "CLR Fundamentals," each object that resides on the managed heap carries with it some additional metadata. More specifically, each object is prefixed by an additional 8 bytes. Figure 5-3 shows an example of a small object heap segment.

In Figure 5-3, we can see that the first 4 bytes of any object located on the managed heap is the sync block index followed by an additional 4 bytes that indicate the method table pointer.

Allocating Memory

Now that we understand how the CLR heap manager, at a high level, structures the memory available to applications, we can take a look at how allocation requests are satisfied. We already know that the CLR heap manager consists of one or more

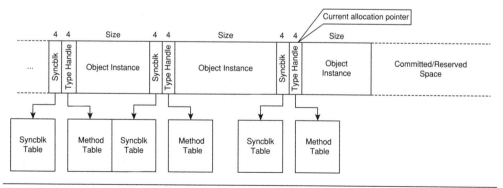

Figure 5-3   Example of a small object heap segment

segments and that memory allocations are allotted from one of the segments and returned to the caller. How is this memory allocation performed? Figure 5-4 illustrates the process that the CLR heap manager goes through when a memory allocation request arrives.

In the most optimal case, when a GC is not needed for the allocation to succeed, an allocation request is satisfied very efficiently. The two primary tasks performed in that scenario are those of simply advancing a pointer and clearing the memory region. The act of advancing the allocation pointer implies that new allocations are simply tacked on after the last allocated object in the segment. When another allocation request is satisfied, the allocation pointer is again advanced, and so forth. Please note that this allocation scheme is quite different than the Windows heap manager in the sense that the Windows heap manager does not guarantee

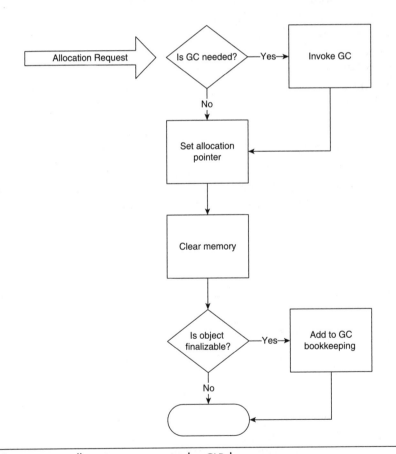

Figure 5-4 Memory allocation process in the CLR heap manager

locality of objects on the heap in the same fashion. An allocation request on the Windows heap manager can be satisfied from any given free block anywhere in the segment. The other scenario to consider is what happens when a GC is required due to breaching a memory threshold. In this case, a GC is performed and the allocation attempt is tried again. The last interesting aspect from Figure 5-4 is that of checking to see if the allocated object is finalizable. Although not, strictly speaking, a function of the managed heap, it is important to call out as it is part of the allocation process. If an object is finalizable, a record of it is stored in the GC to properly manage the lifetime of the object. We will discuss finalizable objects in more detail later in the chapter.

Before we move on and discuss the garbage collector internals, let's take a look at a very simple application that performs a memory allocation. The source code behind the application is shown in Listing 5-1.

Listing 5-1   Simple memory allocation

```
using System;
using System.Text;
using System.Runtime.Remoting;

namespace Advanced.NET.Debugging.Chapter5
{
    class Name
    {
        private string first;
        private string last;

        public string First { get { return first; } }
        public string Last { get { return last; } }

        public Name(string f, string l)
        {
            first = f; last = l;
        }
    }

    class SimpleAlloc
    {
        static void Main(string[] args)
```

(continues)

5. MANAGED HEAP AND GARBAGE COLLECTION

Listing 5-1 Simple memory allocation *(continued)*

```
    {
        Name name = null;

        Console.WriteLine("Press any key to allocate memory");
        Console.ReadKey();

        name = new Name("Mario", "Hewardt");

        Console.WriteLine("Press any key to exit");
        Console.ReadKey();
    }
  }
}
```

The source code and binary for Listing 5-1 can be found in the following folders:

- Source code: `C:\ADND\Chapter5\SimpleAlloc`
- Binary: `C:\ADNDBin\05SimpleAlloc.exe`

The source code in Listing 5-1 is painfully simple, but the more interesting question is, how do we find that particular memory allocation on the managed heap using the debuggers? Fortunately, the SOS debugger extension has a few handy commands that enable us to gain some insight into the contents of the managed heap. The command we will use in this particular example is the `DumpHeap` command. By default, the `DumpHeap` command lists all the objects that are stored on the managed heap together with their associated address, method table, and size. Let's run our `05SimpleAlloc.exe` application under the debugger and break execution when the `Press any key to allocate memory` prompt is shown. When execution breaks into the debugger, run the `DumpHeap` command. A partial listing of the output of the command is shown in the following:

```
0:004> !DumpHeap
  Address        MT      Size
790d8620   790fd0f0        12
790d862c   790fd8c4        28
790d8648   790fd8c4        32
790d8668   790fd8c4        32
790d8688   790fd8c4        28
790d86a4   790fd8c4        24
790d86bc   790fd8c4        24
...
...
...
```

```
total 2379 objects
Statistics:
      MT     Count    TotalSize  Class Name
79119954        1           12  System.Security.Permissions.ReflectionPermission
79119834        1           12  System.Security.Permissions.FileDialogPermission
791032a8        1          128  System.Globalization.NumberFormatInfo
79100e38        3          132  System.Security.FrameSecurityDescriptor
791028f4        2          136  System.Globalization.CultureInfo
791050b8        4          144  System.Security.Util.TokenBasedSet
790fe284        2          144  System.Threading.ThreadAbortException
79102290       13          156  System.Int32
790f97c4        3          156  System.Security.Policy.PolicyLevel
790ff734        9          180  System.RuntimeType
790ffb6c        3          192  System.IO.UnmanagedMemoryStream
7912d7c0       11          200  System.Int32[]
790fd0f0       17          204  System.Object
79119364        8          256  System.Collections.ArrayList+SyncArrayList
79101fe4        6          336  System.Collections.Hashtable
79100a18       10          360  System.Security.PermissionSet
79112d68       18          504
System.Collections.ArrayList+ArrayListEnumeratorSimple
79104368       21          504  System.Collections.ArrayList
7912d9bc        6          864  System.Collections.Hashtable+bucket[]
7912dae8        8         1700  System.Byte[]
7912dd40       14         2296  System.Char[]
7912d8f8       23        17604  System.Object[]
790fd8c4     2100       132680  System.String
Total 2379 objects
```

The output of the `DumpHeap` command is divided into two sections. The first section contains the entire list of objects located on the managed heap. The `DumpObject` command can be used on any of the listed objects to get further information about the object. The second section contains a statistical view of the managed heap activity by grouping related objects and displaying the method table, count, total size, and the object's type name. For example, the item

```
79100a18       10          360 System.Security.PermissionSet
```

indicates that the object in question is a `PermissionSet` with a method descriptor of `0x79100a18` and that there are `10` instances on the managed heap with a total size of `360` bytes. The statistical view can be very useful when trying to understand an excessively large managed heap and which objects may be causing the heap to grow.

The `DumpHeap` command produces quite a lot of output and it can be difficult to find a particular allocation in the midst of all of the output. Fortunately, the `DumpHeap` command has a variety of switches that makes life easier. For example, the –type and –mt switches enable you to search the managed heap for a given type name or a method table address. If we run the DumpHeap command with the –type switch looking for the allocation our application makes, we get the following:

```
0:003> !DumpHeap -type Advanced.NET.Debugging.Chapter5.Name
 Address       MT      Size
total 0 objects
Statistics:
      MT     Count    TotalSize Class Name
Total 0 objects
```

The output clearly indicates that there are no allocations on the managed heap of the given type. Of course, this makes perfect sense because our sample application has not performed its allocation. Resume execution of the application until you see the **Press any key to exit** prompt. Again, break execution and run the DumpHeap command again with the –type switch:

```
0:004> !DumpHeap -type Advanced.NET.Debugging.Chapter5.Name
Address       MT      Size
01ca6c7c 002030cc     16
total 1 objects
Statistics:
      MT     Count    TotalSize Class Name
002030cc       1            16 Advanced.NET.Debugging.Chapter5.Name
Total 1 objects
```

This time, we can see that we have an instance of our type on the managed heap. The output follows the same structure as the default DumpHeap output by first showing the instance specific data (address, method table, and size) followed by the statistical view, which shows the managed heap only having one instance of our type.

The DumpHeap command has several other useful switches depending on the debugging scenario at hand. Table 5-1 details the switches available.

This concludes our high-level discussion of the Windows memory architecture and how the CLR heap manager fits in. We've looked at how the CLR heap manager organizes memory to provide an efficient memory management scheme as well as the process that the CLR heap manager goes through when a memory allocation request arrives at its doorstep. The next big question is how the GC itself functions, its relationship to the CLR heap manager, and how memory is freed after it has been considered discarded.

Table 5-1   DumpHeap Switches

Switch	Description
-stat	Limits output to managed heap statistics
-strings	Limits output to strings stored on the managed heap
-short	Limits output to just the address of the objects on the managed heap
-min	Filters based on the minimum object size specified
-max	Filters based on the maximum object size specified
-thinlock	Outputs objects with associated thinlocks
-startAtLowerBound	Begin walking the heap at a lower bound
-mt	Limit output to the specified method table
-type	Limit output to the specified type name (substring match)

ARE THERE OTHER TYPES OF CLR HEAPS? In addition to the CLR heap, which is the heap typically used during "day-to-day" memory allocations, there are other types of heaps. For example, when the JIT compiler translates IL to machine code, it uses its own heap. Another example is the CLR loader, which utilizes yet another heap. The internals of these heaps are for the most part undocumented and typically not traversed (outside of SOS) during a debug session.

Garbage Collector Internals

The CLR GC is a highly efficient, scalable, and reliable automatic memory manager. Much time and effort went into researching the optimal behavioral characteristics of the GC. Before delving into the details of the CLR GC, it is important to state the definition of what the GC is and also what assumptions were made during its design and implementation. Let's begin by looking at some of the key assumptions.

- The CLR GC assumes that everything is garbage unless otherwise told. This means that the GC is ready to collect *all* objects on the managed heap unless told otherwise. In essence, it implements a *reference tracking* scheme for all live objects in the system (we will define what live means shortly) where objects without any references to them are considered garbage and can be collected.
- The CLR GC assumes that all objects on the managed heap will be *short lived (or ephemeral)*. In other words, the GC attempts to collect short-lived objects more often than long-lived objects operating under the assumption that if an object has been around for a while, chances are it will be around for a little longer and there is no need to attempt to collect that object again.
- The CLR GC tracks an object's age via the use of generations. Young objects are placed in generation 0 and older objects in generations 1 and 2. As an object grows older, it is promoted from one generation to the next. As such, a generation can be said to define the age of an object.

Based upon the assumptions above, we can arrive at a definition of the CLR GC: It is a *reference tracking* and *generational* garbage collector.

Let's look at each of the parts of the definition more concretely and begin with how generations define the age of an object.

Generations

The CLR GC defines three generations very innovatively called generation 0, generation 1, and generation 2. Each of the generations contains objects of a certain age where generation 0 contains newly allocated objects and generation 2 contains the oldest of objects. An object moves from one generation to the next by surviving a garbage collection. By surviving, it's implied that the object was still being referenced (or is still rooted) at the time of the garbage collection. Each of the generations can be garbage collected at any time, but the frequency of garbage collections depend on the generation. Remember from the previous section that one of the assumptions that the CLR makes is that most objects are going to be short-lived (i.e., live in generation 0). Due to that assumption, generation 0 is collected far more frequently than generation 2 in hopes to prune these short-lived objects quicker. Figure 5-5 shows the overall algorithm when it comes to how the generations are garbage collected.

In Figure 5-5, we can see that the triggering of a garbage collection is by new allocation request and when the budget for generation 0 has been exceeded. If so, the garbage collector collects all objects that have no roots associated with them and promotes all objects *with* roots to generation 1. Much in the same way that generation 0 has a budget defined, so does generation 1; and if, as part of promoting objects from generation 0 to generation 1, the budget is exceeded, the GC repeats the process of

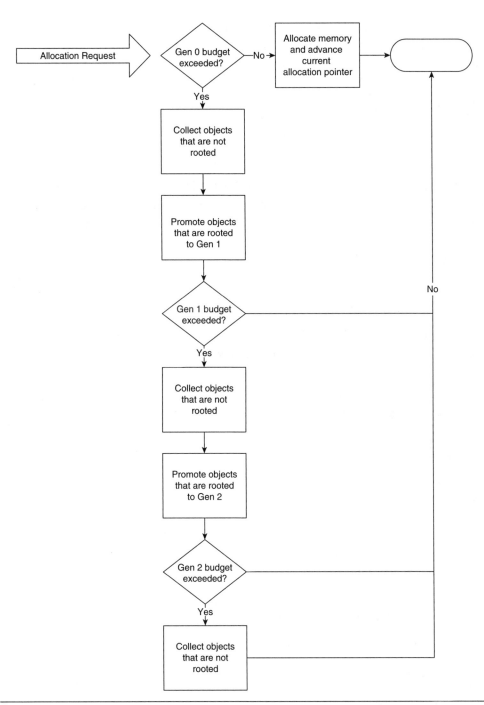

Figure 5-5 High-level overview of generational garbage collection algorithm

collecting objects with no roots in generation 1 and promoting objects with roots to generation 2. The process repeats itself for generation 2. If, while promoting to generation 2, the GC cannot collect any objects and the budget for generation 2 is exceeded, the CLR heap manager tries to allocate another segment that will hold generation 2 objects. If the creation of a new segment fails, an `OutOfMemoryException` is thrown. The CLR heap manager also releases segments if they are not in use anymore; we will discuss this process in more detail later in the chapter.

WHAT ELSE CAN TRIGGER A GARBAGE COLLECTION? In addition to a garbage collection occurring due to the allocation of memory and exceeding the thresholds for generation 0, 1, and 2, respectively, a couple of other scenarios exist that can cause it to happen. First, a garbage collection can be forced via the `GC.Collect` and related APIs. Secondly, the garbage collector is very cognizant of memory usage in the system as a whole. Through careful collaboration with the operating system, the garbage collector can kick start a collection if the system as a whole is found to be under extreme memory pressure.

Let's take a practical look at how an object is collected and promoted. Listing 5-2 shows the source code behind the application we will use to illustrate the generational concepts.

Listing 5-2 Example source code to illustrate generational concepts

```
using System;
using System.Text;
using System.Runtime.Remoting;

namespace Advanced.NET.Debugging.Chapter5
{
    class Name
    {
        private string first;
        private string last;

        public string First { get { return first; } }
        public string Last { get { return last; } }

        public Name(string f, string l)
        {
            first = f; last = l;
        }
    }
```

```
class Gen
{
    static void Main(string[] args)
    {
        Name n1 = new Name("Mario", "Hewardt");
        Name n2 = new Name("Gemma", "Hewardt");

        Console.WriteLine("Allocated objects");

        Console.WriteLine("Press any key to invoke GC");
        Console.ReadKey();

        n1 = null;
        GC.Collect();

        Console.WriteLine("Press any key to invoke GC");
        Console.ReadKey();

        GC.Collect();

        Console.WriteLine("Press any key to exit");
        Console.ReadKey();
    }
}
```

The source code and binary for Listing 5-2 can be found in the following folders:

- Source code: `C:\ADND\Chapter5\Gen`
- Binary: `C:\ADNDBin\05Gen.exe`

In Listing 5-2, we have defined a simple type called `Name`. In the `Main` method, we instantiate two instances of the `Name` type, both of which end up going to generation 0 as new allocations. When the user has been prompted to `Press any key to invoke GC`, we set the `n1` instance to `null`, which indicates that it can be garbage collected because it no longer has any roots. Next, the garbage collection occurs and collects `n1` and promotes `n2` to generation 1. Finally, the last garbage collection promotes `n2` to generation 2 because it is still rooted.

Let's run the application under the debugger and see how we can verify our theories on how `n1` and `n2` are collected and promoted. When the application is running under the debugger, resume execution until the first `Press any key to invoke GC` prompt. At that point, we need to break execution and find the addresses to the two object instances, which can easily be done via the `ClrStack` command as shown in the following:

```
0:000> !ClrStack -a
OS Thread Id: 0x1c0c (0)
ESP        EIP
0028f3b4 77709a94 [NDirectMethodFrameSlim: 0028f3b4]
 Microsoft.Win32.Win32Native.ReadConsoleInput(IntPtr, InputRecord ByRef, Int32,
Int32 ByRef)
0028f3cc 793e8f28 System.Console.ReadKey(Boolean)
    PARAMETERS:
        intercept = 0x00000000
    LOCALS:
        <no data>
        0x0028f3dc = 0x00000001
        <no data>
        <no data>
        <no data>
        <no data>
        <no data>
        <no data>
        <no data>

0028f40c 793e8e33 System.Console.ReadKey()
0028f410 003000f3 Advanced.NET.Debugging.Chapter5.Gen.Main(System.String[])
    PARAMETERS:
        args = 0x01c55818
    LOCALS:
        <CLR reg> = 0x01da5938
        <CLR reg> = 0x01da5948

0028f65c 79e7c74b [GCFrame: 0028f65c]
```

The addresses of the two objects on the managed heap are `0x01da5938` and `0x01da5948`. How can we figure out which generation objects on the managed heap belong to? The answer to that lies in understanding the correlation between managed heap segments and generations. As previously discussed, each managed heap consists of one or more segments where the objects reside. Furthermore, part of the segment(s) is dedicated to a given generation. Figure 5-6 shows an example of a hypothetical managed heap segment.

In Figure 5-6, the managed heap segment is divided into three generations, each with its own starting address managed by the CLR heap manager. Generations 0 and 1 are part of a single segment known as the ephemeral segment where short-lived objects live. Because the GC goes under the assumption that most objects are short

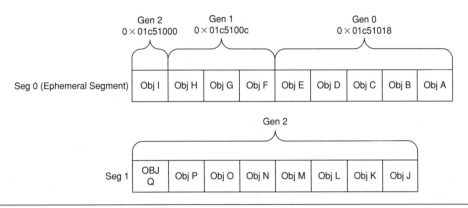

Figure 5-6 Hypothetical managed heap segment

lived, most objects are not expected to live past generation 0 or, at a maximum, generation 1. Objects that live in generation 2 are the oldest objects and get collected very infrequently. It is possible that generation 2 can also be part of the ephemeral segment even though generation 2 is not collected as often. By looking at an object's address and knowing the address ranges for each of the generations, we can find out which generation an object belongs to. How do we know what the generational starting addresses for the CLR heap manager are? The answer lies in a command called `eeheap`. The `eeheap` command displays various memory statistics of data consumed by internal CLR data structures. By default, `eeheap` displays verbose data, meaning that information related to the GC as well as the loader is displayed. To display information only about the GC, the `-gc` switch can be used. Let's run the command in our existing debug session and see what we get:

```
0:004> !eeheap -gc
Number of GC Heaps: 1
generation 0 starts at 0x01da1018
generation 1 starts at 0x01da100c
generation 2 starts at 0x01da1000
ephemeral segment allocation context: none
 segment     begin allocated      size
002c7db0 790d8620  790f7d8c 0x0001f76c(128876)
01da0000 01da1000  01da8010 0x00007010(28688)
Large object heap starts at 0x02da1000
 segment     begin allocated      size
02da0000 02da1000  02da3250 0x00002250(8784)
Total Size    0x289cc(166348)
```

```
GC Heap Size    0x289cc(166348)
```

Part of the output shows clearly the starting addresses of each of the generations. If we look at the object addresses in the debug session of our sample application, we can see the following:

```
<CLR reg> = 0x01da5938
<CLR reg> = 0x01da5948
```

Both of these addresses corresponding to our objects fall within the address range of generation 0 (starting at `0x01da1018`), hence we can conclude that both of them live within the realm of that generation. This makes perfect sense because we are currently in the code flow where the objects were just allocated and we are pending a garbage collection. If we resume execution of the application and subsequently break execution again the next time we see the `Press any key to invoke GC`, we should see some difference in which generation the objects belong to. If we look at the source code, we can see that prior to invoking a garbage collection, we set the `n1` reference to `null`, which in essence makes the object rootless and one that should be garbage collected. Furthermore, `n2` is still rooted and as such should be promoted to generation 1 during the garbage collection. Let's take a look by following the same process as earlier: find the object addresses, use the `eeheap` command to find the generational address ranges, and see which generation the object falls into:

```
0:000> !ClrStack -a
OS Thread Id: 0x1910 (0)
ESP       EIP
0021f394 77709a94 [NDirectMethodFrameSlim: 0021f394]
 Microsoft.Win32.Win32Native.ReadConsoleInput(IntPtr, InputRecord
ByRef, Int32, Int32 ByRef)
0021f3ac 793e8f28 System.Console.ReadKey(Boolean)
    PARAMETERS:
        intercept = 0x00000000
    LOCALS:
        <no data>
        0x0021f3bc = 0x00000001
        <no data>
        <no data>
        <no data>
        <no data>
        <no data>
        <no data>
        <no data>
        <no data>
```

```
0021f3ec 793e8e33 System.Console.ReadKey()
0021f3f0 01690111 Advanced.NET.Debugging.Chapter5.Gen.Main(System.String[])
    PARAMETERS:
        args = 0x01da5818
    LOCALS:
        <CLR reg> = 0x00000000
        <CLR reg> = 0x01da5948


0021f644 79e7c74b [GCFrame: 0021f644]
0:000> !eeheap -gc
Number of GC Heaps: 1
generation 0 starts at 0x01da6c00
generation 1 starts at 0x01da100c
generation 2 starts at 0x01da1000
ephemeral segment allocation context: none
 segment    begin allocated     size
002c7db0 790d8620  790f7d8c 0x0001f76c(128876)
01da0000 01da1000  01da8c0c 0x00007c0c(31756)
Large object heap starts at 0x02da1000
 segment    begin allocated     size
02da0000 02da1000  02da3240 0x00002240(8768)
Total Size    0x295b8(169400)
```

```
GC Heap Size    0x295b8(169400)
```

The most interesting part of the output is in the **eeheap** command output. We can see now that the generational address ranges have changed slightly. More specifically, the starting address of generation 0 has changed from `0x01da1018` to `0x01da6c00`, which in essence implies that generation 1 has become bigger (because the starting address of generation 1 remains unchanged). If we correlate the address of our **n2** object (`0x01da5948`) with the generational address ranges that the **eeheap** command displayed, we can see that the **n2** object falls into generation 1. Again, this is fully expected because **n2** previously lived in generation 0 and was still rooted at the time of the garbage collection, thereby promoting the object to the next generation. I will leave it as an exercise to you to see what happens on the final garbage collection in the sample application.

Although the SOS debugger extension provides the means of finding out which generation any given object belongs to, it is a somewhat tedious process as it requires that addresses be checked against potentially changing generational addresses within any given managed heap segment. Furthermore, there is no concrete way to list all the objects that fall into any given generation, making it hard to get an overall picture of the per generation utilization. Fortunately, the SOSEX extension comes to the rescue with a command named dumpgen. With the dumpgen command, you can easily get a list of all objects that belong to the generation specified as an argument to the command. For example, using the same sample application as shown in Listing 5-2, here is the output when running dumpgen:

```
0:000> !dumpgen 0
01da6c00           12 **** FREE ****
01da6c0c           68 System.Char[]
2 objects, 80 bytes
0:000> !dumpgen 1
01da100c           12 **** FREE ****
01da1018           12 **** FREE ****
01da1024           72 System.OutOfMemoryException
01da106c           72 System.StackOverflowException
01da10b4           72 System.ExecutionEngineException
01da10fc           72 System.Threading.ThreadAbortException
01da1144           72 System.Threading.ThreadAbortException
01da118c           12 System.Object
01da1198           28 System.SharedStatics
01da11b4          100 System.AppDomain
...
...
...
01da5948           16 Advanced.NET.Debugging.Chapter5.Name
01da5958           28 Microsoft.Win32.Win32Native+InputRecord
01da5974           12 System.Object
01da5980           20 Microsoft.Win32.SafeHandles.SafeFileHandle
01da5994           36 System.IO.__ConsoleStream
01da59b8           28 System.IO.Stream+NullStream
...
...
...
```

We can see that there aren't a lot of objects in generation 0; instead, we have a ton of objects in generation 1 including our n2 instance at address 0x01da5948. The dumpgen command really makes life easier when looking at generation specific data.

What About GC.Collect()?

As you have seen, the source code in Listing 5-2 (as well as throughout the chapter) contains calls to GC.Collect(). The GC.Collect() API does pretty much what the name implies. It forces a garbage collection to occur irrespective of whether it is needed. The last part of the previous statement is extremely important: *irrespective of whether it is needed*. The GC continuously fine tunes itself throughout the execution of the application to ensure that it behaves optimally under the application's circumstances. By invoking `GC.Collect()`, and thereby forcing a garbage collection, it can wreak havoc with the GC's fine-tuning algorithm. Under normal circumstances, it is therefore *highly* recommended not to use the API. The usage of the API in the book is solely to make the examples more deterministic.

So far, we have discussed how objects live in managed heap segments divided into generations and how these objects are either garbage collected or promoted to the next generation, depending on if they are still referenced (or still rooted). One question that still remains is what it means for an object to be rooted. The next section introduces the notion of roots, which are at the heart of the decision-making process the GC uses to determine if an object can be collected.

Roots

One of the most fundamental aspects of a garbage collection is that of being able to determine which objects are still being referenced and which objects are not and can be considered for garbage collection. Contrary to popular belief, the GC itself does not implement the logic for detecting which objects are still being referenced; rather, it uses other components in the CLR that have far more knowledge about the lifetimes of the objects. The CLR uses the following components to determine which objects are still referenced:

- Just In Time compiler. The JIT compiler is the component responsible for translating IL to machine code and has detailed knowledge of which local variables were considered active at any given point in time. The JIT compiler maintains this information in a table that it subsequently references when the GC asks for objects that are still considered to be alive.

RETAIL VERSUS DEBUG BUILDS Please note that there *can* be a difference between retail and debug builds when it comes to the JIT compiler tracking the aliveness of local variables. In retail builds, the JIT compiler can get rather aggressive and consider a local variable dead even before it goes out of scope (assuming it is not being used). This can present some really interesting challenges when debugging, and the decision was therefore made to keep all local variables alive until the end of the scope in debug builds.

- Stack walker. This comes into play when unmanaged calls are made to the execution engine. During these calls, it is imperative that any managed objects used during the call also be part of the reference tracking system.
- Handle table. The CLR maintains a set of handle tables on a per application domain basis that can contain, for example, pointers to pinned reference types on the managed heap. During a GC inquiry, these handle tables are probed for live references to objects on the managed heap.
- Finalize queue. We will discuss the notion of object finalizers shortly, but for the time being, view objects with finalizers as objects that can be considered dead from an application's perspective but still need to be kept alive for cleanup purposes.
- If the object is a member of any of the above categories.

During the probing phase, the GC also marks all the objects according to their state (rooted). When all components have been probed, the GC goes ahead and starts the garbage collection of all objects by promoting all objects that are still considered rooted. An interesting question in regards to roots is, Given an address to an object on the managed heap, is it possible to see if the object is rooted or not; and if so, what the reference chain of object is? Again, we turn to the SOS extension and a command named `gcroot`. The `gcroot` command uses a technique similar to the earlier one utilized by the GC to find the aliveness of the object. Let's take a look at some sample code. Listing 5-3 shows the source code of an application that defines a set of types and references to those types at various scopes.

Listing 5-3   Sample application to illustrate object roots

```
using System;
using System.Text;
using System.Threading;

namespace Advanced.NET.Debugging.Chapter5
{
    class Name
    {
        private string first;
        private string last;

        public string First { get { return first; } }
        public string Last { get { return last; } }

        public Name(string f, string l)
```

```
        {
            first = f; last = l;
        }
    }

    class Roots
    {
        public static Name CompleteName = new Name ("First", "Last");

        private Thread thread;
        private bool shouldExit;

        static void Main(string[] args)
        {
            Roots r = new Roots();
            r.Run();
        }

        public void Run()
        {
            shouldExit = false;

            Name n1 = CompleteName;

            thread = new Thread(this.Worker);
            thread.Start(n1);

            Thread.Sleep(1000);

            Console.WriteLine("Press any key to exit");
            Console.ReadKey();

            shouldExit = true;

        }

        public void Worker(Object o)
        {
            Name n1 = (Name)o;
            Console.WriteLine("Thread started {0}, {1}",
                            n1.First,
                            n1.Last);

            while (true)
            {
                // Do work
```

(continues)

Listing 5-3 Sample application to illustrate object roots *(continued)*

```
            Thread.Sleep(500);
            if (shouldExit)
                break;
        }
    }
}
}
```

The source code and binary for Listing 5-3 can be found in the following folders:

- Source code: `C:\ADND\Chapter5\Roots`
- Binary: `C:\ADNDBin\05Roots.exe`

The source code in Listing 5-3 declares a static instance of the `Name` type. The main part of the application declares a reference to the static instance in the `Run` method as well as starts up a thread passing the reference to the newly created thread. The method that the new thread executes uses the reference passed to it until the user hits any key, at which point both the worker thread and the application terminate. The object we are interested in tracking for this exercise is the `CompleteName` static field. From the source code, we can glean the following characteristics about `CompleteName`:

- We have a static reference to the object instance at the `Roots` class level serving as our first root to the object.
- In the `Run` method, we assign a local variable reference (`n1`) to the object instance serving as our second root. The `n1` local variable is not used after the thread has started and is subject to becoming invalid even before the end of the method scope (in retail builds). In debug builds, the reference is guaranteed to remain valid until the end of the scope is reached.
- In the `Run` method, we pass the local variable reference `n1` to the thread method during thread startup serving as our third root.

Let's run the application under the debugger and manually break execution when the `Press any key to exit` prompt is displayed. The first thing we need to find is the address to the object we are interested in (and dumping the object for good measure) followed by running the `gcroot` command on the address:

```
0:005> ~0s
eax=002cef9c ebx=002cef94 ecx=792274ec edx=79ec9058 esi=002cedf0 edi=00000000
eip=77709a94 esp=002ceda0 ebp=002cedc0 iopl=0        nv up ei pl zr na pe nc
cs=001b ss=0023 ds=0023 es=0023 fs=003b gs=0000              efl=00000246
ntdll!KiFastSystemCallRet:
77709a94 c3                  ret
0:000> !ClrStack -a
OS Thread Id: 0x2358 (0)
ESP       EIP
002cef6c 77709a94 [NDirectMethodFrameSlim: 002cef6c]
 Microsoft.Win32.Win32Native.ReadConsoleInput(IntPtr, InputRecord ByRef, Int32,
Int32 ByRef)
002cef84 793e8f28 System.Console.ReadKey(Boolean)
    PARAMETERS:
        intercept = 0x00000000
    LOCALS:
        <no data>
        0x002cef94 = 0x00000001
        <no data>
        <no data>
        <no data>
        <no data>
        <no data>
        <no data>
        <no data>
        <no data>

002cefc4 793e8e33 System.Console.ReadKey()
002cefc8 00890212 Advanced.NET.Debugging.Chapter5.Roots.Run()
    PARAMETERS:
        this = 0x01c758e0
    LOCALS:
        <CLR reg> = 0x01c758d0

002cefe8 0089013f Advanced.NET.Debugging.Chapter5.Roots.Main(System.String[])
    PARAMETERS:
        args = 0x01c75888
    LOCALS:
        <CLR reg> = 0x01c758e0

002cf208 79e7c74b [GCFrame: 002cf208]
0:000> !do 0x01c758d0
Name: Advanced.NET.Debugging.Chapter5.Name
MethodTable: 001b311c
```

```
EEClass: 001b13a0
Size: 16(0x10) bytes
 (C:\ADNDBin\05Roots.exe)
Fields:
        MT    Field   Offset         Type VT    Attr    Value Name
790fd8c4 4000001       4      System.String  0 instance 01c75898 first
790fd8c4 4000002       8      System.String  0 instance 01c758b4 last
0:000> !gcroot 0x01c758d0
Note: Roots found on stacks may be false positives. Run "!help gcroot" for
more info.
Scan Thread 0 OSTHread 2358
ESP:2cefbc:Root:01c758d0(Advanced.NET.Debugging.Chapter5.Name)
Scan Thread 1 OSTHread 1630
Scan Thread 3 OSTHread 254c
ESP:47df428:Root:01c758d0(Advanced.NET.Debugging.Chapter5.Name)
ESP:47df42c:Root:01c758d0(Advanced.NET.Debugging.Chapter5.Name)
ESP:47df438:Root:01c758d0(Advanced.NET.Debugging.Chapter5.Name)
ESP:47df4d0:Root:01c75984(System.Threading.ThreadHelper)->
01c758d0(Advanced.NET.Debugging.Chapter5.Name)
ESP:47df4d8:Root:01c75984(System.Threading.ThreadHelper)->
01c758d0(Advanced.NET.Debugging.Chapter5.Name)
ESP:47df4f4:Root:01c75984(System.Threading.ThreadHelper)->
01c758d0(Advanced.NET.Debugging.Chapter5.Name)
ESP:47df500:Root:01c75984(System.Threading.ThreadHelper)->
01c758d0(Advanced.NET.Debugging.Chapter5.Name)
ESP:47df5c0:Root:01c758d0(Advanced.NET.Debugging.Chapter5.Name)->
01c758d0(Advanced.NET.Debugging.Chapter5.Name)
ESP:47df5c4:Root:01c75998(System.Threading.ParameterizedThreadStart)->
01c75984(System.Threading.ThreadHelper)
ESP:47df754:Root:01c758d0(Advanced.NET.Debugging.Chapter5.Name)->
01c75984(System.Threading.ThreadHelper)
ESP:47df758:Root:01c75998(System.Threading.ParameterizedThreadStart)->
01c75984(System.Threading.ThreadHelper)
ESP:47df764:Root:01c75998(System.Threading.ParameterizedThreadStart)->
01c75984(System.Threading.ThreadHelper)
ESP:47df76c:Root:01c758d0(Advanced.NET.Debugging.Chapter5.Name)->
01c75984(System.Threading.ThreadHelper)
DOMAIN(0037FCF8):HANDLE(Pinned):a13fc:Root:02c71010(System.Object[])->
01c758d0(Advanced.NET.Debugging.Chapter5.Name)
```

As you can see from the `gcroot` output, the command scans a number of
different sources to find and build the reference chain to the object specified.
Regardless of the source, the output of the `GCRoot` command results in the
following general format:

```
<root>-><reference 1>-><reference 2>-><reference X>-><object>
```

Depending on the source probed, each of the elements takes on a slightly different format as shown.

- Local variables on a threads stack. The `root` element typically looks like the following: `<stack register>:<stack pointer>:Root:<object>`. The `stack register` depends on the architecture. For example, on x86 machines it shows as `ESP` and on x64 machines it shows as `RSP`. The `stack pointer` shows the location on the stack where the object is rooted, and the `object address` is the address of the object that is holding a reference to the next object in the reference chain. Let's take a look at an example:

```
ESP:47df428:Root:01c758d0(Advanced.NET.Debugging.Chapter5.Name)
```

We can see that there is a local variable located on stack (`ESP`) location `0x047df428`. Furthermore, the output tells us that this constitutes a root to the object at address `0x01c758d0`, which is a reference to the `Advanced.NET.Debugging.Chapter5.Name` type.

- Handle tables. All handle tables are scanned as part of `GCRoot` execution looking for references to the specified object. If a reference is found, the output of the command takes on the following general syntax: `DOMAIN(<address>):HANDLE(<type>):<handleaddress>:Root:<object>`. The `domain address` field indicates the address of the application domain to which the handle reference belongs. The `handle type` specifies the type of the handle. The possible handle types are Weak, WeakTrac Resurrection, Normal, and Pinned.

    Next is the `handle address`, which is the address to the handle itself. Please keep in mind that the handle type is a value type and if you want to dump out the contents you must use the `DumpVC` command rather than `DumpObj`. Finally, the `root object` address is shown. Let's take a look at an example:

```
DOMAIN(002EFCD8):HANDLE(Pinned):2813fc:Root:02c81010
(System.Object[])->01c858d0(Advanced.NET.Debugging.
Chapter5.Name)
```

The preceding output indicates that the object at address `0x01c858d0` is rooted by an object that resides in the handle table corresponding to the application domain with address `0x002efcd8`. Furthermore, the address of the handle value holding the reference is located at address `0x002813fc` and the type of the handle value is pinned. Lastly, the actual object that holds the reference is at address `0x02c81010`, which is of type `System.Object[]`.

■ F-reachable queue. The f-reachable queue is scanned to see if there are any references to the specified object. If a root reference to the object is found on the f-reachable queue, it will be displayed in the following general format: `Finalizer queue:Root:<object address>(<object type>)`. The first part of the output indicates that the source of the root is the f-reachable queue. Next, the address of the referenced object is displayed, followed by the object type. What follows is an example of the output of `GCRoot` when run against an object that is on the f-reachable queue:

```
Finalizer
queue:Root:01d15750(Advanced.NET.Debugging.Chapter5.Name)
```

In the preceding output, we can see that the object at address `0x01d15750` of type `Advanced.NET.Debugging.Chapter5.Name` is rooted by the f-reachable queue.

■ The last source of output for the `GCRoot` command is if an object is a member of any of the preceding categories.

One of the potential problems with `gcroot` and local variables is that it may not always be accurate, thereby producing false positives. To convince ourselves that the stack locations listed in the output are accurate, we have to manually inspect the stack location and correlate it to source code so that we can see whether the local variable is in fact still referencing the object. For example, assume we have the following very simple function:

```
public void Run()
{
    Name n1 = new Name("A", "B");

    Console.WriteLine("Press any key to exit");
    Console.ReadKey();
}
```

In the source code, we have a simple instance of the Name class assigned to the `n1` local variable. If we ran the `GCRoot` command on the `n1` reference, we would expect to only see one reference on the thread stack:

```
0:000> !GCRoot 0x01e9580c
Note: Roots found on stacks may be false positives. Run "!help gcroot" for
more info.
Scan Thread 0 OSTHread 1638
ESP:1df29c:Root:01e9580c(Advanced.NET.Debugging.Chapter5.Name)
ESP:1df2a0:Root:01e9580c(Advanced.NET.Debugging.Chapter5.Name)
Scan Thread 2 OSTHread 14ac
```

The output clearly shows that thread 0 apparently has two references to the object on the thread stack. How is this possible? The way that the GCRoot command works is by assuming that *every* address on the stack is an address to an object. It tries to verify this assumption by utilizing various metadata information. In light of this, objects that are (or were) previously present on the stack are treated as first class references to those objects and listed in the output of GCRoot. If you suspect that the output of GCRoot, in as far as thread stacks is concerned, is incorrect, the best approach is to use the U command to unassemble the stack frames and correlate the stack registers in the GCRoots output to the unassembled code to see which objects are truly valid.

Finalization

The garbage collection mechanism described so far assumes that objects that are collected do not require any special cleanup code. At times, objects that encapsulate other resources require that these resources be cleaned up as part of object destruction. A great example is an object that wraps an underlying native resource such as a file handle. Without explicit cleanup code, the memory behind the managed object is cleaned up by the GC, but the underlying handle that the object encapsulates is not (because GC has no special knowledge of native handles). The net result is naturally a resource leak. To provide a proper cleanup mechanism, the CLR introduces what is known as finalizers. A finalizer can be compared to destructors in the native C++ world. Whenever an object is freed (or garbage collected), the destructor (or finalizer) is run. In C#, a finalizer is declared very similarly to a C++ destructor by using the ~<class name>() notation. An example is shown in the following listing:

```
public class MyClass
{
    …
    …
    …
    ~MyClass()
    {
        // Cleanup code
    }
}
```

When the class is compiled into IL, the finalize method gets translated into a function called `Finalize`. The key thing about objects with finalizers is that the garbage collector treats them a little differently than other objects. Because the garbage collector is in fact an *automatic* memory manager, it also has the responsibility of executing all finalization code that an object may have during a garbage collection. To keep tabs on which objects have finalizers, the garbage collector maintains a queue called a finalization queue. Objects that are created on the managed heap and contain finalizers are automatically placed on the finalization queue during creation. Please note that the finalization queue does *not* contain objects that are considered garbage, but rather it contains all objects with finalizers that are alive on the managed heap. When an object with a finalizer becomes rootless and a garbage collection occurs, the GC places the object on a different queue known as the f-reachable queue. This queue contains all objects with defined finalizers that are considered to be garbage and need to have their finalizers executed. All objects on the f-reachable queue are considered roots to those objects, meaning that the object is still alive. It is important to note that the finalizer code for each of the objects on the f-reachable queue is not executed as part of the garbage collection phase. Instead, each .NET process contains a special thread known as the finalization thread. The finalization thread wakes up, on request of the GC, and checks the state of the f-reachable queue. If there are any objects on the f-reachable queue, the finalization thread picks them up one by one and executes the finalize methods.

WHY NOT EXECUTE THE FINALIZE METHODS AS PART OF THE GARBAGE COLLECTION? Because finalize methods contain managed code and during a GC managed code threads are suspended, the finalizer thread runs outside of the boundary of the GC.

When the garbage collection finishes, objects with finalizers are on the f-reachable queue (rooted and alive) until the finalization thread executes the finalize methods. At that point, the object is removed from the f-reachable queue, is considered rootless, and can be truly reclaimed by the garbage collector. The next time a garbage collection is started, the objects are collected. Figure 5-7 illustrates an example of the finalization process.

Step 1 in Figure 5-7 consists of allocating Obj D and Obj E, both of which contain finalize methods. As part of the allocation, the objects are placed on the managed heap as well as on the finalization queue to indicate that the objects need to be finalized when no longer in use. In step 2, Obj D and Obj E have both become rootless when a garbage collection occurs. At that point, both objects are moved from the finalization queue to the f-reachable queue to indicate that the finalize methods are

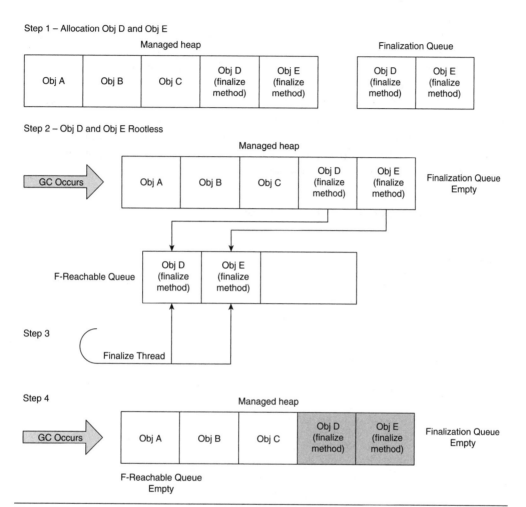

Figure 5-7   Example of finalization process

now ready to be run. At some point in the future (nondeterministic), step 3 is executed and the finalizer thread wakes up and starts running the finalize methods for both of the objects. Even after the finalizer has finished, both objects are still rooted on the f-reachable queue. Lastly, in step 4, another garbage collection occurs and the objects are removed from the f-reachable queue (no longer rooted) and then collected from the managed heap by the garbage collector.

An interesting aspect of having a dedicated thread executing the finalize methods is that the CLR does not place any guarantees when the thread wakes up and executes. As such, it is possible that it will take some time before an object with a finalizer is actually cleaned up. When dealing with objects that aggregate scarce resources, it may not always be feasible to wait for a long period of time for the resource to be reclaimed. In such situations, it is best to implement an explicit and deterministic cleanup pattern such as the `IDisposable` and/or `Close` patterns. Finally, having a dedicated thread also means that you have no control over the state of that thread, and making assumptions based on state can break your application.

Let's take a look at a concrete example of an object with a finalize method and see if we can track the object during a garbage collection. Listing 5-4 shows the source code of the application we will be utilizing.

Listing 5-4   Simple object with a finalize method

```
using System;
using System.Text;
using System.Runtime.InteropServices;

namespace Advanced.NET.Debugging.Chapter5
{
    class NativeEvent
    {
        private IntPtr nativeHandle;

        public IntPtr NativeHandle { get { return nativeHandle; } }

        public NativeEvent(string name)
        {
            nativeHandle = CreateEvent(IntPtr.Zero,
                                       false,
                                       true,
                                       name);
        }

        ~NativeEvent()
        {
            if(nativeHandle!=IntPtr.Zero)
            {
                CloseHandle(nativeHandle);
                nativeHandle=IntPtr.Zero;
            }
        }
    }
```

```
        [DllImport("kernel32.dll")]
        static extern IntPtr CreateEvent(IntPtr lpEventAttributes,
                                         bool bManualReset,
                                         bool bInitialState,
                                         string lpName);

        [DllImport("kernel32.dll")]
        static extern IntPtr CloseHandle(IntPtr lpEvent);
}

class Finalize
{
    static void Main(string[] args)
    {
        Finalize f = new Finalize();
        f.Run();
    }

    public void Run()
    {
        NativeEvent nEvent = new NativeEvent("MyNewEvent");

        //
        // Use nEvent
        //

        nEvent = null;

        Console.WriteLine("Press any key to GC");
        Console.ReadKey();

        GC.Collect();

        Console.WriteLine("Press any key to GC");
        Console.ReadKey();

        GC.Collect();

        Console.WriteLine("Press any key to exit");
        Console.ReadKey();
    }

}
}
```

The source code and binary for Listing 5-4 can be found in the following folders:

- Source code: `C:\ADND\Chapter5\Finalize`
- Binary: `C:\ADNDBin\05Finalize.exe`

The source code in Listing 5-4 declares a type called `NativeEvent` that simply wraps the creation of a Windows event using the .NET interoperability services. Because the net result of creating a native event is a handle, the handle must be closed during object destruction to avoid a handle leak in the application. The closing of the handle is implemented in the `NativeEvent` finalize method. The main part of the application is implemented in the `Finalize` class. More specifically, the `Run` method declares an instance of the `NativeEvent` class, sets the local variable reference to `null` (indicating that it can be garbage collected), followed by a couple of forced garbage collections. What do we expect to happen to the `NativeEvent` instance we declared at the point of the first garbage collection? From our previous discussion, we expect that prior to the garbage collection, the object is in the finalization queue. Furthermore, when the garbage collection occurs, the object is deemed rootless and moved to the f-reachable queue where it maintains a reference to the object so that the finalization thread can run the `Finalize` method. It's important to remember that the execution of the finalization thread does not happen during the garbage collection, but rather it happens out of band at any time. When the `Finalize` method has run, the object can be fully collected during the next garbage collection. Let's see if we can use the debuggers to verify our earlier theory. Run `05Finalize.exe` under the debugger and break execution when the first `Press any key to GC` prompt appears. When we have broken into the debugger, we can use the `FinalizeQueue` command to show the state of the finalizable objects in the process:

```
0:004> !FinalizeQueue
SyncBlocks to be cleaned up: 0
MTA Interfaces to be released: 0
STA Interfaces to be released: 0
```

```
generation 0 has 6 finalizable objects (003d3160->003d3178)
generation 1 has 0 finalizable objects (003d3160->003d3160)
generation 2 has 0 finalizable objects (003d3160->003d3160)
Ready for finalization 0 objects (003d3178->003d3178)
Statistics:
      MT    Count    TotalSize Class Name
00123128        1           12 Advanced.NET.Debugging.Chapter5.NativeEvent
7911c9c8        1           20 Microsoft.Win32.SafeHandles.SafePEFileHandle
```

```
791037c0       1            20 Microsoft.Win32.SafeHandles.SafeFileMappingHandle
79103764       1            20 Microsoft.Win32.SafeHandles.SafeViewOfFileHandle
79101444       1            20 Microsoft.Win32.SafeHandles.SafeFileHandle
790fe704       1            56 System.Threading.Thread
Total 6 objects
```

There are several pieces of useful information in the output. First, the finalization queues for each generation are shown. In this particular case, generation 0 has 6 finalizable objects and generations 1 and 2 have none. For each of the finalization queues, the `FinalizeQueue` command also shows the address range of the queue itself for that particular generation. For example, generation 0's finalization queue starts at address `0x003d3160` and ends at address `0x003d3178`. We can use the `dd` command to dump the queue as shown here:

```
0:004> dd 003d3160 16
003d3160    01fc1df0 01fc5090 01fc5964 01fc5998
003d3170    01fc683c 01fc6850
```

The elements in the queue can be looked at further by using the `do` command. If we want to look at the object at address `0x01fc5964` in more detail, we would use the command shown here:

```
0:004> !do 01fc5964
Name: Advanced.NET.Debugging.Chapter5.NativeEvent
MethodTable: 00123128
EEClass: 00121804
Size: 12(0xc) bytes
 (C:\ADNDBin\05Finalize.exe)
Fields:
      MT    Field   Offset                 Type VT    Attr      Value Name
791016bc  4000001        4     System.IntPtr  1 instance         1f0 nativeHandle
```

The next piece of useful information from the `FinalizeQueue` command is the f-reachable queue, which is shown in the following output:

```
Ready for finalization 0 objects (000c3178->000c3178)
```

The output indicates that at this point there are no objects that are ready to be finalized. This makes perfect sense because a garbage collection has not yet occurred.

The final piece of output in the `FinalizeQueue` command is the statistics section, which shows a summarized list of all objects in either the finalization queue or the f-reachable queue.

Before we resume execution, we need to discuss the magic finalization thread that exists in all managed processes. What does the stack trace of this thread look like? To find the answer, use the ~*kn command to display the stack traces of all the threads in the process including frame numbers. In the output, one thread in particular looks interesting:

```
     2  Id: 1a10.c10 Suspend: 1 Teb: 7ffdd000 Unfrozen
# ChildEBP RetAddr
00 011cf604 77709254 ntdll!KiFastSystemCallRet
01 011cf608 7618c244 ntdll!ZwWaitForSingleObject+0xc
02 011cf678 79e789c6 KERNEL32!WaitForSingleObjectEx+0xbe
03 011cf6bc 79e7898f mscorwks!PEImage::LoadImage+0x1af
04 011cf70c 79e78944 mscorwks!CLREvent::WaitEx+0x117
05 011cf720 79ef2220 mscorwks!CLREvent::Wait+0x17
06 011cf73c 79fb997b mscorwks!WKS::WaitForFinalizerEvent+0x4a
07 011cf750 79ef3207 mscorwks!WKS::GCHeap::FinalizerThreadWorker+0x79
08 011cf764 79ef31a3 mscorwks!Thread::DoADCallBack+0x32a
09 011cf7f8 79ef30c3 mscorwks!Thread::ShouldChangeAbortToUnload+0xe3
0a 011cf834 79fb9643 mscorwks!Thread::ShouldChangeAbortToUnload+0x30a
0b 011cf85c 79fb960d mscorwks!ManagedThreadBase_NoADTransition+0x32
0c 011cf86c 79fba09b mscorwks!ManagedThreadBase::FinalizerBase+0xd
0d 011cf8a4 79f95a2e mscorwks!WKS::GCHeap::FinalizerThreadStart+0xbb
0e 011cf93c 76184911 mscorwks!Thread::intermediateThreadProc+0x49
0f 011cf948 776ee4b6 KERNEL32!BaseThreadInitThunk+0xe
10 011cf988 776ee489 ntdll!_RtlUserThreadStart+0x23
11 011cf9a0 00000000 ntdll!_RtlUserThreadStart+0x1b
```

Frames 6 and 7 in the stack trace indicate that in fact this is the finalizer thread for the process. Frame 6 in particular shows that the thread is currently waiting for finalizer events (or objects that need to be finalized). Let's set a breakpoint on the return address of frame 6 (`0x79fb997b`), which will trigger any time the finalizer thread is awakened to perform work:

```
bp 79fb997b
```

When the breakpoint is set, resume execution and press any key to trigger the first garbage collection. You'll notice that a breakpoint is hit, as shown in the following:

```
0:003> g
 Breakpoint 0 hit
eax=00000001 ebx=00000001 ecx=7618c42d edx=77709a94 esi=00000000 edi=00493a48
eip=79fb997b esp=00b7f768 ebp=00b7f770 iopl=0         nv up ei pl nz na po nc
cs=001b  ss=0023  ds=0023  es=0023  fs=003b  gs=0000              efl=00000202
mscorwks!WKS::GCHeap::FinalizerThreadWorker+0x79:
79fb997b 3bde            cmp     ebx,esi
```

The breakpoint corresponds to the finalizer thread breakpoint set earlier and indicates that the finalizer is ready to execute the Finalize methods on the objects in the f-reachable queue. How do we find out what objects are in the f-reachable queue? You guessed it: by using the `FinalizeQueue` command:

```
0:002> !FinalizeQueue
SyncBlocks to be cleaned up: 0
MTA Interfaces to be released: 0
STA Interfaces to be released: 0
```

```
generation 0 has 0 finalizable objects (003d3170->003d3170)
generation 1 has 4 finalizable objects (003d3160->003d3170)
generation 2 has 0 finalizable objects (003d3160->003d3160)
Ready for finalization 2 objects (003d3170->003d3178)
Statistics:
      MT     Count    TotalSize Class Name
00123128         1           12 Advanced.NET.Debugging.Chapter5.NativeEvent
7911c9c8         1           20 Microsoft.Win32.SafeHandles.SafePEFileHandle
791037c0         1           20 Microsoft.Win32.SafeHandles.SafeFileMappingHandle
79103764         1           20 Microsoft.Win32.SafeHandles.SafeViewOfFileHandle
79101444         1           20 Microsoft.Win32.SafeHandles.SafeFileHandle
790fe704         1           56 System.Threading.Thread
```

This time, the output states that there are two objects in the f-reachable queue, starting at address `0x003d3160`, that the finalization thread is about to execute. If we dump out the contents of the f-reachable queue and each of the objects, we can see the following:

```
0:002> dd 003d3170 12
003d3170    01fc5090 01fc5964
0:002> !do 01fc5090
Name: Microsoft.Win32.SafeHandles.SafePEFileHandle
MethodTable: 7911c9c8
EEClass: 791fb61c
Size: 20(0x14) bytes
 (C:\Windows\assembly\GAC_32\mscorlib\2.0.0.0__b77a5c561934e089\mscorlib.dll)
Fields:
      MT    Field   Offset                 Type VT     Attr    Value Name
791016bc 40005c1        4        System.IntPtr  1 instance   3eab28 handle
79102290 40005c2        8        System.Int32   1 instance        4 _state
7910be50 40005c3        c      System.Boolean   1 instance        1 _ownsHandle
7910be50 40005c4        d      System.Boolean   1 instance        1
_fullyInitialized
0:002> !do 01fc5964
Name: Advanced.NET.Debugging.Chapter5.NativeEvent
```

```
MethodTable: 00123128
EEClass: 00121804
Size: 12(0xc) bytes
 (C:\ADNDBin\05Finalize.exe)
Fields:
      MT    Field   Offset                   Type VT    Attr      Value Name
791016bc  4000001        4         System.IntPtr  1 instance        1f0 nativeHandle
```

The first object is of type `SafePEFileHandle` and the second object is of type `NativeEvent`, which happens to be the object we are interested in. If we resume execution, the finalizer thread executes the Finalize method of our `NativeEvent` class. What happens to the objects on the f-reachable queue after finalization has completed? Well, the objects are removed from the f-reachable queue, which renders them rootless; they will be collected during the next garbage collection.

This concludes our discussion of finalization. As you can see, there is a lot of work being done under the hood whenever a finalizable type comes into play. Not only does the CLR need additional data structures (such as the finalization queue and f-reachable queue), but it also spins up a dedicated thread to run the `Finalize` methods for each object that is being collected. Furthermore, an object with a `Finalize` does not get collected in just one garbage collection, but rather two, which in essence means that the objects with `Finalize` methods always get promoted to generation 1 before they are truly dead, making it a far more expensive object to work with.

Reclaiming GC Memory

We have discussed the GC in quite a bit of detail. We now know exactly what the GC does when an object is considered garbage. The one missing piece of information is what the GC does with the memory that becomes available after an object is garbage collected. Does the memory get put on some sort of free list and then reused when another allocation request arrives? Does the memory get freed? Is fragmentation ever a problem on the managed heap? The answer is a combination of all three. If a collection that occurs in generations 0 and 1 leaves a gap on the managed heap, the garbage collector compacts all live objects so that they reside next to each other and coalesces any free blocks on the managed heap into a larger block that is located after the last live object (starting at the current allocation pointer). Figure 5-8 shows an example of the compacting and coalescing.

In Figure 5-8, the initial state of the managed heap contains five rooted objects (A through E). At some point during execution, objects B and D become rootless and are candidates to be reclaimed during a garbage collection. When the garbage collection occurs, the memory occupied by objects B and D is reclaimed, which leads to

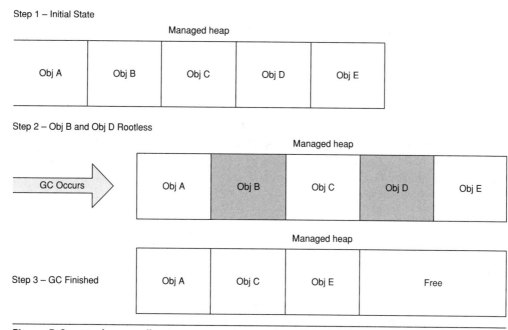

Figure 5-8   Garbage collection compacting and coalescing phase

gaps on the managed heap. To remove these gaps, the garbage collector compacts the remaining live objects (Obj A, C, and E) and coalesces the two free blocks (used to hold Obj B and D) into one free block. Lastly, the current allocation pointer is updated as a result of the compacting and coalescing.

The ephemeral segment contains both generation 0 and generation 1 (and also part of generation 2), but generation 2 can consist of multiple managed heap segments. As more and more objects make it to generation 2, the need to grow generation 2 also increases. The way that the CLR heap manager grows generation 2 is by allocating more segments. When objects in generation 2 are collected, the CLR heap manager decommits memory in the segments, and when a segment is no longer needed, it is entirely freed. In certain situations and allocation patterns, generation 2 grows and shrinks quite frequently, leading to a large number of calls to allocate and free virtual memory (`VirtualAlloc` and `VirtualFree` APIs). Two common drawbacks of this approach are that these calls can be expensive because a transition to kernel mode is required as well as the potential to fragment the VM address space. As such, CLR 2.0 introduces a feature called VM hoarding, which essentially does not free segments but rather keeps the segments on a standby list that can be utilized when more memory is required. To utilize the VM hoarding feature, the CLR host itself must specify that it wants to use the feature.

FULL VERSUS PARTIAL GARBAGE COLLECTION A garbage collection that collects all three generations due to breaching all three generational thresholds is known as a full garbage collection. In contrast, garbage collection in only generation 0 or generation 0 and 1 is simply known as a garbage collection.

Because the cost of a compaction is directly proportional to the size of the object (the bigger the object, the costlier the compaction), the garbage collector introduces another type of heap called the large object heap (LOH). Objects that are large enough to severely hurt the performance of a compaction are placed on the LOH, which we will discuss next.

Large Object Heap

The large object heap (LOH) consists of objects that are greater than or equal to 85,000 bytes in size. The decision to separate objects of that size into its own heap is related to the fact that during the compacting phase of a garbage collection, the cost of compacting an object is directly proportional to the size of the object being compacted. Rather than having large objects on the standard heap eating up garbage collection time during compaction, the LOH was created. The LOH is best viewed as an extension of generation 2, and a collection of the LOH can only be done after a generation 2 collection has occurred, implying that a collection of the LOH is only done during a full garbage collection. Because compacting large objects is very expensive, the GC avoids compacting the LOH altogether and instead uses a process known as sweeping that keeps a free list that is used to keep track of available memory in the LOH segment(s). Figure 5-9 shows an example of a LOH with two segments.

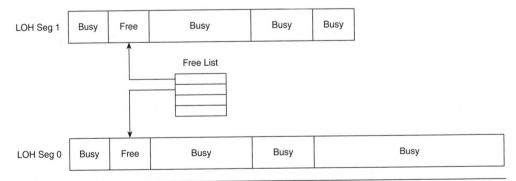

Figure 5-9 LOH example

Please note that although the LOH does not perform any compaction, it does do coalescing of adjacent free blocks. That is, if you ever end up with two free adjacent blocks, the GC coalesces those blocks into a larger block and adds it to the free list (while also removing the two smaller blocks).

To find out the current state of the LOH in the debugger, we can again use the `eeheap –gc` command, which includes details on the LOH:

```
0:004> !eeheap -gc
Number of GC Heaps: 1
generation 0 starts at 0x01fc6c18
generation 1 starts at 0x01fc100c
generation 2 starts at 0x01fc1000
ephemeral segment allocation context: none
 segment    begin allocated     size
00308030 790d8620  790f7d8c 0x0001f76c(128876)
01fc0000 01fc1000  01fc8c24 0x00007c24(31780)
Large object heap starts at 0x02fc1000
 segment     begin allocated     size
02fc0000 02fc1000   02fc3240 0x00002240(8768)
Total Size    0x295d0(169424)
```

```
GC Heap Size    0x295d0(169424)
```

The LOH section in the command output shows the starting point of the LOH as well as per-segment information such as the segment, start, and end address of the segment and total size of the segment. In the preceding example, we can see that the LOH has one segment (`0x02fc000`) starting at address `0x02fc1000` and ending at `0x02fc3240` with a total size of `0x00002240`. The last piece of information is the total size of all segments in the LOH. One interesting question related to the LOH is how the contents of the LOH can be dumped. There are a couple of options that both revolve around using `DumpHeap` command switches. The first switch of interest is the `–min` switch, which tells the `DumpHeap` command that you are only interested in objects of the specified size. Because we know that LOH objects are greater than or equal to 85,000 bytes in size, we can use the following command:

```
0:004> !DumpHeap -min 85000
 Address      MT    Size
02c53250 7912dae8    100016
total 1 objects
Statistics:
     MT    Count   TotalSize Class Name
7912dae8      1       100016 System.Byte[]
```

Here, we can see that there is one object of size `100016` on the LOH. You can verify or convince yourself that the object is in fact on the LOH by looking at the address. If the address of the object falls within the LOH segments addresses, it must be located on the LOH (with the exception of free objects, which can reside both in the SOH as well as the LOH).

The next option we have is to specify a starting address for the `DumpHeap` command. If we specify the starting address of the LOH, we can ask the command to dump out all objects on the LOH. The switch to use is the `—startAtLowerBound` switch, which takes the address as a parameter. Using the same LOH as earlier, the following command can be used:

```
0:004> !DumpHeap -startAtLowerBound 02c51000
  Address       MT      Size
02c51000 002a6360       16 Free
02c51010 7912d8f8     4096
02c52010 002a6360       16 Free
02c52020 7912d8f8     4096
02c53020 002a6360       16 Free
02c53030 7912d8f8      528
02c53240 002a6360       16 Free
02c53250 7912dae8   100016
02c6b900 002a6360       16 Free
total 9 objects
Statistics:
      MT    Count    TotalSize   Class Name
002a6360        5           80      Free
7912d8f8        3         8720   System.Object[]
7912dae8        1       100016   System.Byte[]
Total 9 objects
```

Again, we see the object of size `100016`, but even more interesting is that we see objects that are *smaller than 85,000 bytes* on the LOH. What are these objects and how did they end up on the LOH? The answer is that these very, very small objects are placed there by the CLR heap manager, which uses them for its own purposes. Generally speaking, you always see a select few objects with a size less than 85,000 bytes exclusively used by the GC.

Let's take a look at a small sample application that allocates a single large object of size 10,000 bytes (see Listing 5-5). We will then use the debuggers to see if we can locate the object on the LOH and see what happens when the object is collected.

Listing 5-5 Sample application demonstrating LOH

```
using System;
using System.Text;
using System.Runtime.InteropServices;

namespace Advanced.NET.Debugging.Chapter5
{
    class LOH
    {
        static void Main(string[] args)
        {
            LOH l = new LOH();
            l.Run();
        }

        public void Run()
        {
            byte[] b = null;
            Console.WriteLine("Press any key to allocate on LOH");
            Console.ReadKey();

            b = new byte[100000];

            Console.WriteLine("Press any key to GC");
            Console.ReadKey();

            b = null;
            GC.Collect();

            Console.WriteLine("Press any key to exit");
            Console.ReadKey();
        }

    }
}
```

The source code and binary for Listing 5-5 can be found in the following folders:

- Source code: `C:\ADND\Chapter5\LOH`
- Binary: `C:\ADNDBin\05LOH.exe`

Let's run the application in the debugger and break execution when the `Press any key to allocate on LOH` is displayed. At this point, we haven't yet created our big allocation, but it never hurts to take a look at the LOH heap to see what, if anything, is already on it:

```
0:004> !eeheap -gc
Number of GC Heaps: 1
generation 0 starts at 0x01f01018
generation 1 starts at 0x01f0100c
generation 2 starts at 0x01f01000
ephemeral segment allocation context: none
 segment    begin allocated      size
004a8008 790d8620   790f7d8c 0x0001f76c(128876)
01f00000 01f01000   01f5c334 0x0005b334(373556)
Large object heap starts at 0x02f01000
 segment    begin allocated      size
02f00000 02f01000   02f03250 0x00002250(8784)
Total Size    0x7ccf0(511216)
```

```
GC Heap Size   0x7ccf0(511216)
0:004> !dumpheap -startatlowerbound 02f01000
 Address      MT      Size
02f01000 00496360      16 Free
02f01010 7912d8f8    4096
02f02010 00496360      16 Free
02f02020 7912d8f8    4096
02f03020 00496360      16 Free
02f03030 7912d8f8     528
02f03240 00496360      16 Free
total 7 objects
Statistics:
      MT    Count    TotalSize Class Name
00496360      4           64       Free
7912d8f8      3         8720 System.Object[]
Total 7 objects
```

We start by finding the starting point of the LOH by using the `eeheap` command. The starting point in this case is `0x02f01000`. Then, we feed the starting address to the `dumpheap` command using the `—startatlowerbound` switch to output all objects on the LOH. In the output, we can see that the only objects that are on the LOH are the mysterious object arrays that are smaller than 85,000 bytes. Other than that, we have no other objects present. Next, resume execution and again manually break execution when the `Press any key to GC` is shown.

We issue the same `dumpheap` command as before to see if we can spot our 100KB allocation:

```
0:003> !dumpheap -startatlowerbound 02f01000
 Address       MT     Size
02f01000 00496360       16 Free
02f01010 7912d8f8     4096
02f02010 00496360       16 Free
02f02020 7912d8f8     4096
02f03020 00496360       16 Free
02f03030 7912d8f8      528
02f03240 00496360       16 Free
02f03250 7912dae8   100016
02f1b900 00496360       16 Free
total 9 objects
Statistics:
      MT    Count    TotalSize Class Name
00496360       5           80      Free
7912d8f8       3         8720 System.Object[]
7912dae8       1       100016 System.Byte[]
Total 9 objects
```

We can see that our allocation is stored at address `0x02f03250` on the LOH. Next, we resume execution until we see the **Press any key to exit** prompt. At this point, a garbage collection has occurred, so let's see what the LOH looks like by using the same `dumpheap` command again:

```
0:003> !dumpheap -startatlowerbound 02f01000
 Address       MT     Size
02f01000 00496360       16 Free
02f01010 7912d8f8     4096
02f02010 00496360       16 Free
02f02020 7912d8f8     4096
02f03020 00496360       16 Free
02f03030 7912d8f8      528
total 6 objects
Statistics:
      MT    Count    TotalSize Class Name
00496360       3           48      Free
7912d8f8       3         8720 System.Object[]
```

This time, we can see how the object has been removed from the LOH and the free blocks available as a result of the collection.

Pinning

As we saw in the Releasing GC Memory section, the garbage collector employs a technique known as compaction to reduce fragmentation on the GC heap. When a compaction occurs, objects may end up moving around on the heap so that they can be placed together, thereby avoiding gaps. As part of the object move, because the address of the object changes, all references to the object are also updated. This works well assuming all references to the object are contained within the CLR, but quite often it is necessary for .NET applications to work outside of the boundary of the CLR by using the interoperability services (such as platform invocation or COM interoperability). If a reference to a managed object is passed to an underlying native API, the object might be moved while the native API is reading and/or writing to the memory, causing serious problems because the CLR clearly cannot notify the native API of the address change. Figure 5-10 illustrates the problem.

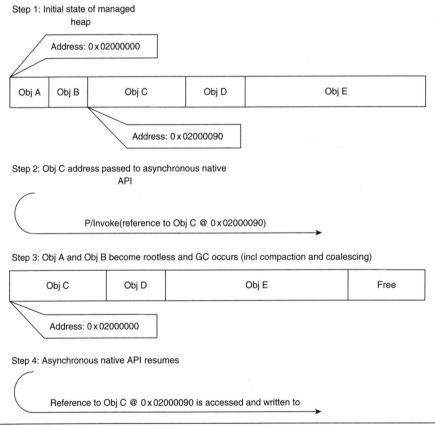

Figure 5-10 Interoperability services and GC compaction problem

From the flow in Figure 5-10, we can see that the initial state of the managed heap includes five objects starting with Obj A at address 0x02000000. At a certain point, a platform invocation call to an asynchronous native API is required. Furthermore, the address of Obj C (0x02000090) needs to be passed to the API. Upon successfully calling the asynchronous native API, a garbage collection occurs causing Obj A and Obj B to be collected. This leaves a gap of two free objects on the managed heap and the garbage collector dutifully rectifies the problem by compacting the managed heap and therefore moving Obj C to address 0x02000000. It also coalesces the two free blocks and places them at the end of the heap. After the garbage collection has finished, the asynchronous API call we made earlier decides to write to the address initially passed to it (0x02000090), which originally held Obj C. As you can see, with the asynchronous API writing to that address, we will experience a managed heap corruption as the memory is no longer occupied by Obj C.

Because the invocation of native code is such a common task, a solution had to be devised that allowed for safe invocation in light of a compacting garbage collector. The solution is called pinning and refers to the capability to pin specific objects on the managed heap. When an object is pinned, the garbage collector will not move the object for any reason until the object is unpinned. If Obj C in Figure 5-10 was pinned prior to invoking the asynchronous native API, the managed heap corruption would not have occurred due to the garbage collector not moving Obj C during the compaction phase.

Let's take a look at an example of a simple application that performs pinning and see what it looks like in the debugger. Listing 5-6 shows the source code of the application.

Listing 5-6   Sample application using pinning

```
using System;
using System.Text;
using System.Runtime.InteropServices;

namespace Advanced.NET.Debugging.Chapter5
{
    class Pinning
    {
        static void Main(string[] args)
        {
            Pinning p = new Pinning();
            p.Run();
        }
```

(continues)

Listing 5-6 *Sample application using pinning* *(continued)*

```
public void Run()
{
    SByte[] b1 = null;
    SByte[] b2 = null;
    SByte[] b3 = null;
    Console.WriteLine("Press any key to alloc");
    Console.ReadKey();

    b1 = new SByte[100];
    b2 = new SByte[200];
    b3 = new SByte[300];

    GCHandle h1 = GCHandle.Alloc(b1, GCHandleType.Pinned);
    GCHandle h2 = GCHandle.Alloc(b2, GCHandleType.Pinned);
    GCHandle h3 = GCHandle.Alloc(b3, GCHandleType.Pinned);

    Console.WriteLine("Press any key to GC");
    Console.ReadKey();

    GC.Collect();

    Console.WriteLine("Press any key to exit");
    Console.ReadKey();

    h1.Free(); h2.Free(); h3.Free();
}

}
}
```

The source code and binary for Listing 5-6 can be found in the following folders:

- Source code: `C:\ADND\Chapter5\Pinning`
- Binary: `C:\ADNDBin\05Pinning.exe`

The sample application shown in Listing 5-6 illustrates how to use the `GCHandle` type to pin objects. The `Run` method declares three arrays of the `SByte` type and creates `GCHandles` for each of the allocations specifying that the objects be pinned. The application then forces a garbage collection and exits. Let's run the application under the debugger and see if we can track the allocated memory and how it gets pinned.

Resume execution of the application until you see the `Press any key to GC` prompt. At this point, we manually break execution and use a command called `GCHandles`. The `GCHandles` command displays a list of all the handles available in the process:

```
0:004> !GCHandles
GC Handle Statistics:
Strong Handles: 15
Pinned Handles: 7
Async Pinned Handles: 0
Ref Count Handles: 0
Weak Long Handles: 0
Weak Short Handles: 1
Other Handles: 0
Statistics:
      MT    Count   TotalSize Class Name
790fd0f0        1          12 System.Object
790feba4        1          28 System.SharedStatics
790fcc48        2          48 System.Reflection.Assembly
790fe17c        1          72 System.ExecutionEngineException
790fe0e0        1          72 System.StackOverflowException
790fe044        1          72 System.OutOfMemoryException
790fed00        1         100 System.AppDomain
790fe704        2         112 System.Threading.Thread
79100a18        4         144 System.Security.PermissionSet
790fe284        2         144 System.Threading.ThreadAbortException
7912ee44        3         636 System.SByte[]
7912d8f8        4        8736 System.Object[]
Total 23 objects
```

The `GCHandles` command walks the handle tables and looks for all types of different handles (strong, weak, pinned, etc.) and displays a summary of the results as well as a statistical section with detailed information on each type found. In the preceding output, we can see that we have 15 strong handles, 7 pinned handles, and 1 weak short handle. In addition, in the `Statistics` section, we can see the three `SByte` arrays that we allocated and pinned. The `GCHandles` command provides a good overview of the handle activity in any given process, but if further information is required, such as the type of handle for each of the types listed in the `Statistics` section, we have to use an additional command called `objsize`. One of the functions of the `objsize` command is to output the size of the object passed in as an argument. If no arguments are specified, it scans all the referenced objects in the process and outputs the size as well as other useful information:

```
0:004> !objsize
Scan Thread 0 OSTHread 2558
ESP:2fed54: sizeof(01d9599c) =              20 (        0x14) bytes
   (Microsoft.Win32.SafeHandles.SafeFileHandle)
ESP:2fee18: sizeof(01d96d9c) =             312 (       0x138) bytes (System.SByte[])
ESP:2fee20: sizeof(01d96c58) =             112 (        0x70) bytes (System.SByte[])
ESP:2fee24: sizeof(01d96cc8) =             212 (        0xd4) bytes (System.SByte[])
ESP:2fee30: sizeof(01d958b4) =              12 (         0xc) bytes
   (Advanced.NET.Debugging.Chapter5.Pinning)
…
…
…
Scan Thread 2 OSTHread 2c80
DOMAIN(004DFD10):HANDLE(Strong):1c119c: sizeof(01d958a4) =
            16 (        0x10) bytes (System.Object[])
…
…
…
DOMAIN(004DFD10):HANDLE(WeakSh):1c12fc: sizeof(01d91de8) =
            56 (        0x38) bytes (System.Threading.Thread)
DOMAIN(004DFD10):HANDLE(Pinned):1c13e4: sizeof(01d96d9c) =
           312 (       0x138) bytes (System.SByte[])
DOMAIN(004DFD10):HANDLE(Pinned):1c13e8: sizeof(01d96cc8) =
           212 (        0xd4) bytes (System.SByte[])
DOMAIN(004DFD10):HANDLE(Pinned):1c13ec: sizeof(01d96c58) =
           112 (        0x70) bytes (System.SByte[])
DOMAIN(004DFD10):HANDLE(Pinned):1c13f0: sizeof(02d93030) =
           708 (       0x2c4) bytes (System.Object[])
DOMAIN(004DFD10):HANDLE(Pinned):1c13f4: sizeof(02d92020) =
          4276 (      0x10b4) bytes (System.Object[])
DOMAIN(004DFD10):HANDLE(Pinned):1c13f8: sizeof(01d9118c) =
            12 (         0xc) bytes (System.Object)
DOMAIN(004DFD10):HANDLE(Pinned):1c13fc: sizeof(02d91010) =
         19332 (      0x4b84) bytes (System.Object[])
```

The output has been abbreviated, but clearly shows that our **SByte** arrays have been pinned as shown by **HANDLE(Pinned)**.

Although the notion of pinning objects solves the problem of movable objects during native code invocations, it does present a problem to the garbage collector; the problem is that of fragmentation (one of the problems that compaction is meant to solve). If there are a lot of interleaved pinned objects on the managed heap, situations may occur where there isn't enough contiguous free space available. Figure 5-11 shows a hypothetical example of a fragmented managed heap due to excessive pinning.

In the layout illustrated in Figure 5-11, we can see that we have several free smaller blocks intertwined with live objects (Obj A through D). If a garbage collection

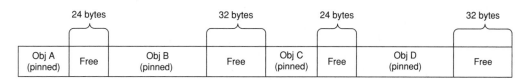

Figure 5-11 Hypothetical example of a fragmented managed heap

should occur, the layout of the managed heap will remain unchanged. The reason for that is simple: The garbage collector cannot perform a compaction due to all live objects being pinned and hence not movable. Because the free blocks are not adjacent, it also cannot perform coalescing. Even though we have free blocks available, memory allocation requests may in fact fail if the size of the requested allocation is greater than 32 bytes. We will take a look at a real-world managed heap fragmentation problem in detail later in the chapter.

WHAT ABOUT THE LOH? Earlier, we discussed the LOH and how it is swept rather than compacted. This essentially means that objects on the LOH never move. Does that mean that we can skip pinning objects on the LOH? The answer is a resounding no! If you don't pin objects on the LOH, you are making a very dangerous implementation assumption that the LOH will *never ever* utilize compaction. That is an implementation detail that can change between CLR versions. It is therefore imperative that objects on the LOH always be pinned in case the implementation changes.

Garbage Collection Modes

The last topic we will discuss are the modes that the garbage collector runs in. There are three primary modes of operation:

- Nonconcurrent workstation
- Concurrent workstation
- Server

We've already discussed the difference between server and workstation in general, and it boils down to the server mode creating one heap and one GC thread per processor. All garbage collection related activities are performed by the dedicated GC thread on the processor it is assigned to. What we haven't discussed is the notion of concurrent and nonconcurrent garbage collections. In the nonconcurrent workstation mode, the garbage collector suspends all managed threads for the *entire* duration of the garbage collection. Only when the garbage collection is finished does it resume all the managed threads in the process. This may work fine if there isn't a need for super-fast responsiveness, but in cases such as GUI applications, quick response times are very critical. Hence, the introduction of the concurrent workstation mode where, during a garbage collection, the managed threads are not suspended for the entire duration of the garbage collection but are allowed to wake up periodically and do work before being put back to sleep again for the garbage collector to do some more work. This increases the responsiveness of the application but can make garbage collection slightly slower.

Debugging Managed Heap Corruptions

A heap corruption is best defined as a bug that violates the integrity of the heap and causes strange behaviors to occur in an application. The symptoms of a heap corruption are vast and can range from subtle and random behaviors or a flat-out crash that stops an application in its tracks. For example, consider an application that has an object whose state controls the frequency with which work items are pulled from a queue. If a thread inadvertently changes the frequency due to corrupting the memory of the object, work items may be pulled off much quicker than the system can handle, or, conversely, work items may not be pulled out at all, causing processing delays. In a situation like this, tracking down the culprit can be difficult because the behavior is exhibited after the corruption has already taken place. In fact, when working with heap corruptions, the best case scenario is a crash that happens as close to the source of the corruption as possible, eliminating the need for a lot of painful historic back tracking of how the heap ended up being corrupted in the first place.

Due to the subtle nature of heap corruption symptoms, it is also one of the trickiest categories of bugs to debug. To begin with, what causes a heap corruption to occur? Generally speaking, there are probably as many different causes for heap corruptions as there are symptoms, but one very common cause is that of not properly managing the memory that the application owns. Problems such as reuse after free, dangling pointers, buffer overruns, and so on can all be possible heap corruption culprits. The good news is that the CLR eliminates many of these problems by effectively managing the memory on the application's behalf. For example, reuse after free is no longer possible because an object isn't collected while rooted, buffer overruns are trapped and surfaced as an exception, and dangling pointers are not easily achieved. Although the CLR very effectively eliminates a lot of the heap corruption culprits, it does so only when the code runs within the confines of the managed execution environment. Often, it is necessary for a managed code application to call into native code and pass data to the native API. The second that the code transitions into the native world, the data that reside on the managed heap and are passed to the native code are no longer under the protection of the CLR and can cause all sorts of problems unless carefully managed before making the transition. For example, buffer overruns are no longer trapped and the compacting nature of the GC can cause pointers to become stale. The managed to native code interaction is one of the biggest heap corruption culprits in the managed world.

CAN THERE BE MANAGED HEAP CORRUPTIONS WITHOUT NATIVE CODE INVOLVEMENT? Although it is possible for a managed heap to become corrupted without any native code interactions, it is a very rare occurrence and usually indicates a bug in the CLR itself.

In this part of the chapter, we will look at an example of an application that suffers from a heap corruption. Listing 5-7 illustrates the application's source code.

Listing 5-7 Example of an application that suffers from a heap corruption

```
using System;
using System.Text;
using System.Runtime.InteropServices;

namespace Advanced.NET.Debugging.Chapter5
{
    class Heap
    {
        static void Main(string[] args)
        {
            Heap h = new Heap();
            h.Run();
        }
        public void Run()
        {
```

(continues)

Listing 5-7 Example of an application that suffers from a heap corruption *(continued)*

```
        byte[] b = new byte[50];
        for (int i = 0; i < 50; i++)
            b[i] = 15;


        Console.WriteLine("Press any key to invoke native method");
        Console.ReadKey();

        InitBuffer(b, 50);

        Console.WriteLine("Press any key to exit");
        Console.ReadKey();
    }


    [DllImport("05Native.dll")]
    static extern void InitBuffer(byte[] buffer, int size);


    }
}
```

The source code and binary for Listing 5-7 can be found in the following folders:

- Source code: `C:\ADND\Chapter5\Heap`
- Binary: `C:\ADNDBin\05Heap.exe and C:\ADNDBin\05Native.dll`

Note that to better illustrate the debug session, the native source code is not shown. The application in Listing 5-6 allocates a byte array (50 elements) and calls into a native API to initialize the memory by passing in the byte array as well as the size of the array. If we run the application under the debugger, we can very quickly see that an access violation occurs:

```
...
...
...
Press any key to invoke native method
 ModLoad: 71190000 711ab000   C:\ADNDBin\05Native.dll
ModLoad: 63f70000 64093000   C:\Windows\WinSxS\x86_microsoft.vc90.debugcrt
_1fc8b3b9a1e18e3b_9.0.21022.8_none_96748342450f6aa2\MSVCR90D.dll
(1b00.26e4): Access violation - code c0000005 (first chance)
First chance exceptions are reported before any exception handling.
This exception may be expected and handled.
eax=77767574 ebx=00000001 ecx=01c659a4 edx=01c66ad8 esi=01c66868 edi=00000017
eip=7936ab16 esp=0031edac ebp=00000017 iopl=0         nv up ei pl nz na pe nc
```

```
cs=001b  ss=0023  ds=0023  es=0023  fs=003b  gs=0000          efl=00010206
*** WARNING: Unable to verify checksum for
C:\Windows\assembly\NativeImages_v2.0.50727_32\
mscorlib\5b3e3b0551bcaa722c27dbb089c431e4\mscorlib.ni.dll
mscorlib_ni+0x2aab16:
7936ab16 ff90a4000000    call    dword ptr [eax+0A4h] ds:0023:77767618=????????
0:000> !ClrStack
OS Thread Id: 0x26e4 (0)
ESP        EIP
0031edac 7936ab16 System.IO.StreamWriter.Flush(Boolean, Boolean)
0031edcc 7936b287 System.IO.StreamWriter.Write(Char[], Int32, Int32)
0031edec 7936b121 System.IO.TextWriter.WriteLine(System.String)
0031ee04 7936b036 System.IO.TextWriter+SyncTextWriter.WriteLine(System.String)
0031ee10 793e9d86 System.Console.WriteLine(System.String)
0031ee1c 00810171 Advanced.NET.Debugging.Chapter5.Heap.Run()
0031ee48 008100a7 Advanced.NET.Debugging.Chapter5.Heap.Main(System.String[])
0031f068 79e7c74b [GCFrame: 0031f068]
```

What is interesting about the access violation is the stack trace of the offending thread. It looks like the access violation occurred while making our second call to the `Console.WriteLine` method (right after our call to the native `InitBuffer` API). Even if we assume that a heap corruption is taking place, why is it failing in some seemingly random place in the code base? Again, it is important to remember that a heap corruption rarely breaks at the point of the corruption; rather, it breaks at some seemingly random place later in the execution flow. This would certainly qualify as random because we certainly do not expect a call to `Console.WriteLine` to ever fail with an access violation. Armed with the knowledge that an access violation has occurred and that the access violation occurred in a rather strange part of the execution flow, we can now *theorize* that we have a possible heap corruption on our hands. The big question is, how do we verify our theory? Remember our earlier definition of a heap corruption: a violation of the integrity of the heap. If we can walk all objects on the heap, and verify the validity of each object, we can say for sure whether the integrity has been violated. Although it's possible to walk the entire managed heap by hand, it is a time-consuming process to say the least. Fortunately, the SOS `VerifyHeap` command automates this process for us. The `VerifyHeap` command walks the entire managed heap, validating each object along the way, and reports the results of the validation. If we run the command in our debug session, we can see the following:

```
0:000> !VerifyHeap
-verify will only produce output if there are errors in the heap
object 01c65968: does not have valid MT
curr_object : 01c65968
Last good object: 01c65928
```

```
object 02c61010: bad member 01c65968 at 02c61084
object 02c61010: bad member 01c65984 at 02c6109c
object 02c61010: bad member 01c659fc at 02c61444
object 02c61010: bad member 01c659e4 at 02c61448
object 02c61010: bad member 01c659f0 at 02c6144c
object 02c61010: bad member 01c659c8 at 02c6158c
curr_object : 02c61010
Last good object: 02c61000
```

In the preceding output, we can see that there seems to be a number of problems with our managed heap. More specifically, the first error encountered seems to be with the object located at address 0x01c65968 not having a valid MT (method table). We can easily verify this by hand by dumping out the contents of that address using the dd command:

```
0:000> dd 01c65968 l1
01c65968   3b3a3938
0:000> dd 3b3a3938 l1
3b3a3938   ????????
```

The method table of the object located at address 0x01c65968 seems to be 0x3b3a3938, which furthermore is shown to be an invalid address. At this point, we know we are working with a corrupted heap starting with an object at address 0x01c65968, but what we don't know yet is how it got corrupted. A useful technique in situations like this is to investigate objects surrounding the corrupted memory area. For example, what does the previous object look like? The output of VerifyHeap shows the address of the last good object to be 0x01c65928. If we dump out the contents of that object, we can see the following:

```
0:000> !do 01c65928
Name: System.Byte[]
MethodTable: 7912dae8
EEClass: 7912dba0
Size: 62(0x3e) bytes
Array: Rank 1, Number of elements 50, Type Byte
Element Type: System.Byte
Fields:
None
0:000> !objsize 01c65928
sizeof(01c65928) =            64 (           0x40) bytes (System.Byte[])
```

The object in question appears to be a byte array with 50 elements, which also looks very similar to the byte array that we created in our application. Furthermore, because the `do` command is capable of displaying details of the object, the object's metadata seems to be structurally intact. Please note that the `objsize` command was used to get the total size (including members of the object) of the object (`64`). The next interesting piece of information to look at is the contents of the array itself. We can use the `dd` command to display the entire object in raw memory form:

```
0:000> dd 01c65928
01c65928   7912dae8 00000032 03020100 07060504
01c65938   0b0a0908 0f0e0d0c 13121110 17161514
01c65948   1b1a1918 1f1e1d1c 23222120 27262524
01c65958   2b2a2928 2f2e2d2c 33323130 37363534
01c65968   3b3a3938 3f3e3d3c 43424140 47464544
01c65978   4b4a4948 4f4e4d4c 53525150 57565554
01c65988   5b5a5958 5f5e5d5c 63626160 67666564
01c65998   6b6a6968 6f6e6d6c 73727170 77767574
```

In the output, we can see that the 64 bytes that the object occupies begin with the method table indicating the type of the array followed by the number of elements in the array followed by the array contents itself. The next object begins at address `0x01c65928` ((starting address of object)+`0x40`(total size of object)). If we look at the contents of the last good object (`0x01c65928`), we can see that the array contains incremental integer values. Furthermore, when the end of the last good object is reached, we still see a progression of the incremental integer values spilling over to what is considered the next object on the heap (`0x01c65968`). This observation yields a very important clue as to what may potentially be happening. If the object at address `0x01c65928` was incorrectly written and allowed to write past the end of the object boundary, we would corrupt the next object in the heap. Figure 5-12 illustrates the scenario.

Figure 5-12 Managed heap corruption

At this point, we have a pretty good understanding of the data shown to us in the debugger. By code reviewing the parts of the application that manipulate our byte array, we can see that when we pass the byte array to the native `InitBuffer` API the function does not respect the boundaries of the object and writes past the end of the object, causing the subsequent object on the heap to become corrupted (as output by the `VerifyHeap` command).

There is one additional piece of information that was displayed by the `VerifyHeap` command earlier:

```
object 02c61010: bad member 01c65968 at 02c61084
object 02c61010: bad member 01c65984 at 02c6109c
object 02c61010: bad member 01c659fc at 02c61444
object 02c61010: bad member 01c659e4 at 02c61448
object 02c61010: bad member 01c659f0 at 02c6144c
object 02c61010: bad member 01c659c8 at 02c6158c
curr_object : 02c61010
Last good object: 02c61000
```

`VerifyHeap` is telling us that there exists an object located at address `0x02c61010` that contains a member that references the corrupted object starting at address `0x01c65968`. As a matter of fact, there are multiple lines stating that the same object is referencing a number of different members of the corrupted object at various addresses (`0x01c65968`, `0x01c65984`, `0x01c659fc`, etc). In essence, `VerifyHeap` not only tells us which object is corrupted, but any other object on any of the heaps that references the corrupt object will also be displayed.

VerifyHeap and GC Interference

We have seen how the `VerifyHeap` command can make troubleshooting managed heap corruptions more efficient by walking the heap and reporting inconsistencies that can be a result of a heap corruption. There are times, however, when `VerifyHeap` can yield results that may not be as a result of a heap corruption. An example of that is if the CLR is in *the middle* of doing a garbage collection. During a garbage collection, the GC may end up compacting the heap, which involves moving objects around. For example, if a move was currently in progress, the `VerifyHeap` command may very well fail or give inaccurate information due to the heap being reorganized.

One of the built-in diagnostic aids that the garbage collector includes is the capability to perform heap verification before and after garbage collection occurs. To enable these diagnostics, set the environment variable `COMPLUS_HeapVerify=1`.

The sample application we used to demonstrate how the managed heap can become corrupted was based on using the interoperability services to invoke native code. Depending on how the heap is corrupted by the native code, as well as the timing of garbage collections, there may not be any signs of a heap corruption being present until much later after the native code has already done the damage, making it difficult to backtrack to the source of the problem. To aid in this troubleshooting process, an MDA was added called the gcUnmanagedToManaged MDA. Essentially, the MDA aims at reducing the time gap between when the corruption actually occurs in native code and when the next GC occurs. The way this is accomplished is by forcing a garbage collection when the interoperability call transitions back from unmanaged to managed code, thereby pinpointing the problem much earlier in the process. Let's enable the MDA (please see Chapter 1, "Introduction to the Tools" on how to enable MDAs) and rerun our sample application under the debugger to see if we can trap the heap corruption earlier:

```
...
...
...
Press any key to invoke native method
 ModLoad: 71190000 711ab000   C:\ADNDBin\05Native.dll
ModLoad: 63f70000 64093000   C:\Windows\WinSxS\x86_microsoft.vc90.
debugcrt_1fc8b3b9a1e18e3b_9.0.21022.8_none_96748342450f6aa2\MSVCR90D.dll
(19d8.258c): Access violation - code c0000005 (first chance)
First chance exceptions are reported before any exception handling.
This exception may be expected and handled.
eax=3b3a3938 ebx=02d81010 ecx=00960184 edx=01d8598c esi=00020000 edi=00001000
eip=79f66846 esp=0025ec54 ebp=0025ec74 iopl=0  nv up ei pl nz na po nc
cs=001b  ss=0023  ds=0023  es=0023  fs=003b  gs=0000         efl=00010202
mscorwks!WKS::gc_heap::mark_object_simple+0x16c:
79f66846 0fb708          movzx   ecx,word ptr [eax]       ds:0023:3b3a3938=????
0:000> k
ChildEBP RetAddr
0025ec74 79f66932 mscorwks!WKS::gc_heap::mark_object_simple+0x16c
0025ec88 79fbc552 mscorwks!WKS::GCHeap::Promote+0x8d
0025eca0 79fbc3c9 mscorwks!PinObject+0x10
0025ecc4 79fc37b9 mscorwks!ScanConsecutiveHandlesWithoutUserData+0x26
0025ece4 79fba942 mscorwks!BlockScanBlocksWithoutUserData+0x26
0025ed08 79fba917 mscorwks!SegmentScanByTypeMap+0x55
0025ed60 79fba807 mscorwks!TableScanHandles+0x65
0025edc8 79fbb9a2 mscorwks!HndScanHandlesForGC+0x10d
0025ee0c 79fbaaf8 mscorwks!Ref_TracePinningRoots+0x6c
0025ee30 79f669f6 mscorwks!CNameSpace::GcScanHandles+0x60
0025ee70 79f65d57 mscorwks!WKS::gc_heap::mark_phase+0xae
```

```
0025ee94 79f6614c mscorwks!WKS::gc_heap::gc1+0x62
0025eea8 79f65f5d mscorwks!WKS::gc_heap::garbage_collect+0x261
0025eed4 79f6dfa1 mscorwks!WKS::GCHeap::GarbageCollectGeneration+0x1a9
0025eee4 79f6df4b mscorwks!WKS::GCHeap::GarbageCollectTry+0x2d
0025ef04 7a0aea3d mscorwks!WKS::GCHeap::GarbageCollect+0x67
0025ef8c 7a12addd mscorwks!MdaGcUnmanagedToManaged::TriggerGC+0xa7
0025f020 79e7c74b mscorwks!FireMdaGcUnmanagedToManaged+0x3b
0025f030 79e7c6cc mscorwks!CallDescrWorker+0x33
0025f0b0 79e7c8e1 mscorwks!CallDescrWorkerWithHandler+0xa3
0:000> !ClrStack
OS Thread Id: 0x258c (0)
ESP       EIP
0025efdc 79f66846 [NDirectMethodFrameStandalone: 0025efdc]
 Advanced.NET.Debugging.Chapter5.Heap.InitBuffer(Byte[], Int32)

0025efec 00a80165 Advanced.NET.Debugging.Chapter5.Heap.Run()
0025f018 00a800a7 Advanced.NET.Debugging.Chapter5.Heap.Main(System.String[])
0025f240 79e7c74b [GCFrame: 0025f240]
```

We can see here that the native stack trace that caused the access violation looks a lot different than our earlier stack trace. It now looks like we are hitting the problem during a garbage collection. Where in our managed code flow did the garbage collection occur? If we look at the managed code stack trace, we can see that we now get the access violation during our call to the native `InitBuffer` API.

If you ever suspect that a heap corruption might be taking place due to a native API invocation, enabling the gcUnmanagedtoManaged MDA can save a ton of debugging time.

Debugging Managed Heap Fragmentation

Earlier in the chapter, we described a phenomenon known as heap fragmentation, in which free and busy blocks are arranged and interleaved on the managed heap in such a way that they can cause problems in applications that surface as OutOfMemory exceptions; in reality, enough memory is free, just not in a contiguous fashion. The CLR heap manager utilizes a technique known as compacting and coalescing to reduce the risk of heap fragmentation. In this section, we will take a look at an example that can cause heap fragmentation to occur and how we can use the debuggers to identify that a heap fragmentation is in fact occurring and the reasons behind it. The example is shown in Listing 5-8.

Listing 5-8   Heap fragmentation example

```
using System;
using System.Text;
using System.Runtime.InteropServices;

namespace Advanced.NET.Debugging.Chapter5
{
    class Fragment
    {
        static void Main(string[] args)
        {
            Fragment f = new Fragment();
            f.Run(args);
        }

        public void Run(string[] args)
        {
            if (args.Length < 2)
            {
                Console.WriteLine("05Fragment.exe <alloc. size> <max mem in MB>");
                return;
            }

            int size = Int32.Parse(args[0]);
            int maxmem = Int32.Parse(args[1]);
            byte[][] nonPinned = null;
            byte[][] pinned = null;
            GCHandle[] pinnedHandles = null;

            int numAllocs=maxmem*1000000/size;

            pinnedHandles = new GCHandle[numAllocs];

            pinned = new byte[numAllocs / 2][];
            nonPinned = new byte[numAllocs / 2][];

            for (int i = 0; i < numAllocs / 2; i++)
            {
                nonPinned[i] = new byte[size];
                pinned[i] = new byte[size];
        pinnedHandles[i] =
GCHandle.Alloc(pinned[i], GCHandleType.Pinned);
            }
```

(continues)

Listing 5-8 Heap fragmentation example *(continued)*

```
Console.WriteLine("Press any key to GC & promo to gen1");
Console.ReadKey();

GC.Collect();

Console.WriteLine("Press any key to GC  & promo to gen2");
Console.ReadKey();

GC.Collect();

Console.WriteLine("Press any key to GC(free non pinned");
Console.ReadKey();

for (int i = 0; i < numAllocs / 2; i++)
{
    nonPinned[i] = null;
}

GC.Collect();

Console.WriteLine("Press any key to exit");
Console.ReadKey();
        }
    }
}
```

The source code and binary for Listing 5-8 can be found in the following folders:

- Source code: `C:\ADND\Chapter5\Fragment`
- Binary: `C:\ADNDBin\05Fragment.exe`

The application enables the user to specify an allocation size and the maximum amount of memory that the application should consume. For example, if we want the allocation size to be 50,000 bytes and the overall memory consumption limit to be 100MB, we would run the application as following:

```
C:\ADNDBIN\05Fragment 50000 100
```

The application proceeds to allocate memory, in chunks of the specified allocation size, until the limit is reached. After the allocations have been made, the application performs a couple of garbage collections to promote the surviving objects to generation 2 and then makes the nonpinned objects rootless, followed by another garbage collection that subsequently releases the nonpinned allocations. Let's take a look by running the application under the debugger with an allocation size of `50000` and a max memory threshold of 1GB.

After the `Press any key to GC and promo to Gen1` prompt is displayed, the application has finished allocating all the memory and we can take a look at the managed heap using the `DumpHeap —stat` command:

```
0:004> !DumpHeap -stat
total 22812 objects
Statistics:
      MT      Count    TotalSize Class Name
79119954          1           12 System.Security.Permissions.ReflectionPermission
79119834          1           12 System.Security.Permissions.FileDialogPermission
791197b0          1           12 System.Security.PolicyManager
...
...
...
791032a8          2          256 System.Globalization.NumberFormatInfo
79101fe4          6          336 System.Collections.Hashtable
7912d9bc          6          864 System.Collections.Hashtable+bucket[]
7912dd40         10         2084 System.Char[]
00395f68        564        13120 Free
7912d8f8         14        17348 System.Object[]
791379e8          1        80012 System.Runtime.InteropServices.GCHandle[]
79141f50          2        80032 System.Byte[][]
790fd8c4       2108       132148 System.String
7912dae8      20002   1000240284 System.Byte[]
Total 22812 objects
```

The output of the command shows a few interesting fields. Because we are looking specifically for heap fragmentation symptoms, any listed `Free` blocks should be carefully investigated. In our case, we seem to have `564` free blocks occupying a total size of `13120`. Should we be worried about these free blocks causing heap fragmentation? Generally speaking, it is useful to look at the total size of the free blocks in comparison to the overall size of the managed heap. If the size of the free blocks is large in comparison to the overall heap size, heap fragmentation may be an issue and should be investigated further. Another important consideration to be made is that of which generation the possible heap fragmentation is occurring in. In generation 0, fragmentation is typically not a problem because the CLR heap manager can allocate using any free blocks that may be available. In generation 1 and 2 however, the only way for the free blocks to be used is by promoting objects to each respective generation. Because generation 1 is part of the ephemeral segment, which there can only be one of, generation 2 is most commonly the generation of interest when looking at heap fragmentation problems. Let's take a look at what our heap looks like by using the **eeheap —gc** command:

```
0:004> !eeheap -gc
Number of GC Heaps: 1
generation 0 starts at 0x56192a54
generation 1 starts at 0x55d91000
generation 2 starts at 0x01c21000
ephemeral segment allocation context: none
 segment     begin allocated     size
003a80e0 790d8620   790f7d8c 0x0001f76c(128876)
01c20000 01c21000   0282db84 0x00c0cb84(12635012)
04800000 04801000   05405ee4 0x00c04ee4(12603108)
05800000 05801000   06405ee4 0x00c04ee4(12603108)
06a50000 06a51000   07655ee4 0x00c04ee4(12603108)
07a50000 07a51000   08655ee4 0x00c04ee4(12603108)
...
...

...
4fd90000 4fd91000   50995ee4 0x00c04ee4(12603108)
50d90000 50d91000   51995ee4 0x00c04ee4(12603108)
51d90000 51d91000   52995ee4 0x00c04ee4(12603108)
52d90000 52d91000   53995ee4 0x00c04ee4(12603108)
53d90000 53d91000   54995ee4 0x00c04ee4(12603108)
54d90000 54d91000   55995ee4 0x00c04ee4(12603108)
55d90000 55d91000   5621afd8 0x00489fd8(4759512)
Large object heap starts at 0x02c21000
 segment     begin allocated     size
02c20000 02c21000   02c23250 0x00002250(8784)
Total Size  0x3ba38e90(1000574608)
-----------------------------------------
GC Heap Size  0x3ba38e90(1000574608)
```

The last line of the output tells us that the total GC Heap Size is right around 1GB. You may also notice that there is a rather large list of segments. Because we are allocating a rather large amount of memory, the ephemeral segment gets filled up pretty quickly and new generation 2 segments get created. We can verify this by looking at the starting address of generation 2 in the preceding output (`0x01c21000`) and correlating the start addresses of each segment in the segment list. Let's get back to the free blocks we saw earlier. In which generations are they located? We can find out by using the **dumpheap —type Free** command. An abbreviated output follows:

```
0:004> !DumpHeap -type Free
 Address       MT      Size
01c21000 00395f68      12 Free
01c2100c 00395f68      24 Free
01c24c44 00395f68      12 Free
01c24c50 00395f68      12 Free
01c24c5c 00395f68    6336 Free
01e299d0 00395f68      12 Free
0202a6f4 00395f68      12 Free
0222b418 00395f68      12 Free
0242c13c 00395f68      12 Free
0262ce60 00395f68      12 Free
04801000 00395f68      12 Free
0480100c 00395f68      12 Free
04a01d30 00395f68      12 Free
04c02a54 00395f68      12 Free
04e03778 00395f68      12 Free
0500449c 00395f68      12 Free
052051c0 00395f68      12 Free
05801000 00395f68      12 Free
0580100c 00395f68      12 Free
05a01d30 00395f68      12 Free
05c02a54 00395f68      12 Free
05e03778 00395f68      12 Free
0600449c 00395f68      12 Free
062051c0 00395f68      12 Free
06a51000 00395f68      12 Free
06a5100c 00395f68      12 Free
06c51d30 00395f68      12 Free
06e52a54 00395f68      12 Free
07053778 00395f68      12 Free
0725449c 00395f68      12 Free
074551c0 00395f68      12 Free
07a51000 00395f68      12 Free
07a5100c 00395f68      12 Free
07c51d30 00395f68      12 Free
07e52a54 00395f68      12 Free
08053778 00395f68      12 Free
0825449c 00395f68      12 Free
084551c0 00395f68      12 Free
08a51000 00395f68      12 Free
08a5100c 00395f68      12 Free
08c51d30 00395f68      12 Free
08e52a54 00395f68      12 Free
09053778 00395f68      12 Free
0925449c 00395f68      12 Free
```

```
094551c0 00395f68          12 Free
09a51000 00395f68          12 Free
09a5100c 00395f68          12 Free
09c51d30 00395f68          12 Free
09e52a54 00395f68          12 Free
0a053778 00395f68          12 Free
0a25449c 00395f68          12 Free
0a4551c0 00395f68          12 Free
0aee1000 00395f68          12 Free
0aee100c 00395f68          12 Free
0b0e1d30 00395f68          12 Free
0b2e2a54 00395f68          12 Free
0b4e3778 00395f68          12 Free
...
...
...
55192a54 00395f68          12 Free
55393778 00395f68          12 Free
5559449c 00395f68          12 Free
557951c0 00395f68          12 Free
55d91000 00395f68          12 Free
55d9100c 00395f68          12 Free
55f91d30 00395f68          12 Free
56192a54 00395f68          12 Free
02c21000 00395f68          16 Free
02c22010 00395f68          16 Free
02c23020 00395f68          16 Free
02c23240 00395f68          16 Free
total 564 objects
Statistics:
      MT    Count     TotalSize Class Name
00395f68      564         13120      Free
Total 564 objects
```

By looking at the address of each of the free blocks and correlating the address to the segments from the `eeheap` command, we can see that a great majority of the free objects reside in generation 2. With a total free size of 13120 in a heap that is right around 1GB in size, the fragmentation now is only a small fraction of one percent. Nothing to worry about (yet). Let's resume the application and keep pressing any key when prompted until you see the `Press any key to exit` prompt. At that point, break into the debugger and again run the `DumpHeap –stat` command to get another view of the heap:

```
0:004> !DumpHeap -stat
total 22233 objects
Statistics:
      MT       Count    TotalSize Class Name
79119954         1            12 System.Security.Permissions.ReflectionPermission
79119834         1            12 System.Security.Permissions.FileDialogPermission
791197b0         1            12 System.Security.PolicyManager
00113038         1            12 Advanced.NET.Debugging.Chapter5.Fragment
791052a8         1            16 System.Security.Permissions.UIPermission
79117480         1            20 System.Security.Permissions.EnvironmentPermission
791037c0         1            20 Microsoft.Win32.SafeHandles.SafeFileMappingHandle
79103764         1            20 Microsoft.Win32.SafeHandles.SafeViewOfFileHandle
...
...
...
7912d8f8        12         17256 System.Object[]
791379e8         1         80012 System.Runtime.InteropServices.GCHandle[]
79141f50         2         80032 System.Byte[][]
790fd8c4      2101        131812 System.String
00395f68     10006     496172124 Free
7912dae8     10002     500120284 System.Byte[]
Total 22233 objects
```

This time, we can see that the amount of free space has grown considerably. From the output, there are `10006` instances of free blocks occupying a total of `496172124` bytes of memory. To find out how this total amount correlates to our overall heap size, we once again use the `eeheap —gc` command:

```
0:004> !eeheap -gc
Number of GC Heaps: 1
generation 0 starts at 0x55d9100c
generation 1 starts at 0x55d91000
generation 2 starts at 0x01c21000
ephemeral segment allocation context: none
 segment     begin allocated      size
003a80e0 790d8620  790f7d8c 0x0001f76c(128876)
01c20000 01c21000  02821828 0x00c00828(12585000)
04800000 04801000  053f9b88 0x00bf8b88(12553096)
...
...
...
54d90000 54d91000  55989b88 0x00bf8b88(12553096)
55d90000 55d91000  562190b0 0x004880b0(4751536)
Large object heap starts at 0x02c21000
 segment     begin allocated      size
```

```
02c20000 02c21000  02c23240 0x00002240(8768)
Total Size  0x3b6725f4(996615668)
```

GC Heap Size 0x3b6725f4(996615668)

The total GC heap size is reported as 996615668 bytes. Overall, we can say that the heap is approximately 50% fragmented. This can easily be verified by looking at the verbose output of the DumpHeap command:

```
0:004> !DumpHeap
 Address        MT      Size
...

...

...
55ff381c 7912dae8    50012
55fffb78 00395f68    50012 Free
5600bed4 7912dae8    50012
56018230 00395f68    50012 Free
5602458c 7912dae8    50012
560308e8 00395f68    50012 Free
5603cc44 7912dae8    50012
56048fa0 00395f68    50012 Free
560552fc 7912dae8    50012
56061658 00395f68    50012 Free
5606d9b4 7912dae8    50012
56079d10 00395f68    50012 Free
5608606c 7912dae8    50012
560923c8 00395f68    50012 Free
5609e724 7912dae8    50012
560aaa80 00395f68    50012 Free
560b6ddc 7912dae8    50012
560c3138 00395f68    50012 Free
560cf494 7912dae8    50012
560db7f0 00395f68    50012 Free
560e7b4c 7912dae8    50012
560f3ea8 00395f68    50012 Free
56100204 7912dae8    50012
5610c560 00395f68    50012 Free
...

...

...
```

From the output, we can see that a pattern has emerged. We have a block of size 50012 that is allocated and in use followed by a free block of the same size that is considered free. We can use the DumpObj command on the allocated object to find out more details:

```
0:004> !DumpObj 5606d9b4
Name: System.Byte[]
MethodTable: 7912dae8
EEClass: 7912dba0
Size: 50012(0xc35c) bytes
Array: Rank 1, Number of elements 50000, Type Byte
Element Type: System.Byte
Fields:
None
```

This object is a byte array, which corresponds to the allocations that our application is creating. How did we end up with such an allocation pattern (allocated, free, allocated, free) to begin with? We know that the garbage collector should perform compacting and coalescing to avoid this scenario. One of the situations that can cause the garbage collector not to compact and coalesce is if there are objects on the heap that are pinned (i.e., nonmoveable). To find out if that is indeed the case in our application, we need to see if there are any pinned handles in the process. We can utilize the `GCHandles` command to get an overview of handle usage in the process:

```
0:004> !GCHandles
GC Handle Statistics:
Strong Handles: 15
Pinned Handles: 10004
Async Pinned Handles: 0
Ref Count Handles: 0
Weak Long Handles: 0
Weak Short Handles: 1
Other Handles: 0
Statistics:
      MT    Count    TotalSize Class Name
790fd0f0        1           12 System.Object
790feba4        1           28 System.SharedStatics
790fcc48        2           48 System.Reflection.Assembly
790fe17c        1           72 System.ExecutionEngineException
790fe0e0        1           72 System.StackOverflowException
790fe044        1           72 System.OutOfMemoryException
790fed00        1          100 System.AppDomain
790fe704        2          112 System.Threading.Thread
79100a18        4          144 System.Security.PermissionSet
790fe284        2          144 System.Threading.ThreadAbortException
7912d8f8        4         8744 System.Object[]
7912dae8    10000    500120000 System.Byte[]
Total 10020 objects
```

The output of `GCHandles` tells us that we have `10004` pinned handles. Further more, in the `statistics` section, we can see that 10,000 of those handles are used to pin byte arrays. At this point, we are almost there and can do a quick code review that shows that half of the byte array allocations made in the application are explicitly pinned, causing the heap to get fragmented.

Excessive or prolonged pinning is one of the most common reasons behind fragmentation of the managed heap. If pinning is necessary, the developer must ensure that pinning is short lived in order not to interfere too much with the garbage collector.

How Much Is Too Much?

In our preceding example, initially, the heap fragmentation was a fraction of one percent. At that point, we really didn't have to pay too much attention to it as it was too small to concern us. Later, we noticed that the fragmentation grew to 50%, which caused an in-depth investigation to figure out the reason for it. Is there a magical percentage of when one should start worrying? There is no hard number, but generally speaking if the heap is between 10% and 30% fragmented, due diligence should be exercised to ensure that it is not a long-running problem.

In the preceding example, we looked at fragmentation as it relates to the managed heap. It is also possible to encounter situations where the virtual memory managed by the Windows virtual memory manager gets fragmented. In those cases, the CLR heap manager may not be able to grow its heap (i.e., allocate new segments) to accommodate allocation requests. The `address` command can be used to get in-depth information on the systems virtual memory state.

Debugging Out of Memory Exceptions

Even though the CLR heap manager and the garbage collector work hard to ensure that memory is automatically managed and used in the most efficient way possible, bad programming can still cause serious issues in .NET applications. In this part of the chapter, we will take a look at how a .NET application can exhaust enough memory to fail with an `OutOfMemoryException` and how we can use the debuggers to figure out the source of the problem. It is important to note that the example we will use illustrates how memory can be exhausted in the managed world and does not cover the various ways in which resources can be leaked in native code when invoked via the interoperability services layer. In Chapter 7, "Interoperability," we will look at an example of a native resource leak caused by improper invocations from managed code.

The application we will use to illustrate the problem is shown in Listing 5-9.

Listing 5-9 Example of an application that causes an eventual OutOfMemoryException

```
using System;
using System.IO;
using System.Xml.Serialization;

namespace Advanced.NET.Debugging.Chapter5
{
    public class Person
    {
        private string name;
        private string social;
        private int age;

        public string Name
        {
            get { return name; }
            set { this.name=value;}
        }

        public string SocialSecurity
        {
            get { return social; }
            set { this.social= value; }
        }

        public int Age
        {
            get { return age; }
            set { this.age = value; }
        }

        public Person() {}
        public Person(string name, string ss, int age)
```

(continues)

Listing 5-9 Example of an application that causes an eventual
OutOfMemoryException *(continued)*

```
        {
            this.name = name; this.social = ss; this.age = age;
        }
    }

class OOM
{
    static void Main(string[] args)
    {
        OOM o = new OOM();
        o.Run();
    }

    public void Run()
    {
        XmlRootAttribute root = new XmlRootAttribute();
        root.ElementName = "MyPersonRoot";
        root.Namespace = "http://www.contoso.com";
        root.IsNullable = true;

        while (true)
        {
            Person p = new Person();
            p.Name = "Mario Hewardt";
            p.SocialSecurity = "xxx-xx-xxxx";
            p.Age = 99;

            XmlSerializer ser = new
                XmlSerializer(typeof(Person), root);
            Stream s = new
                FileStream("c:\\ser.txt", FileMode.Create);

            ser.Serialize(s, p);
            s.Close();
        }
    }
}
```

The source code and binary for Listing 5-9 can be found in the following folders:

- Source code: `C:\ADND\Chapter5\OOM`
- Binary: `C:\ADNDBin\05OOM.exe`

The application is pretty straightforward and consists of a `Person` class and an `OOM` class. The `OOM` class contains a `Run` method that sits in a tight loop creating instances of the `Person` class and serializes the instance into XML stored in a file on the local drive. When we run this application, we would like to monitor the memory consumption to see if it steadily increases over time, which could eventually lead to an `OutOfMemoryException` being thrown. What tools do we have at our disposal to monitor the memory consumption of a process? We have several options. The most basic option is to simply use task manager (shortcut `SHIFT-CTRL-ESC`). Task manager can display per-process memory information such as the working set, commit size, and paged/nonpaged pool. By default, only the Memory (Private Working Set) is enabled. To enable other process information, the Select Columns menu choice on the View menu can be used. The Windows Task Manager has several different tabs, and the tab of most interest when looking at per-process details is the Processes tab. The Processes tab shows a number of rows where each row represents a running process. Each of the columns in turn shows a specific piece of information about the process. Figure 5-13 shows an example of Windows Task Manager with a number of different memory details enabled in the Processes tab.

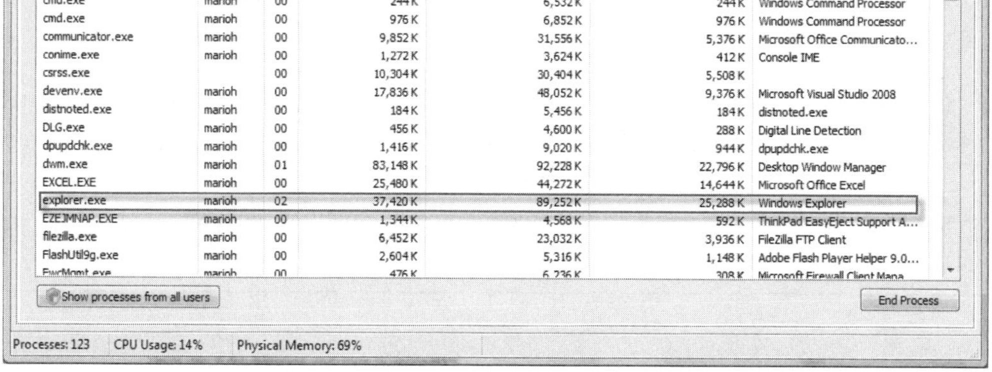

Figure 5-13 Example of Windows Task Manager Processes tab

In Figure 5-13, we can see, for example, that `explorer.exe`'s working set size is 37,420K. Before we can move forward and effectively utilize Windows Task Manager for memory-related investigations, we have to have a clear understanding of what each of the possible memory-related columns means. Table 5-2 details the most commonly used columns and their descriptions.

PRE-WINDOWS VISTA TASK MANAGER Some much-needed changes were made in Windows Vista and later versions to better capture the memory-related process information. Prior to Windows Vista, Windows Task Manager had a column named VM size, which, contrary to popular belief, indicated the amount of private bytes a process was consuming. Similarly, the Mem Usage column corresponds to the working set (including shared memory) of the process. Finally, a feature we will utilize in Chapter 8, "Postmortem Debugging," is the capability to create dump files simply by right-clicking on the process and choosing the Create Dump File item.

Let's run `0500M.exe` and watch the Memory – Working Set, Memory – Private Working Set, and Memory – Commit Size columns. Table 5-3 shows the results taken at periodic (approximately 60-second) intervals.

Table 5-2 Windows Task Manager Memory-Related Columns

Column	Description
Memory – Working Set	Amount of memory in the private working set as well as the shared memory
Memory – Peak Working Set	Maximum amount of working set used by the process
Memory – Working Set Delta	Amount of change in the working set
Memory – Private Working Set	Amount of memory the process is using minus shared memory
Memory – Commit Size	Amount of virtual memory committed by the process

Table 5-3   Memory Usage of 00500M.exe

Interval	Working Set (K)	Private Working Set (K)	Commit Size (K)
1	18,000	7,000	16,000
2	24,000	11,000	19,000
3	28,000	13,000	22,000
4	33,000	16,000	25,000
5	38,000	19,000	28,000
6	42,000	22,000	30,000

From Table 5-3, we can see that we have a steady increase across the board. Both the working set sizes as well as the commit size are continuously growing. If this application is allowed to run indefinitely, chances are high that it could eventually run out of memory and an `OutOfMemoryException` would be thrown. Although using the Windows Task Manager is useful to get an overview of the memory consumed, what information does it present to us as far as figuring out the source of the excessive memory consumption? Is the memory located on the native heap or the managed heap? Is it located on the heap period or elsewhere?

To find the answers to those questions, we need a more granular tool to aid us: the Windows Reliability and Performance Monitor. The Windows Reliability and Performance Monitor tool is a powerful and extensible tool that can be used to investigate the state of the system as a whole or on a per-process basis. The tool uses several different data sources such as performance counters, trace logs, and configuration information. During .NET debug sessions, performance counters is the most commonly used data source. A performance counter is an entity that is responsible for publishing a specific performance characteristic of an application or service at regular time intervals or under specific conditions. For example, a Web service servicing credit card transactions can publish a performance counter that shows how many failed transactions have occurred over time. The Windows Reliability and Performance tool knows where to gather the performance counter data and displays the results in a nice graphical and historical view. To run the tool, click the Windows Start button and type `perfmon.exe` in the search tool (prior to Windows Vista, select run and then type `perfmon.exe`). Figure 5-14 shows an example of the start screen of the tool.

The left-hand pane shows the different data sources available to the tool. As mentioned earlier, performance counters are used heavily when diagnosing .NET applications and are located under the Monitoring Tools node under Performance Monitor. The right-hand pane shows the data associated with the current data source

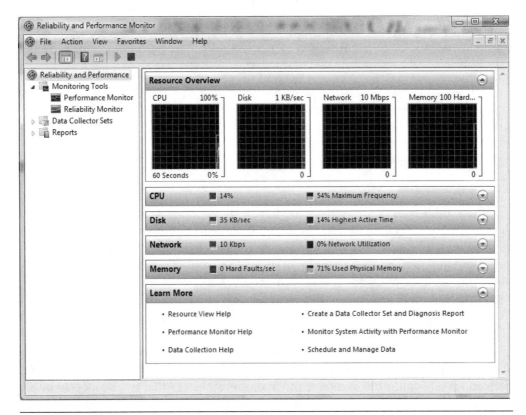

Figure 5-14   Windows Reliability and Performance Monitor

selected. When first launched, the tool shows an overview of the system state including CPU, Disk, Memory, and Network utilization. Figure 5-15 shows the tool after the Performance Monitor item is selected.

The right-hand pane now displays a visual representation of the selected performance counters over time. By default, the Processor Time counter is always selected when the tool is first launched. To add counters, right-click in the right pane and select Add Counters, which brings up the Add Counters dialog shown in Figure 5-16.

The Add Counters dialog has two parts. The first part is the left side's Available Counters options, which shows a drop-down list of all available counter categories as well as the instances of the available objects that the performance counters can collect and display data on. For example, if the .NET CLR Memory performance counter category is selected, the list of available instances shows the processes that are available. The right pane simply shows all the performance counters that have been added.

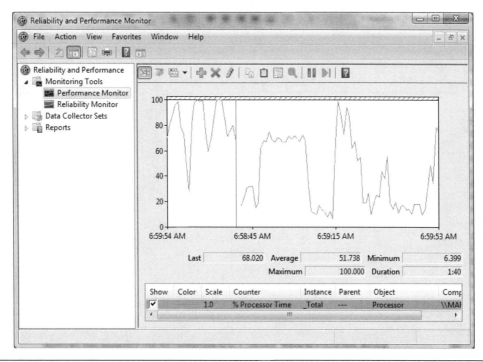

Figure 5-15 Performance Monitor

Now that we know how to add and display performance counters in the tool, let's try it out on our sample application. The first question we have to answer before blindly adding random performance counters is, which CLR counters are we specifically interested in based on the symptoms we are seeing? Table 5-4 shows the available CLR performance counter categories as well as their associated descriptions.

Based on the plethora of available categories, in our specific example, we are interested in finding out more details on the memory consumption (.NET CLR Memory) of our sample application. Table 5-5 shows the specific counters available in this category as well as their descriptions.

To monitor our sample application's memory usage, let's pick the # total bytes counter as well as the # total committed bytes counter. This can give us valuable clues as to whether the memory is on the managed heap or elsewhere in the process. Start the `0500M.exe` application followed by launching the Windows Reliability and Performance Monitoring tool. Add the two counters and specify the `0500M.exe` instance in the list of available instances. Figure 5-17 shows the output of the tool after about two minutes of `0500M.exe` runtime.

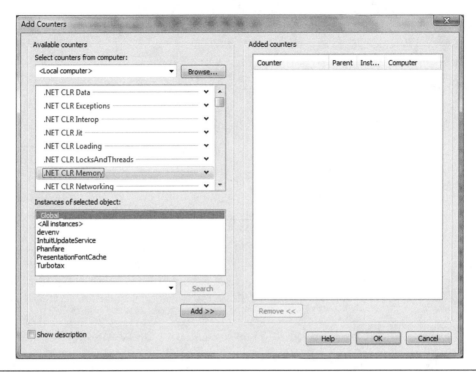

Figure 5-16 Add Counters dialog

The counters look pretty stable with no major uptick. Yet, if we look at the 05OOM process in Windows Task Manager, we can see that memory consumption is increasing quite a bit. Where is the memory coming from? At this point, we have eliminated the managed heap as being the cause for memory usage growth, and our strategy is now to use the other various counters available to see if we can spot an uptick. For example, let's choose the bytes in loader heap and current assemblies (both under the .NET CLR Loading category) and see what the output shows. (See Figure 5-18.)

Note that you may have to change the vertical scale maximum (under properties) to a larger number depending on how long the application has been executing. In Figure 5-18, the vertical scale maximum has been set to 5000. This time, we can see some more interesting data. Both the bytes in loader heap and current assemblies performance counters are slowly increasing over time. One of our theories is that we are looking at a potential assembly leak. To verify this, we can attach the debugger to the `05OOM.exe` process (`ntsd —pn 05oom.exe`) and use the `eeheap -loader` command:

Table 5-4 CLR-Specific Performance Counters Categories

Category	Description
.NET CLR Data	Runtime statistics on data (such as SQL) performance
.NET CLR Exceptions	Runtime statistics on CLR exception handling such as number of exceptions thrown
.NET CLR Interop	Runtime statistics on the interoperability services such as number of marshalling operations
.NET CLR Jit	Runtime statistics on the Just In Time compiler such as number of methods JITTED
.NET CLR Loading	Runtime statistics on the CLR class/assembly loader such as total number of bytes in the loader heap
.NET CLR LocksAndThreads	Runtime statistics on locks and threads such as the contention rate of a lock
.NET CLR Memory	Runtime statistics on the managed heap and garbage collector such as the number of collections in each generation
.NET CLR Networking	Runtime statistics on networking such as datagrams sent and received
.NET CLR Remoting	Runtime statistics on remoting such as remote calls per second
.NET CLR Security	Runtime statistics on security the total number of runtime checks

Table 5-5 .NET CLR Memory Performance Counters

Performance Counter	Description
# Bytes in all heaps	The total number of bytes in all heaps (gen 0, gen 1, gen 2, and large object heap).
# GC Handles	Total number of GC handles.
# Gen 0 collections	Total number of generation 0 garbage collections.
# Gen 1 collections	Total number of generation 1 garbage collections.
# Gen 2 collections	Total number of generation 2 garbage collections.

(continues)

5. MANAGED HEAP AND GARBAGE COLLECTION

Table 5-5 .NET CLR Memory Performance Counters *(continued)*

Performance Counter	Description
# Induced GC	Total number of times a call to `GC.Collect` has been made.
# Pinned objects	Total number of pinned objects in the managed heap during the last garbage collection. Please note that it only displays the number of pinned objects from the generations that were collected. As such, if a garbage collection resulted in only generation 0 being collected, this number only states how many pinned objects were in that generation.
# of Sink blocks in use	Current number of sync blocks in use. Useful when diagnosing performance problems related to heavy synchronization usage.
# Total committed bytes	Total number of virtual bytes committed by the CLR heap manager.
# Total reserved bytes	Total number of virtual bytes reserved by the CLR heap manager.
% Time in GC	Percentage of total elapsed time spent in the garbage collector since the last garbage collection.
Allocated bytes/sec	Number of allocated bytes per second. Updated at the beginning of every garbage collection.
Finalization Survivors	The number of garbage-collected objects that survives a collection due to waiting for finalization.
Gen 0 heap size	Maximum number of bytes that can be allocated in generation 0.
Gen 0 Promoted bytes/sec	Number of promoted bytes per second in generation 0.
Gen 1 heap size	Current number of bytes in generation 1.
Gen 1 Promoted bytes/sec	Number of promoted bytes per second in generation 1.
Gen 2 heap size	Current number of bytes in generation 1.
Large object heap size	Current size of the large object heap.
Process ID	Process identifier of process being monitored.
Promoted finalization – Memory from gen 0	The number of bytes that are promoted to generation 1 due to waiting to be finalized.
Promoted memory from Gen 0	The number of bytes promoted from generation 0 to generation 1 (minus objects that are waiting to be finalized).
Promoted memory from Gen 1	The number of bytes promoted from generation 1 to generation 2 (minus objects that are waiting to be finalized).

```
0:003> !eeheap -loader
Loader Heap:
```

```
System Domain: 7a3bc8b8
LowFrequencyHeap: Size: 0x0(0)bytes.
HighFrequencyHeap: 002a2000(8000:1000) Size: 0x1000(4096)bytes.
StubHeap: 002aa000(2000:2000) Size: 0x2000(8192)bytes.
Virtual Call Stub Heap:
  IndcellHeap: Size: 0x0(0)bytes.
  LookupHeap: Size: 0x0(0)bytes.
  ResolveHeap: Size: 0x0(0)bytes.
  DispatchHeap: Size: 0x0(0)bytes.
  CacheEntryHeap: Size: 0x0(0)bytes.
Total size:  0x3000(12288)bytes
```

```
Shared Domain: 7a3bc560
LowFrequencyHeap: 002d0000(2000:1000) Size: 0x1000(4096)bytes.
HighFrequencyHeap: 002d2000(8000:1000) Size: 0x1000(4096)bytes.
StubHeap: 002da000(2000:1000) Size: 0x1000(4096)bytes.
Virtual Call Stub Heap:
  IndcellHeap: 00870000(2000:1000) Size: 0x1000(4096)bytes.
  LookupHeap: 00875000(2000:1000) Size: 0x1000(4096)bytes.
  ResolveHeap: 0087b000(5000:1000) Size: 0x1000(4096)bytes.
  DispatchHeap: 00877000(4000:1000) Size: 0x1000(4096)bytes.
  CacheEntryHeap: 00872000(3000:1000) Size: 0x1000(4096)bytes.
Total size:  0x7000(28672)bytes
```

```
Domain 1: 304558
LowFrequencyHeap: 002b0000(2000:2000) 00ca0000(10000:10000) 01cf0000(10000:10000)
04070000(10000:10000) 04170000(10000:10000)
...
...
...
 165e0000(10000:10000) 166b0000(10000:10000) 16770000(10000:10000)
16830000(10000:10000) 16900000(10000:10000) 169c0000(10000:10000)
16a80000(10000:a000) Size: 0x16fc000(24100864)bytes.
HighFrequencyHeap: 002b2000(8000:8000) 03e50000(10000:10000) 04370000(10000:10000)
046c0000(10000:10000) 04a10000(10000:10000)
...
...
...
15bf0000(10000:10000) 15f30000(10000:10000) 16270000(10000:10000)
165a0000(10000:10000) 168f0000(10000:a000) Size: 0x572000(5709824)bytes.
StubHeap: 002ba000(2000:1000) Size: 0x1000(4096)bytes.
Virtual Call Stub Heap:
  IndcellHeap: Size: 0x0(0)bytes.
  LookupHeap: Size: 0x0(0)bytes.
```

```
    ResolveHeap: 002ca000(6000:1000) Size: 0x1000(4096)bytes.
    DispatchHeap: 002c7000(3000:1000) Size: 0x1000(4096)bytes.
    CacheEntryHeap: 002c2000(4000:1000) Size: 0x1000(4096)bytes.
Total size: 0x1c71000(29822976)bytes
```

```
Jit code heap:
LoaderCodeHeap: 165f0000(10000:b000) Size: 0xb000(45056)bytes.
LoaderCodeHeap: 15de0000(10000:10000) Size: 0x10000(65536)bytes.
LoaderCodeHeap: 15600000(10000:10000) Size: 0x10000(65536)bytes.
...
...
...
LoaderCodeHeap: 04710000(10000:10000) Size: 0x10000(65536)bytes.
LoaderCodeHeap: 009e0000(10000:10000) Size: 0x10000(65536)bytes.
Total size: 0x23b000(2338816)bytes
```

```
Module Thunk heaps:
Module 790c2000: Size: 0x0(0)bytes.
Module 002d2564: Size: 0x0(0)bytes.
...
...
...
Module 168f8e40: Size: 0x0(0)bytes.
Module 168f93b8: Size: 0x0(0)bytes.
Module 168f9930: Size: 0x0(0)bytes.
Total size: 0x0(0)bytes
```

```
Module Lookup Table heaps:
Module 790c2000: Size: 0x0(0)bytes.
Module 002d2564: Size: 0x0(0)bytes.
Module 002d21d8: Size: 0x0(0)bytes.
...
...
...
Module 168f93b8: Size: 0x0(0)bytes.
Module 168f9930: Size: 0x0(0)bytes.
Total size: 0x0(0)bytes
```

Total LoaderHeap size: 0x1eb6000(32202752)bytes

==

The first two domains (system and shared) seem to look reasonable, but the default application domain has a ton of data in it. More specifically, it contains the bulk of the overall loader heap (size 32202752). Why does the application domain contain so much data? We can get further information about the default application domain by using the `DumpDomain` command and specifying the address of the default application domain (found in output from the previous `eeheap` command):

```
0:003> !DumpDomain 304558
```

```
Domain 1: 00304558
LowFrequencyHeap: 0030457c
HighFrequencyHeap: 003045d4
StubHeap: 0030462c
Stage: OPEN
SecurityDescriptor: 00305ab8
Name: 05OOM.exe
Assembly: 0030d1b0
[C:\Windows\assembly\GAC_32\mscorlib\2.0.0.0__b77a5c561934e089\mscorlib.dll]
ClassLoader: 002fc988
SecurityDescriptor: 0030dfd8
  Module Name
790c2000 C:\Windows\assembly\GAC_32\mscorlib\2.0.0.0__b77a5c561934e089\mscorlib.dll
002d2564 C:\Windows\assembly\GAC_32\mscorlib\2.0.0.0__b77a5c561934e089\sortkey.nlp
002d21d8 C:\Windows\assembly\GAC_32\mscorlib\2.0.0.0__b77a5c561934e089\sorttbls.nlp

Assembly: 0032f1b8 [C:\ADNDBin\05OOM.exe]
ClassLoader: 002fd168
SecurityDescriptor: 00330f30
  Module Name
002b2c3c C:\ADNDBin\05OOM.exe

Assembly: 0033bb98
[C:\Windows\assembly\GAC_MSIL\System.Xml\2.0.0.0__b77a5c561934e089\System.Xml.dll]
ClassLoader: 002fd408
SecurityDescriptor: 00326b18
  Module Name
639f8000
C:\Windows\assembly\GAC_MSIL\System.Xml\2.0.0.0__b77a5c561934e089\System.Xml.dll
...
...
...
Assembly: 00346408 [4ql4a3hq, Version=0.0.0.0, Culture=neutral,
PublicKeyToken=null]
ClassLoader: 003423a8
SecurityDescriptor: 00346380
  Module Name
002b46f8 4ql4a3hq, Version=0.0.0.0, Culture=neutral, PublicKeyToken=null
```

```
Assembly: 003465a0 [lx4qjutk, Version=0.0.0.0, Culture=neutral, PublicKeyToken=null]
ClassLoader: 00342488
SecurityDescriptor: 00346518
  Module Name
002b4ce4 lx4qjutk, Version=0.0.0.0, Culture=neutral, PublicKeyToken=null

Assembly: 003466b0 [udslhfbo, Version=0.0.0.0, Culture=neutral, PublicKeyToken=null]
ClassLoader: 003424f8
SecurityDescriptor: 00346628
  Module Name
002b5258 udslhfbo, Version=0.0.0.0, Culture=neutral, PublicKeyToken=null

...
...
...
...
```

As we can see, there are numerous assemblies loaded into the default application domain. Furthermore, the names of the assemblies seem rather random. Why are all these assemblies being loaded? Our code in Listing 5-9 certainly doesn't directly load any assemblies, which means that these assemblies have to be dynamically generated. To further investigate what these assemblies contain, we can pick one of them and dump out the associated module information using the `DumpModule` command:

```
0:003> !DumpModule 002b5258
Name: udslhfbo, Version=0.0.0.0, Culture=neutral, PublicKeyToken=null
Attributes: PEFile
Assembly: 003466b0
LoaderHeap: 00000000
TypeDefToMethodTableMap: 00ca2df8
TypeRefToMethodTableMap: 00ca2e10
MethodDefToDescMap: 00ca2e6c
FieldDefToDescMap: 00ca2ed0
MemberRefToDescMap: 00ca2ef8
FileReferencesMap: 00ca2fec
AssemblyReferencesMap: 00ca2ff0
MetaData start address: 00cc07c8 (4344 bytes)
```

Next, we dump the metadata of the module using the `dc` command specifying the starting address and the ending address (starting address + size of metadata):

```
0:003> dc 00cc07c8 00cc07c8+0n4344
00cc07c8    424a5342 00010001 00000000 0000000c   BSJB............
00cc07d8    302e3276 3730352e 00003732 00050000   v2.0.50727......
00cc07e8    0000006c 00000528 00007e23 00000594   l...(...#~......
```

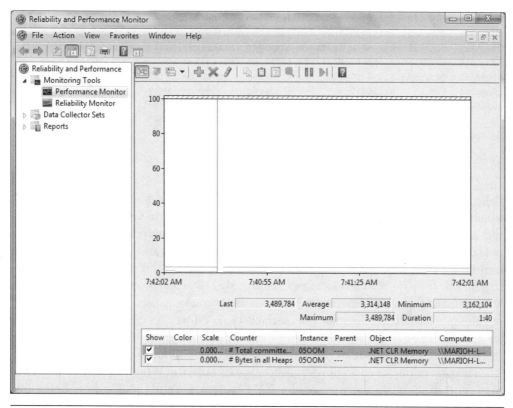

Figure 5-17   Monitoring 05OOM.exe total and committed bytes

```
00cc07f8   0000077c 72745323 73676e69 00000000   |...#Strings....
...
...
...
00cc0d58   00000000 6f4d3c00 656c7564 6475003e   .....<Module>.ud
00cc0d68   66683173 642e6f62 58006c6c 65536c6d   slhfbo.dll.XmlSe
00cc0d78   6c616972 74617a69 576e6f69 65746972   rializationWrite
00cc0d88   72655072 006e6f73 7263694d 666f736f   rPerson.Microsof
00cc0d98   6d582e74 65532e6c 6c616972 74617a69   t.Xml.Serializat
00cc0da8   2e6e6f69 656e6547 65746172 7734164    ion.GeneratedAss
00cc0db8   6c626d65 6d580079 7265536c 696c6169   embly.XmlSeriali
00cc0dc8   6974617a 65526e6f 72656461 73726550   zationReaderPers
00cc0dd8   58006e6f 65536c6d 6c616972 72657a69   on.XmlSerializer
00cc0de8   65500031 6e6f7372 69726553 7a696c61   1.PersonSerializ
00cc0df8   58007265 65536c6d 6c616972 72657a69   er.XmlSerializer
```

```
00cc0e08   746e6f43 74636172 73795300 2e6d6574   Contract.System.
00cc0e18   006c6d58 74737953 582e6d65 532e6c6d   Xml.System.Xml.S
00cc0e28   61697265 617a696c 6e6f6974 6c6d5800   erialization.Xml
00cc0e38   69726553 7a696c61 6f697461 6972576e   SerializationWri
00cc0e48   00726574 536c6d58 61697265 617a696c   ter.XmlSerializa
00cc0e58   6e6f6974 64616552 58007265 65536c6d   tionReader.XmlSe
00cc0e68   6c616972 72657a69 6c6d5800 69726553   rializer.XmlSeri
...
...
...
```

Now we are getting somewhere. From the output of the metadata, we can see that the module associated with the assembly contains references to some form of XML serialization. Furthermore, it seems that the module contains XML serialization types that are specific to the serialization of the `Person` class in our code. Based on this evidence, we can now hypothesize that the XML serialization code in our application is causing all of these dynamic assemblies to be generated. The next step is the documentation for the `XmlSerializer` class. MSDN clearly states that using the `XmlSerializer` class for performance reasons may in fact create a specialized dynamic assembly to handle the serialization. More specifically, seven of the `XmlSerializer` constructors result in dynamic assemblies being generated, whereas the remaining two have reuse logic that reduces the number of dynamic assemblies.

The preceding scenario illustrates how we can use the Windows Task Manager to monitor the overall memory usage of a .NET application and the Windows Reliability and Performance Monitor tool to drill down into the CLR specifics. The scenario assumes that we had the luxury of running and monitoring the application live. In many cases, the application simply runs until it runs out of memory and throws an `OutOfMemoryException`. If we let our sample application run indefinitely, the `OutOfMemoryException` would have been reported as follows:

```
(1830.1f20): CLR exception - code e0434f4d (first/second chance not available)
eax=0027ed2c ebx=e0434f4d ecx=00000001 edx=00000000 esi=0027edb4 edi=00338510
eip=775842eb esp=0027ed2c ebp=0027ed7c iopl=0         nv up ei pl nz na po nc
cs=001b  ss=0023  ds=0023  es=0023  fs=003b  gs=0000            efl=00000202
*** ERROR: Symbol file could not be found.  Defaulted to export symbols for
kernel32.dll -
kernel32!RaiseException+0x58:
```

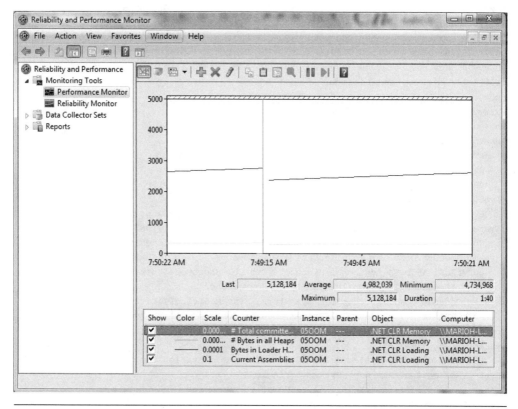

Figure 5-18 Monitoring O5OOM.exe current assemblies and bytes in loader heap performance counters

As discussed earlier, to get further information on the managed exception, we can use the `PrintException` command:

```
0:000> kb
ChildEBP RetAddr  Args to Child
0027ed7c 79f071ac e0434f4d 00000001 00000001 kernel32!RaiseException+0x58
0027eddc 79f0a780 51e10dac 00000001 00000000
 mscorwks!RaiseTheExceptionInternalOnly+0x2a8
*** WARNING: Unable to verify checksum for System.ni.dll
0027ee80 7a53e025 0027f14c 79f0a3d9 0027f338 mscorwks!JIT_Rethrow+0xbf
0027ef4c 7a53d665 51df597c 00000000 51de0050 System_ni+0xfe025
0027ef80 7a4d078a 51df597c 51de0050 638fcb39 System_ni+0xfd665
*** WARNING: Unable to verify checksum for System.Xml.ni.dll
0027efec 638fb6e5 00000000 51de02cc 00000000 System_ni+0x9078a
```

```
0027f078 638fa683 51ddff88 00000000 51de02cc System_Xml_ni+0x15b6e5
0027f09c 63960d09 00000000 00000000 00000000 System_Xml_ni+0x15a683
0027f0c4 6396090c 00000000 00000000 00000000 System_Xml_ni+0x1c0d09
0027f120 79e7c74b 00000000 0027f158 0027f1b0 System_Xml_ni+0x1c090c
00000000 00000000 00000000 00000000 00000000 mscorwks!CallDescrWorker+0x33
0:000> !PrintException 51e10dac
Exception object: 51e10dac
```

Exception type: System.OutOfMemoryException

```
Message: <none>
InnerException: <none>
StackTrace (generated):
    SP       IP       Function
    0027EE94 7942385A mscorlib_ni!System.Reflection.Assembly.Load
(Byte[], Byte[], System.Security.Policy.Evidence)+0x3a
    0027EEB0 7A4BF513 System_ni!Microsoft.CSharp.CSharpCodeGenerator.FromFileBatch
(System.CodeDom.Compiler.CompilerParameters, System.String[])+0x3ab
    0027EF00 7A53E025 System_ni!Microsoft.CSharp.CSharpCodeGenerator.FromSourceBatch
(System.CodeDom.Compiler.CompilerParameters, System.String[])+0x1f1
    0027EF58 7A53D665 System_ni!Microsoft.CSharp.CSharpCodeGenerator.System.CodeDom.
Compiler.ICodeCompiler.CompileAssemblyFromSourceBatch
(System.CodeDom.Compiler.CompilerParameters, System.String[])+0x29
    0027EF8C 7A4D078A System_ni!System.CodeDom.Compiler.CodeDomProvider.
CompileAssemblyFromSource(System.CodeDom.Compiler.CompilerParameters,
System.String[])+0x16
    0027EF98 638FCB39 System_Xml_ni!System.Xml.Serialization.Compiler.Compile
(System.Reflection.Assembly, System.String,
System.Xml.Serialization.XmlSerializerCompilerParameters,
System.Security.Policy.Evidence)+0x269
    0027F000 638FB6E5
System_Xml_ni!System.Xml.Serialization.TempAssembly.GenerateAssembly
(System.Xml.Serialization.XmlMapping[], System.Type[], System.String,
System.Security.Policy.Evidence,
System.Xml.Serialization.XmlSerializerCompilerParameters,
System.Reflection.Assembly, System.Collections.Hashtable)+0x7e9
    0027F094 638FA683 System_Xml_ni!System.Xml.Serialization.TempAssembly..ctor
(System.Xml.Serialization.XmlMapping[], System.Type[], System.String, System.String,
System.Security.Policy.Evidence)+0x4b
    0027F0B4 63960D09 System_Xml_ni!System.Xml.Serialization.XmlSerializer..ctor
(System.Type, System.Xml.Serialization.XmlAttributeOverrides, System.Type[],
System.Xml.Serialization.XmlRootAttribute, System.String, System.String,
System.Security.Policy.Evidence)+0xed
    0027F0E4 6396090C System_Xml_ni!System.Xml.Serialization.XmlSerializer..ctor
(System.Type, System.Xml.Serialization.XmlRootAttribute)+0x28
      0027F0F4 009201D6 05OOM!Advanced.NET.Debugging.Chapter5.OOM.Run()+0xe6
      0027F118 009200A7
05OOM!Advanced.NET.Debugging.Chapter5.OOM.Main(System.String[])+0x37
```

```
StackTraceString: <none>
HResult: 8007000e
There are nested exceptions on this thread. Run with -nested for details
```

At this point, the application has already failed and we can't rely on runtime monitoring tools to gauge the application's memory usage. In situations like this, we have to rely solely on the debugger commands to analyze where the memory is being consumed. Unfortunately, there is no single cookbook recipe on the exact commands and steps to take, but as a general rule of thumb, utilizing the various diagnostics commands (such as `eeheap`, `dumpheap`, `dumpdomain`, etc.) can give invaluable clues as to where in the CLR the memory is being consumed. The excessive memory consumption can, of course, also be as a result of a native code leak, which we will see an example of in Chapter 7, "Interoperability."

Immediately Break on OutOfMemoryException

When a process gets into a situation where it is running out of memory, things can get very tricky and the application may not be able to properly handle the condition. Because an `OutOfMemoryException` gets propagated up the chain and does not fault the process until the exception is deemed unhandled, a lot of code may still get executed as part of the unwinding making troubleshooting more difficult in certain situations. Furthermore, if the code is hosted in a process that it does not own, the process may catch all kinds of exceptions and continue running. To ensure that an `OutOfMemoryException` always breaks under the debugger, the CLR introduced a registry value called `GCBreakOnOOM` (DWORD) under the following registry path: `HKEY_LOCAL_MACHINE\SOFTWARE\Microsoft\.NET Framework`. The value can be set to 1, in which case an event log message is logged; it can be set to 2, in which case the out of memory condition causes a break in the debugger; or it can be set to 4, in which case a more extensive event log is written that includes memory statistics at the point where the out of memory condition was encountered.

Summary

Effective debugging of tricky application problems in the managed heap and garbage collector requires a solid internal understanding of how these components work. In this chapter, we took a detailed tour of how the CLR heap manager and garbage collector functions. We started by looking at the high-level architecture and how the

CLR heap manager fits into the overall Windows memory architecture followed by an in-depth discussion of the various concepts (generations, roots, finalization, etc.) utilized by the garbage collector. Sample code was shown in tandem with the debugger and associated tools to illustrate how these concepts work in practice. Lastly, we looked at a number of examples of common programming mistakes and how they manifest themselves in the CLR. The examples included how to track down the source of heap corruptions on the managed heap, how to track down the source of out-of-memory situations, and how to debug faulty finalization code.

## CHAPTER 6

SYNCHRONIZATION

In this chapter, we will take a close look at common synchronization problems and how to troubleshoot and find the root cause as efficiently as possible. The chapter starts out by explaining the basic synchronization primitives available in the CLR, is followed by a number of practical debugging scenarios showcasing the most common synchronization problems, and then discusses how to use the debuggers to get at the root cause.

Synchronization Basics

The Windows operating system is a preemptive and multithreaded operating system. Multithreading refers to the capability to run any number of threads concurrently. If the system is a single processor machine, Windows creates the illusion of concurrent thread execution by allowing each thread to run for a short period of time (known as a time quantum). When that time quantum is exhausted, the thread is put to sleep and the processor switches to another thread (known as a context switch), and so on. On a multiprocessor machine, two or more threads are capable of running concurrently (one thread per physical processor).

By being preemptive, all active threads in the system must be able to yield control of the processor to another thread at any point in time. Given that the operating system can take away control from a thread, developers must take care to always be in a state where control can safely be taken away.

If all applications were single threaded, or if all the threads were running in isolation, synchronization would not be a problem. Alas, for efficiency sake, dependent multithreading is the norm today and also the source of a lot of bugs in applications. Dependent multithreading occurs when two or more threads need to work in tandem to complete a task. Code execution for a given task may, for example, be broken up between one or more threads (with or without shared resources) and hence the threads need to "communicate" with each other in regards to the order of thread execution. This communication is referred to as thread synchronization and is crucial to any multithreaded application.

Thread Synchronization Primitives

Internally, the Windows operating system represents a thread in a data structure known as the thread execution block (TEB). This data structure contains various attributes such as the thread identifier, last error, local storage, and so on. Listing 6-1 shows an abbreviated output of the different elements of the TEB data structure.

Listing 6-1   Abbreviated output of the TEB data structure

```
0:000> dt _TEB
ntdll!_TEB
   +0x000 NtTib             : _NT_TIB
   +0x01c EnvironmentPointer : Ptr32 Void
   +0x020 ClientId          : _CLIENT_ID
   +0x028 ActiveRpcHandle   : Ptr32 Void
   +0x02c ThreadLocalStoragePointer : Ptr32 Void
   +0x030 ProcessEnvironmentBlock : Ptr32 _PEB
   +0x034 LastErrorValue    : Uint4B
   +0x038 CountOfOwnedCriticalSections : Uint4B
   ...
   ...
   ...
   +0xfca RtlExceptionAttached : Pos 9, 1 Bit
   +0xfca SpareSameTebBits : Pos 10, 6 Bits
   +0xfcc TxnScopeEnterCallback : Ptr32 Void
   +0xfd0 TxnScopeExitCallback : Ptr32 Void
   +0xfd4 TxnScopeContext   : Ptr32 Void
   +0xfd8 LockCount         : Uint4B
   +0xfdc ProcessRundown    : Uint4B
   +0xfe0 LastSwitchTime    : Uint8B
   +0xfe8 TotalSwitchOutTime : Uint8B
   +0xff0 WaitReasonBitMap  : _LARGE_INTEGER
```

All in all, on a Windows Vista machine, the TEB data structure contains right around 98 different elements. Although most of these elements aren't typically used when debugging .NET synchronization problems, it is important to be aware that Windows carries a lot of information about any given thread to accurately schedule execution. Much in the same way that Windows includes a thread data structure to maintain the state of a thread, so does the CLR. The CLR's version of the thread data structure is, not surprisingly, called `Thread`. Although the internals of the `Thread` class is not made public, we can utilize the SOS debugger extension commands outlined in Chapter 3, "Basic Debugging Tasks," to gain insight into the mechanics of CLR threads.

One very useful command is the `threads` command, which outputs a summary of all the CLR threads currently in the process as well as individual state for each thread:

```
0:003> !threads
ThreadCount: 2
UnstartedThread: 0
BackgroundThread: 1
PendingThread: 0
DeadThread: 0
Hosted Runtime: no
                                 PreEmptive   GC Alloc           Lock
      ID OSID ThreadOBJ    State    GC        Context    Domain  Count APT
Exception
   0   1 108c 00191ec8     a020 Enabled  00000000:00000000 0015d080     0 MTA
   2   2  990 0019b900     b220 Enabled  00000000:00000000 0015d080     0 MTA
(Finalizer)
```

The output of the command is detailed in Chapter 3. Although the `threads` command gives us some insight into the CLR representation of a thread (such as the thread state, CLR thread ID, OS thread ID, etc.), the internal CLR representation is far more extensive. Even though the internal representation is not made public, we can use the Rotor source code to gain some insight into the general structure of the Thread class. The Rotor source files of interest are `threads.h` and `threads.cpp` located under the `sscli20\clr\src\vm folder`. Listing 6-2 shows a few examples of data members that are part of the `Thread` class.

Listing 6-2 Abbreviated version of the CLR Thread class

```
class Thread
{
    ...
    ...
    ...
    volatile ThreadState m_State;

    DWORD m_dwLockCount;
    DWORD m_ThreadId;
    LockEntry *m_pHead;
    LockEntry m_embeddedEntry;
    ...
    ...
    ...
}
```

6. SYNCHRONIZATION

The m_State member contains the state of the thread (such as alive, aborted, etc.). The m_dwLockCount member indicates how many locks are currently held by the thread. The m_ThreadId member corresponds to the managed thread ID, and the last two members (m_pHead, m_embeddedEntry) correspond to the reader/writer lock state of the thread. If we need to take a closer look at a CLR thread (including the members above), we have to first find a pointer to an instance of a Thread class. This can easily be done by first using the threads command and looking at the ThreadOBJ column, which corresponds to the underlying Thread instance:

```
0:000> !threads
ThreadCount: 2
UnstartedThread: 0
BackgroundThread: 2
PendingThread: 0
DeadThread: 0
Hosted Runtime: no
                                      PreEmptive   GC Alloc          Lock
       ID OSID ThreadOBJ   State      GC       Context       Domain
   Count APT Exception
   0     1 47c8 003b4528     220 Enabled   01ebb070:01ebbfe8 003afe20    0 STA
XXXX     2 1120 003c3b28    b220 Enabled   00000000:00000000 003afe20
       0 STA (Finalizer)
0:000> dd 003b4528
003b4528  79f96af0 00000220 00000000 ffffffff
003b4538  00000000 00000000 00000000 00000001
003b4548  00000000 003b4550 003b4550 003b4550
003b4558  00000000 00000000 baad0000 003b1120
003b4568  01ebb070 01ebbfe8 0001afd0 00000000
003b4578  00000000 00000000 00000000 baadf00d
003b4588  003b4be8 003c90b0 003c91d0 000000e8
003b4598  003c90b0 003e3248 00000000 00000100
```

We can see that the threads command shows that the first thread pointer is located at address 0x003b4528. We can then use the dd command to dump out the contents of the pointer. What if we want to find out the contents of the m_State member? To accomplish this, we have to first figure out the offset of this member in the object's memory layout. A couple of different strategies can be used. The first strategy is to look at the class definition and see if there are any members in close proximity that you already know the value of. If that is the case, you can simply dump out the contents of the object until you find the known member and subsequently find the target member by relative offset. The other strategy is to simply look at all the members in the class definition and find the offset of the target member by simply adding up all the sizes of previous members leading up to the member of interest. Let's use the latter strategy to find the m_State member. Looking at the class definition, we can see that the m_State member is in fact the very first member of the class. It then stands to reason that if we were to dump out the contents of the thread pointer, the very first field should be the state of the thread:

```
0:000> dd 003b4528
003b4528  79f96af0 00000220 00000000 ffffffff
003b4538  00000000 00000000 00000000 00000001
003b4548  00000000 003b4550 003b4550 003b4550
003b4558  00000000 00000000 baad0000 003b1120
003b4568  01ebb070 01ebbfe8 0001afd0 00000000
003b4578  00000000 00000000 00000000 baadf00d
003b4588  003b4be8 003c90b0 003c91d0 000000e8
003b4598  003c90b0 003e3248 00000000 00000100
```

Interestingly enough, the first element (0x79f96af0) doesn't seem to resemble a thread's state. As a matter of fact, if we use the ln (list near) command, we can see the following:

```
0:000> ln 79f96af0
(79f96af0)   mscorwks!Thread::'vftable'   |   (79f96b28)   mscorwks!Thread::Thread
Exact matches:
mscorwks!Thread::'vftable' = <no type information>
```

We are seeing the virtual function table pointer of the object. Although not terribly interesting from a debugging perspective, it can come in handy to convince ourselves that the pointer we are looking at is in fact a pointer to a valid thread object. Because we can safely ignore this pointer for our current purposes, the next value is 0x00000220. This value looks like it may represent a bitmask of sorts but to interpret this bitmask in the context of a thread state, we must first enumerate the various bits that constitute a thread state. The Thread class contains an enumeration that represents a thread's state called the ThreadState enumeration. This enumeration can yield important clues when debugging synchronization problems. Although the entire enumeration contains close to one hundred fields, some are more important than others when debugging synchronization issues. Table 6-1 shows the most interesting fields of the ThreadState enumeration.

6. SYNCHRONIZATION

Table 6-1   ThreadState Enumeration

Field Name	Value	Description
TS_Unknown	0x00000000	State of a newly initialized thread.
TS_AbortRequested	0x00000001	A thread abort has been requested.
TS_GCSuspendPending	0x00000002	This state indicates that the GC has requested that this thread be suspended and that the thread is trying to find a safe spot to suspend itself.
TS_LegalToJoin	0x00000020	Thread is in a state where it can enter a Join.
TS_Background	0x00000200	Thread is a background thread.
TS_Unstarted	0x00000400	Thread has never been started.
TS_Dead	0x00000800	Thread is dead, meaning that the underlying OS thread is gone but the managed representation of the thread may still reside in memory.
TS_ThreadPoolThread	0x00800000	Thread is a thread pool thread.
TS_AbortInitiated	0x10000000	Indicates that a thread abort has begun.
TS_Finalized	0x20000000	The underlying managed thread object has been finalized and can be collected.
TS_FailStarted	0x40000000	Thread failed to start.

Based on Table 6-1 and our previous state 0x00000220, we can infer the following:

- The thread is a background thread (0x00000200).
- The thread is in a state where it can enter a Join (0x00000020).
- The thread is a newly initialized thread (0x00000000).

THREAD CLASS DISCLOSURE Although it may be useful to see the "internals" of a thread, it is important to realize that there is a good reason why this information is internal and not exposed through the threads command. Much of the information is an implementation detail and Microsoft reserves the right to change it at any time. Taking a dependency on these internal mechanisms is a dangerous prospect and should be avoided at all cost. Secondly, Rotor is a *reference* implementation and does not guarantee that the internals mimic the CLR source code in detail.

Now that we have discussed how the CLR represents a thread internally, it is time to take a look at some of the most common synchronization primitives that the CLR exposes as well as how they are represented in the CLR itself.

Events

The event is a kernel mode primitive accessible in user mode via an opaque handle. An Event is a synchronization object that can take on one of two states: signaled or nonsignaled. When an event goes from the nonsignaled state to the signaled state (indicating that a particular event has occurred), a thread waiting on that event object is awakened and allowed to continue execution. Event objects are very commonly used to synchronize code flow execution between multiple threads. For example, the native Win32 API `ReadFile` can read data asynchronously by passing in a pointer to an OVERLAPPED structure. Figure 6-1 illustrates the flow of events.

The `ReadFile` returns to the caller immediately and processes the read operation in the background. The caller is then free to do other work. After the caller is ready for the results of the read operation, it simply waits (using the `WaitForSingleObject` API) for the state of the event to become signaled. When

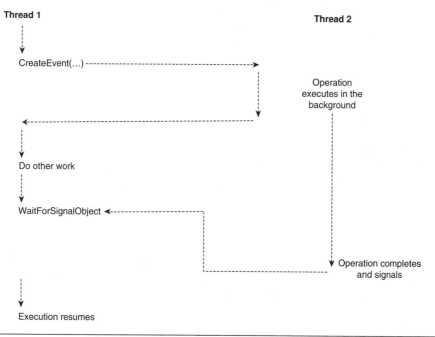

Figure 6-1 Asynchronous API flow

the background read operations succeeds, the event is set to a signaled state, thereby waking up the calling thread, and allows execution to continue.

There are two forms of event objects: manual reset and auto reset. The key difference between the two is what happens when the event is signaled. In the case of a manual reset event, the event object remains in the signaled state until explicitly reset, thereby allowing any number of threads waiting for the event object to be released. In contrast, the auto reset event only allows one waiting thread to be released before being automatically reset to the nonsignaled state. If there are no threads waiting, the event remains in a signaled state until the first thread tries to wait for the event. In the .NET framework, the manual reset event is exposed in the System.Threading.ManualResetEvent class and the auto reset event is exposed in the System.Threading.AutoResetEvent class.

To take a closer look at an instance of either of the two classes of events, we can use the do command as shown in the following:

```
0:000> !do 0x01c9ad4c
Name: System.Threading.AutoResetEvent
MethodTable: 791124e4
EEClass: 791f5ff0
Size: 24(0x18) bytes
 (C:\Windows\assembly\GAC_32\mscorlib\2.0.0.0__b77a5c561934e089\mscorlib.dll)
Fields:
      MT    Field   Offset                 Type VT    Attr    Value Name
790fd0f0  400018a        4         System.Object  0 instance 00000000 __identity
791016bc  40005b3        c        System.IntPtr  1 instance      204 waitHandle
79112728  40005b4        8 ...es.SafeWaitHandle  0 instance 01c9ad64 safeWaitHandle
7910be50  40005b5       10       System.Boolean  1 instance        0
 hasThreadAffinity
791016bc  40005b6      994        System.IntPtr  1   shared    static InvalidHandle

0:000> !do 0x01c9ad78
Name: System.Threading.ManualResetEvent
MethodTable: 7911a1e8
EEClass: 7911a170
Size: 24(0x18) bytes
 (C:\Windows\assembly\GAC_32\mscorlib\2.0.0.0__b77a5c561934e089\mscorlib.dll)
Fields:
      MT    Field   Offset                 Type VT    Attr    Value Name
790fd0f0  400018a        4         System.Object  0 instance 00000000 __identity
791016bc  40005b3        c        System.IntPtr  1 instance      208 waitHandle
79112728  40005b4        8 ...es.SafeWaitHandle  0 instance 01c9ad90 safeWaitHandle
7910be50  40005b5       10       System.Boolean  1 instance        0
 hasThreadAffinity
791016bc  40005b6      994        System.IntPtr  1   shared    static InvalidHandle
          >> Domain:Value  0016ff10:ffffffff <<
```

Because the Event classes in the `System.Threading` namespace are simply wrappers over the underlying Windows kernel objects, the `waitHandle` member of the classes can be used to gain more insight into the underlying kernel mode object. We can use the `handle` debugger command with the `waitHandle` value:

```
0:000> !handle 204 8
Handle 204
  Object Specific Information
    Event Type Auto Reset
    Event is Waiting
```

Here, we can see that the `waitHandle` with value `204` corresponds to an auto reset event that is currently in a waiting state.

Mutex

A mutex is a kernel mode synchronization construct that can be used to synchronize threads both within a process as well as across multiple processes (by naming the mutex during creation). Generally speaking, if your synchronization chores are all within the same process you should use a monitor or other user mode synchronization primitives. If, on the other hand, you need to synchronize across processes, a named mutex is the right approach. Because a mutex is a kernel mode construct, the user mode code accesses the mutex using the System.Threading.Mutex class. To get more information about a mutex while debugging in user mode, you can use the `dumpobj` extension command to see the individual fields of the mutex.

```
0:000> !do 0x01eb58bc
Name: System.Threading.Mutex
MethodTable: 79117d00
EEClass: 791f94d8
Size: 24(0x18) bytes
  (C:\Windows\assembly\GAC_32\mscorlib\2.0.0.0__b77a5c561934e089\mscorlib.dll)
Fields:
      MT    Field   Offset                 Type VT    Attr    Value Name
790fd0f0  400018a      4      System.Object  0 instance 00000000
  __identity
791016bc  40005b3      c         System.IntPtr  1 instance      1fc
  waitHandle
79112728  40005b4      8  ...es.SafeWaitHandle  0 instance 01eb5958
  safeWaitHandle
7910be50  40005b5     10      System.Boolean  1 instance        1
hasThreadAffinity
```

```
791016bc  40005b6      994         System.IntPtr  1    shared   static InvalidHandle
    >> Domain:Value  003bfdc0:ffffffff <<
7910be50  40005fd      9a0         System.Boolean 1    shared   static dummyBool
    >> Domain:Value  003bfdc0:NotInit  <<
```

The layout of the Mutex class is very similar to that of the two previous event classes we discussed. In the same way that the event classes contained a `waitHandle`, so does the Mutex class. This `waitHandle` can be used in conjunction with the `handle` command to get more detailed information on the mutex:

```
0:000> !handle 1fc 8
Handle 1fc
  Object Specific Information
    Mutex is Free
```

Semaphore

A semaphore is a kernel mode synchronization object accessible from user mode. It is similar to a mutex in the sense that it allows exclusive access to a resource. The main difference, however, is that a semaphore employs resource counting, thereby allowing X number of threads access to the resource. A great example of when to use a semaphore is in a system that has four USB ports that are accessed by a piece of code. Because there are four USB ports, we would like to allow four threads to concurrently use one of the available USB ports. To accomplish this, we would create a semaphore with a max resource count of four. As threads try to acquire the semaphore, the reference count (initialized to 4) is checked as to whether it is greater than 0, and if it is, it allows the acquisition and decrements the reference count. When the reference count reaches 0, a thread trying to acquire the semaphore is put to sleep until a thread releases the semaphore and the reference count is incremented. As with events and mutexes, you would use the `do` command followed by the `handle` extension command in the debugger to get extended information on a semaphore.

```
0:000> !do 0x01d159ac
Name: System.Threading.Semaphore
MethodTable: 7a76397c
EEClass: 7a763904
Size: 24(0x18) bytes
  (C:\Windows\assembly\GAC_MSIL\System\2.0.0.0__b77a5c561934e089\System.dll)
Fields:
      MT    Field   Offset               Type VT    Attr    Value Name
790fd0f0  400018a        4        System.Object  0 instance 00000000 __identity
791016bc  40005b3        c        System.IntPtr  1 instance      238 waitHandle
```

```
79112728   40005b4        8 ...es.SafeWaitHandle  0 instance 01d159c4 safeWaitHandle
7910be50   40005b5       10        System.Boolean  1 instance        0
 hasThreadAffinity
791016bc   40005b6      994        System.IntPtr   1   shared    static InvalidHandle
    >> Domain:Value  0018fdc0:ffffffff <<
79102290   4001066      8c8        System.Int32    1   static           0 MAX_PATH
0:000> !handle 238
Handle 238
  Type          Semaphore
0:000> !handle 238 8
Handle 238
  Object Specific Information
    Semaphore Count 0
    Semaphore Limit 3
```

Monitor

A monitor is best viewed as a construct that monitors access to an object and creating a lock on it thereby not allowing other threads to obtain access until the owning thread explicitly leaves (or unlocks) the monitor. In contrast with the earlier synchronization primitives discussed, a monitor is not just a wrapper around core Windows synchronization primitives, rather a first class .NET citizen. To use the monitor, the System.Threading.Monitor class should be used. The Monitor class cannot be instantiated; rather it contains a set of static methods that can be used to acquire a lock. The two most common methods are Enter and Exit. The Enter method acquires an exclusive lock on the specified object (assuming the object is not locked already) and the Exit method releases an exclusive lock on the specified object. For example, the following code snippet locks on object db1:

```
Monitor.Enter(db1);
// Do work
Monitor.Exit(db1);
```

In C#, there is a more convenient lock statement that can be used to acquire and release an exclusive lock. Even though the lock statement doesn't seem to have anything to do with monitors, in reality, it is just a shortcut form for calling the Monitor.Enter and Monitor.Exit methods. This can easily be seen by looking at the intermediate language (IL) that is generated for a lock statement. Figure 6-2 shows an example of the IL that is generated from the following code:

```
lock (someObj)
{
    Console.WriteLine("I'm locked now");
}
```

The IL shows that the lock statement is expanded to automatically enter a monitor (as illustrated by the boxed statements) followed by wrapping the protected region of code in a try/finally to ensure that the monitor is released at the end of the scope.

Because the Monitor class is an object that cannot be instantiated, there is really no state that we can look at in the debugger per se. In light of this, who keeps track of which locks are available and the state of each lock? The answer is that each object that is locked also keeps the information necessary to maintain the integrity of the locks as part of the object's layout. We'll look into the internals of this bookkeeping in the "Synchronization Internals" section of this chapter.

ReaderWriterLock(Slim)

The Monitor class previously discussed allows exclusive access to an object from a single thread at a time. Although this works great in cases where writes are very frequent, the Monitor suffers in performance where there are more reads than writes and when the lock is heavily contended. To address this performance issue, the ReaderWriterLock(Slim) was introduced. A ReaderWriterLock allows multiple concurrent threads read access while limiting write operations to a single thread at a time. In contrast with the Monitor class, the ReaderWriterLock class itself contains a state that controls access to the lock:

```
0:000> !do 0x01e86cdc
Name: System.Threading.ReaderWriterLock
MethodTable: 79108ba4
EEClass: 79108b40
Size: 44(0x2c) bytes
```

```
IL_001e:  dup
IL_001f:  stloc.s    CS$2$0000
IL_0021:  call       void [mscorlib]System.Threading.Monitor::Enter(object)
IL_0026:  nop
.try
{
  IL_0027:  nop
  IL_0028:  ldstr      "I'm locked now"
  IL_002d:  call       void [mscorlib]System.Console::WriteLine(string)
  IL_0032:  nop
  IL_0033:  nop
  IL_0034:  leave.s    IL_003f
} // end .try
finally
{
  IL_0036:  ldloc.s    CS$2$0000
  IL_0038:  call       void [mscorlib]System.Threading.Monitor::Exit(object)
  IL_003d:  nop
  IL_003e:  endfinally
} // end handler
```

Figure 6-2 IL generated by the lock statement

```
(C:\Windows\assembly\GAC_32\mscorlib\2.0.0.0__b77a5c561934e089\mscorlib.dll)
Fields:
```

MT	Field	Offset	Type	VT	Attr	Value	Name
791016bc	4000626	4	System.IntPtr	1	instance	0	_hWriterEvent
791016bc	4000627	8	System.IntPtr	1	instance	0	_hReaderEvent
791016bc	4000628	c	System.IntPtr	1	instance	0	_hObjectHandle
79102290	4000629	10	System.Int32	1	instance	0	_dwState
79102290	400062a	14	System.Int32	1	instance	0	_dwULockID
79102290	400062b	18	System.Int32	1	instance	1	_dwLLockID
79102290	400062c	1c	System.Int32	1	instance	0	_dwWriterID
79102290	400062d	20	System.Int32	1	instance	1	
_dwWriterSeqNum							
7910480c	400062e	24	System.Int16	1	instance	0	_wWriterLevel

The _hWriterEvent and _hReaderEvent are both handles to underlying events that control access to the reader and writer queues, respectively. The handles are regular Windows events. The _dwState field indicates the various internal states that the lock can be in (such as reader, writer, waiting reader, waiting writer, etc.). The _dwULockID and _dwLLockID fields are internal identifiers of who is holding the lock. The _dwWriterID is the thread ID of the thread owning the lock and finally, the _wWriterLevel is the recursive lock count of the owning writer thread.

READERWRITERLOCKSLIM The ReaderWriterLock is an extremely nice mechanism when dealing with synchronizing access to critical sections of code. However, in comparison to a Monitor, the ReaderWriterLock suffers from poor performance. In light of this, another type of ReaderWriterLock was introduced, called the ReaderWriterLockSlim. In addition to improving performance over its predecessor, it also has greatly simplified rules for recursion and upgrading/downgrading lock state. It is highly recommended that developers use this more efficient lock.

Thread Pool

One common way of creating a new thread is by using the System.Threading.Thread class and specifying a method or delegate that will be executed after the thread starts. For simple and scoped scenarios, this approach works well, but in scenarios where you have a relatively large number of requests, a better approach is to use a pool of threads that can be efficiently managed by the runtime. The `System.Threading.ThreadPool` class exposes this functionality to the developer. There is exactly one thread pool per process and the default allotted number of threads is 250 (1000 I/O completion threads). The minimum number of threads that will always be available in the thread pool is the number of processors on the system. A developer can queue a task to the thread pool using the `QueueUserWorkItem` method available on the `ThreadPool` class. One caveat to be aware of is that any state that is set at the thread level is retained when the thread is given back to the thread pool. If the same thread is used to service another request that is incompatible with the threads state, the application will more than likely fail.

To find out the state of the thread pool during the debugging, the SOS debugger extension `threadpool` command can be used:

```
0:014> !threadpool
CPU utilization 10%
Worker Thread: Total: 9 Running: 9 Idle: 0 MaxLimit: 500 MinLimit: 2
Work Request in Queue: 92
--------------------------------------
Number of Timers: 0
--------------------------------------
Completion Port Thread:Total: 0 Free: 0 MaxFree: 4 CurrentLimit: 0
MaxLimit: 1000 MinLimit: 2
```

The first part of the output of the thread pool command shows worker threads statistics. The current machine wide CPU utilization (10%), total number of worker threads (9), number of running worker threads (9), as well as number of idle worker threads (0). In addition, it also shows what the maximum and minimum limits are for the pool (500 and 2). The next line shows the number of requests that are waiting to be serviced in the queue (92). If the application is utilizing the thread pool to keep timers, the total number of timers is shown (0). The last part of the output shows data on the completion ports threads.

Synchronization Internals

As we alluded to earlier, thread synchronization primitives such as a Monitor needs to carry with it a certain amount of bookkeeping information to know if the monitor is locked, the owning thread, waiting threads, and so on. In this part of the chapter, we take a look at how the CLR manages lock information.

Object Header

As briefly mentioned in Chapter 2, "CLR Fundamentals," each object on the managed heap has an associated object header that contains a plethora of information regarding the state of the object. Examples of information stored in the object header are hash codes, lock information, sync block index, and so on. Figure 6-3 shows an example of a managed heap illustrating how each object has an associated object header.

The sheer amount of *potential* information that can be stored in the object is greater than the size of object header itself (machine-word-size). The idea behind this concept is that any given object may (or may not) require all the information depending on the execution flow. As long as the execution flow (for example, just getting the hash code of the object) stays within the limits of the size of the object header, it will be stored in the object header. What happens if additional information needs to be stored when the header is full? In these cases, the CLR employs what is known as header inflation by creating an instance of a separate data structure called a sync block and copies all information currently stored in the object header into the sync block. The sync block is stored in non GC memory and accessed through an index into a sync block table. For the object to know how to locate the sync block associated with the particular object, the object header is now changed to contain the sync table index where the sync block is located. Figure 6-4 illustrates the concept of an object header and sync block.

Step 1 in Figure 6-4 shows an object that has an object header with the value `0x0f78734a`. In step 2, another piece of information needs to be stored in the object header but unfortunately doesn't fit. As a result, the CLR inflates the header by creating a sync block that is stored at index 1 in the sync block table. The object header is then set to the value of `0x08000001` to indicate the header now contains a sync block index of 1. How does the CLR know whether the information in the object header refers to a sync block index or simply other data stored in the header?

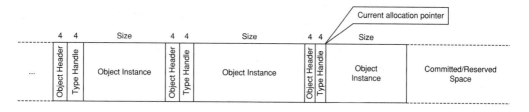

Figure 6-3 Example of managed heap and object layouts

6. SYNCHRONIZATION

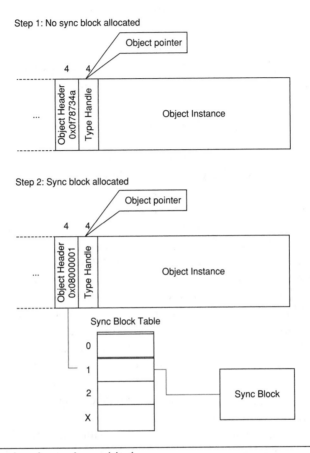

Figure 6-4 Object header and sync blocks

The answer lays in the organization of the object header bits. If the 0x08000000 mask is set in the object header, the rest of the object header contains either a hash code or a sync block index. We can further narrow it down by determining if the 0x04000000 mask is also set, in which case the header contains a hash code. If that mask is not set, the rest of the header is a sync block index. As mentioned before, the object header can store quite a lot of different information. To get an in-depth view of the different types of information, please see the Rotor source code at the following location:

```
sscli20\clr\src\vm\syncblk.h
```

Sync Blocks

To take a pragmatic look at sync blocks, Listing 6-3 is used to help clarify the importance of the sync block and how it relates to locks.

Listing 6-3 Simple example of an acquired lock

```
using System;
using System.Text;
using System.Threading;

namespace Advanced.NET.Debugging.Chapter6
{
    class Simple
    {
        static void Main(string[] args)
        {
            Simple s = new Simple();
            s.Run();
        }

        public void Run()
        {
            this.GetHashCode();

            Console.WriteLine("Press any key to acquire lock");
            Console.ReadLine();
            Monitor.Enter(this);
            Console.WriteLine("Press any key to release lock");
            Console.ReadLine();
            Monitor.Exit(this);
            Console.WriteLine("Press any key to exit");
            Console.ReadLine();
        }
    }
}
```

The source code and binary for Listing 6-3 can be found in the following folders:

- Source code: `C:\ADND\Chapter6\Simple`
- Binary: `C:\ADNDBIN\06Simple.exe`

As you can see, the sample code in Listing 6-3 is very straightforward. It simply acquires a lock on the `this` object at the beginning of the `Run` method and promptly releases it at the end. For the time being, please ignore the `GetHashCode` call at the beginning of the function. We will see the importance of this somewhat innocent statement later. Next, we run the application under the debugger and break execution (either manually or via breakpoints) when the `Press any key to acquire lock` prompt is shown. At this point, we want to take a look at the sync block for the `Simple` object and verify that no locks have been acquired. Because the sync block data structure is for the most part undocumented, we have to use the `syncblk` command to get more detailed information. The `syncblk` command can either run without any arguments, in which case it outputs the list of sync blocks for objects that are owned by a thread; alternatively, the `syncblk` command can take an argument to a specific sync block index. Where do we find the sync block index for a particular object? Remember that an object pointer points to the type handle field followed by the actual object instance data. The 4 bytes preceding the type handle is also part of the object layout and contains the object header of the object. We can use the `dd` command to dump out the contents of the object header index by simply subtracting 4 from the object pointer. For example, in our existing debug session, the sequence of commands to get the sync block index is illustrated in the following:

```
0:000> !ClrStack -a
OS Thread Id: 0x462c (0)
...
...
...
0018f080 793a3350 System.IO.StreamReader.ReadBuffer()
    PARAMETERS:
        this = 0x01e36cb8
    LOCALS:
        <no data>

0018f090 793aaa2f System.IO.StreamReader.ReadLine()
    PARAMETERS:
        this = 0x01e36cb8
    LOCALS:
        <no data>
        <no data>
        <no data>
        <no data>

0018f0a4 79497b5a System.IO.TextReader+SyncTextReader.ReadLine()
    PARAMETERS:
        this = 0x01e37028

0018f0ac 793e99f0 System.Console.ReadLine()
```

```
0018f0b0 0093011b Advanced.NET.Debugging.Chapter6.Simple.Run()
    PARAMETERS:
        this = 0x01e358a0

0018f0b8 009300a7 Advanced.NET.Debugging.Chapter6.Simple.Main(System.String[])
    PARAMETERS:
        args = 0x01e35890
    LOCALS:
        <CLR reg> = 0x01e358a0

0018f2e0 79e7c74b [GCFrame: 0018f2e0]
0:000> !do 0x01e358a0
Name: Advanced.NET.Debugging.Chapter6.Simple
MethodTable: 002e3038
EEClass: 002e1210
Size: 12(0xc) bytes
 (C:\ADNDBin\06Simple.exe)
Fields:
None
0:000> dd 0x01e358a0-0x4 l1
01e3589c 0f78734a
```

The preceding sequence of commands illustrated is a three-step process:

1. We use the ClrStack -a command to dump out all the call stack of the thread as well as all its parameters. The bottommost frame corresponds to our Main method, which in turn contains a local variable that contains the reference to our instance of the Simple class.
2. To convince ourselves that we are in fact working with the correct object (of type Simple), we use the do command.
3. Lastly, we use the dd command to dump out the object header, which resides at the object pointer minus 4 bytes.

The current value of the object header (0x0f78734a) indicates that we are looking at the object's hash code (and not a sync block index). It's important to understand that we have yet to acquire the lock on the object and it's therefore possible that the sync block has not yet been created. Let's resume execution until you see the Press any key to release lock prompt, at which point you again break into the debugger. After you have broken into the debugger, you use the same three-step process to get the pointer from ClrStack, use do to convince yourself that you working with the correct object, and then finally the dd command to dump out the sync block index. Why go through the first two steps again? Isn't the object pointer constant after all? Keep in mind that the garbage collector is free to move the object around at any time, and the location of the object may change. For the sake of brevity, the output in the following listing only lists the sync block step:

```
0:000> dd 0x01e358a0-0x4 l1
01e3589c 08000001
```

This time, the sync block index looks more reasonable (0x08000001). From our earlier discussion on the object header, we know that the presence of bitmask 0x0800000 indicates that we are dealing with a sync block index. If we use the syncblk command specifying 0x1 as the argument, we can now see

```
0:000> !syncblk 0x1
Index SyncBlock MonitorHeld Recursion Owning Thread Info  SyncBlock Owner
    1 00322fd4           1         1 003044f0  462c   0   01e358a0
Advanced.NET.Debugging.Chapter6.Simple
---------------------------------
Total           1
CCW             0
RCW             0
ComClassFactory 0
Free            0
```

The output of the syncblk command contains two primary sections. The first section includes information relative to the lock being held. The meaning of the columns is shown in Table 6-2.

Table 6-2   Syncblk Column Description

Column	Description
Index	The sync block index.
SyncBlock	Address to the sync block data structure (undocumented).
MonitorHeld	Number of monitors held.
Recursion	How many times one and the same thread has acquired the lock.
Owning thread info	First item is the pointer to the internal thread data structure, the second item is the OS thread id, and the third item is the debugger thread id.
SyncBlock Owner	First item is the pointer to the object whose lock is being held, and the item is the type of the object on which the lock is second held.

The other section of interest is not directly related to locks, but rather contains the total number of sync blocks in the sync block table, the number of Runtime Callable Wrappers (RCW) as well as the total number of COM Callable Wrappers (CCW). Finally, the `Free` line indicates how many sync blocks are available in the sync block table.

Thin Locks

Understanding what happens internally when a lock is acquired on an object is incredibly useful when dealing with common synchronization problems such as deadlocks. The `syncblk` command can be used to quickly identify which thread is holding which lock to determine the source of the deadlock. Now, before we move onto discussing some of the most common synchronization problems and how they can be debugged, we have yet to explain that mysterious line in Listing 6-3:

```
this.GetHashCode();
```

The reason the above statement was added to the sample code was to ensure that a sync block was created. As mentioned before, the object header can be used to manage locks that have been acquired on the object. However, that is not the only use of the object header. It can also be used to store other information about the object (such as hash codes, COM interoperability data, and application domain index). If the object is not synchronized (i.e., a lock has never been taken) and if the application didn't perform an operation causing the object header to be used, the sync block will simply not exist for that object. In our previous example, by calling `GetHashCode`, we essentially forced the creation of a sync block to illustrate how it is managed by the CLR. Can a lock be managed without the existence of a sync block? Yes, CLR 2.0 introduced what is known as a thin lock to allow for a far more efficient mechanism of managing locks. In the case of a thin lock, the only piece of information that is stored in the object header is the thread ID of the acquiring thread (i.e., no sync block). Based on this single piece of information, we can also infer that the thin lock is simply a spinning lock (because more information would be required to implement a lock that would efficiently wait). The thin lock does not, however, spin indefinitely; rather, only until a threshold has been reached. If the lock cannot be acquired as the threshold is passed, an actual sync block is created that allows the storage of information required to do an efficient wait (such as an event).

In essence, the CLR uses the following algorithm to determine when to use a sync block versus a thin lock for synchronization purposes:

- If a sync block already exists, use the sync block to store lock information; otherwise,
- Determine whether a thin lock will fit in the current object header.

   Yes. Store thread id in the object header. If, subsequently, more information needs to be stored, a sync block is automatically created and the current object header contents are moved to the new sync block.

   No. Create a new sync block, move the current object header's content into the new sync block, and store lock.

We can easily verify this by simply moving the `GetHashCode` call in our sample code to right after the first lock acquisition. For brevity's sake, the source code isn't listed but can be found in the following location:

- Source code: `C:\ADND\Chapter6\Simple2`
- Binary: `C:\ADNDBIN\06Simple2.exe`

Let's run the application under the debugger and verify the preceding theory by following three steps:

1. Prior to the lock being acquired, dump out the sync block and make sure it's empty.
2. Acquire the lock, break execution, and verify that a thin lock has been created.
3. Get the hash code, break execution, and verify that the thin lock has now been replaced by a sync block.

Step 1 is shown in the following:

```
0:000> !do 0x01e1ad1c
Name: Advanced.NET.Debugging.Chapter6.Simple
MethodTable: 000d3188
EEClass: 000d1298
Size: 12(0xc) bytes
 (C:\ADNDBin\06Simple2.exe)
Fields:
None
0:000> dd 0x01e1ad1c-0x4 l1
01e1ad18  00000000
```

We can see that the sync block index is 0. The next step is to acquire the lock (without `GetHashCode` method being called) and make sure we get a thin lock:

```
0:003> !do 0x01e1ad1c
Name: Advanced.NET.Debugging.Chapter6.Simple
MethodTable: 000d3188
EEClass: 000d1298
Size: 12(0xc) bytes
 (C:\ADNDBin\06Simple2.exe)
Fields:
None
ThinLock owner 1 (002f70e0), Recursive 0
```

Interestingly enough, the `do` command can detect the presence of a thin lock, as shown in the last line of output. The line simply states that a thin lock has been acquired on the object with a thread object pointer of `0x002f70e0` and a recursive count of 0. We can also verify this by looking at the object header, which should contain the thread ID of the owning thread:

```
0:003> dd 0x01e1ad1c-0x4 l1
01e1ad18  00000001
0:003> !threads
ThreadCount: 2
UnstartedThread: 0
BackgroundThread: 1
PendingThread: 0
DeadThread: 0
Hosted Runtime: no
                                  PreEmptive   GC Alloc          Lock
     ID OSID ThreadOBJ    State   GC      Context       Domain
  Count APT Exception
0     1 22cc 002f70e0     a020 Enabled  01c8bd38:01c8c328 0008fdf8    2 MTA
2     2 cdf0 000a3ae0     b220 Enabled  00000000:00000000 0008fdf8
   0 MTA (Finalizer)
```

We can see that the owning thread is the thread with a CLR thread id of 1 and that the pointer to the thread is `0x002f70e0`, which corresponds to the output of the `do` command.

Next, we execute the `GetHashCode` method and again break execution and check on the sync block and thin lock states:

```
0:000> !do 0x01e1ad1c
Name: Advanced.NET.Debugging.Chapter6.Simple
MethodTable: 000d3188
EEClass: 000d1298
Size: 12(0xc) bytes
 (C:\ADNDBin\06Simple2.exe)
Fields:
```

```
None
0:000> dd 0x01e1ad1c-0x4 l1
01e1ad18  08000001
0:000> !syncblk 0001
Index SyncBlock MonitorHeld Recursion Owning Thread Info  SyncBlock Owner
    1 003231fc           1          1 002f70e0  4c98   0   01e1ad1c
  Advanced.NET.Debugging.Chapter6.Simple
-------------------------------
Total            1
CCW              0
RCW              0
ComClassFactory  0
Free             0
```

As per our expectations, this time, the output of the `do` command is lacking the thin lock statement indicating that the lock may have been moved into the sync block. We then use the `syncblk` command to verify that it in fact contains a valid lock.

Another neat trick when working with thin locks is using the `-thinlock` with the `dumpheap` command, which searches through all objects on the managed heap that have a thin lock associated with them. Using the same `06Simple2.exe` application, we can run the command after the lock has been acquired:

```
0:000> !dumpheap -thinlock
 Address        MT     Size
01e1bcdc 79191d38       16     ThinLock owner 1 (002f70e0) Recursive 0
```

The output shows the address (`0x01e1bcdc`) and method table (`0x79191d38`) of the object on which a lock is held as well as the thread object pointer (`0x002f70e0`).

Synchronization Scenarios

Now that we are armed with the knowledge of the different synchronization primitives, the powerful debugger commands available to look into the primitives, as well as how these primitives are kept internally, we can now turn our attention to investigating the most common types of synchronization problems. We'll begin our discussion with a simple dead lock scenario.

Basic Deadlock

Deadlocks are perhaps the most common and frustrating problems that developers encounter when writing multithreaded applications. In essence, a deadlock occurs when two or more threads hold protected resources and refuse to let go of those resources until others have let go of theirs. Because none of the threads are willing to release their protected resources, ultimately, none of the threads ever make any progress. They simply sit there and wait for the others to make a move and a deadlock ensues. There are numerous ways that a deadlock can occur, and we will take look at some common ones throughout this chapter. However, before getting into some of the more complicated cases, we will illustrate a simple and simulated deadlock scenario. This will give you a good idea of what a deadlock looks like in the debugger and the commands that can be used to get to the bottom of the deadlock.

The sample application we will use to illustrate the deadlock is rather simplistic and is shown in Listing 6-4.

Listing 6-4   Sample application that results in a deadlock

```
using System;
using System.Text;
using System.Threading;

namespace Advanced.NET.Debugging.Chapter6
{
    internal class DBWrapper1
    {
        private string connectionString;

        public DBWrapper1(string conStr)
        {
            this.connectionString = conStr;
        }
    }

    internal class DBWrapper2
    {
        private string connectionString;

        public DBWrapper2(string conStr)
        {
            this.connectionString = conStr;
        }
    }

    class Deadlock
    {
        private static DBWrapper1 db1;
        private static DBWrapper2 db2;
```

(continues)

Listing 6-4 *Sample application that results in a deadlock* *(continued)*

```csharp
static void Main(string[] args)
{
    db1 = new DBWrapper1("DBCon1");
    db2 = new DBWrapper2("DBCon2");

    Thread newThread = new Thread(ThreadProc);
    newThread.Start();

    Thread.Sleep(2000);
    lock (db2)
    {
        Console.WriteLine("Updating DB2");
        Thread.Sleep(2000);
        lock (db1)
        {
            Console.WriteLine("Updating DB1");
        }
    }
}

private static void ThreadProc()
{
    Console.WriteLine("Start worker thread");
    lock (db1)
    {
        Console.WriteLine("Updating DB1");
        Thread.Sleep(3000);
        lock (db2)
        {
            Console.WriteLine("Updating DB2");
        }
    }
}
}
```

The source code and binary for Listing 6-4 can be found in the following folders:

- Source code: `C:\ADND\Chapter6\DeadLock`
- Binary: `C:\ADNDBIN\06DeadLock.exe`

The application is a multithreaded application (2 threads) that utilizes two different databases wrapped in helper classes (DBWrapper1 and DBWrapper2). Each thread needs access to both databases to be able to perform its work. Because the underlying database access API(s) are not thread safe, the application utilizes two monitors (via `lock` statement), each protecting one database. To avoid polluting the sample code, the code that utilizes the databases are simulated by simply putting the thread to sleep for a number of milliseconds. When you run this application, you will quickly see that it never finishes. In this simple application, you may have already spotted the problem in the code, but let's attach a debugger to a running instance and see what is happening. The first step is to dump out all the threads currently running in the process, which is illustrated in Listing 6-5.

Listing 6-5   All CLR thread stacks currently running in the process

```
0:004> ~*e!clrstack
OS Thread Id: 0xaec (0)
ESP        EIP
0013f328 7c90e514 [GCFrame: 0013f328]
0013f3f8 7c90e514 [HelperMethodFrame_1OBJ: 0013f3f8]
 System.Threading.Monitor.Enter(System.Object)
0013f450 00cb017b Advanced.NET.Debugging.Chapter6.Deadlock.Main(System.String[])
0013f69c 79e7be1b [GCFrame: 0013f69c]
OS Thread Id: 0x2e8 (1)
Unable to walk the managed stack. The current thread is likely not a
managed thread. You can run !threads to get a list of managed threads in
the process
OS Thread Id: 0x9d4 (2)
Failed to start stack walk: 80004005
OS Thread Id: 0xe1c (3)
ESP        EIP
00dbf75c 7c90e514 [GCFrame: 00dbf75c]
00dbf82c 7c90e514 [HelperMethodFrame_1OBJ: 00dbf82c]
 System.Threading.Monitor.Enter(System.Object)
00dbf884 00cb02f4
Advanced.NET.Debugging.Chapter6.Deadlock.ThreadProc()
00dbf8b4 793d70fb
System.Threading.ThreadHelper.ThreadStart_Context(System.Object)
00dbf8bc 793608fd
System.Threading.ExecutionContext.Run(System.Threading.ExecutionContext,
System.Threading.ContextCallback, System.Object)
00dbf8d4 793d71dc System.Threading.ThreadHelper.ThreadStart()
00dbfaf8 79e7be1b [GCFrame: 00dbfaf8]
OS Thread Id: 0x5ec (4)
Unable to walk the managed stack. The current thread is likely not a
managed thread. You can run !threads to get a list of managed threads in
the process
```

Please note the usage of the ~*e!clrstack command, which dumps out the stack traces for all threads (native and managed) in the process. Albeit simplistic, the output illustrates a very common recognition technique for deadlocks. Two (or more) threads each waiting to acquire a different lock, but nothing seems to be happening. To verify that our assumption of a deadlock is indeed correct, we need to take a closer look at the objects involved. How do we find the address of the object that each thread is waiting on? We'll look at a couple of different approaches starting with the more manual approach of looking at each of the threads that are waiting in more detail. Let's start with thread 0:

```
0:004> ~0s
eax=00000000 ebx=0013f0c4 ecx=0013f390 edx=7c90e514 esi=00000000 edi=7ffd6000
eip=7c90e514 esp=0013f09c ebp=0013f138 iopl=0         nv up ei pl zr na pe nc
cs=001b  ss=0023  ds=0023  es=0023  fs=003b  gs=0000            efl=00000246
ntdll!KiFastSystemCallRet:
7c90e514 c3              ret
0:000> !ClrStack -a
OS Thread Id: 0xaec (0)
ESP      EIP
0013f328 7c90e514 [GCFrame: 0013f328]
0013f3f8 7c90e514 [HelperMethodFrame_1OBJ: 0013f3f8]
System.Threading.Monitor.Enter(System.Object)
0013f450 00cb017b Advanced.NET.Debugging.Chapter6.Deadlock.Main(System.String[])
    PARAMETERS:
        args = 0x01281a00
    LOCALS:
        0x0013f458 = 0x01281ae0
        0x0013f454 = 0x01281ab4
        0x0013f450 = 0x01281aa8

0013f69c 79e7be1b [GCFrame: 0013f69c]
```

This tells us that the Main method is attempting to acquire a lock. The Main method, however, attempts to acquire two locks, so which lock statement does the call stack correspond to? The third frame from the output of ClrStack tells us that the EIP (instruction pointer) at the point of entering the monitor is 0x00cb017b. We can now use the U command to show the annotated assembly code in that location. The abbreviated output is shown in the following listing:

```
0:000> !u 00cb017b
Normal JIT generated code
Advanced.NET.Debugging.Chapter6.Deadlock.Main(System.String[])
Begin 00cb0070, size 17c
00cb0070 55              push    ebp
```

```
00cb0071 8bec              mov     ebp,esp
00cb0073 57                push    edi
00cb0074 56                push    esi
...
...
...
00cb0142 a1cc1e2802        mov     eax,dword ptr ds:[02281ECCh]
00cb0147 8945d4            mov     dword ptr [ebp-2Ch],eax
00cb014a 8b4dd4            mov     ecx,dword ptr [ebp-2Ch]
00cb014d e8873b1c79        call    mscorwks!JIT_MonEnterWorker (79e73cd9)
00cb0152 90                nop
00cb0153 90                nop
00cb0154 8b0d44302802      mov     ecx,dword ptr ds:[2283044h]
00cb015a e8198d7078        call    mscorlib_ni+0x2f8e78 (793b8e78)
 (System.Console.WriteLine(System.String), mdToken: 06000764)
00cb015f 90                nop
00cb0160 b9d0070000        mov     ecx,7D0h
00cb0165 e806767278        call    mscorlib_ni+0x317770 (793d7770)
 (System.Threading.Thread.Sleep(Int32), mdToken: 0600125e)
00cb016a 90                nop
00cb016b a1c81e2802        mov     eax,dword ptr ds:[02281EC8h]
00cb0170 8945d0            mov     dword ptr [ebp-30h],eax
00cb0173 8b4dd0            mov     ecx,dword ptr [ebp-30h]
00cb0176 e85e3b1c79        call    mscorwks!JIT_MonEnterWorker (79e73cd9)
>>> 00cb017b 90               nop
00cb017c 90                nop
00cb017d 8b0d48302802      mov     ecx,dword ptr ds:[2283048h]
00cb0183 e8f08c7078        call    mscorlib_ni+0x2f8e78 (793b8e78)
 (System.Console.WriteLine(System.String), mdToken: 06000764)
...
...
...
```

Based on the instruction pointer at which the Enter call was made (0x00cb0176) and the output of the U command, we can see that prior to where the instruction pointer is currently located there was another monitor Enter call made at location 0x00cb014d. At this point, we know that it is the second lock statement in the Main method that is causing us to wait indefinitely. Simple code inspection also tells us that it is trying to take a lock on object db1 of type DBWrapper1. What is the address of db1? Because db1 is a static variable, we can find it by looking at the locals shown in the ClrStack output. By using the do command on each of the addresses, we find that the db1 instance is located at address 0x01281aa8:

```
0:000> !do 0x01281aa8
Name: Advanced.NET.Debugging.Chapter6.DBWrapper1
```

```
MethodTable: 009130d4
EEClass: 009113a4
Size: 12(0xc) bytes
 (C:\ADNDBin\06Deadlock.exe)
Fields:
      MT    Field  Offset                  Type VT     Attr     Value Name
790f9244  4000001      4       System.String  0 instance 01281a10
connectionString
```

Now that we have the address of the object instance that the `Main` method is waiting to acquire a lock on, we can check on the sync block for that object to see if it is held by another thread (remember that if it was held by a thin lock, the `do` command would have shown it):

```
0:000> dd 0x01281aa8-0x4 l1
01281aa4  08000003
```

The sync block index is `0003`, which we can pass to the `syncblk` command as shown in the following:

```
0:000> !syncblk 0003
Index SyncBlock MonitorHeld Recursion Owning Thread Info  SyncBlock Owner
    3 001aa934           3         1 001aa218  f74    3    01281aa8
Advanced.NET.Debugging.Chapter6.DBWrapper1
--------------------------------
Total          3
CCW            0
RCW            0
ComClassFactory 0
Free           0
```

From the output of the `syncblk` command, we can see that the object instance is locked by a thread with debugger thread id `0x3`. Let's switch over to that thread and see if there is anything preventing that thread from releasing the lock:

```
0:000> ~3s
eax=8bcf97d4 ebx=00dbf4f8 ecx=ffffffff edx=ffffffff esi=00000000 edi=7ffde000
eip=7c90e514 esp=00dbf4d0 ebp=00dbf56c iopl=0         nv up ei pl zr na pe nc
cs=001b  ss=0023  ds=0023  es=0023  fs=003b  gs=0000             efl=00000246
ntdll!KiFastSystemCallRet:
7c90e514 c3              ret
0:003> !ClrStack
OS Thread Id: 0xf74 (3)
```

```
ESP        EIP
00dbf75c 7c90e514 [GCFrame: 00dbf75c]
00dbf82c 7c90e514 [HelperMethodFrame_1OBJ: 00dbf82c]
 System.Threading.Monitor.Enter(System.Object)
00dbf884 00cb02f4
Advanced.NET.Debugging.Chapter6.Deadlock.ThreadProc()
00dbf8b4 793d70fb
System.Threading.ThreadHelper.ThreadStart_Context(System.Object)
00dbf8bc 793608fd System.Threading.ExecutionContext.Run(System.Threading.
ExecutionContext, System.Threading.ContextCallback, System.Object)
00dbf8d4 793d71dc System.Threading.ThreadHelper.ThreadStart()
00dbfaf8 79e7be1b [GCFrame: 00dbfaf8]
```

From the call stack of the thread with debugger thread ID 0x3, we can see that it is our worker thread that is also stuck waiting on acquiring a lock. We can use the same mechanism we used earlier to find which lock it is waiting on by following these steps:

1. Unassemble the `ThreadProc` method using the `U` command.
2. Find which monitor `Enter` call is causing the thread to get stuck (remember that the `ThreadProc` method has two lock statements).
3. Dump out the contents of the object whose lock the thread is trying to acquire.

In our debug session, the object that the worker thread is trying to acquire a lock on is the `db2` object instance. Looking closely at the `db2` object instance sync block, we can see the following:

```
0:003> !syncblk 0002
Index SyncBlock MonitorHeld Recursion Owning Thread Info  SyncBlock Owner
    2 001aa904           3         1 00190d88      dc  0     01281ab4
    Advanced.NET.Debugging.Chapter6.DBWrapper2
---------------------------------
Total             3
CCW               0
RCW               0
ComClassFactory 0
Free              0
```

The output clearly shows us that the lock is held by a thread with debugger thread ID 0x0. This is also the same thread we looked at earlier that was holding a lock on the `db1` object instance. The picture should now be clear. The first thread in our process is holding the second database lock while waiting for the first database lock to become available. The second thread holds the lock associated with the first database lock while waiting for the second to become available. The net result is the following: a deadlocked application.

Now that we know which threads are deadlocking on what, the final step is to do source code analysis to try and break the deadlock. From our simple example, it should be quite evident why the deadlock happened and how it can be broken.

So far, we have shown how to manually root cause a deadlock, which can be quite a tedious process. Fortunately, there are a few commands that make the process more automated. The first command we will take a look at is the `syncblk` command (without any arguments). If you run the `syncblk` command without any arguments, it shows the contents of the entire sync block table, which can be useful as it gives a concise view of all the locks held in the system. In our sample application, the output of the `syncblk` command is shown in the following:

```
0:003> !syncblk
Index SyncBlock MonitorHeld Recursion Owning Thread Info   SyncBlock Owner
    2 001aa904           3         1 00190d88    dc    0   01281ab4
Advanced.NET.Debugging.Chapter6.DBWrapper2
    3 001aa934           3         1 001aa218   f74    3   01281aa8
Advanced.NET.Debugging.Chapter6.DBWrapper1
-------------------------------
Total             3
CCW               0
RCW               0
ComClassFactory   0
Free              0
```

The output clearly states all the locks that are being held and if you suspect a deadlock situation based on the call stacks in the application, this can quickly yield valuable clues in regards to the lock state of the process. Even though the `syncblk` command shows the overall lock state of all the objects, you will still have to do some analysis to determine if a deadlock is present. For example, you have to look at each of the threads to determine if they are, in fact, deadlocked and which objects they are deadlocked on. This manual process has further been automated by the SOSEX debugger extension in a command called `dlk` (deadlock). The `dlk` command analyzes the sync block contents and outputs the result if a deadlock is detected. In our preceding sample, the `dlk` command yields the following:

```
0:003> !dlk
Deadlock detected:
CLR thread 1 holds sync block 001aa904
OBJ:01281ab4[Advanced.NET.Debugging.Chapter6.DBWrapper2]
         waits sync block 001aa934
```

```
OBJ:01281aa8[Advanced.NET.Debugging.Chapter6.DBWrapper1]
CLR thread 3 holds sync block 001aa934
OBJ:01281aa8[Advanced.NET.Debugging.Chapter6.DBWrapper1]
          waits sync block 001aa904
OBJ:01281ab4[Advanced.NET.Debugging.Chapter6.DBWrapper2]
CLR Thread 1 is waiting at
Advanced.NET.Debugging.Chapter6.Deadlock.Main(System.String[])(+0x67
 IL)(+0xd2 Native) [c:\Publishing\ADND\Code\Chapter6\Deadlock\06Deadlock.cs, @
45,17]
CLR Thread 3 is waiting at
Advanced.NET.Debugging.Chapter6.Deadlock.ThreadProc()(+0x30 IL)(+0x46 Native)
[c:\Publishing\ADND\Code\Chapter6\Deadlock\06Deadlock.cs, @ 59,17]
```

The output clearly shows that a potential deadlock has been detected and that thread 1 holds a lock on object DBWrapper2 and is waiting on DBWrapper1. Furthermore, thread 3 holds a lock on DBWrapper1 and is waiting on DBWrapper2. In addition, the last part of the output also shows the exact location where each of the threads is stuck waiting.

Please note that the previous discussion assumes that the lock is stored in the sync block. If a thin lock is involved, the same overall strategy applies with the exception of using the dumpheap -thinlock command rather than the syncblk command to find out which objects are locked and which thread owns which lock. Also, at the time of this writing, the SOSEX dlk command does not work with thin locks.

This wraps up our discussion of how to debug a deadlock. Although we have shown a deadlock in the context of a monitor, it is important to note that any synchronization primitive can yield a deadlock if not used properly.

Orphaned Lock Exceptions

Writing well-behaved code in the presence of exceptions can be a daunting task, especially when coupled with multithreading. In this section, we will take a look at a scenario that involves an application that makes (poor) use of exceptions. The application code is listed in Listing 6-6.

Listing 6-6 Orphaned locks sample application

```
using System;
using System.Text;
using System.Threading;

namespace Advanced.NET.Debugging.Chapter6
{
    internal class DBWrapper1
```

(continues)

Listing 6-6 Orphaned locks sample application *(continued)*

```csharp
{
    private string connectionString;

    public DBWrapper1(string conStr)
    {
        this.connectionString = conStr;
    }
}

class Exc
{
    private static DBWrapper1 db1;

    static void Main(string[] args)
    {
        db1 = new DBWrapper1("DB1");

        Thread newThread = new Thread(ThreadProc);
        newThread.Start();

        Thread.Sleep(500);
        Console.WriteLine("Acquiring lock");
        Monitor.Enter(db1);

        //
        // Do some work
        //

        Console.WriteLine("Releasing lock");
        Monitor.Exit(db1);
    }

    private static void ThreadProc()
    {
        try
        {
            Monitor.Enter(db1);
            Call3rdPartyCode(null);
            Monitor.Exit(db1);
        }
        catch (Exception)
        {
            Console.WriteLine("3rd party code threw an exception");
        }
    }
```

```
        private static void Call3rdPartyCode(Object obj)
        {
            if (obj == null)
            {
                throw new NullReferenceException();
            }

            //
            // Do some work
            //
        }
    }
}
```

The source code and binary for Listing 6-6 can be found in the following folders:

- Source code: `C:\ADND\Chapter6\Exception`
- Binary: `C:\ADNDBIN\06Exception.exe`

As you can see, the code in Listing 6-6 is pretty straightforward. The main thread starts by creating a new worker thread. After the thread has been successfully created, it then tries to acquire a lock on the `db1` instance. After it is done, it releases the lock and terminates.

The worker threads job is to call into some third-party code (perhaps a dynamically loaded assembly) while holding a lock on the `db1` instance. The code also makes an attempt at being exception safe by wrapping the call with a try/catch statement attempting to catch all exceptions thrown and dump an error to console if an exception is thrown.

Although the application is a very poorly designed application, it nevertheless illustrates a very common problem. Before we get into all the different problems with the application, let's run it and see what the final outcome is:

```
C:\ADNDBin>06Exception.exe
3rd party code threw an exception
Acquiring lock
```

All that appears to be happening is that the application hangs when trying to acquire a lock. Let's take a look at the state of the threads in the process by attaching the debugger to the process and dumping out all the threads, illustrated in Listing 6-7.

Listing 6-7 Sample application thread state

```
0:004> ~*e!clrstack
OS Thread Id: 0x1530 (0)
ESP       EIP
0025ec6c 77d99a94 [GCFrame: 0025ec6c]
0025ed3c 77d99a94 [HelperMethodFrame_1OBJ: 0025ed3c]
 System.Threading.Monitor.Enter(System.Object)
0025ed94 01bf0111
Advanced.NET.Debugging.Chapter6.Exc.Main(System.String[])
0025efc4 79e7c74b [GCFrame: 0025efc4]
OS Thread Id: 0x1aec (1)
Unable to walk the managed stack. The current thread is likely not a
managed thread. You can run !threads to get a list of managed threads in
the process
OS Thread Id: 0x1e00 (2)
Failed to start stack walk: 80004005
OS Thread Id: 0x1640 (3)
Unable to walk the managed stack. The current thread is likely not a
managed thread. You can run !threads to get a list of managed threads in
the process
OS Thread Id: 0x15b0 (4)
Unable to walk the managed stack. The current thread is likely not a
managed thread. You can run !threads to get a list of managed threads in the process
```

Listing 6-7 indicates that the main thread is waiting to acquire a lock but is not able to (the rest of the threads are unmanaged). To find out why, we have to dump out the lock in question and see what information it may provide us. To dump out the lock, we have to first find the object in question (of type DBWrapper1). We can use the dumpstackobjects command as follows:

```
0:000> !dumpstackobjects
OS Thread Id: 0xd330 (0)
ESP/REG  Object    Name
ecx      01deadb0 Advanced.NET.Debugging.Chapter6.DBWrapper1
002df144 01deadb0 Advanced.NET.Debugging.Chapter6.DBWrapper1
002df198 01deadbc System.Threading.ThreadStart
002df19c 01deaddc System.Threading.Thread
002df1a0 01deaddc System.Threading.Thread
002df1a8 01deadbc System.Threading.ThreadStart
002df1b0 01deaddc System.Threading.Thread
002df1c4 01decc0c System.IO.StreamWriter
002df1e4 01deaeb4 System.Char[]
002df20c 01deaddc System.Threading.Thread
```

```
002df218 01deadb0 Advanced.NET.Debugging.Chapter6.DBWrapper1
002df234 01dead28 System.Object[]    (System.String[])
002df2f4 01dead28 System.Object[]    (System.String[])
002df4a8 01dead28 System.Object[]    (System.String[])
002df4d0 01dead28 System.Object[]    (System.String[])
```

We can then use the object pointer in the output to get the object header:

```
0:000> dd 01deadb0-0x4 l1
01deadac  08000002
```

As we can see, the object header indicates that a sync block has been created for the object. To get lock information, we use the `syncblk` command:

```
0:000> !syncblk 002
Index SyncBlock MonitorHeld Recursion Owning Thread Info  SyncBlock Owner
    2 00443994           3         1 00442208    0 XXX    01deadb0
 Advanced.NET.Debugging.Chapter6.DBWrapper1
-------------------------------
Total          2
CCW            0
RCW            0
ComClassFactory 0
Free           0
```

The output clearly tells us that the object is locked. What is surprising about the output is the Owning Thread Info column, which includes XXX as the indicator of the debugger thread id and 0 for the OS thread id. What does XXX mean? It simply means that the CLR was unable to map the OS thread id to a debugger thread. One very common reason for this is that the thread that at one point or another acquired a lock on the object has since gone away *without releasing* the lock. To further convince ourselves, we can also use the `threads` command:

```
0:000> !threads
ThreadCount: 3
UnstartedThread: 0
BackgroundThread: 1
PendingThread: 0
DeadThread: 1
Hosted Runtime: no
                               PreEmptive   GC Alloc           Lock
      ID OSID ThreadOBJ    State   GC       Context      Domain
  Count APT Exception
   0    1 d330 00417130   200a020 Enabled  01deaee0:01dec328 0040fe20      0 MTA
```

```
    2     2 cb7c 00423b40     b220 Enabled   00000000:00000000 0040fe20     0 MTA
(Finalizer)
XXXX   3    0 00442208         9820 Enabled   00000000:00000000 0040fe20     1 Ukn
```

The output tells us that 1 thread is considered dead and the thread in question is marked with XXX in the thread list. Dead threads are only output until they are finalized.

The next question to answer is how do we know what this seemingly dead thread was up to prior to terminating? To answer that question, it is important to do a little bit of code review in conjunction with the data that the debugger outputs. In our particular example, the only other thread is our worker thread, so could it be the culprit? Possibly, as it definitely tries to acquire a lock:

```
Monitor.Enter(db1);
Call3rdPartyCode(null);
Monitor.Exit(db1);
```

The only problem is that it also releases the lock properly after the call to the third-party code, hence the lock should be in a good state. Although that may be our first impression, looking closer at the code reveals the seemingly innocent try/catch block that surrounds the locking code. Essentially, because the thread is calling into some third-party code, it wants to do everything it can to protect itself from the code throwing any type of exception and therefore tries to catch all exceptions that may come out of it. Although one could argue that this isn't the best way of protecting yourself, there is an even bigger problem looming on the horizon. What actually happens if the third-party code throws an exception? Well, the catch all filter is executed where it simply outputs an error to the console window and exits. Did we release the lock that was acquired prior to calling the third-party code? Absolutely not. The only code that gets executed in this scenario is the catch filter, and we end up with an orphaned lock. Now we know why the application hung: a worker thread orphaned a lock while going about its business. In addition to the poor attempt of trying to protect itself by catching all exceptions, the question of holding a lock while calling into some third-party code is brought up. Is that a safe thing to do? Generally speaking, the answer is no. Because you have no idea of what this third-party code may do, holding a lock while calling it can lead to other devastating problems. Imagine that the third-party code tried to call back on some API that required the same lock to be acquired (from a different thread). If the API isn't designed to handle re-entrancy, a deadlock will occur. As a general rule of thumb, developers must exercise extreme caution when dealing with third-party code and trying to protect their code from all the different mishaps that can result.

Let's say that the developer who wrote the code in Listing 6-6 was set against making any substantial changes to it. Is there anything he can do to make it at least behave slightly better? Absolutely. He can make sure that the lock is released properly even in the presence of exceptions by making sure it is released in the exception handling code. To place truly strong guarantees, an alternative is to have a finally block where the lock is released. Finally, to make the code more readable, you can also use the `lock` statement, discussed earlier, that essentially translates into `Monitor.Enter` and `Monitor.Exit` (in a finally block).

Thread Abortion

In the last section, we discussed how a lock can become orphaned by not properly releasing the lock. Are there other situations in which a lock can be orphaned even if the code to release the lock was properly written? As you've probably already guessed, the answer is a resounding yes. The most common scenario in which this can happen is the use of the `Thread.Abort` method. Although CLR thread abortions make every attempt at cleanly terminating a thread, there are a lot of scenarios where aborting a thread can cause problems. Let's take a look at a scenario that is a slight variation of the one used to illustrate how a lock can be orphaned due to a thread abortion. The source code for the scenario is shown in Listing 6-8.

Listing 6-8 Orphaned lock sample application

```
using System;
using System.Threading;

namespace Advanced.NET.Debugging.Chapter6
{
    class Abort
    {
        public void WorkerThread()
        {
            try
            {
                //
                // Do some work
                //
            }
            finally
            {
                // Do some cleanup while holding a lock
                lock (this)
```

(continues)

Listing 6-8 Orphaned lock sample application *(continued)*

```
                {
                }
            }
        }

        public static void Main(string[] args)
        {
            Abort abort = new Abort();
            Thread worker = new Thread(abort.WorkerThread);
            lock (abort)
            {
                worker.Start();

                Console.WriteLine("Acquired lock");
                Thread.Sleep(2000);

                Console.WriteLine("Aborting worker thread");
                worker.Abort();
            }
        }
    }
}
```

The source code and binary for Listing 6-8 can be found in the following folders:

- Source code: `C:\ADND\Chapter6\Abort`
- Binary: `C:\ADNDBIN\06Abort.exe`

The idea behind the code is that the main thread starts a new thread that does some background work. The main thread then waits for a little bit until it determines to abort the worker thread (perhaps thinking that it was stuck). If we execute the application, we observe the following:

```
C:\ADNDBin>06Abort.exe
Acquired lock
Aborting worker thread
```

The application simply sits there and never finishes. Let's attach the debugger and follow the same process as in the previous scenario to debug the application. We begin by dumping out all the threads to see if any of them are stuck (native threads omitted):

```
0:004> ~*e!clrstack
OS Thread Id: 0x135c (0)
ESP       EIP
0013f3e8 7c90e514 [HelperMethodFrame_1OBJ: 0013f3e8]
System.Threading.Thread.AbortInternal()
0013f440 793d750c System.Threading.Thread.Abort()
0013f450 00cb013d Advanced.NET.Debugging.Chapter6.Abort.Main(System.String[])
0013f69c 79e7be1b [GCFrame: 0013f69c]
OS Thread Id: 0x388 (3)
ESP       EIP
00dbf754 7c90e514 [GCFrame: 00dbf754]
00dbf824 7c90e514 [HelperMethodFrame_1OBJ: 00dbf824]
System.Threading.Monitor.Enter(System.Object)
00dbf87c 00cb0209 Advanced.NET.Debugging.Chapter6.Abort.WorkerThread()
00dbf8b4 793d70fb
System.Threading.ThreadHelper.ThreadStart_Context(System.Object)
00dbf8bc 793608fd
System.Threading.ExecutionContext.Run(System.Threading.ExecutionContex
t, System.Threading.ContextCallback, System.Object)
00dbf8d4 793d71dc System.Threading.ThreadHelper.ThreadStart()
00dbfaf8 79e7be1b [GCFrame: 00dbfaf8]
```

From the output, we can see that there are two threads of interest. The first thread, the main thread (id 0), appears to be stuck in a call to the `Abort` method. The second thread (id 3) appears to be stuck in a call to `Monitor.Enter`.

To better understand the state of the two threads, it is important to understand what exactly happens under the covers when a thread is aborted. When a thread is aborted, a `ThreadAbortException` is thrown in the target thread. This in turn gives the thread the capability to do some amount of cleanup before terminating. For threads that ensure cleanup is properly done, the scenario can be viewed as cooperative thread abortion (in contrast with the `TerminateThread` API in Windows). Based on the knowledge that a `ThreadAbortException` should have been thrown and should have terminated our worker thread, why is it still stuck waiting for the monitor? Let's verify that our worker thread did in fact receive a thread abort request:

```
0:004> !threads
ThreadCount: 3
UnstartedThread: 0
BackgroundThread: 1
PendingThread: 0
DeadThread: 0
Hosted Runtime: no
                             PreEmptive   GC Alloc        Lock
      ID OSID ThreadOBJ    State    GC      Context    Domain
```

```
Count APT Exception
    0    1 135c 00190d28    200a020 Enabled   00000000:00000000 0015bf10      1 MTA
    2    2 13d4 0019aa40       b220 Enabled   00000000:00000000 0015bf10      0 MTA
(Finalizer)
    3    3  388 001a9d30    200b021 Enabled   00000000:00000000 0015bf10      0 MTA
```

The state of the worker thread is 0x0200b021. The key is the first bit (1). Referencing Table 6-1, we can see that it indicates that an abort has been requested (TS_AbortRequested). To summarize our findings so far, we know that the main thread started a new thread, the main thread attempted to abort the new thread (and is stuck doing so), and the new thread received the abort request but is refusing to terminate. The answer to this problem lies in the fact that the worker thread received a request to abort while executing its finally block. For obvious reasons, aborting a thread while executing the finally block is not allowed and hence a deadlock ensues.

Lock Statement and Thread Abortions

Is the lock statement guaranteed to always release the lock in the case of thread abortions? The answer is maybe. The key lies in looking at the IL code that is generated when the lock statement is used.

```
  IL_0008:  call        void [mscorlib]System.Threading.Monitor::Enter(object)
  IL_000d:  nop
  .try
  {
    IL_000e:  nop
    IL_000f:  ldstr       "Test"
    IL_0014:  call        void
Advanced.NET.Debugging.Chapter6.Abort::Call3rdPartyCode(object)
    IL_0019:  nop
    IL_001a:  nop
    IL_001b:  leave.s     IL_0025
  } // end .try
  finally
  {
    IL_001d:  ldloc.0
    IL_001e:  call        void [mscorlib]System.Threading.Monitor::Exit(object)
    IL_0023:  nop
    IL_0024:  endfinally
  } // end handler
```

The basic idea behind the lock statement is to first acquire the lock (IL_0008), followed by wrapping the region of code executing under the protection of the lock in a try/finally. In the finally clause, the monitor is then released. Now, if the thread executing this code is aborted, the finally clause is invoked and the lock is released. If we look closer at the IL, we see an interesting nop instruction (IL_000d). The nop instruction is inserted by the compiler to support various debugging specific scenarios (such as setting breakpoints). The key here is to understand that the nop instruction is inserted prior to the try block; this means that if a thread is aborted while it is executing the nop instruction, the thread abort exception will never be caught and hence the monitor's state will remain locked. Please note that this is only applicable when building debug builds (where optimizations are turned off). It is, nonetheless, a very interesting scenario under which you may be running against debug builds during development and end up chasing a deadlock that would otherwise never surface in production.

Finalizer Hangs

In Chapter 5, "Managed Heap and Garbage Collection," we took a tour of the CLR memory manager and looked at several examples of interesting bugs that can wreak havoc in an application. In this part of the chapter, we will take a look at another interesting managed heap problem that is a direct result of poorly synchronized threads. The application we will use to illustrate the problem is partially shown in Listing 6-9.

Listing 6-9 *Application exhibiting memory leak symptoms*

```
using System;
using System.IO;
using System.Runtime.InteropServices;
using System.Management;

namespace Advanced.NET.Debugging.Chapter6
{
    class Wmi
    {
        private ManagementClass obj;
        private byte[] data;

        public Wmi(byte[] data)
        {
            this.data = data;
        }

        public void ProcessData()
        {
            obj = new ManagementClass("Win32_Environment");
            obj.Get();
```

(continues)

Listing 6-9 Application exhibiting memory leak symptoms *(continued)*

```
        //
        // Use data member reference
        //
    }

    ~Wmi()
    {
        //
        // Clean up any native resources
        //
    }
}

class Worker
{
    public Worker()
    {
        Init();
    }

    public void ProcessData(byte[] data)
    {
        Process(data);
    }

    ~Worker()
    {
        UnInit();
    }

    [DllImport("06Native.dll")]
    static extern void Init();

    [DllImport("06Native.dll")]
    static extern void UnInit();

    [DllImport("06Native.dll")]
    static extern void Process(byte[] data);
}

class OOMFin
{
    private Worker worker;

    static void Main(string[] args)
```

```
    {
        if (args.Length < 1)
        {
            Console.WriteLine("06Finalize.exe <num iterations>");
            return;
        }

        OOMFin o = new OOMFin();
        o.Run(Int32.Parse(args[0]));
    }

    public void Run(int iterations)
    {
        Initialize();

        for (int i = 0; i < iterations; i++)
        {
            byte[] b = new byte[10000];
            Wmi w = new Wmi(b);
            w.ProcessData();
        }

        GC.Collect();

        Console.WriteLine("Press any key to exit");
        Console.ReadKey();
    }

    private void Initialize()
    {
        byte[] b = new byte[100];

        worker = new Worker();
        worker.ProcessData(b);

        worker = null;
        GC.Collect();
    }
    }
}
```

The source code and binary for Listing 6-9 can be found in the following folders:

- Source code: `C:\ADND\Chapter6\Finalize`
- Binary: `C:\ADNDBin\06Finalize.exe` and `05Native.dll`

The application consists of a `Worker` class, which uses the interoperability services to process inbound data. The driver class is called `OOMFin` and contains the `Run` method that uses the `Worker` class and subsequently sits in a tight loop using the `Wmi` class to retrieve the environment block data from the system. The number of iterations can be controlled on the command line:

```
C:\ADNDBin\06Finalize.exe <number of iterations>
```

The application source code is relatively straightforward and nothing in it indicates that there should be any memory-related issues. Let's run the application under the debugger and specify `10000` iterations. After the application has completed and we suspect that memory is being too aggressively consumed, we are tasked with finding out the state of the memory by using the available debugger commands. Let's start by using the `eeheap-loader` command to see if there is anything unusual about the output:

```
0:007> !eeheap -loader
Loader Heap:
--------------------------------
System Domain: 7a3bc8b8
...

...

...
Total size:  0x3000(12288)bytes
--------------------------------
Shared Domain: 7a3bc560
...

...

...
Total size:  0x5000(20480)bytes
--------------------------------
Domain 1: 34fd48
...

...

...
Total size:  0x8000(32768)bytes
--------------------------------
Jit code heap:
LoaderCodeHeap: 00a60000(10000:1000) Size: 0x1000(4096)bytes.
Total size:  0x1000(4096)bytes
--------------------------------
```

```
Module Thunk heaps:
...
...
...
Total size: 0x0(0)bytes
--------------------------------
Module Lookup Table heaps:
...
...
...
Total size: 0x0(0)bytes
--------------------------------
Total LoaderHeap size: 0x11000(69632)bytes
```

The total size for the loader heap is 69632 bytes, nothing unusually high; so we can fairly safely say that at this point in time we do not suspect that there is any problem with the loader heap. Next, let's take a look at the managed heap by using the eeheap -gc command:

```
0:007> !eeheap -gc
Number of GC Heaps: 1
generation 0 starts at 0x125c2280
generation 1 starts at 0x123f63f4
generation 2 starts at 0x01fa1000
ephemeral segment allocation context: none
 segment     begin allocated       size
003872b8 7a733370  7a754b98 0x00021828(137256)
00367b38 790d8620  790f7d8c 0x0001f76c(128876)
01fa0000 01fa1000  02f9ee78 0x00ffde78(16768632)
054a0000 054a1000  0649f31c 0x00ffe31c(16769820)
07830000 07831000  0882e0d4 0x00ffd0d4(16765140)
0ada0000 0ada1000  0bd9f5cc 0x00ffe5cc(16770508)
0d250000 0d251000  0e24e0d4 0x00ffd0d4(16765140)
0f220000 0f221000  1021e0d4 0x00ffd0d4(16765140)
111f0000 111f1000  11d99830 0x00ba8830(12224560)
121f0000 121f1000  125c428c 0x003d328c(4010636)
Large object heap starts at 0x02fa1000
 segment     begin allocated       size
02fa0000 02fa1000  02fa4240 0x00003240(12864)
Total Size  0x6fb166c(117118572)
--------------------------------
GC Heap Size  0x6fb166c(117118572)
```

6. SYNCHRONIZATION

The total size of the managed heap is right around 117MB, which is not terribly high; but considering that the application is about to exit and that it forced a garbage collection earlier, it may be worthwhile to investigate this statistic more. To get some more information about the managed heap, we use the `DumpHeap -stat` command:

```
0:007> !DumpHeap -stat
total 226604 objects
Statistics:
      MT    Count    TotalSize Class Name
79119954        1          12
System.Security.Permissions.ReflectionPermission
79119834        1          12
System.Security.Permissions.FileDialogPermission
791197b0        1          12 System.Security.PolicyManager
...

...

...
6758707c    10000      120000
System.Management.IWbemClassObjectFreeThreaded
790fa9d8    10000      160000 System.__ComObject
000c3104    10000      160000 Advanced.NET.Debugging.Chapter6.Wmi
79104368    10003      240072 System.Collections.ArrayList
790fd8c4     4972      270224 System.String
67585310    10000      280000 System.Management.ManagementScope
67589900    20001      320016 System.Management.WbemDefPath
67584c28    20001      400020 System.Management.ManagementPath
67583f10    10000      480000
System.Management.ManagementNamedValueCollection
67584b74    10000      560000 System.Management.ConnectionOptions
79101fe4    10024      561344 System.Collections.Hashtable
67583650    10000      640000 System.Management.ManagementClass
7912d9bc    10024     1443528 System.Collections.Hashtable+bucket[]
67583fcc    60000     1920000
System.Management.IdentifierChangedEventHandler
003563b0    11301     9406484      Free
7912dae8    10003   100120360 System.Byte[]
Total 226604 objects
```

From the output, we can see that we still have `10000` instances of the `Wmi` class that we use in our application. The type that is occupying the most memory is the byte array, which we also know is being held by the `Wmi` type. Why do we still have all these `Wmi` types lying around? The code that uses the type is very straightforward and all instances should be collected without problems:

```
for (int i = 0; i < iterations; i++)
{
    byte[] b = new byte[10000];
    Wmi w = new Wmi(b);
    w.ProcessData();
}
```

Because the Wmi instances still appear rooted, we can find out what the reference chain is by using the GCRoot command, which takes an address to the object in question. To find the address, we first use the DumpHeap -type command:

```
0:007> !DumpHeap -type Advanced.NET.Debugging.Chapter6.Wmi
Address         MT        Size
01fa72b4  000c3104         16
01fac2a8  000c3104         16
01faec9c  000c3104         16
...
...
...
125b2c9c  000c3104         16
125b73dc  000c3104         16
125bbb1c  000c3104         16
125c025c  000c3104         16
total 10000 objects
Statistics:
      MT    Count    TotalSize Class Name
000c3104    10000       160000 Advanced.NET.Debugging.Chapter6.Wmi
Total 10000 objects
0:007> !GCRoot 125bbb1c
Note: Roots found on stacks may be false positives. Run "!help gcroot" for
more info.
Scan Thread 0 OSTHread 2bdc
Scan Thread 1 OSTHread 23f4
Finalizer queue:Root:125bbb1c(Advanced.NET.Debugging.Chapter6.Wmi)
```

We chose the object located at address 0x125bbb1c and fed that address to the GCRoot command. Interestingly enough, the object seems to be rooted by the f-reachable queue. The fact that it is on the f-reachable queue makes perfect sense because it has a Finalize method; it is not clear why it hasn't been collected yet. Let's use the FinalizeQueue command to glance at the state of the f-reachable queue:

```
0:007> !FinalizeQueue
SyncBlocks to be cleaned up: 50000
```

```
MTA Interfaces to be released: 0
STA Interfaces to be released: 0
--------------------------------
generation 0 has 3 finalizable objects (10c0ec0c->10c0ec18)
generation 1 has 3 finalizable objects (10c0ec00->10c0ec0c)
generation 2 has 4 finalizable objects (10c0ebf0->10c0ec00)
Ready for finalization 29998 objects (10c0ec18->10c2c0d0)
Statistics:
      MT     Count  TotalSize Class Name
7911c9c8         1        20 Microsoft.Win32.SafeHandles.SafePEFileHandle
79112728         1        20 Microsoft.Win32.SafeHandles.SafeWaitHandle
791037c0         1        20 Microsoft.Win32.SafeHandles.SafeFileMappingHandle
79103764         1        20 Microsoft.Win32.SafeHandles.SafeViewOfFileHandle
79101444         1        20 Microsoft.Win32.SafeHandles.SafeFileHandle
79108ba4         1        44 System.Threading.ReaderWriterLock
790fe704         1        56 System.Threading.Thread
7910a5c4         1        60 System.Runtime.Remoting.Contexts.Context
6758707c     10000    120000 System.Management.IWbemClassObjectFreeThreaded
000c3104     10000    160000 Advanced.NET.Debugging.Chapter6.Wmi
67583650     10000    640000 System.Management.ManagementClass
Total 30008 objects
```

It looks like there are close to 3000 objects on the f-reachable queue but the question still remains, why haven't these objects already been finalized? One possible theory is that the finalizer thread in the process hasn't awakened yet to do the work associated with running all the `Finalize` methods on the f-reachable queue. Let's check the state of the finalizer thread:

```
0:007> !Threads
ThreadCount: 2
UnstartedThread: 0
BackgroundThread: 1
PendingThread: 0
DeadThread: 0
Hosted Runtime: no
                                        PreEmptive  GC Alloc              Lock
        ID OSID ThreadOBJ    State      GC          Context      Domain
   Count APT Exception
     0   1 2bdc 00354448     a020 Enabled   125c2e0c:125c4280 0034fd48     0 MTA
     1   2 23f4 00358d68     b220 Enabled   00000000:00000000 0034fd48     0 MTA
(Finalizer)
0:007> ~1s
eax=00358d68 ebx=00000000 ecx=041af6c0 edx=041af6cc esi=70627138 edi=00000000
eip=77419a94 esp=041af800 ebp=041af864 iopl=0         nv up ei pl nz ac po cy
cs=001b  ss=0023  ds=0023  es=0023  fs=003b  gs=0000             efl=00000213
ntdll!KiFastSystemCallRet:
```

```
77419a94 c3              ret
0:001> k
ChildEBP RetAddr
041af7fc 77419254 ntdll!KiFastSystemCallRet
041af800 774033b4 ntdll!ZwWaitForSingleObject+0xc
041af864 7740323c ntdll!RtlpWaitOnCriticalSection+0x155
041af88c 706214e4 ntdll!RtlEnterCriticalSection+0x152
041af964 000ba26b 05Native!UnInit+0x34
WARNING: Frame IP not in any known module. Following frames may be wrong.
041af9a8 79fbcca7 0xba26b
041af9c8 79fbcca7 mscorwks!MethodTable::SetObjCreateDelegate+0xc5
041afa2c 79fbcc15 mscorwks!MethodTable::SetObjCreateDelegate+0xc5
041afa4c 79fbcbb7 mscorwks!MethodTable::CallFinalizer+0x76
041afa60 79f6acb6 mscorwks!SVR::CallFinalizer+0xb2
041afab0 79f6abf7 mscorwks!WKS::GCHeap::TraceGCSegments+0x170
041afb38 79fb99d6 mscorwks!WKS::GCHeap::TraceGCSegments+0x2b6
041afb50 79ef3207 mscorwks!WKS::GCHeap::FinalizerThreadWorker+0xe7
041afb64 79ef31a3 mscorwks!Thread::DoADCallBack+0x32a
041afbf8 79ef30c3 mscorwks!Thread::ShouldChangeAbortToUnload+0xe3
041afc34 79fb9643 mscorwks!Thread::ShouldChangeAbortToUnload+0x30a
041afc5c 79fb960d mscorwks!ManagedThreadBase_NoADTransition+0x32
041afc6c 79fba09b mscorwks!ManagedThreadBase::FinalizerBase+0xd
041afca4 79f95a2e mscorwks!WKS::GCHeap::FinalizerThreadStart+0xbb
041afd48 77584911 mscorwks!Thread::intermediateThreadProc+0x49
```

Interestingly enough, it looks like the finalizer thread is in the process of executing a finalize method. To find out which object it is executing the method on, we use the `ClrStack` command to get a managed call stack:

```
0:001> !ClrStack
OS Thread Id: 0x23f4 (1)
ESP       EIP
041af994 77419a94 [NDirectMethodFrameStandalone: 041af994]
Advanced.NET.Debugging.Chapter6.Worker.UnInit()
041af9a4 00a6030d Advanced.NET.Debugging.Chapter6.Worker.Finalize()
```

As shown by the output, the finalizer thread is executing the `Finalize` method of our `Worker` type. The `NDirectMethodFrameStandalone` indicates that a managed to native transition is occurring. If we go back to our native call stack, the top part shows:

```
041af7fc 77419254 ntdll!KiFastSystemCallRet
041af800 774033b4 ntdll!ZwWaitForSingleObject+0xc
041af864 7740323c ntdll!RtlpWaitOnCriticalSection+0x155
041af88c 706214e4 ntdll!RtlEnterCriticalSection+0x152
041af964 000ba26b 05Native!UnInit+0x34
```

In essence, the finalizer thread is executing the `Finalize` method of our `Worker` type, which in turn uses the interoperability services to call into a native module (`05Native`), which in turn attempts to enter a critical section, but appears to be getting stuck. A closer look at the source code shows that the `ProcessData` function we call from the `Initialize` method in our `OOMFin` class enters a critical section but never, subsequently, releases the critical section. The `UnInit` function in turn attempts to enter the critical section, but because it is already locked, the call waits indefinitely. Because the usage of the `Worker` class (which also has a `Finalize` method) precedes the usage of the `Wmi` class, the `Worker` class instance ends up on the f-reachable queue before any of our numerous `Wmi` instances, which also means that the finalizer thread will pick that instance up first and immediately get stuck. Now, because the finalizer thread simply picks up objects on the f-reachable queue in a serialized fashion, any object that causes the finalizer thread to fail (or get stuck in this case), *will prevent the finalizer thread from executing the rest of the Finalize methods on the f-reachable queue* causing the objects never to get cleaned up and garbage collected. The net result is that memory consumption will grow in an unbounded fashion and eventually will result in an `OutOfMemoryException`.

As we've seen in this part of the chapter, using a Finalize method can be far from trivial. Great care must be taken to ensure that there are no inadvertent bugs (such as a deadlock) in the Finalize code because even the smallest of bugs can cause not only that specific object not to be cleaned up but also all other objects that follow on the f-reachable queue.

Summary

Multithreading may seem like a trivial programming exercise. After all, it's pretty simple. You spin up a number of threads and have them work in parallel to accomplish some task. As we've seen throughout the chapter, the area of concurrency and synchronization is far from trivial. One could even argue that its one of the top areas prone to bugs. Extreme care must be taken to ensure that all threads live and work together in harmony. Small mistakes in this logic can have substantial and devastating consequences.

In this chapter, we took a look at some very common mistakes made when dealing with multithreaded applications and synchronization. We started with a brief overview of the different synchronization primitives available in the CLR and how those primitives are organized in the runtime. A number of scenarios such as deadlocks, orphaned locks, thread abortions, and finalization deadlocks were shown, as well as how to find the root cause using the debuggers.

## CHAPTER 7

INTEROPERABILITY

When .NET 1.0 was first introduced back in 2002, the .NET team was faced with the question of how much support it should provide for interacting with legacy code written outside of the brand new managed runtime. Because the success of the new platform depended, to a large degree, on the adoption rate, the .NET team decided to provide a rich and seamless integration with existing native code. The two primary areas of focus were allowing managed code to call into native code via COM (or vice versa); or, alternatively, call into exported DLL functions. Managed code calling into COM (or vice versa) is called COM interoperability (also called interop) and calls into exported DLL functions are referred to as Platform Invocation Services (P/Invoke). In this chapter, we take a look at how COM interoperability and platform invocation works internally and also some of the most interesting problems that can occur when managed code and native code interact improperly.

Platform Invocation

The Platform Invocation Services (P/Invoke) is the part of the CLR that is responsible for ensuring that managed code can call into the wide range of functions that are exported from native DLLs. Although the .NET framework does a tremendous job of neatly wrapping most of the functions available in Win32, not all of them are currently covered. In cases where you need to call a function that is not wrapped, P/Invoke offers the functionality needed to develop your own wrapper. At a high level, the process for P/Invoking to a native function is

1. Define a managed code function that corresponds to the native function.
2. Annotate the managed code function definition with the DllImport attribute to indicate that it's intended to represent a native function.
3. Call the managed code function definition, which causes the CLR to load the DLL and transition to the native function during the call sequence.

Below is an example of a simple P/Invoke managed method definition corresponding to the Win32 `Beep` (simply plays a tone on the speaker) API defined in `kernel32.dll`.

```
BOOL WINAPI Beep(
    __in DWORD dwFreq,
    __in DWORD dwDuration
);
```

```
[DllImport("kernel32.dll", SetLastError=true)]
private static extern bool Beep(uint freq, uint dur);
```

The `DllImport` attribute is used to indicate that the function corresponds to a P/Invoke definition and that the specified function resides in `kernel32.dll`. Furthermore, `SetLastError` is used to indicate that we want the function to set the last error when exiting. Let's take a look at what an application that uses this P/Invoke definition looks like under the debugger. Listing 7-1 shows a very simplistic application.

Listing 7-1   Application that P/Invokes to the Beep function

```
using System;
using System.Text;
using System.Runtime.InteropServices;
using System.Runtime.Remoting;

namespace Advanced.NET.Debugging.Chapter7
{
    class BeepSample
    {
        static void Main(string[] args)
        {
            Beep(1000, 2000);
        }

        [DllImport("kernel32.dll", SetLastError=true)]
        private static extern bool Beep(uint freq, uint dur);
    }
}
```

The source code and binary for Listing 7-1 can be found in the following folders:

- Source code: `C:\ADND\Chapter7\Beep`
- Binary: `C:\ADNDBin\07Beep.exe`

Now, let's run the application under the debugger and set a breakpoint on the kernel32.dll Beep function. That way, when the breakpoint hits, we can take a look at the stack trace and see if we can glean some information on what the runtime does to enable us to call into native code:

```
0:000> bp kernel32!Beep
0:000> g
ModLoad: 75d10000 75dd6000   C:\Windows\system32\ADVAPI32.dll
ModLoad: 76fb0000 77073000   C:\Windows\system32\RPCRT4.dll
...

...

...
ModLoad: 76150000 76195000   C:\Windows\system32\iertutil.dll
ModLoad: 75b40000 75b54000   C:\Windows\system32\Secur32.dll
ModLoad: 77590000 775bd000   C:\Windows\system32\ws2_32.dll
ModLoad: 77560000 77566000   C:\Windows\system32\NSI.dll
ModLoad: 79060000 790b6000   C:\Windows\Microsoft.NET\Framework\
v2.0.50727\mscorjit.dll
Breakpoint 0 hit
eax=00123060 ebx=00448720 ecx=000003e8 edx=000007d0 esi=0029f160 edi=0029f390
eip=75e666e8 esp=0029f12c ebp=0029f148 iopl=0         nv up ei pl zr na pe nc
cs=001b  ss=0023  ds=0023  es=0023  fs=003b  gs=0000              efl=00000246
KERNEL32!Beep:
75e666e8 6a2c            push    2Ch
0:000> !ClrStack
OS Thread Id: 0x146c (0)
ESP       EIP
0029f160 75e666e8 [NDirectMethodFrameStandalone: 0029f160]
 Advanced.NET.Debugging.Chapter7.BeepSample.Beep(UInt32, UInt32)
0029f170 00a80092 Advanced.NET.Debugging.Chapter7.BeepSample.Main(System.String[])
0029f390 79e7c74b [GCFrame: 0029f390]
```

In the output of the ClrStack command, we can see that the Main method is calling into our P/Invoke Beep signature. Notice that the frame corresponding to our Beep method is prefixed with the following:

```
[NDirectMethodFrameStandalone: 0029f160]
```

The NDirectMethodFrameStandalone indicates that a transition to native code is taking place. We can get some verification of that fact by taking the address specified (0x0029f160) and dumping out the contents:

```
0:000> dd 0029f160
0029f160 79e73620 0029f390 00123040 00a80092
0029f170 01e75874 79e7c74b 0029f180 0029f1c0
```

```
0029f180   0029f200 79e7c6cc 0029f250 00000000
0029f190   0029f220 00000000 0012c040 0029f1f0
0029f1a0   79f07fee 0029f390 be1faf39 0029f3dc
0029f1b0   0029f240 00000000 0029f390 00448720
0029f1c0   00000000 00000000 00000000 00000000
0029f1d0   00000001 00000000 79e7c1fa 0029f19c
```

The first element looks like it may be a code address, so let's use the `ln` command to see if it resolves to anything:

```
0:000> ln 79e73620
(79e73620)   mscorwks!NDirectMethodFrameStandalone::'vftable'   |
  (79e73688)   mscorwks!NDirectMethodFrameSlim::'vftable'
Exact matches:
    mscorwks!NDirectMethodFrameStandalone::'vftable' = <no type information>
```

Sure enough, the output shows that the address corresponds to the virtual function table of the `NDirectMethodFrameStandalone` object. We can further dump out the virtual function table and use the `ln` command on some of the function addresses to see what it contains:

```
0:000> dd 79e73620 14
79e73620   79fc1a7d 79e730fc 7a0a3e0a 79e74034
0:000> ln 79fc1a7d
...
...
...
Exact matches:
    mscorwks!DelegateTransitionFrame::GcScanRoots = <no type information>
    mscorwks!NDirectMethodFrame::GcScanRoots = <no type information>
```

Although the `NDirectMethodFrame` is largely undocumented, much information can be gleaned about the object by simply digging around the various functions that it contains. The key to remember is that anytime you see an `NDirectMethodFrame` statement in the stack, you know that the code just transitioned from managed code into the native world.

So far, we've seen a very simple example of a P/Invoke application and what the transition to native code looks like in the debugger. The transition frame (as abstracted by the `NDirectMethodFrame` object) needs to be able to handle all sorts of different schemes depending on the complexity of the native function that is being called. Perhaps the most critical of these schemes is the marshalling that takes place during the transition. Marshalling simply refers to the conversion of various data representations that are not compatible in the two worlds (managed and native). For simple data types such as an `int` or `bool`, the marshalling is for the most part automatic, but with other more complex data types, the CLR may need help from the caller to properly identify how the data should be marshaled. Let's take a look at a slightly more complicated P/Invoke call as shown in Listing 7-2.

Listing 7-2 P/Invoke example

```
using System;
using System.Text;
using System.Runtime.InteropServices;
using System.Runtime.Remoting;

namespace Advanced.NET.Debugging.Chapter7
{
    class PInvoke
    {
        private const int TableSize = 50;

        [StructLayout(LayoutKind.Sequential, CharSet = CharSet.Ansi)]
        public class Node
        {
            public string First;
            public string Last;
            public string Social;
            public UInt32 Age;
        }

        [StructLayout(LayoutKind.Sequential)]
        public class Table
        {
            [MarshalAs(UnmanagedType.ByValArray, SizeConst = TableSize)]
            public IntPtr[] Nodes;

            public IntPtr Aux;
        }

        static void Main(string[] args)
        {
            PInvoke p = new PInvoke();
            p.Run();
        }
```

(continues)

Listing 7-2   P/Invoke example *(continued)*

```
public void Run()
{
    Node[] nodes = new Node[TableSize];
    nodes[0] = new Node();
    nodes[0].First = "First Name 1";
    nodes[0].Last = "Last Name 1";
    nodes[0].Social = "Social 1";
    nodes[0].Age = 30;

    nodes[1] = new Node();
    nodes[1].First = "First Name 2";
    nodes[1].Last = "Last Name 2";
    nodes[1].Social = "Social 2";
    nodes[1].Age = 31;

    nodes[2] = new Node();
    nodes[2].First = "First Name 3";
    nodes[2].Last = "Last Name 3";
    nodes[2].Social = "Social 3";
    nodes[2].Age = 32;

    Table t = new Table();
    t.Aux = IntPtr.Zero;

    t.Nodes = new IntPtr[TableSize];
    for (int i = 0; i < TableSize && nodes[i] != null; i++)
    {
        int nodeSize = Marshal.SizeOf(typeof(Node));
        t.Nodes[i] = Marshal.AllocHGlobal(nodeSize);
        Marshal.StructureToPtr(nodes[i], t.Nodes[i], false);
    }

    int tableSize = Marshal.SizeOf(typeof(Table));
    IntPtr pTable = Marshal.AllocHGlobal(tableSize);
    Marshal.StructureToPtr(t, pTable, false);

    Myfunc(pTable);
}

[DllImport("05Native.dll")]
private static extern void Myfunc(IntPtr ptr);
}
}
```

The source code and binary for Listing 7-2 can be found in the following folders:

- Source code: `C:\ADND\Chapter7\PInvoke`
- Binary: `C:\ADNDBin\07PInvoke.exe and 05Native.dll`

The source code in Listing 7-2 shows a slightly more complex P/Invoke call. Rather than passing simple data types to the native function, it accepts a pointer to a `Table` structure that contains an array of the `Node` type. The `Node` type in turn contains a set of basic types (`string` and `int`). Due to the complex nature of the data being passed from managed to native code, we can no longer rely on the standard marshaler; instead, we have to provide specific instructions on how the different elements of the complex type should be marshaled. Those instructions come in the form of attributes applied at the type level or the member level. For example, both the `Node` type and the `Table` type have the attribute `StructLayout` applied to them specifying the layout kind to be sequential (meaning all members are laid out sequentially in memory). Furthermore, the `Nodes` array in the `Table` type has the attribute `MarshalAs` applied to it specifying that the array should be treated as an array of value types. In addition to annotating the different elements of the data structure being passed to native code, we also have to write explicit marshaling code that makes sure that we allocate the memory needed for the type as well as calling the `Marshal.StructureToPtr` method that copies the elements from the data type to the newly allocated memory according to the marshaling annotations we added. When all the preparation code has been put in place, we can finally make the actual call to the native method passing in the pointer to the newly created and marshaled `Table` type. Although relying on the default marshaler is clearly far easier, there are times when custom (or explicit) marshaling is needed and writing explicit marshaling can be a daunting and error prone task. The net effects of buggy marshaling code can range from immediate crashes to very subtle problems that do not surface right away; and knowing how to use the debugger to troubleshoot these problems is essential. Let's start by using our example in Listing 7-2 as an illustration on how to do some basic debugging steps on properly written marshaling code. Start by running `07Pinvoke.exe` under the debugger and set a breakpoint on the native function we are calling (`Myfunc` located in the `05Native.dll` module).

```
0:000> bp 05native!MyFunc
Bp expression '05native!MyFunc' could not be resolved, adding deferred bp
0:000> g
ModLoad: 76730000 767f6000   C:\Windows\system32\ADVAPI32.dll
ModLoad: 761a0000 76263000   C:\Windows\system32\RPCRT4.dll
```

...

...

...

```
Breakpoint 0 hit
eax=000c3078 ebx=00249fe8 ecx=0026eb98 edx=79ec7f60 esi=001df258 edi=001df4bc
eip=6f2e1590 esp=001df228 ebp=001df240 iopl=0         nv up ei pl zr na pe nc
cs=001b  ss=0023  ds=0023  es=0023  fs=003b  gs=0000         efl=00000246
05Native!Myfunc:
6f2e1590 55                   push    ebp
```

After the breakpoint is reached, we can look at the argument passed to the function:

```
0:000> dv
         ptr = 0x0026eb98
0:000> dd 0x0026eb98 l3
0026eb98  00270078 00270090 002700a8
0:000> dd 00270078 l4
00270078  00272a48 0025eb40 0025eda0 0000001e
0:000> da 00272a48
00272a48  "First Name 1"
```

The `dv` command displays the parameters to the function (`0x0026eb98`), which corresponds to an instance of the `Table` structure. We then use the `dd` command to display the pointers to the nodes contained within the array. Subsequently, we again use the `dd` command to display the contents of the first node in the array and the `da` command on the first element to display the first element, which happens to be a string representing the first name. To convince ourselves that the parameter is indeed intact and proper, we could continue using this strategy for the rest of the nodes and elements. Always remember to set a breakpoint in the native code function being called followed by verification that the data passed is proper by using the plethora of dump commands.

So far, we have discussed the P/Invoke method of calling into native code, but there is another interoperability layer that is commonly used called the COM Interoperability layer.

COM Interoperability

The Component Object Model (COM) is a binary interface that was introduced by Microsoft in 1993. It provides a common way of defining language neutral components that can be created and used across machine boundaries. Even though COM was introduced as a *standard*, it enjoyed most of its success on the Windows platform where the number of available COM objects grew rapidly. Due to this success and with the advent of .NET, a key feature was to allow managed code to easily interact with existing COM objects and thus the COM interoperability layer was born. COM interop is simply a way to interact with native code and more specifically native code implemented as COM objects. The interaction can be bidirectional in the sense that managed code can call into existing native code COM objects as well as native code calling into managed objects exposed as COM objects. We'll focus our discussion on the most common type of COM interop, namely at how .NET allows managed code to call into a native code COM object.

Runtime Callable Wrapper

Earlier in the chapter, we discussed the P/Invoke layer and how it can be used to interact with native code modules (DLLs). At a high level, the algorithm used by the P/Invoke layer is

1. Load the specified module (DLL) into the process address space.
2. Find the address of the function of interest.
3. Marshall data.
4. Call the function.

COM interop is slightly more complicated because it has its own registration, instantiation, lifetime management, and marshaling semantics. Rather than requiring each managed code application to implement the necessary code to locate, instantiate, acquire interfaces, and manage the marshaling, the COM interop layer has the capability to generate all the code necessary and produce what is known as an interop assembly. The interop assembly is best viewed as a managed proxy to the underlying COM object with a familiar .NET object model rather making it easier to program against. To get a better idea of how this mechanism works, we will be using a simple COM object that exposes one method called Add. Due to the simplicity, we won't worry about the actual native code; rather, we will only list the interface definition for the COM object as shown in Listing 7-3.

Listing 7-3   IDL for simple COM object

```
interface IBasicMath : IUnknown
{
    [helpstring("method Add")]
    HRESULT Add([in] LONG num1, [in] LONG num2, [out] LONG* res);
};
```

The binary for Listing 7-3 can be found in the following folders:

■ Binary: `C:\ADNDBin\07PInvoke07ComObj.dll`

REGISTERING COM BINARIES All COM objects must register themselves in a well-known location in the registry so that the COM system can locate the corresponding binaries. To register a COM object, the `regsvr32.exe` can be used. For example, to use the sample COM object in Listing 7-3, you must first run the following: `regsvr32 07ComObj.dll`.

The `Add` method simply takes two numbers as input and stores the result in the third out parameter. To use the COM object shown in Listing 7-3 from managed, we can use the code shown in Listing 7-4.

Listing 7-4 Sample managed code using a simple COM object

```
using System;
using System.Text;
using System.Runtime.InteropServices;
using System.Runtime.Remoting;
using COMInterop;

namespace Advanced.NET.Debugging.Chapter7
{
    class COMInteropSample
    {
        [STAThread]
        static void Main(string[] args)
        {
            int result;
            BasicMathClass s = new BasicMathClass();
            s.Add(1, 2, out result);
            Console.WriteLine("Result= " + result);
        }
    }
}
```

The source code and binary for Listing 7-4 can be found in the following folders:

■ Source code: `C:\ADND\Chapter7\COMInterop`
■ Binary: `C:\ADNDBin\07COMInterop.exe and 07Managed.dll`

As you can see, calling into a native code COM object is a very straightforward process. We simply instantiate an instance of the `BasicMathClass` type and call the corresponding `Add` method. Where is the `BasicMatchClass` type defined? The answer to that lies in what is known as a primary interop assembly (PIA). As you can see in Listing 7-4, we added a using statement for the `COMInterop` namespace. This namespace and contained types was generated by using a tool called `tlbimp.exe` (part of the .NET SDK). `Tlbimp.exe` can generate a PIA by simply pointing it to the COM binary. In the preceding example, the following command was run to generate the `07Managed.dll` PIA:

```
TlbImp.exe 07ComObj.dll /out:07Managed.dll /namespace:COMInterop
```

So far, we've discussed the three high-level entities involved in a COM interop scenario: the COM binary, the managed client, and the PIA. There is a forth entity involved that sits behind the scenes and gets created at runtime: the Runtime Callable Wrapper (RCW). Figure 7-1 illustrates all four entities working in tandem to allow for a seamless interop experience.

The process illustrated in Figure 7-1 starts with the managed client calling the method defined in the COM object as defined in the PIA. The CLR creates an instance of the RCW (one per CoClass) by using information from the PIA. The RCW then intercepts the call to the method, translates the arguments into native types, transitions, and invokes the method in native code.

Another aspect of the RCW is that it handles the lifetime of the underlying COM object. COM object lifetimes are managed by a reference counting scheme, which simply means that anytime an interface to the object is acquired, the reference count is incremented. Conversely, when an interface is no longer needed, the reference count is decremented. When the reference count reaches 0, the instance can safely be discarded. The RCW keeps track of the number of references that has been made

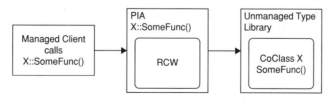

Figure 7-1   The four primary entities involved in COM interoperability

and ensures that the reference count is incremented/decremented accordingly. When a managed client is done using the RCW and there are no outstanding references, the RCW gets collected and all associated COM objects are freed.

DETERMINISTICALLY RELEASING COM OBJECTS Because the RCW decrements and cleans up any references to the underlying COM objects after there are no references to the actual RCW, it means that COM objects are not cleaned up until the garbage collector cleans up the RCW. There is a way to force the release of a COM object by using the `Marshal.ReleaseComObject` method.

Let's run the application in Listing 7-4 (`07ComInterop.exe`) under the debugger and see if we can use the debugger to gain some insight into the underpinnings of the COM interop call. Start by setting a breakpoint on the native function on the COM object `Add` function, resume execution until the breakpoint hits, and then dump out the managed call stack:

```
0:000> bp 07ComObj!CBasicMath::Add
Bp expression '07ComObj!CBasicMath::Add' could not be resolved, adding deferred bp
0:000> g
ModLoad: 76730000 767f6000   C:\Windows\system32\ADVAPI32.dll
ModLoad: 761a0000 76263000   C:\Windows\system32\RPCRT4.dll
...
...
...
Breakpoint 0 hit
eax=5c701573 ebx=004d8610 ecx=00000003 edx=5c718704 esi=0025efa8 edi=0025f1ec
eip=5c707900 esp=0025ef60 ebp=0025ef90 iopl=0         nv up ei pl zr na pe nc
cs=001b  ss=0023  ds=0023  es=0023  fs=003b  gs=0000             efl=00000246
07ComObj!CBasicMath::Add:
5c707900 55              push    ebp
0:000> !ClrStack -a
OS Thread Id: 0x26f4 (0)
ESP        EIP
0025efa8 5c707900 [ComPlusMethodFrameStandaloneCleanup: 0025efa8]
  COMInterop.BasicMathClass.Add(Int32, Int32, Int32 ByRef)
0025efc0 004800b8 Advanced.NET.Debugging.Chapter7.COMInteropSample.Main
(System.String[])
    PARAMETERS:
        args = 0x01f358c8
    LOCALS:
```

```
0x0025efc4 = 0x00000000
<CLR reg> = 0x01f36268
```

```
0025f1ec 79e7c74b [GCFrame: 0025f1ec]
```

The topmost frame of the managed stack shows the call into the `Add` method in the PIA, which under the covers handles the transition to native code (as indicated by the `ComPlusMethodFrameStandaloneCleanup`).

There are a few SOS commands that can be used to get COM interop related information. First, as we have alluded to in earlier parts of the book, some of the SOS commands show what is known as the apartment type. Here is an example of the `threads` command in our debug session:

```
0:000> !threads
ThreadCount: 2
UnstartedThread: 0
BackgroundThread: 1
PendingThread: 0
DeadThread: 0
Hosted Runtime: no
                                PreEmptive   GC Alloc         Lock
      ID OSID ThreadOBJ    State    GC     Context        Domain
   Count APT Exception
   0   1 26f4 004d8610     6020 Enabled  01f36278:01f38004 004d1328    0 STA
   2   2 2a00 004da6c0     b220 Enabled  00000000:00000000 004d1328    0 MTA
(Finalizer)
```

An apartment is a logical construct that is tightly coupled to the COM threading model. At a high level, one of the key aspects of COM is to allow components with different threading requirements to work together. For example, a COM component that is not written to handle concurrent calls can use the single threaded apartment (STA), which causes the COM subsystem to serialize all calls made to the component. Conversely, components that handle concurrent calls can use the multi threaded apartment (MTA) model, in which case no attempts are made by COM to serialize the calls. When any given thread wants to use a COM component, it must choose the apartment model accordingly. By default, all .NET threads are in the MTA. In Listing 7-4, we explicitly changed the main thread by applying the `STAThread` attribute on the `Main` method (primarily because the COM object itself is registered as using the STA model). The `APT` column of the output of the `threads` command shows which apartment model the thread is utilizing (STA, MTA).

Another command that shows COM interop related information is the `syncblk` command.

```
0:000> !syncblk
Index SyncBlock MonitorHeld Recursion Owning Thread Info  SyncBlock Owner
------------------------
Total            1
CCW              0
RCW              1
ComClassFactory 0
Free             0
```

The output of the `syncblk` command shows the total number of RCWs that the CLR has instantiated and that are active. This count can come in useful when you want to get a quick overview of the current RCW usage.

The last command of interest is the `COMState` command. The `COMState` command outputs detailed COM information for each thread in the process:

```
0:000> !COMState
    ID    TEB   APT    APTId CallerTID Context
 0 2ff8 7ffde000 STA     a84         0 0024b228
 1 2c14 7ffdd000 Ukn
 2  508 7ffdc000 MTA       0         0 0024b398
 3 2400 7ffdb000 Ukn
 4 2eb8 7ffda000 Ukn       0         0 00000000
```

The most interesting aspect of the output is the `APT` column, which shows the apartment model of the thread.

Now that we have discussed how managed code applications can call into native code COM objects and what information we can see in regard to this interoperability under the debugger, it's time to turn our attention to the most common pitfalls of using both the P/Invoke and COM interop layers and how we can use our newly gained understanding and debugging techniques to arrive at the root cause.

Debugging P/Invoke Calls

Earlier in the chapter, we talked about how the P/Invoke layer allows managed code to call into native code. The complexity of performing this task depends entirely on the complexity of the native function being called. For example, we have to make sure that the managed code signature representing the native function is defined properly or, in cases where the default marshaler isn't sufficient, we have to write our own marshaling code. The additional code has to be carefully written to avoid subtle bugs in the application. In this section of the book, we will take a look at a couple of examples where the native code invocation from managed code isn't properly written, what the symptoms are, and finally how we can use the debuggers and tools to efficiently troubleshoot.

Calling Conventions

A calling convention is nothing more than a contract between the caller of a function and the function itself. It specifies a set of rules that both parties must agree on for the call to be made properly. As can be seen in Table 7-1, a few different types of calling conventions are available. The main difference between these calling conventions lies in how parameters are passed to the calling function and how they are cleaned up from the sack.

When using P/Invoke to call a native function, it is critical that the correct calling convention is used. If an incorrect calling convention is used, the application will exhibit problems that can be very hard to detect. By default, the P/Invoke layer uses the `Winapi` calling convention, which is strictly speaking not a calling convention but rather instructs the runtime to use the default platform calling convention—for example, on Windows, the default is `StdCall` and on Windows CE, it is `Cdecl`. However, you can also specify a different calling convention by using the `CallingConvention` field of the `DllImport` attribute. The last column in Table 5-1 shows the mapping between the native calling convention and the `DllImport CallingConvention` field.

Let's take a look at an application that performs a P/Invoke call. We will use the same application as shown earlier in Listing 7-2, with the exception of the P/Invoke signature, which has changed slightly to illustrate how an application behaves when a calling convention is explicitly specified.

Table 7-1 Calling Conventions

Calling Convention	Arguments	Cleanup	DllImport CallingConvention
Stdcall	Stack (right to left)	Called function	StdCall
Cdecl	Stack (right to left)	Calling function	Cdecl
Fastcall	Registers/stack (right to left)	Called function	FastCall (Not supported)
Thiscall	Registers/stack (right to left)	Called function	ThisCall

7. INTEROPERABILITY

The source code and binary for this example can be found in the following folders:

- Source code: `C:\ADND\Chapter7\Sig`
- Binary: `C:\ADNDBin\07Sig.exe` and `05Native.dll`

If we run the application, we can quickly see that an exception is thrown:

```
C:\ADNDBin>07Sig.exe

Unhandled Exception: System.AccessViolationException: Attempted to
 read or write protected memory. This is often an indication that
 other memory is corrupt.
   at Advanced.NET.Debugging.Chapter7.PInvoke.Myfunc(IntPtr ptr)

   at Advanced.NET.Debugging.Chapter7.PInvoke.Run() in
c:\Publishing\ADND\Code\Chapter7\Sig\07Sig.cs:line 72
   at
Advanced.NET.Debugging.Chapter7.PInvoke.Main(String[] args) in
c:\Publishing\ADND\Code\Chapter7\Sig\07Sig.cs:line 33
```

The exception that is thrown indicates that an access violation occurred. An access violation is nothing more than an instruction accessing memory that is considered to be invalid. The easiest way to debug these types of problems is to simply run the application under the debugger until the access violation occurs and then look at the state of the application to identify the root cause:

```
...
...
...

(21a0.2608): Access violation - code c0000005 (first chance)
First chance exceptions are reported before any exception handling.
This exception may be expected and handled.
eax=00000000 ebx=00078570 ecx=deda8173 edx=79ec7f60 esi=002deeb8 edi=002dee88
eip=6c7615c6 esp=002dedb0 ebp=002dee88 iopl=0         nv up ei pl nz ac po nc
cs=001b  ss=0023  ds=0023  es=0023  fs=003b  gs=0000              efl=00010212
05Native!Myfunc+0x36:
6c7615c6 833c8100        cmp     dword ptr [ecx+eax*4],0 ds:0023:deda8173=????????
```

As per expectations, a first chance access violation is raised when executing the `cmp` instruction located at address `0x6c7615c6`. Is it possible to find out which line in the source code this `cmp` instruction corresponds to? One easy way to instruct the debugger to output source code/line information is to use the `lines` command:

```
0:000> !lines
Line number information will be loaded
```

Now, any time we ask for a call stack source code location and line number, information will be included (if private symbols are available):

```
0:000> k
ChildEBP RetAddr
002dee88 001ba307 05Native!Myfunc+0x36
[c:\workzone\05native\05native\05native.cpp @ 75]
WARNING: Frame IP not in any known module. Following frames may be wrong.
002def00 79e7c74b 0x1ba307
002def10 79e7c6cc mscorwks!CallDescrWorker+0x33
002def90 79e7c8e1 mscorwks!CallDescrWorkerWithHandler+0xa3
002df0cc 79e7c783 mscorwks!MethodDesc::CallDescr+0x19c
002df0e8 79e7c90d mscorwks!MethodDesc::CallTargetWorker+0x1f
...
...
...
```

From the output, we can see that the source file is 05native.cpp and the line number is 75. Here is the source code for the Myfunc function:

```
__declspec(dllexport) VOID Myfunc(TABLE* ptr)
{
[75]          for(int i=0; ptr->Coll[i]!=NULL; i++)
     {
          printf("First: %s, Last: %s, Social: %s, Age: %d\n",
               ptr->Coll[i]->First,
               ptr->Coll[i]->Last,
               ptr->Coll[i]->Social,
               ptr->Coll[i]->Age);
     }
}
```

Based on the fact that we are seeing a cmp instruction and that line 75 corresponds to our for loop, we can safely assume that the for loop conditional (ptr->Coll[i]!=NULL) is being executed. Let's deconstruct the conditional further. The ptr pointer is passed as a parameter to the function, so we should be able to use the dv command to get the address of it:

```
0:000> dv /V
002dee80 @ebp-0x08           i = 0
002dee90 @ebp+0x08           ptr = 0xdeda8173
```

From the output, we can see that the pointer value is `0xdeda8173`. Because the pointer value corresponds to a `TABLE` structure, which in turn contains an array of nodes, we would expect the pointer to point to memory that contains a number of other pointers each corresponding to a node instance. If we dump out the pointer, we see the following:

```
0:000> dd 0xdeda8173
deda8173  ???????? ???????? ???????? ????????
deda8183  ???????? ???????? ???????? ????????
deda8193  ???????? ???????? ???????? ????????
deda81a3  ???????? ???????? ???????? ????????
deda81b3  ???????? ???????? ???????? ????????
deda81c3  ???????? ???????? ???????? ????????
deda81d3  ???????? ???????? ???????? ????????
deda81e3  ???????? ???????? ???????? ????????
```

Not a good sign. The question marks in the output indicate that the memory pointed to is invalid. Where did the pointer value come from? We already know that the pointer is being passed from our managed code application. If we look at the signature of our native `Myfunc` function, we can see that it is declared as

```
__declspec(dllexport) VOID Myfunc(TABLE* ptr)
```

Because it doesn't explicitly state a calling convention, the default calling convention `cdecl` applies (parameters are passed on the stack from right to left). Based on the output of the `dv` command, we expect that the parameter will be placed in stack location `ebp+0x8`. We can also very clearly see that the pointer is invalid. The big question still remains: Where is the correct pointer located? Let's restart the application and set a breakpoint in `Myfunc` before the access violation occurs. After the breakpoint hits, let's take a look at the state of our stack again:

```
...
...
...
Breakpoint 0 hit
eax=001d3078 ebx=002b8548 ecx=002d27f8 edx=79ec7f60 esi=001bef08 edi=001bf174
eip=6c761590 esp=001beedc ebp=001beef0 iopl=0         nv up ei pl zr na pe nc
cs=001b  ss=0023  ds=0023  es=0023  fs=003b  gs=0000           efl=00000246
05Native!Myfunc:
6c761590 55              push    ebp
0:000> dv /V
001beee0 @ebp+0x08              ptr = 0xb87bc271
0:000> dd 0xb87bc271 l1
b87bc271  ????????
```

Again, we can see that the pointer points to invalid memory (as indicated by question marks). However, the set of register values is interesting. For example, if we look at the contents of the `ecx` register, we see the following:

```
0:000> dd 002d27f8
002d27f8    002dcd20 002d2678 002d2738 00000000
002d2808    00000000 00000000 00000000 00000000
002d2818    00000000 00000000 00000000 00000000
002d2828    00000000 00000000 00000000 00000000
002d2838    00000000 00000000 00000000 00000000
002d2848    00000000 00000000 00000000 00000000
002d2858    00000000 00000000 00000000 00000000
002d2868    00000000 00000000 00000000 00000000
0:000> dd 002dcd20 14
002dcd20    002dab80 002d1148 002d1178 0000001e
0:000> da 002dab80
002dab80    "First Name 1"
```

The contents of the `ecx` pointer looks strikingly similar to what we would expect the function parameter to be; yet, the function seems to be picking up an invalid pointer value from the stack. The key to remember in this scenario is that there is a calling convention that explicitly uses the `ecx` register when passing arguments to functions. The calling convention is called `ThisCall`. The `ThisCall` calling convention always places the 'this' pointer in the `ecx` register and the rest of the arguments on the stack. Is it possible that the `ThisCall` calling convention was used and was causing a mismatch with the native functions calling convention (`cdecl`)? To answer that question, we look at the managed code method signature for our P/Invoke function and see the following:

```
[DllImport("05Native.dll", CallingConvention = CallingConvention.ThisCall)]
private static extern void Myfunc(IntPtr ptr);
```

Sure enough, a mistake was made when specifying the calling convention of the `Myfunc` function causing a mismatch to occur that left the native code function looking for the argument on the stack when in reality it was passed via the `ecx` register. Quite a lot of debugging just to identify what seems like a rather trivial problem of mismatched calling conventions. Fortunately, there exists an MDA that aids in this process. The `pInvokeStackImbalance` MDA can be used to identify certain types of calling convention mismatches that result in the stack becoming imbalanced as part of the function call. To enable this MDA, please use the following configuration file (see Chapter 1, "Introduction to the Tools," for details on enabling MDA):

```
<?xml version="1.0" encoding="UTF-8" ?>
<mdaConfig>
  <assistants>
```

```
    <pInvokeStackImbalance  />
  </assistants>
</mdaConfig>
```

Please note that this MDA only catches mismatched calling convention problems that result in the stack being imbalanced. There are certain types of calling convention mismatches (such as `ThisCall` versus `Cdecl`) that do not cause this MDA to trip; because of this, manual debugging is still required.

Delegates

We have looked at how to interoperate with synchronous native code functions. What about asynchronous functions that require a function pointer that is invoked throughout the lifetime of the asynchronous operation? Can a managed code function be passed as function pointer to native code? Absolutely. The P/Invoke layer can take a managed code delegate and convert it into a function pointer, which the native function can subsequently use. Let's take a look at an example. Listing 7-5 shows a managed code application that calls the following native asynchronous method:

```
typedef void (__stdcall  *PCALLBACK) (ULONG result);

__declspec(dllexport) VOID __stdcall AsyncProcess(PCALLBACK ptr)
```

The native function is called `AsyncProcess` and takes a function pointer to a function that takes a `ULONG` as a parameter that indicates the result of the operation. The basic idea behind the `AsyncProcess` function is that it returns immediately and does its work in parallel (by spawning another thread). When completed, the worker thread calls into the specified function with the result. The managed application that uses this function is shown in Listing 7-5.

Listing 7-5 Managed application calling native asynchronous function

```
using System;
using System.Text;
using System.Runtime.InteropServices;
using System.Runtime.Remoting;
using System.Threading;

namespace Advanced.NET.Debugging.Chapter7
{
    class PInvoke
```

```
    {
        public delegate void Callback(int result);

        public static void Main()
        {
            Callback c = new Callback(MyCallback);

            AsyncProcess(c);

            // Do additional work

            Console.WriteLine("Press any key to exit");
            Console.ReadKey();

        }

        public static void MyCallback(int result)
        {
            Console.WriteLine("Result= " + result);
        }

        [DllImport("05Native.dll")]
        private static extern void AsyncProcess(Callback callBack);
    }
}
```

The source code and binary for Listing 7-5 can be found in the following folders:

- Source code: `C:\ADND\Chapter7\Callback`
- Binary: `C:\ADNDBin\07Callback.exe and 05native.dll`

The application is very straightforward: It creates a delegate instance that matches the function pointer that our native function expects and then calls the native function with the newly created delegate instance. It then prompts the user to press any key to exit before terminating. The delegate is invoked when the native function completes, specifying the result of the operation, which is output to the console. Please note that some of the code in the managed application has been intentionally left out in Listing 7-5 to better illustrate the problem.

If you run the application, you can see that it finishes relatively quickly and prompts you to press any key to exit the application. If you press any key pretty quickly after it finishes, the application simply terminates without displaying the results of the asynchronous operation. If you wait for the asynchronous operation a few more seconds, instead of seeing the result, the dreaded 07Callback.exe Has Stopped Working dialog is shown. What's causing this rather simple application to crash? Judging by the sequence of events, it looks as if the application successfully calls into the `AsyncProcess` function and then simply waits for the result to be delivered on our delegate instance. To get some more information, let's run the application under the debugger:

```
...

...

...

Press any key to exit
(2eb4.36a8) : Unknown exception - code c0000096 (first chance)
(2eb4.36a8): Unknown exception - code c0000096 (!!! second chance !!!)
eax=00000000 ebx=00000000 ecx=765ac379 edx=77629a94 esi=04b3f7a8 edi=04b3f874
eip=00bd0a22 esp=04b3f7a0 ebp=04b3f874 iopl=0         nv up ei pl zr na pe nc
cs=001b  ss=0023  ds=0023  es=0023  fs=003b  gs=0000            efl=00010246
00bd0a22 ee           out     dx,al
```

From the output, we can see that an exception was thrown with code `0xc0000096`. How do we find out what this exception corresponds to? We can use the `error` command and specify the exception code:

```
0:003> !error c0000096
Error code: (NTSTATUS) 0xc0000096 (3221225622) - {EXCEPTION}
  Privileged instruction.
```

The exception seems to indicate that we were executing a privileged instruction causing the fault to occur. Let's dump out the call stack of the offending thread to see if we can get some more insight into where this privileged execution originated:

```
0:003> !lines
Line number information will be loaded
0:003> k
ChildEBP RetAddr
WARNING: Frame IP not in any known module. Following frames may be wrong.
04b3f79c 6de4169c 0xbd0a22
04b3f874 765a4911 05Native!Helper+0x3c
  [c:\workzone\05native\05native\05native.cpp @ 92]
04b3f880 7760e4b6 KERNEL32!BaseThreadInitThunk+0xe
04b3f8c0 7760e489 ntdll!__RtlUserThreadStart+0x23
04b3f8d8 00000000 ntdll!_RtlUserThreadStart+0x1b
```

From the stack, we can see that the helper thread that our native function created executes the `Helper` function, which in turn (at line 92) makes a call to execute
code located at address `0xbd0a22`. If we look at the code for the `Helper` function,
we can see the following:

```
DWORD WINAPI Helper(LPVOID lpParam)
{
      Sleep(2000);
[92]  g_pfunc(5);
      return 1;
}
```

Line 92 corresponds to a function invocation whose address is stored in the
global variable `g_pfunc`. Furthermore, if we look at the `AsyncProcess` function
that we originally called, we can see that it stores the function pointer passed in as
an argument from our managed application in the `g_pfunc` global variable. Based
on these observations, we can conclude that the managed application called the
`AsyncProcess` method (passing in our delegate), which saved the function
pointer in a global variable, created a new thread to handle the request and then
returned immediately. The new thread subsequently performs the work and
attempts to call back on the function pointer stored in the global variable. Let's
now take a look at the code that caused the exception to be raised in the first
place:

```
0:003> u 0xbd0a22
00bd0a22 ee              out     dx,al
00bd0a23 fe              ???
00bd0a24 ee              out     dx,al
00bd0a25 fe              ???
00bd0a26 ee              out     dx,al
00bd0a27 fe              ???
00bd0a28 ee              out     dx,al
00bd0a29 fe              ???
```

As we can see, the instructions located at address `0xbd0a22` look invalid (it's
never a good thing to see `???` in the disassembly). The next big question is, why did
we end up with an invalid function address? Let's rerun the application under the
debugger but this time set a breakpoint on the `AsyncProcess` function to see if the
function pointer (i.e., delegate) we passed in looked reasonable to begin with:

```
0:000> bp 05native!AsyncProcess
0:000> g
```

```
...
...
...
Breakpoint 0 hit
eax=6de01050 ebx=00385c90 ecx=79ee2457 edx=80000000 esi=001df240 edi=001df1d8
eip=6de01d40 esp=001df194 ebp=001df228 iopl=0         nv up ei ng nz na pe nc
cs=001b  ss=0023  ds=0023  es=0023  fs=003b  gs=0000          efl=00000286
05Native!AsyncProcess:
6de01d40 55               push    ebp
0:000> dv
        ptr = 0x008d0a22
    hThread = 0xffffffff
        dwId = 0x1df150
0:000> u 0x008d0a22
008d0a22 b8080a8d00      mov     eax,8D0A08h
008d0a27 e948000000      jmp     008d0a74
008d0a2c ab              stos    dword ptr es:[edi]
008d0a2d ab              stos    dword ptr es:[edi]
008d0a2e ab              stos    dword ptr es:[edi]
008d0a2f ab              stos    dword ptr es:[edi]
008d0a30 ab              stos    dword ptr es:[edi]
008d0a31 ab              stos    dword ptr es:[edi]
```

After the breakpoint has been hit, the output of the local variables (using the dv command) shows that the function pointer is 0x008d0a22. When we disassemble that address, we see a mov instruction followed by a jmp instruction. This looks far more reasonable than our previous disassembly. These two instructions form what is known as the thunk code that the P/Invoke layer adds whenever a call is made from native to managed code. This is very much similar to the work that the P/Invoke layer has to do when going from managed to native code such as marshaling data. At this point, we have verified that at the point where AsyncProcess is invoked, the delegate passed from our managed code application to the native AsyncProcess function is indeed valid. Somehow, after the call is made, the code located at that specific function pointer changes and when the Helper function attempts to use it, a crash ensues. Let's set a breakpoint on the Helper function and once again check the state of the function pointer:

```
0:000> bp 05native!Helper
0:000> g
Breakpoint 1 hit
eax=765a48ff ebx=00000000 ecx=00000000 edx=6de011c2 esi=00000000 edi=00000000
eip=6de01660 esp=0496ff88 ebp=0496ff90 iopl=0         nv up ei pl zr na pe nc
cs=001b  ss=0023  ds=0023  es=0023  fs=003b  gs=0000          efl=00000246
05Native!Helper:
6de01660 55               push    ebp
```

```
0:003> X 05native!g_pfunc
6de07138 05Native!g_pfunc = 0x008d0a22
```

After the breakpoint hits, we use the X command to resolve the g_pfunc symbol to get the address where the function pointer is stored (0x008d0a22). Next, we disassemble the address to convince ourselves that the instructions are still correct:

```
0:003> u 0x008d0a22
008d0a22 b8080a8d00      mov     eax,8D0A08h
008d0a27 e948000000      jmp     008d0a74
008d0a2c ab              stos    dword ptr es:[edi]
008d0a2d ab              stos    dword ptr es:[edi]
008d0a2e ab              stos    dword ptr es:[edi]
008d0a2f ab              stos    dword ptr es:[edi]
008d0a30 ab              stos    dword ptr es:[edi]
008d0a31 ab              stos    dword ptr es:[edi]
```

The output is identical to our previous disassembly and we can safely conclude that the thunk instructions are still valid. The last check we want to perform is to set a breakpoint at the point where the call to the address is actually made followed by checking the thunk code one last time:

```
0:003> u 05native!Helper
05Native!Helper:
6de01660 55              push    ebp
6de01661 8bec            mov     ebp,esp
6de01663 81ecc0000000    sub     esp,0C0h
6de01669 53              push    ebx
6de0166a 56              push    esi
6de0166b 57              push    edi
6de0166c 8dbd40ffffff    lea     edi,[ebp-0C0h]
6de01672 b930000000      mov     ecx,30h
0:003> u
05Native!Helper+0x17:
6de01677 b8cccccccc      mov     eax,0CCCCCCCCh
6de0167c f3ab            rep stos dword ptr es:[edi]
6de0167e 8bf4            mov     esi,esp
6de01680 68d0070000      push    7D0h
6de01685 ff158481e06d    call    dword ptr [05Native!_imp__Sleep (6de08184)]
6de0168b 3bf4            cmp     esi,esp
6de0168d e8a4faffff      call    05Native!ILT+305(__RTC_CheckEsp) (6de01136)
6de01692 8bf4            mov     esi,esp
0:003> u
05Native!Helper+0x34:
6de01694 6a05            push    5
```

```
6de01696 ff153871e06d    call      dword ptr [05Native!g_pfunc (6de07138)]
6de0169c 3bf4             cmp       esi,esp
6de0169e e893fafffff     call      05Native!ILT+305(__RTC_CheckEsp) (6de01136)
6de016a3 b801000000       mov       eax,1
6de016a8 5f               pop       edi
6de016a9 5e               pop       esi
6de016aa 5b               pop       ebx
0:003> bp 6de01696
0:003> g
Press any key to exit
Breakpoint 1 hit
eax=00000000 ebx=00000000 ecx=765ac379 edx=77629a94 esi=0485fbd0 edi=0485fc9c
eip=6de01696 esp=0485fbcc ebp=0485fc9c iopl=0         nv up ei pl zr na pe nc
cs=001b  ss=0023  ds=0023  es=0023  fs=003b  gs=0000          efl=00000246
05Native!Helper+0x36:
6de01696 ff153871e06d    call      dword ptr [05Native!g_pfunc
 (6de07138)] ds:0023:6de07138=00ca0a22
0:003> u 0xbd0a22
00bd0a22 ee               out       dx,al
00bd0a23 fe               ???
00bd0a24 ee               out       dx,al
00bd0a25 fe               ???
00bd0a26 ee               out       dx,al
00bd0a27 fe               ???
00bd0a28 ee               out       dx,al
00bd0a29 fe               ???
```

This time, we can see that the thunk code is invalid again. We can now safely conclude that when the Helper function first executes everything looks good with the function pointer, but by the time it actually makes the call the pointer contents have changed and become invalid. How is that possible? The key to understanding what is happening is to remember that a delegate is a first class object and citizen of the managed world. As such, a delegate instance is stored on the managed heap and is subject to the same GC rules, meaning that during a garbage collection, the delegate instance may be collected (if rootless) or moved around to a different location. Earlier, we stated that some code had been omitted from Listing 7-5. More specifically, after the AsyncProcess call was made, the application released the reference on the delegate instance and invoked the GC, which in turn caused the object delegate to be cleaned up. Furthermore, the cleanup of the delegate instance occurred before the native Helper function had attempted a callback. The net result when the callback actually occurred was that it called into a piece of memory no longer representing the delegate. In this particular case, we were actually lucky because the application faulted with an exception. In other situations, we may have had invalid code that caused random writes in memory and did not fault straight away, where root cause analysis would have been far more time consuming further down the road.

What is the right solution to this problem? The answer lies in making sure that any objects used in managed to native code transitions are pinned (please see Chapter 5, "Managed Heap and Garbage Collection," for more information on pinning) *throughout the duration* of the operation. Although it's true that the P/Invoke layer automatically pins objects when a P/Invoke call is made, the objects are also automatically unpinned after that particular function call is done and transitions back to managed code. This works well for synchronous calls, but in the case of an asynchronous call, delegates may still be referenced in the native code function only to be used later (after the initial call returns).

Because the symptoms of a collected delegate being used by native code can be very elusive and take time to surface, is there a way to enable additional instrumentation so that the problem surfaces right away? Fortunately, the answer is yes and comes in the form of an MDA. The `callbackOnCollectedDelegate` MDA maintains a number of the thunks of collected delegates and anytime a callback occurs on a collected delegate the MDA checks the thunk list and reports an error. To enable the MDA, the following configuration file should be used:

```
<mdaConfig>
  <assistants>
    <callbackOnCollectedDelegate listSize="1500" />
  </assistants>
</mdaConfig>
```

The `listSize` attribute corresponds to the number of thunks you want the MDA to keep in memory. If we enable this MDA for our application and run it in the debugger, we will see the following output when the call to the collected delegate occurs:

```
Press any key to exit
ModLoad: 60340000 60348000   C:\Windows\Microsoft.NET\Framework\
v2.0.50727\culture.dll
<mda:msg xmlns:mda="http://schemas.microsoft.com/CLR/2004/10/mda">
  <!--
        A callback was made on a garbage collected delegate of type
        '07Callback!Advanced.NET.Debugging.Chapter7.PInvoke+Callback::Invoke'. This
may
        cause application
crashes, corruption and data loss. When passing delegates to
```

```
      unmanaged code,
 they must be kept alive by the managed application until it is
      guaranteed that they will never be called.
  -->
 <mda:callbackOnCollectedDelegateMsg break="true">
   <delegate
 name="07Callback!Advanced.NET.Debugging.Chapter7.PInvoke+Callback::Invoke"/>
   </mda:callbackOnCollectedDelegateMsg>
</mda:msg>
```

The output of the MDA clearly states that a call was made on a collected delegate as well as specifying the type of the delegate. It is highly recommended that this MDA be enabled when testing any application that performs interoperability with native code because bugs introduced as part of this interoperability can be very difficult to track down otherwise.

WHAT IS THE DEFAULT CALLING CONVENTION OF A DELEGATE? Delegates use the `stdcall` calling convention and care must be taken to ensure that the native callback definition matches the `stdcall` calling convention.

P/Invoke Log

There is another useful MDA called the `pInvokeLog` MDA that, when enabled, outputs detailed information on each of the P/Invoke calls made in the managed application. The configuration to enable this MDA is shown below:

```
<mdaConfig>
  <assistants>
    <pInvokeLog>
      <filter>
        <match dllName="05native.dll"/>
        <match dllName="kernel32.dll"/>
      </filter>
    </pInvokeLog>
  </assistants>
</mdaConfig>
```

The filter section allows you to specify which DLLs that you are interested in tracing P/Invoke calls to. In the preceding example, all P/Invoke calls to `05native.dll` and `kernel32.dll` will be traced in the debugger. An example trace is shown below:

```
<mda:msg xmlns:mda="http://schemas.microsoft.com/CLR/2004/10/mda">
  <mda:pInvokeLogMsg>
    <method name="07Sig!Advanced.NET.Debugging.Chapter7.PInvoke::Myfunc"/>
    <dllImport dllName="C:\ADNDBin\05Native.dll" entryPoint="Myfunc"/>
  </mda:pInvokeLogMsg>
</mda:msg>
```

Debugging Interop Leaks

In a perfect world, managed code applications would never need to interoperate with native code (at least directly). Instead, there would exist well-tested and reliable .NET wrappers for all the existing native code components out there. Unfortunately, we do not live in a perfect world and interoperability is a necessity. For the most part, if the native library is properly written, creating a managed wrapper around the library is relatively straightforward. There are cases, however, when the native library suffers from certain deficiencies. These deficiencies can range from functional code bugs to serious memory corruption problems. In this part of the chapter, we will take a look at some common pitfalls related to memory leaks when working with native libraries. Please note that this discussion is not meant to exhaustively illustrate all the tools available to debug native memory leaks, but rather show a few common tools and techniques. For more exhaustive information on how to debug native memory leaks, please see Chapter 9, "Resource Leaks," in Mario Hewardt and Daniel Pravat's *Advanced Windows Debugging*, (Boston, MA: Addison-Wesley, 2008).

The example managed code application we will use in this part of the chapter can be found in the following folders:

- Source code: `C:\ADND\Chapter7\Date`
- Binary: `C:\ADNDBin\07Date.exe` and `05native.dll`

To make the example as effective as possible, for the time being, please refrain from looking at the source.

The command-line syntax for the application is shown below:

```
07Date.exe <number of iterations>
```

Table 7-2 Memory Usage Based on Iterations

Iterations	Memory (Private Working Set)	Commit
1000	2,240K	8,784K
10,000	4,576K	11,124K
100,000	26,388K	32,948K
1,000,000	245,020K	251,588K

The number of iterations corresponds to the number of P/Invoke calls the managed application performs before simply printing out the current date in the console. You can think of this application as a contrived and simulated P/Invoke stress test. Before we run the application, please start task manager (CTRL-SHIFT-ESC) and make sure that the Memory (Private Working Set) and Commit Size columns are shown. (These can be enabled by choosing View, Select Columns.) Next, let's run the application specifying a different number of iterations each time, as shown in Table 7-2. The memory usage is recorded at the end of each application run after a garbage collection was invoked.

As we can see from Table 7-2, the memory usage goes up with each increase in iterations. With the last run (1 million iterations), the committed memory was an astonishing 250MB. Now that we suspect something unusual happening with our application's memory, how do we go about debugging it? In Chapter 5, we already looked at how to do some simple analysis using the eeheap command. Let's run the application under the debugger (specifying 1 million iterations), break execution once the Press any key to exit prompt is displayed, and run the eeheap -gc command:

```
0:004> !eeheap -gc
Number of GC Heaps: 1
generation 0 starts at 0x01d56510
generation 1 starts at 0x01d5100c
generation 2 starts at 0x01d51000
ephemeral segment allocation context: none
 segment    begin allocated   size
002e7828 790d8620  790f7d8c 0x0001f76c(128876)
01d50000 01d51000  01d5851c 0x0000751c(29980)
Large object heap starts at 0x02d51000
 segment    begin allocated    size
02d50000 02d51000  02d53240 0x00002240(8768)
Total Size   0x28ec8(167624)
------------------------------
GC Heap Size    0x28ec8(167624)
```

The last line of the output tells us that the size of the managed heap is 167624 bytes. That's a far cry from the 250MB that the application seems to be consuming. Because it doesn't appear that the excessive memory usage is based on the managed heap, let's use the address command to get a summary view of the memory usage in the process:

```
0:004> !address -summary
ProcessParametrs 002916e8 in range 00290000 002fc000
Environment 00290808 in range 00290000 002fc000


-------------------- Usage SUMMARY ------------------------
    TotSize (       KB)    Pct(Tots) Pct(Busy)    Usage
    3f36000 (    64728) : 03.09%     17.31%     : RegionUsageIsVAD
   692c8000 ( 1723168) : 82.17%     00.00%     : RegionUsageFree
    2a7e000 (    43512) : 02.07%     11.64%     : RegionUsageImage
    4fe000 (     5112) : 00.24%     01.37%     : RegionUsageStack
      5000 (       20) : 00.00%     00.01%     : RegionUsageTeb
   fe70000 (   260544): 12.42%     69.68%     : RegionUsageHeap
         0 (        0) : 00.00%     00.00%     : RegionUsagePageHeap
      1000 (        4) : 00.00%     00.00%     : RegionUsagePeb
         0 (        0) : 00.00%     00.00%     :
RegionUsageProcessParametrs
         0 (        0) : 00.00%     00.00%     :
RegionUsageEnvironmentBlock
     Tot: 7fff0000 (2097088 KB) Busy: 16d28000 (373920 KB)


-------------------- Type SUMMARY ------------------------
    TotSize (       KB)    Pct(Tots)    Usage
   692c8000 ( 1723168) : 82.17%     : <free>
    2a7e000 (    43512) : 02.07%     : MEM_IMAGE
    1e12000 (    30792) : 01.47%     : MEM_MAPPED
   12498000 (   299616) : 14.29%     : MEM_PRIVATE


-------------------- State SUMMARY ------------------------
    TotSize (       KB)    Pct(Tots)    Usage
   13ec7000 (   326428) : 15.57%     : MEM_COMMIT
   692c8000 ( 1723168) : 82.17%     : MEM_FREE
    2e61000 (    47492) : 02.26%     : MEM_RESERVE

Largest free region: Base 146e0000 - Size 41f50000 (1080640 KB)
```

In the Usage Summary section of the output, we see an interesting line corresponding to RegionUsageHeap where the size is 260,544KB. This line indicates that the native Windows heap size is right around 260MB, which closely matches the memory consumption that was reported by Task Manager.

At this point, we have identified that the managed heap is very small in comparison to the overall memory usage and that most of the memory is located on the native Windows heap. The big question, though, is why all this memory was allocated on the native heap to begin with. As you might have suspected, it has to do with the P/Invoke calls that are being made from our managed application. Let's take a look at the source code of the application shown in Listing 7-6.

Listing 7-6 Sample managed application using P/Invoke

```
using System;
using System.Text;
using System.Runtime.InteropServices;
using System.Runtime.Remoting;
using System.Threading;

namespace Advanced.NET.Debugging.Chapter7
{
    class PDate
    {
        public static void Main(string[] args)
        {
            if (args.Length != 1)
            {
                Console.WriteLine("Please specify number of iterations");
                return;
            }

            int it = Int32.Parse(args[0]);

            StringBuilder date=new StringBuilder(100);
            for (int i = 0; i < it; i++)
            {
                GetDate(date);
            }

            GC.Collect();
            Console.WriteLine("Press any key to exit");
            Console.Read();
        }

        [DllImport("05Native.dll", CharSet = CharSet.Unicode)]
        private static extern void GetDate(StringBuilder date);
    }
}
```

As can be seen in Listing 7-6, the application sits in a tight loop invoking the native function `GetDate` through P/Invoke. The `GetDate` function expects a string that, upon success, will contain the current system date. After completing the P/Invoke iterations, it forces a garbage collection and prompts before exiting. Next, let's take a look at the native code function:

```
__declspec(dllexport) VOID __stdcall GetDate(WCHAR* pszDate)
{
    SYSTEMTIME time;

    WCHAR* pszTmpDate=new WCHAR[100];

    GetSystemTime(&time);

    wsprintf(pszTmpDate,
        L"%d-%d-%d",
        time.wMonth,
        time.wDay,
        time.wYear);
    wcscpy(pszDate, pszTmpDate);
}
```

It should be pretty trivial to spot the problem. Basically, the function uses a temporary buffer to store the current system date before copying the contents of that buffer to the string pointer passed in as a parameter. Unfortunately, the developer forgot to free the memory associated with the temporary buffer and, hence, a memory leak ensues.

As we've seen with this relatively straightforward and leaking application, care must be taken when analyzing out of memory or high memory utilization. It is not always sufficient to simply analyze the managed heap to arrive at explanations behind the excessive memory usage. There are times when the managed heap looks perfectly reasonable and requires us to venture outside of the managed heap to see if there are any detectable patterns with the overall memory consumption of the process.

Can't We Use Native Leak Detection Tools?

There are some pretty fancy native code memory leak detection tools (such as UMDH and LeakDiag) that not only tell you about potential leaks but also the complete callstack of the allocating thread. Unfortunately, those tools do not work well with managed code because the tool is unable to get a nice managed code callstack. For example, the callstack shown in UMDH might look like this:

```
002cefc0 003fa2ac 05Native!GetDate+0x67
002cf080 79e7c74b 0x3fa2ac
```

```
002cf090  79e7c6cc  mscorwks!CallDescrWorker+0x33
002cf110  79e7c8e1  mscorwks!CallDescrWorkerWithHandler+0xa3
002cf254  79e7c783  mscorwks!MethodDesc::CallDescr+0x19c
002cf270  79e7c90d  mscorwks!MethodDesc::CallTargetWorker+0x1f
002cf284  79eefb9e  mscorwks!MethodDescCallSite::Call+0x18
002cf3e8  79eef830  mscorwks!ClassLoader::RunMain+0x263
002cf650  79ef01da  mscorwks!Assembly::ExecuteMainMethod+0xa6
002cfb20  79fb9793  scorwks!SystemDomain::ExecuteMainMethod+0x43f
002cfb70  79fb96df  mscorwks!ExecuteEXE+0x59
002cfbb8  70d1573d  mscorwks!_CorExeMain+0x15c
002cfbc4  70d6ae72  mscoreei!_CorExeMain+0x25
002cfbd0  70d65121  mscoree!GetMetaDataInternalInterface+0x2d5
002cfbe4  7760e4b6  mscoree!CorExeMain+0x8
002cfc24  7760e489  ntdll!__RtlUserThreadStart+0x23
002cfc3c  00000000  ntdll!_RtlUserThreadStart+0x1b
```

This is not tremendously useful because we don't know which part of the managed code ended up calling the native function; but it is somewhat useful because it clearly tells us that a managed code thread called a native function via P/Invoke. We could then look at those particular calls and see if we can spot anything wrong.

Debugging COM Interop Finalization

In Chapter 5, we took a look at the common problem of misbehaving finalizers. Objects with associated Finalize methods must be carefully coded to ensure that the Finalize method always returns to avoid an accumulation of objects on the finalize queue that will eventually lead to an out of memory situation. In this part of the chapter, we will take a look at an example that utilizes Finalize methods and COM interop and see if there are any peculiarities that could arise. Listing 7-7 illustrates the sample application we will use in our discussion.

Listing 7-7   Sample COM interop example with finalizable objects

```
using System;
using System.Text;
using System.Runtime.InteropServices;
using System.Runtime.Remoting;
using System.Threading;
using System.Management;
using COMInterop;
```

```
namespace Advanced.NET.Debugging.Chapter7
{
    class Wmi
    {
        private ManagementClass obj;
        private byte[] data;

        public Wmi(byte[] data)
        {
            this.data = data;
        }

        public void ProcessData()
        {
            obj = new ManagementClass("Win32_Environment");
            obj.Get();

            //
            // Use data member reference
            //
        }

        ~Wmi()
        {
            //
            // Clean up any native resources
            //
        }
    }

    class Worker
    {
        public Worker()
        {
            Init();
        }

        public void ProcessData(byte[] data)
        {
            Process(data);
        }
```

(continues)

Listing 7-7 Sample COM interop example with finalizable objects *(continued)*

```csharp
    ~Worker()
    {
        UnInit();
    }

    [DllImport("05Native.dll")]
    static extern void Init();

    [DllImport("05Native.dll")]
    static extern void UnInit();

    [DllImport("05Native.dll")]
    static extern void Process(byte[] data);
}


class Data
{
    BasicMathClass data;

    public Data(BasicMathClass data)
    {
        this.data = data;
    }

    ~Data()
    {
        int result;
        data.Add(1, 2, out result);
    }
}

class Fin
{
    private static BasicMathClass s;
    private static Worker worker;

    static void Main(string[] args)
    {
        if (args.Length != 1)
        {
            Console.WriteLine("07Fin.exe <num iterations");
            return;
        }
```

```csharp
            Thread newThread =
                    new Thread(new ThreadStart(Helper));
            newThread.SetApartmentState(ApartmentState.STA);
            newThread.IsBackground=true;
            newThread.Start();

            Thread.Sleep(2000);
            Data d = new Data(s);

            d = null;
            GC.Collect();
            GC.Collect();

            Initialize();

            for (int i = 0; i < Int32.Parse(args[0]); i++)
            {
                byte[] b = new byte[10000];
                Wmi w = new Wmi(b);
                w.ProcessData();
            }

            GC.Collect();

            Console.WriteLine("Press any key to exit");
            Console.ReadKey();
        }

        private static void Initialize()
        {
            byte[] b = new byte[100];

            worker = new Worker();
            worker.ProcessData(b);

            worker = null;
            GC.Collect();
        }

        static void Helper()
        {
            s = new BasicMathClass();
            Thread.Sleep(60000*5);
        }


    }
}
```

The source code and binary for Listing 7-7 can be found in the following folders:

- Source code: `C:\ADND\Chapter7\Fin`
- Binary: `C:\ADNDBin\07Fin.exe`

In a nutshell, the application does the following:

1. Creates a new thread that instantiates our basic Math COM object and goes to sleep.
2. Creates an instance of the Data type and promptly releases the reference to the instance.
3. Forces a garbage collection (GC).
4. Creates a number of Wmi instances where the number of instances can be specified on the command line.
5. Forces a GC.
6. Waits for user to press any key to exit.

Based on the preceding execution sequence, there seems to be nothing out of the ordinary with the application code (short of some poor design decisions). Let's run the application and monitor the memory consumption using Task Manager. Table 7-3 shows the memory consumption with different number of iterations specified on the command line (`07Fin.exe <num iterations>`).

Table 7-3 shows a steady increase in memory consumption even after the application forced garbage collections before exiting. Simply by looking at the increased memory utilization, it is fairly safe to assume that if we were to specify a large enough iteration number the application would fault with an `OutOfMemoryException`. To determine the cause of the increase in memory, we again turn to our memory diagnostics strategy of running the application under the debugger and looking at the managed heap statistics. In the debug output that follows, the number of iterations specified was `1000`.

Table 7-3 Memory Consumption of 07Fin.exe with Different Number of Iterations

Iterations	Memory (Private Working Set)	Commit
100	6,172K	15,832K
1,000	27,044K	36,060K
10,000	224,228K	238,216K

7. Interoperability

```
...
...
...
Press any key to exit
(430c.477c): Break instruction exception - code 80000003 (first chance)
eax=7ffd8000 ebx=00000000 ecx=00000000 edx=7765d094 esi=00000000 edi=00000000
eip=77617dfe esp=0651fdcc ebp=0651fdf8 iopl=0         nv up ei pl zr na pe nc
cs=001b  ss=0023  ds=0023  es=0023  fs=003b  gs=0000         efl=00000246
ntdll!DbgBreakPoint:
77617dfe cc              int     3
0:007> !eeheap -gc
Number of GC Heaps: 1
generation 0 starts at 0x028f540c
generation 1 starts at 0x028237b4
generation 2 starts at 0x01eb1000
ephemeral segment allocation context: none
 segment     begin allocated     size
004b6368 7a733370   7a754b98 0x00021828(137256)
00477790 790d8620   790f7d8c 0x0001f76c(128876)
01eb0000 01eb1000   028f7418 0x00a46418(10773528)
Large object heap starts at 0x02eb1000
 segment     begin allocated     size
02eb0000 02eb1000   02eb4240 0x00003240(12864)
Total Size  0xa8a5ec(11052524)
------------------------------
GC Heap Size  0xa8a5ec(11052524)
```

We let the application run until the `Press any key to exit` prompt is displayed, at which point we break into the debugger and use the `eeheap -gc` command to take a look at the overall statistics of the managed heap. The reported size is approximately 11MB. On the other hand, Task Manager is reporting a committed size of 36MB. Because the managed heap is only a portion of the overall memory consumption, perhaps there are unmanaged resources at play:

```
0:007> !address -summary
 ProcessParametrs 004216e8 in range 00420000 00520000
 Environment 00420808 in range 00420000 00520000

---------- Usage SUMMARY -------------------------------------
   TotSize (      KB)  Pct(Tots) Pct(Busy)  Usage
   44c7000 (   70428) : 03.36%    45.47%    : RegionUsageIsVAD
  768b2000 ( 1942216) : 92.61%    00.00%    : RegionUsageFree
   379f000 (   56956) : 02.72%    36.78%    : RegionUsageImage
    7ff000 (    8188) : 00.39%    05.29%    : RegionUsageStack
      8000 (      32) : 00.00%    00.02%    : RegionUsageTeb
```

```
    12d0000 (   19264) : 00.92%    12.44%    : RegionUsageHeap
          0 (       0) : 00.00%    00.00%    : RegionUsagePageHeap
       1000 (       4) : 00.00%    00.00%    : RegionUsagePeb
          0 (       0) : 00.00%    00.00%    :
RegionUsageProcessParametrs
          0 (       0) : 00.00%    00.00%    :
RegionUsageEnvironmentBlock
        Tot: 7fff0000 (2097088 KB) Busy: 0973e000 (154872 KB)

---------- Type SUMMARY ------------------------------------
    TotSize (       KB)   Pct(Tots)   Usage
    768b2000 ( 1942216) : 92.61%   : <free>
    379f000 (   56956) : 02.72%   : MEM_IMAGE
    2314000 (   35920) : 01.71%   : MEM_MAPPED
    3c8b000 (   61996) : 02.96%   : MEM_PRIVATE

---------- State SUMMARY -----------------------------------
    TotSize (       KB)   Pct(Tots)   Usage
    6a6f000 (  108988) : 05.20%   : MEM_COMMIT
    768b2000 ( 1942216) : 92.61%   : MEM_FREE
    2ccf000 (   45884) : 02.19%   : MEM_RESERVE

Largest free region: Base 06520000 - Size 51940000 (1336576 KB)
```

From the output of the `address` command, we can see that there is approximately 19MB of Windows heap usage. Although some of that may be accounted for by internal CLR data structures, most of it can reasonably be assumed to be due to our managed code using (in our case indirectly via the `System.Management` namespace) native resources. What's interesting though is that even if we were using native resources, indirectly, they should have been cleaned up when we did a forced GC at the end of the application. The key to remember is that .NET types that wrap native resources very commonly utilize Finalize methods to clean up the native resources. Is it possible that all the object instances have not yet been finalized by the finalizer thread? Let's take a look by using the `FinalizeQueue` command, which shows statistics on objects that are still pending Finalize execution:

```
0:007> !FinalizeQueue
SyncBlocks to be cleaned up: 5000
MTA Interfaces to be released: 0
STA Interfaces to be released: 0
------------------------------------
generation 0 has 3 finalizable objects (05bd1260->05bd126c)
generation 1 has 3 finalizable objects (05bd1254->05bd1260)
generation 2 has 5 finalizable objects (05bd1240->05bd1254)
```

```
Ready for finalization 3000 objects (05bd126c->05bd414c)
Statistics:
      MT    Count   TotalSize Class Name
000d3868       1          12 Advanced.NET.Debugging.Chapter7.Worker
79112728       1          20 Microsoft.Win32.SafeHandles.SafeWaitHandle
791037c0       1          20 Microsoft.Win32.SafeHandles.SafeFileMappingHandle
79103764       1          20 Microsoft.Win32.SafeHandles.SafeViewOfFileHandle
79101444       1          20 Microsoft.Win32.SafeHandles.SafeFileHandle
7911c9c8       2          40 Microsoft.Win32.SafeHandles.SafePEFileHandle
79108ba4       1          44 System.Threading.ReaderWriterLock
7910a5c4       1          60 System.Runtime.Remoting.Contexts.Context
790fe704       2         112 System.Threading.Thread
6758707c    1000       12000 System.Management.IWbemClassObjectFreeThreaded
000d376c    1000       16000 Advanced.NET.Debugging.Chapter7.Wmi
67583650    1000       64000 System.Management.ManagementClass
Total 3011 objects
```

In the output, we can see that we still have 3000 objects on the finalization queue that are waiting to be cleaned up. What is preventing these objects from being cleaned up? After all, a forced GC should guarantee that the finalizer thread in the process wakes up and starts invoking the Finalize methods on each object in a serialized fashion. Let's take a look at the finalizer thread to make sure it is in a valid state:

```
0:007> !threads
ThreadCount: 3
UnstartedThread: 0
BackgroundThread: 2
PendingThread: 0
DeadThread: 0
Hosted Runtime: no
                                    PreEmptive   GC Alloc         Lock
      ID OSID ThreadOBJ    State    GC      Context        Domain
   Count APT Exception
   0    1 42f8 004669a0     a020 Enabled   028f5f98 : 028f740c 00431288     0 MTA
   2    2 3bd8 00468868     b220 Enabled   00000000:00000000 00431288
      0 MTA (Finalizer)
   3    3 2904 00497248  2007220 Enabled   00000000:00000000 00431288     0 STA
0:007> ~2s
eax=feeefeee ebx=ffffffff ecx=0000032f edx=7fffffff esi=00000000 edi=00000000
eip=77629a94 esp=0404ee18 ebp=0404ee88 iopl=0         nv up ei pl zr na pe nc
cs=001b  ss=0023  ds=0023  es=0023  fs=003b  gs=0000            efl=00000246
ntdll!KiFastSystemCallRet:
77629a94 c3              ret
0:002> k
ChildEBP RetAddr
```

```
0404ee14 77629254 ntdll!KiFastSystemCallRet
0404ee18 765ac244 ntdll!ZwWaitForSingleObject+0xc
0404ee88 765ac1b2 KERNEL32!WaitForSingleObjectEx+0xbe
0404ee9c 774a1f07 KERNEL32!WaitForSingleObject+0x12
0404eec0 775a7f3e ole32!GetToSTA+0xad
0404eeec 775a89d4 ole32!CRpcChannelBuffer::SwitchAptAndDispatchCall+0x132
0404efcc 774be6f5 ole32!CRpcChannelBuffer::SendReceive2+0xef
0404f044 774a0f4f ole32!CAptRpcChnl::SendReceive+0xaf
0404f098 7625364e ole32!CCtxComChnl::SendReceive+0x95
0404f0b0 762536af RPCRT4!NdrProxySendReceive+0x43
0404f0bc 762533e2 RPCRT4!NdrpProxySendReceive+0xc
0404f534 762535f4 RPCRT4!NdrClientCall2+0x5e9
0404f558 761ee20e RPCRT4!ObjectStublessClient+0x6f
0404f568 774a2ed7 RPCRT4!ObjectStubless+0xf
0404f5f0 774f2833 ole32!CObjectContext::InternalContextCallback+0x128
0404f640 7a0bf7db ole32!CObjectContext::ContextCallback+0x87
0404f68c 7a0c04b2 mscorwks!CtxEntry::EnterContextOle32BugAware+0x2b
0404f7ac 7a0bfa13 mscorwks!CtxEntry::EnterContext+0x322
0404f7c0 7a0bfe6f mscorwks!IUnkEntry::MarshalIUnknownToStreamCallback+0x34
0404f808 79ff0959 mscorwks!IUnkEntry::UnmarshalIUnknownForCurrContext+0x45
0404f814 79f831ce mscorwks!IUnkEntry::GetIUnknownForCurrContext+0x31
0404f840 79f823cc mscorwks!RCW::SafeQueryInterfaceRemoteAware+0x16
0404f884 79f82353 mscorwks!RCW::GetComIPForMethodTableFromCache+0x6b
0404f894 79f8243f mscorwks!RCW::GetComIPFromRCW+0x25
0404f8d4 79f82519 mscorwks!ComObject::GetComIPFromRCW+0x40
0404f93c 79f836ce mscorwks!ComObject::GetComIPFromRCWEx+0x66
0404f988 000ca3ee mscorwks!ComObject::StaticGetComIPFromRCWEx+0x50
WARNING: Frame IP not in any known module. Following frames may be wrong.
0404f9f8 79fbcca7 0xca3ee
0404fa18 79fbcca7 mscorwks!MethodTable::SetObjCreateDelegate+0xc5
0404fa7c 79fbcc15 mscorwks!MethodTable::SetObjCreateDelegate+0xc5
0404fa9c 79fbcbb7 mscorwks!MethodTable::CallFinalizer+0x76
0404fab0 79f6acb6 mscorwks!SVR::CallFinalizer+0xb2
0404fb00 79f6abf7 mscorwks!WKS::GCHeap::TraceGCSegments+0x170
0404fb88 79fb99d6 mscorwks!WKS::GCHeap::TraceGCSegments+0x2b6
0404fba0 79ef3207 mscorwks!WKS::GCHeap::FinalizerThreadWorker+0xe7
0404fbb4 79ef31a3 mscorwks!Thread::DoADCallBack+0x32a
0404fc48 79ef30c3 mscorwks!Thread::ShouldChangeAbortToUnload+0xe3
0404fc84 79fb9643 mscorwks!Thread::ShouldChangeAbortToUnload+0x30a
0404fcac 79fb960d mscorwks!ManagedThreadBase_NoADTransition+0x32
0404fcbc 79fba09b mscorwks!ManagedThreadBase::FinalizerBase+0xd
0404fcf4 79f95a2e mscorwks!WKS::GCHeap::FinalizerThreadStart+0xbb
0404fd90 765a4911 mscorwks!Thread::intermediateThreadProc+0x49
0404fd9c 7760e4b6 KERNEL32!BaseThreadInitThunk+0xe
0404fddc 7760e489 ntdll!__RtlUserThreadStart+0x23
0404fdf4 00000000 ntdll!_RtlUserThreadStart+0x1b
```

By using the `threads` command, we can quickly identify which thread in the process corresponds to the finalizer thread (debugger thread id 2). After we know the thread, we can switch to that thread context and dump out the callstack. From the callstack, we can identify that we are in fact looking at a finalizer thread by looking for a frame that contains `FinalizerThreadWorker`. It seems that our particular finalizer thread is in a waiting state (as can be identified by the top frames). There is nothing unusual for a finalizer thread to be in a waiting state per se as it's quite common for it to wait until something is placed on the finalizer queue. The key difference between a properly waiting finalizer thread and ours is that we have a frame with `ole32!GetToSTA`. This implies that the finalizer thread is making a call to an STA COM object and is simply getting stuck. Let's take a look at the source code in Listing 7-7 and see if we can spot any objects that have finalizers that call into a COM object. The `Data` type seems to have a finalizer that calls into the `BasicMathClass` COM object. We can verify that this is the object that is being finalized by simply looking at the managed call stack for the finalizer thread:

```
0:002> !ClrStack
OS Thread Id: 0x3bd8 (2)
ESP        EIP
0404f8f8 77629a94 [GCFrame: 0404f8f8]
0404f9d8 77629a94 [ComPlusMethodFrameStandaloneCleanup: 0404f9d8]
COMInterop.BasicMathClass.Add(Int32, Int32, Int32 ByRef)
0404f9f0 007602e5 Advanced.NET.Debugging.Chapter7.Data.Finalize()
```

Before we continue with the debug session, it is important to understand how the `BasicMathClass` COM object was instantiated. The `Main` method started an STA helper thread, which in turn created the COM object. After it was created, the helper thread simply went to sleep for an extended period of time. Seems like a fairly trivial instantiation. The key, however, lies not in how the COM object itself was created, but how the thread that instantiated the COM object was created. As mentioned earlier, the thread was created in the STA, which means that all calls into the COM object will be serialized by COM. The way that this serialization works, under the covers, is by creating a hidden window and placing messages on the windows message queue that correspond to the method invocations. The STA thread picks up the windows messages in a serialized fashion and executes the COM methods. In order for the STA thread to get the windows messages, it must ensure to process the messages in the message queue. If the thread fails to do so, no messages will be dispatched. The picture should now be clear: The STA thread that created the COM object also promptly went to sleep preventing the processing of messages on the message queue, thereby also preventing any calls on the COM object from being honored. As a matter of fact, any call made on the COM object will simply hang until messages are processed as we can see with the finalizer thread. Furthermore, because a finalizer thread picks up objects to finalize in a serialized fashion, any objects that are still left on the finalize queue will never be collected, causing an increase in memory (and eventually an out of memory exception).

As we've seen, a seemingly innocuous Finalize method that called a simple COM object caused some serious reliability issue in our application. Even though the COM interop layer tries to make life as easy as possible when working with legacy COM code, extreme care must be taken to ensure that the way the interaction works doesn't cause problems in the application.

Early Release of COM Objects

As mentioned before, the lifetime of a COM object is managed by the RCW. If an early release of a COM object is required, you can use the `Marshal.ReleaseComObject` method. To avoid issues such as memory corruptions, care must taken to ensure that the COM object is not in use. The `raceOnRCWCleanup` MDA can be used to catch these problems. The enable the MDA, use the following configuration file:

```
<mdaConfig>
  <assistants>
    <raceOnRCWCleanup/>
  </assistants>
</mdaConfig>
```

Summary

In this chapter, we discussed how the CLR enables managed code to interoperate with native code in a simple and clean fashion. Two main interoperability layers were discussed: P/Invoke and COM interop. Even though the CLR makes it relatively easy to interoperate with native code (in the simplest case, an attribute annotation), great care must be taken to fully understand the nature of the interoperability. We showed how improperly written interoperability can result in serious reliability issues. More specifically, we took a look at examples of improperly written managed applications such as invalid custom marshaling, asynchronous interoperability, interoperability leaks, and COM interoperability and finalization. We showed how to use the debuggers and associated tools to quickly arrive at the root cause as well as a set of MDAs that have been explicitly created to help troubleshoot these difficult problems.

ADVANCED TOPICS

## CHAPTER 8

POSTMORTEM DEBUGGING

Throughout the book, we have looked at quite a few powerful tools available to developers when troubleshooting problematic code. The ultimate goal is to ensure that these tools become integrated into the development process in order to guarantee high quality. These tools are excellent automated ways to find bugs, but they don't, however, make any absolute guarantees that the application will be bug free when it ships.

Inevitably, problems will surface in the application after it has been shipped and will turn up at the most inopportune moments—mainly while the customer uses it. Depending on the severity of the bug, it either can have devastating effects on the customer or merely be a nuisance. In either case, you can expect a phone call from an upset customer asking why the application is not working properly. To remedy the situation and troubleshoot the problem, one option is to ask the customer for remote access to the computer in question. Although it may be feasible at times, customers typically frown upon this, and the answer in many cases is no. The reasons for not granting remote access to a machine vary but typically can be due to the following:

- Customer environment or policy does not allow inbound connections.
- Remote debugging requires that a debugger be attached to one or more processes and implies downtime. If the process is running on a critical server, customers will be reluctant to accept downtime.
- Debugging a process via user mode or kernel mode means that developers have full access to the state of the machine including memory contents. For some customers, this may constitute a privacy issue.

If the customer refuses live access to the machine exhibiting the problem and reproducing the problem locally is not possible, can the problem even be debugged? The answer is yes, and the process of doing so is called postmortem debugging. At a high level, postmortem debugging involves the following steps:

1. Trigger the failure to occur.
2. Take a snapshot of the system state at the point of failure (or even before and after depending of the type of failure).
3. Send the snapshot to engineers for further analysis.

In this chapter, we will take a look at the different ways in which snapshots (also known as dump files) can be generated, the different types of dumps available, and how to analyze them. We will also cover a very powerful dump file aggregation service known as Windows Error Reporting.

Let's start by looking at some of the fundamental dump file topics.

Dump File Fundamentals

As we have mentioned, a dump file is an out of band representation of the state of a given process. The main purpose behind generating a dump file is to analyze application failures without requiring live debugging access to the computer exhibiting the failures. After a dump file has been generated, it can be sent to the appropriate engineer who can then analyze the failure without access to the faulting machine. The engineer simply loads the dump file on his own computer and analyzes the failure using the postmortem capabilities of the debuggers. What information does a dump file contain? Well, that depends entirely on how the dump file was generated. There are two categories of dump files:

- Full dumps
- Mini dumps

A full dump file contains the entire memory space of a process, the executable image, the handle table, and other information used by the debugger. There is no way of customizing the amount of data collected when using the full dump file. However, a full dump file can be converted to a mini dump file using the debuggers.

The contents of mini dump files are variable and can be customized by the dump file generator depending on which generator is used. The information contained within a mini dump file ranges from information on a particular thread to an exhaustive description of the process being dumped. As strange as it may seem, the biggest mini dump file will actually contain more debug information than a full dump file. To that extent, this chapter will focus on the mini dump file construct.

There are a number of tools available that will generate dump files as shown in Table 8-1.

In this section, we will cover how to generate dump files using the Windows Debuggers and ADPlus. Windows Error Reporting will be discussed later in the chapter.

To better illustrate the dump file generation process, we will use a simple application that allocates memory on the heap, writes to that memory, and then faults. Listing 8-1 shows the code for the sample application.

Table 8-1   Tools That Generate Dump Files

Name	Description
Windows Debuggers	The Windows debuggers can generate dumps of different sizes and enable full control of the dump file generation process.
ADPlus	ADPlus is a tool that is part of Debugging Tools for Windows. It acts as a process monitor that is capable of generating dump files whenever a crash or hang occurs. Additionally, it has a notification mechanism that can notify the user of a crash.
Windows Error Reporting	Windows Error Reporting is a service Microsoft provides that allows customers to register with a live error reporting site. Any time a crash occurs in one of the applications owned by a particular customer, an error report is sent from the crashing machine to the Windows Error Reporting Web site. The crash information (including dump file) can be retrieved from the WER service analyzed by the customer postmortem.

Listing 8-1   Simple example of a crashing application

```
using System;
using System.Text;
using System.Runtime.InteropServices;

namespace Advanced.NET.Debugging.Chapter8
{
    class SimpleExc
    {
        static void Main(string[] args)
        {
            SimpleExc s = new SimpleExc();
            s.Run();
        }

        public void Run()
        {
            Console.WriteLine("Press any key to start");
            Console.ReadKey();
```

(continues)

Listing 8-1 Simple example of a crashing application *(continued)*

```
        ProcessData(null);
    }

    public void ProcessData(string data)
    {
        if (data == null)
        {
            throw new ArgumentException("Argument NULL");
        }
        string s = "Hello: " + data;
    }

    }
}
```

The source code and binary for Listing 8-1 can be found in the following folders:

- Source code: `C:\ADND\Chapter8\SimpleExc`
- Binary: `C:\ADNDBin\08SimpleExc.exe`

The source of the failing application should be pretty evident. The call to `ProcessData` results in an `ArgumentException` being thrown due to passing in null. We will start by illustrating how to use the debuggers to generate a dump file.

Generating Dump Files Using the Debuggers

As noted earlier, the application we will be using is illustrated in Listing 8-1. Run the application under the debugger and continue execution until the exception occurs.

```
...
...
...
ModLoad: 77bb0000 77bb6000    C:\Windows\system32\NSI.dll
ModLoad: 79060000 790b6000    C:\Windows\Microsoft.NET\Framework\v2.0.50727
\mscorjit.dll
(1860.958): CLR exception - code e0434f4d (first chance)
(1860.958): CLR exception - code e0434f4d (!!! second chance !!!)
eax=0020eaec ebx=e0434f4d ecx=00000001 edx=00000000 esi=0020eb74 edi=00416bd0
eip=767142eb esp=0020eaec ebp=0020eb3c iopl=0         nv up ei pl nz na po nc
cs=001b  ss=0023  ds=0023  es=0023  fs=003b  gs=0000            efl=00000202
KERNEL32!RaiseException+0x58:
```

```
767142eb c9                  leave
0:000> .loadby sos mscorwks
0:000> !ClrStack
OS Thread Id: 0x958 (0)
ESP       EIP
0020ebc4 767142eb [HelperMethodFrame: 0020ebc4]
0020ec68 00e10177 Advanced.NET.Debugging.Chapter8.SimpleExc.ProcessData
(System.String)
0020ec80 00e1010c Advanced.NET.Debugging.Chapter8.SimpleExc.Run()
0020ec88 00e100a7 Advanced.NET.Debugging.Chapter8.SimpleExc.Main
(System.String[])
0020eeac 79e7c74b [GCFrame: 0020eeac]
```

At this point, we would like to generate a dump file for further postmortem analysis. The single biggest question with generating dump files is how much information to include. As a general rule of thumb, the more state that is stored in the dump file, the more information you will have at your disposal when doing postmortem debugging. The biggest limiting factor is, of course, the size of the dump file. You may find yourself in environments where getting a huge dump file from a highly secure server is not feasible and you may need to work with a stripped-down version.

The means by which a dump file is generated is using the .dump command. The .dump /m option indicates to the debugger that it should generate a mini dump file. Additionally, the .dump /m command can take a number of other options as detailed in Table 8-2.

In addition to the various options that control the contents of the dump file, the name of the dump file must also be specified. When a dump file is generated and a full path is not specified, it will, by default, be generated in the directory from where the debugger was launched. The following example illustrates how to generate a dump file with full memory information using a full path.

```
.dump /mf c:\08dumpfile.dmp
```

Let's run the .dump command on our crashing application:

```
0:000> .dump /mf 08dumpfile.dmp
Creating dumpfile.dmp - mini user dump
Dump successfully written
```

After the debugger is done generating the dump file, you should have a file approximately 64MB in size. To use the dump file, it should be loaded in a new debugger instance using the -z switch. For example, to load the dump file we just generated, the following command should be used:

```
c:\>ntsd –z 08dumpfile.dmp
```

8. POSTMORTEM DEBUGGING

Table 8-2 Options for the .dump Command

Option	Description
a	Generates a complete mini dump with all the options enabled. It includes complete memory data, handle information data, module information, basic memory information, and thread information. Equivalent to using /mfFhut.
f	Generates a mini dump that contains all accessible and committed pages of the owning process.
F	Generates a mini dump that includes all the necessary basic memory information for the debugger to reconstruct the entire virtual memory address space.
h	Generates a mini dump that contains handle information.
u	Generates a mini dump that includes information on unloaded modules. Note that this is only available on Windows Server 2003.
t	Generates a mini dump that includes information on thread times. Thread time information includes created time as well as user and kernel mode times.
i	Generates a mini dump that includes secondary memory information. Secondary memory is any memory (plus a small region surrounding it) that is referenced by a stack pointer or the backing store.
p	Generates a mini dump that includes the process and thread environment blocks.
w	Generates a mini dump that includes all committed read-write private pages.
d	Generates a mini dump that includes all the image data segments.
c	Generates a mini dump that includes all image code segments.
r	Generates a mini dump that is suited for scenarios where privacy is of concern. This option erases (replaces with zeroes) any information not needed in order to recreate the stack (including local variables).
R	Generates a mini dump that is suited to scenarios where privacy is of concern. This option removes the full module paths from the mini dump thereby ensuring the privacy of the user's directory structure.

After the debugger has loaded the dump file, you will see the following debug output:

```
...
...
...
Loading Dump File [c:\08dumpfile.dmp]
User Mini Dump File with Full Memory: Only application data is available
Executable search path is:
Windows Server 2008 Version 6001 (Service Pack 1) MP (2 procs) Free x86 compatible
Product: WinNt, suite: SingleUserTS
Debug session time: Mon Mar  2 06:25:10.000 2009 (GMT-8)
System Uptime: 5 days 7:44:57.406
Process Uptime: 0 days 0:02:39.000
.........................
*** ERROR: Symbol file could not be found.  Defaulted to export symbols for
ntdll.dll -
This dump file has an exception of interest stored in it.
The stored exception information can be accessed via .ecxr.
(1860.958): CLR exception - code e0434f4d (first/second chance not available)
eax=0020eaec ebx=e0434f4d ecx=00000001 edx=00000000 esi=0020eb74 edi=00416bd0
eip=767142eb esp=0020eaec ebp=0020eb3c iopl=0         nv up ei pl nz na po nc
cs=001b  ss=0023  ds=0023  es=0023  fs=003b  gs=0000         efl=00000202
kernel32!RaiseException+0x58:
767142eb c9              leave
```

Near the top of the debug output, you will notice that the debugger gives some basic information about the dump file being loaded. Information includes the location of the dump file, the type of dump file, as well as what information is available. The next interesting piece of information is toward the end of the debugger output where the reason behind the fault is displayed (CLR exception). Armed with this dump file, you can now debug this failure on any machine that you want without physical access to the faulting machine. We will discuss in detail how the postmortem analysis works later in this chapter.

One of the difficulties when generating a dump file explicitly using the debugger is that a debugger has to be attached to the faulty process at the right time. Although that may not seem like a big hurdle, think about scenarios where the crash only reproduces every once in a while and the opportunity to attach the debugger is missed. It would be nice to be able to tell Windows to use the debuggers to generate a dump file any time a process crashes. Fortunately, this mechanism exists and is commonly referred to as the postmortem debugger setup. By default, Windows uses Dr. Watson (deprecated in Windows Vista and later in favor of a new technology) as the postmortem debugger. Dr. Watson generates a dump file any time a process

Table 8-3 Postmortem Debugger Setup

Command Line	Aedebug\Debugger Registry Value	Description
`WinDbg -I`	`winDbg.exe -p %ld -e %ld -g`	Changes the postmortem debugger to be WinDbg. Note that the `-I` must be capitalized.
`cdb -iae`	`cdb.exe -p %ld -e %ld -g`	Changes the postmortem debugger to be cdb.
`ntsd -iae`	`ntsd.exe -p %ld -e %ld -g`	Changes the postmortem debugger to be ntsd.
`drwtsn32 -i`	`drwtsn32 -p %ld -e %ld -g`	Changes the postmortem debugger to be Dr. Watson.

crashes and gives the user the option to send the dump file to Microsoft for further analysis. The postmortem debugger to use can be changed by using the command lines shown in Table 8-3.

Dump File Generation

An important change that occurred in Windows Vista is how the error reporting technology saves dump files locally on the machine. Prior to Windows Vista, Dr. Watson stored generated dump files on the local machine by default. These dump files could be accessed by anyone wanting to debug a particular dump file. In Windows Vista, Dr. Watson has been retired in favor of a more reliable and robust error reporting mechanism. As part of this change, dump files generated on a machine are not stored on the local machine (by default). To change the default behavior, the `ForceQueue` registry setting can be set to 1, which forces all dump files to queued locally prior to being uploaded to Microsoft. The `ForceQueue` registry value is located in the following registry path:

```
HKEY_LOCAL_MACHINE\SOFTWARE\Microsoft\Windows\Windows Error
Reporting
```

After the `ForceQueue` registry value is set to 1, all dump files generated will be stored in the following location:

Processes running in system context or elevated:

```
%ALLUSERSPROFILE %\Microsoft\Windows\WER\[ReportQueue|
ReportArchive]
```

All other processes:

```
%LOCALAPPDATA%\Microsoft\Windows\WER\ [ReportQueue|
ReportArchive]
```

Behind the scenes, when the command lines in Table 8-3 are executed, what happens? The answer is quite simple. They change a few registry values that Windows looks at when it detects a process crash. The registry path used for the postmortem debugger setup is shown below.

```
HKEY_LOCAL_MACHINE\Software\Microsoft\Windows NT\CurrentVersion\AeDebug
```

The `AeDebug` key works perfectly when debugging native code applications; however, with managed code, two other registry values are used to control postmortem managed code debugging. The values are called `DbgManagedDebugger` and `DbgJITDebugLaunchSetting` and are located under the following key:

```
HKEY_LOCAL_MACHINE\SOFTWARE\Microsoft\.NETFramework
```

DbgManagedDebugger

If postmortem debugging has been enabled via the `DbgJITDebugLaunchSettings`, the `DbgManagedDebugger` registry value dictates which debugger should be launched when an unhandled exception is encountered. For example, to set the `ntsd` debugger to be the default debugger when an unhandled exception is encountered in a managed application, set the `DbgManagedDebugger` registry value to

```
c:\program files\debugging tools for windows (x86)\ntsd.exe -p %ld
```

When an unhandled exception is encountered, the debugger specified in the `DbgManagedDebugger` registry value does not necessarily get invoked right away, rather a message box may be displayed that allows you the option of debugging or terminating the application.

One very common question surrounding postmortem debugging is how a dump can automatically be generated in response to faulty applications. The key to enabling this is to set the `DbgManagedDebugger` registry value to the following:

```
ntsd -pv -p %ld -c ".dump /u /ma <path to dump file>; .kill; qd
```

The preceding registry value setting simply says that when a fault occurs, launch the ntsd debugger and issue the dump command to create a dump file followed by quitting by detaching the debug session.

The exact behavior of an unhandled exception can be controlled via the DbgJITDebugLaunchSettings registry value, which is discussed next.

DbgJITDebugLaunchSettings

The DbgJITDebugLaunchSettings registry value dictates the behavior when an unhandled exception is encountered. If this value is set to 0, a message box will be displayed that allows the user to choose what to do about the failure. Please note that the message box will only be displayed for interactive processes and other processes (such as services) will simply terminate. An example of the message box is shown in Figure 8-1.

The postmortem message box simply notifies the user that a problem has occurred in the 08SimpleExc.exe application and gives the user the option of either debugging the failure (Debug button) or terminating the application (Close Program button). If the Debug button is pressed, the DbgManagedDebugger registry value is consulted and the corresponding debugger specified is launched.

If the DbgJITDebugLaunchSettings is set to 1, the faulting application is simply terminated and a stack dump is returned.

If the value is set to 2, the debugger specified in DbgManagedDebugger is launched immediately without displaying a message box.

Finally, if the value is set to 16, the message box discussed earlier is displayed for interactive processes; and for noninteractive processes, the debugger specified in DbgManagedDebugger is launched.

Although the debuggers typically provide more than enough power and flexibility when generating dump files, there is one additional tool that can be used. The tool is called ADPlus.

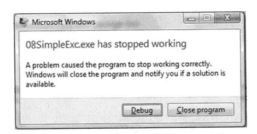

Figure 8-1   Example of a managed code postmortem message box

Generating Dump Files Using ADPlus

ADPlus is a tool that monitors and automates the generation of dump files for one or more faulty processes and has the capability to notify a user or computer when crashes occur. ADPlus is a command-line driven script and Microsoft strongly recommends running ADPlus under the `cscript.exe` interpreter. As a matter of fact, if the default script interpreter is set to something other than `cscript.exe`, a dialog appears asking if you want to change the interpreter to `cscript.exe`. In addition to the command-line options, ADPlus can also work on the basis of configuration files. The configuration files allows for more granular control of the operational flow of ADPlus.

ADPlus can run in one of the following two modes:

- Hang mode is used to troubleshoot processes that exhibit hanging symptoms (such as not making any progress or 100% CPU utilization). ADPlus must be started after the process or processes to monitor have hung.
- Crash mode is used to troubleshoot processes that exhibit crashing behavior. ADPlus must be started before the process crashes.

Let's use crash mode as an example of how to use ADPlus to generate a dump file for `08SimpleExc.exe`. Start by running the `08SimpleExc.exe` application:

```
C:\ADNDBin\08SimpleExc.exe
```

Before pressing any key to resume execution, run the following command line:

```
C:\>adplus.vbs -crash -pn 08SimpleExc.exe -y
 SRV*c:\Symbols*http://msdl.microsoft.com/download/symbols
```

The `-crash` switch puts ADPlus into crash mode, the `-pn` switch tells ADPlus the name of the process to monitor, and the `-y` sets the symbol path to be used throughout the ADPlus execution. The beauty of using the `-pn` switch is that it can monitor any number of instances of any given process name by name.

When execution has finished, ADPlus puts the resulting log files under a directory of the Windows debuggers installation path. The name of the directory takes on the following structure:

```
<runtype>_Mode__Date_<date of run>__Time_<time of run>
```

For example, when ADPlus finished executing, the following directory was created:

```
c:\Program Files\Debugging Tools for Windows (x86)\Crash_Mode__Date_03-02-
2009__Time_08-31-43AM
```

Note that the default path can be changed by using the -o switch.

In the preceding directory, there are several files, but the most important ones are the *.dmp files, which contain all the dump information from the run. As you can see, there are several dump files collected. Why do we have more than one dump file per crash? Well, ADPlus automates the process of collecting dump files and as such generates dump files when certain preset conditions occur during execution. The name of the dump file gives you the necessary clues to figure out the reason the dump file was generated. For example, in our previous run, ADPlus generated the following dump files:

```
PID-4448__08SIMPLEEXC.EXE__1st_chance_Process_Shut_
Down__full_1e20_2009-03-02_08-32-17-440_1160.dmp
```

```
PID-4448__08SIMPLEEXC.EXE__2nd_chance_NET_CLR__full_
1e20_2009-03-02_08-32-08-384_1160.dmp
```

ADPlus generated a full dump file when the first chance process shutdown event occurred, followed by a full dump file when the .NET exception occurred (second chance). Do we need all of these dumps for our particular run? No. In our particular case, the most interesting dump file is the second chance .NET exception. However, there are situations where periodic generation of dump files can be very useful, as it can yield a historical perspective of the systematic deterioration of a process. ADPlus even offers a powerful way for the user to configure how often information should be collected and under what conditions, essentially providing a scripting front end for the debuggers. You can learn more about the scripting capabilities of ADPlus in the debugger documentation. It is important to note that ADPlus does not do anything "magical" via its scripting engine. It simply takes a user-friendly way of specifying debugger directives and translates them into pure and automated debugger commands. You can see how the user-friendly configuration actually translates to the debugger commands by looking at the directory called CDBScripts located in the same directory as the dump files. In our example, the CDBScripts directory contains a file called PID-4448__08SimpleExc.exe.cfg, which contains all the debugger commands used in that ADPlus session.

The last important point about ADPlus is how we can control what type of dump file gets generated when a fault occurs. There are four command-line switches that control this behavior:

- -FullOnFirst. This switch causes ADPlus to generate a full dump file when a first chance exception occurs.
- -MiniOnSecond. This switch causes ADPlus to generate a mini dump file when a second chance exception occurs.
- -NoDumpOnFirst. This switch tells ADPlus not to generate a mini dump file when a first chance exception occurs. This can come in handy as applications sometimes generate first chance exceptions that are gracefully handled.
- -NoDumpOnSecond. This switch tells ADPlus not to generate a mini dump file when a second chance exception occurs.

ADPlus is a convenient, powerful, and flexible tool for monitoring and gathering data from faulty processes. In this section, we covered the basics of the tool, and it is well worth your time to investigate the other powerful features such as the scripting capabilities and defining custom exception handlers that allow you to generate dump files when custom exceptions occur.

Now that we have shown two of the most common ways of generating dump files, it is time to make use of the dump files and see what the troubleshooting process looks like.

Debugging Dump Files

Now that you have been presented with one or more dump files and tasked with the investigation of finding the root cause of the faulty process, what can actually be done using these dump files? Can you dump memory, look at handles, or step through code? Remember that a dump file is simply a static snapshot of the state of a process. As such, setting break points and stepping through code is not possible. Using dump files can be best viewed as manual debugging. By manual, we mean that simply by looking at the state of an application, you will need to manually construct theories about what code has executed to get the application into that state. It should be evident that constructing code execution by state analysis is a much harder proposition than engaging in a live debug session. Nevertheless, plenty of the debugger commands that massage application state into a more digestible form still work when using dump files, and in most cases, with enough patience, the root cause can be found.

Before we take a closer look at the dump files generated in the previous section, there are two critical pieces of information that need to be brought up: symbol files and the data access layer. Because dump files contain no symbolic information, it is critical that symbol files be available when analyzing a dump file. We've already seen the most common symbol commands in action throughout this book. The next critical piece of information is the CLR data access layer (DAC), which is heavily used by the SOS debugger extension to provide you with all the data needed during a debug session.

The Data Access Layer

Contrary to the world of native debugging where a lot can be gleaned from looking at raw memory, in the managed code world, SOS relies heavily on the CLR to provide the debug output and results that we have come to expect. For SOS to properly interpret (or "translate") the raw data that is passed to it, SOS actually makes calls into the CLR (i.e., executing CLR code) to help with this process. The component in the CLR responsible for this functionality is the Data Access Layer (DAC) and is implemented in mscordacwks.dll. Now, because the CLR is continuously undergoing enhancements, the underlying DAC also changes with each version (including hotfixes). You can easily verify this by looking in the installation folder for each of the .NET versions installed on your machine. For example, on my machine, I can see that the mscordacwks.dll is located in the following folder:

```
c:\Windows\Microsoft.NET\Framework\v2.0.50727
```

On a machine running Visual Studio 2010 CTP, however, the file is located in the following folders, indicating that a new version of mscordacwks.dll has been shipped with CLR 4.0:

```
c:\Windows\Microsoft.NET\Framework\v2.0.50727
```

```
c:\Windows\Microsoft.NET\Framework\v4.0.11001
```

Because the debugger requires this component during its operation, being able to tell the debugger where the file is located is crucial. During live debugging, you typically do not have to worry about it because SOS is smart enough and locates the file from the same location where the version of the runtime currently being debugged is located. During postmortem (or dump file) debugging on the other hand, the version of the CLR used in the application may be different than what is available on the machine from where you load and debug the dump file.

Again, it is important to reiterate that the SOS debugger extension calls into the `mscordacwks.dll`, which actually executes CLR code, and thus it is critically important that the debugger use the correct version. Because having the correct version is the key to success, Microsoft publishes most all of the `mscordacwks.dll` that it has shipped on the Microsoft public symbol server. As long as you point the debuggers symbol path to the public symbol server (using `symfix` or related commands), the debugger will be able to find the file. There are scenarios, however, where you still may have to explicitly tell the SOS extension where to find the file. These scenarios include cases where the file isn't available on the public symbol server (rare) or the file wasn't installed to the same location as on the machine where the dump file was generated. To aid in these scenarios, the `cordll` command can be used. The `cordll` command controls the way in which `mscordacwks.dll` is loaded and can be a lifesaver when dealing with potential mismatches. Table 8-4 details the switches available to the `cordll` command.

Table 8-4 Cordll Switches

Switch	Description
-l	Loads debugging modules by probing for the DLL in the default load paths.
-u	Unloads the debugging modules from memory.
-e	Enables CLR debugging.
-d	Disables CLR debugging.
-D	Disables CLR debugging and unloads the debugging modules.
-N	Reloads the debugging modules.
-lp	Specifies the directory path of the debugging modules.
-se	Enables using the short name version of the debugging module, `mscordacwks.dll`.
-sd	Disables using the short name of the debugging module, `mscordacwks.dll`. If this switch is specified, the debugger expects the debugging module to be in the following format: `mscordacwks_<spec>.dll` where `<spec>` is `<architecture>_<architecture>_<file version>`. `<Architecture>` can be either x86 or amd64.
-ve	Enables verbose mode. Verbose mode is very useful when dealing with mismatches because it gives clues as to how the debugger is attempting to load the debug modules.
-vd	Disables verbose mode.

How do you know if you have to worry about using the `cordll` command? Typically, if there is a mismatch of `mscordacwks.dll`, the SOS debugger extension outputs the following error (or variation of the error) when it's unable to execute a command:

```
Failed to load data access DLL, 0x80004005
Verify that 1) you have a recent build of the debugger (6.2.14 or newer)
2) the file mscordacwks.dll that matches your version of mscorwks.dll is
in the version directory
3) or, if you are debugging a dump file, verify that the file
mscordacwks___.dll is on your symbol path.
4) you are debugging on the same architecture as the dump file.
For example, an IA64 dump file must be debugged on an IA64
machine.

You can also run the debugger command .cordll to control the debugger's
load of mscordacwks.dll. .cordll -ve -u -l will do a verbose reload.
If that succeeds, the SOS command should work on retry.

If you are debugging a minidump, you need to make sure that your
executable path is pointing to mscorwks.dll as well.
```

Let's take a look at each of the suggestions that the SOS debugger extension outputs. The first suggestion is pretty straightforward and asks that you make sure that you are running a recent version of the debuggers (6.2.14 or later). The second suggestion is also straightforward and simply asks that you check to make sure you have the version of `mscordacwks.dll` that corresponds to the version of `mscorwks.dll` that is loaded. As previously discussed, the `mscordacwks.dll` should be located in the same folder as the `mscorwks.dll`. The third suggestion gets a little more interesting and asks that if debugging a dump file to make sure that the `mscordacwks___.dll` is in your symbol path. What is the `mscordacwks___.dll`? If you refer back to Table 8-4, you will notice that the `-sd` switch enables the long name for the `mscordacwks.dll`. The long name simply appends the architecture and build number for the DLL to the DLL name. You can then update the symbol path to point to the DLL in question and issue the `cordll` command to reload `mscordacwks.dll`. For example, if the version of `mscordacwks.dll` that was used to generate the dump file is 1.1.1.0 and the architecture is x86, you could rename the `mscordacwks.dll` to `mscordacwks_x86_x86_1.1.1.0.dll`, point the debuggers symbol path to the location of the renamed DLL, and reload the debugging modules using the `cordll` command:

```
0:008> .sympath+ <path to renamed module>
0:008> .cordll -ve -u -l
```

The fourth suggestion asks to ensure that the architecture that you are debugging on is the same as the architecture that the dump file was generated on. Because the debugger actually runs code in the DAC to do its work, it is important that the bitness of the debugger being used to debug the dump file has the exact same bitness that debugger used when creating the dump file. For example, if a 64-bit debugger was used to generate a dump file for a 32-bit process running on a 64-bit system under WOW64, you would not be able to debug that dump file. Instead of using the 64-bit debugger, make sure to use the correct bitness (32-bit) of the debugger to enable the dump file to be debugged.

Finally, the last line in the output asks that if debugging a dump file the executable path is pointing to `mscorwks.dll` as well. The executable path can be controlled in the debugger using the `exepath` command (or `exepath+` command when appending executable paths). For example, if debugging a dump file where `mscorwks.dll` was located in `c:\windows\microsoft.net\framework\v2.0.50727`, you could use the following command to make sure that the executable path is set correctly followed by a reload to ensure it gets picked up by the debugger:

```
0:008> .exepath+ c:\windows\microsoft.net\framework\v2.0.50727
Executable image search path is: c:\windows\microsoft.net\framework\v2.0.50727
0:008> .reload
```

All of the strategies discussed so far assume that the `mscordacwks.dll` is available in one location or another (public symbol server or on the local machine). If you simply cannot find the correct version of the DLL that was being used when the dump file was generated, your best bet is to ask the person who generated the dump if he can send you the corresponding `mscordacwks.dll`. After you've received the file, you can then use the previous strategies to get it loaded.

Ensuring that the correct version of `mscordacwks.dll` has been loaded can be a bit tricky at times and requires a bit of trial and error to get used to. However, when loaded, the SOS debugger extension will be fully functional and debugging can resume.

Dump File Analysis: Unhandled .NET Exception

In the prior section, we generated a dump file of a faulting application and we are now tasked with finding the root cause using only the dump file.

To use a dump file, we have to tell the debugger that we want to analyze a dump file by using the -z switch.

```
C:> ntsd -z C:\08dumpfile.dmp
```

After the debugger has started, the first piece of important information is the CLR exception output.

```
This dump file has an exception of interest stored in it.
The stored exception information can be accessed via .ecxr.
(2dc4.2a08): CLR exception - code e0434f4d (first/second chance not available)
eax=0024ef20 ebx=e0434f4d ecx=00000001 edx=00000000 esi=0024efa8 edi=002c43e8
eip=767142eb esp=0024ef20 ebp=0024ef70 iopl=0         nv up ei pl nz ac po nc
cs=001b  ss=0023  ds=0023  es=0023  fs=003b  gs=0000            efl=00000212
kernel32!RaiseException+0x58:
767142eb c9              leave
```

This tells us immediately that the dump file we are investigating was generated due to a CLR exception. The next logical step is to take a look at the exception details.

```
0:000> kb
ChildEBP RetAddr  Args to Child
0024ef70 79f071ac e0434f4d 00000001 00000001 kernel32!RaiseException+0x58
0024efd0 79f0a629 01b66c20 00000000 00000000
 mscorwks!RaiseTheExceptionInternalOnly+0x2a8
0024f094 01630197 01b658d0 0024f0e0 0024f0fc mscorwks!JIT_Throw+0xfc
WARNING: Frame IP not in any known module. Following frames may be wrong.
00000000 00000000 00000000 00000000 00000000 0x1630197
0:000> !pe 01b66c20
Exception object: 01b66c20
Exception type: System.ArgumentException
Message: Argument NULL
InnerException: <none>
StackTrace (generated):
    SP       IP        Function
    0024F09C 01630197
08SimpleExc!Advanced.NET.Debugging.Chapter8.SimpleExc.ProcessData
(System.String)+0x57
    0024F0B4 01630124
08SimpleExc!Advanced.NET.Debugging.Chapter8.SimpleExc.Run()+0x34
    0024F0C8 016300A7 08SimpleExc!Advanced.NET.Debugging.Chapter8.SimpleExc.Main
(System.String[])+0x37

StackTraceString: <none>
HResult: 80070057
```

Judging from the exception, we can see that our application faulted due to an argument exception where the argument specified in a method call was incorrectly

NULL. The stack trace provided with the exception gives us enough information to do a simple code review to clearly pinpoint the problem. Although this was an extremely trivial example of a dump file, it serves to illustrate that debugging managed code problems postmortem using dump files is fully achievable and all the extremely useful commands in both the SOS and SOSEX debugger extensions are available.

Windows Error Reporting

Anyone who has been using Windows has come across the message box shown in Figure 8-2 at least once.

Figure 8-2 illustrates the signature UI of a technology known as Windows Error Reporting. When presented with this message box, the user has the option to send an error report to Microsoft. If the user chooses to send the error report, it is uploaded over a secure channel (HTTPS) to a Microsoft database where it is categorized (or bucketed) and stored for later analysis. It should come as no surprise that the information that is sent up as part of the error report includes a dump file that helps the developers looking at the problem find the root cause. The applications that can partake in Windows Error Reporting are not limited to Microsoft products. Any

Figure 8-2   Dr. Watson message box

crashing process in Windows will be part of the same scheme. However, to get access to error reports that correspond to your applications, you must first enroll in the Windows Error Reporting Service. In this section, we will take a look at how Windows Error Reporting works, what is sent up as part of the error report, how to enroll in the Windows Error Reporting database, and how to query the service to get the error reports.

Windows Error Reporting Architecture

Windows Error Reporting (WER) is a failure data aggregation service that allows Microsoft and independent software vendors (ISVs) to easily access failure data related to their applications. Figure 8-3 shows the high-level operational flow of the WER service.

There are two primary entities involved in Figure 8-3:

- Computers running applications that exhibit problems and uploads error reports to WER.
- ISV that monitors for failures related to their applications, reported to WER.

Let's say that a given machine somewhere in the world is running an application (illustrated as Process X in Figure 8-3) produced by company ADND. Furthermore, let's say that the application crashes and that the user experiencing the crash is presented with the Dr. Watson UI and asked if he wants to send the error report to Microsoft. The user chooses to do so and the error report is sent using a secure (HTTPS) channel to the WER service. The WER service in turn organizes the error information received into categories (knows as buckets) and stores the error information. To make use of the error reports, a user from company ADND queries the WER service for crashes related to its application and gets the error information reported. If ADND chooses, it can now fix the problem and provide a response so that the next time a user encounters the same crash, Dr. Watson presents the response. The response can come in the form of a fix or other helpful information.

As you can see, the WER service is an incredibly powerful mechanism that provides secure aggregation of error reporting information that ISVs can query to actively gauge the health of their applications. Additionally, ISVs can provide responses to known problems and integrate the responses into the WER feedback loop making it very easy for customers to apply responses when available.

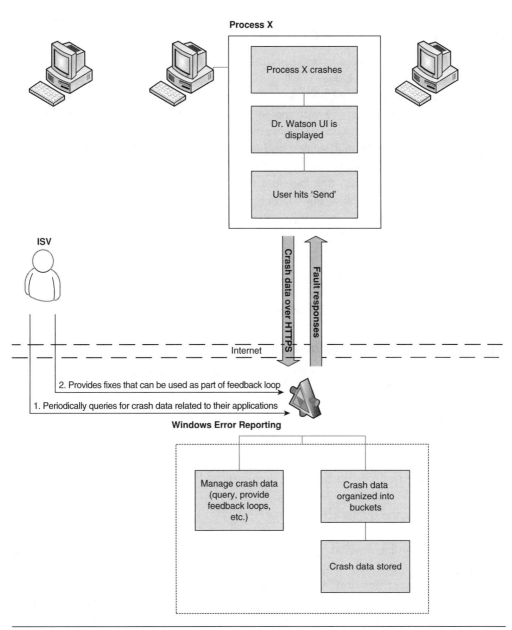

Figure 8-3 High-level overview of WER functionality

The Importance of Sending Error Information

When the Dr. Watson UI rears its head and tells you about an application crash, you may ask yourself: Why bother sending it? Is something ever going to be done about it? The truth of the matter is that Microsoft takes error reporting very seriously. After all, that is why this incredible service was implemented to begin with. Error reporting data is actively monitored and fanned out across the company to the appropriate product groups. When a fix has been identified and ready to be released (typically via Microsoft Update), users can easily apply the fix. In other words, you, the user, have a direct impact on the visibility of bugs and therefore should always make sure to upload the error reports so that Microsoft or other ISVs have the opportunity to analyze the problem and provide a fix.

Throughout the remainder of the discussion of WER, we will be using the 08SimpleExc.exe application used in the previous part of the chapter to practically illustrate the process of using WER.

The first step in using WER is to enroll, which is described next.

Enrolling in Windows Error Reporting

To participate (i.e., query for reports) in WER, an enrollment process must be completed. The enrollment process is broken down into two steps:

- Creating a user account
- Creating a company account

To start the enrollment process, navigate to the following URL:

- https://winqual.microsoft.com/SignUp/

After the page has loaded, you are presented with the account creation page as shown in Figure 8-4.

To create a user account, you must first have a company account. If you have already created a company account, you can either search for that account or locate it using the drop-down list. Clicking the Next button takes you to the account creation page. Because we have not yet created a company account, click the expand button next to Create a Company Account to start the company account creation process as shown in Figure 8-5.

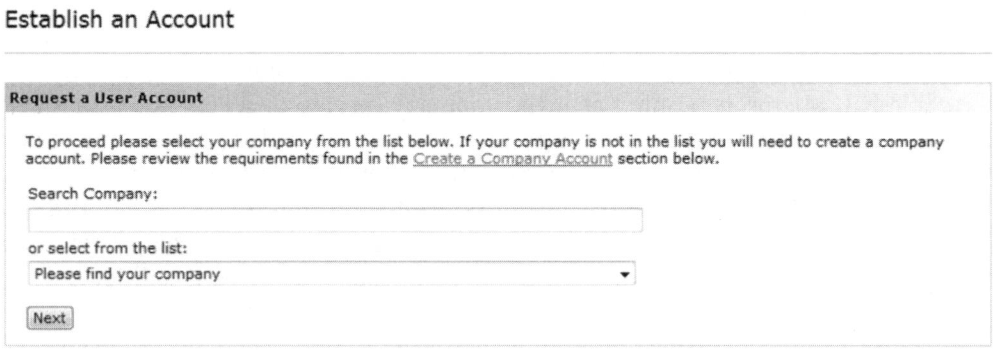

Establish an Account

To proceed please select your company from the list below. If your company is not in the list you will need to create a company account. Please review the requirements found in the Create a Company Account section below.

Search Company:

or select from the list:

Please find your company

Next

Figure 8-4   First page of WER signup process

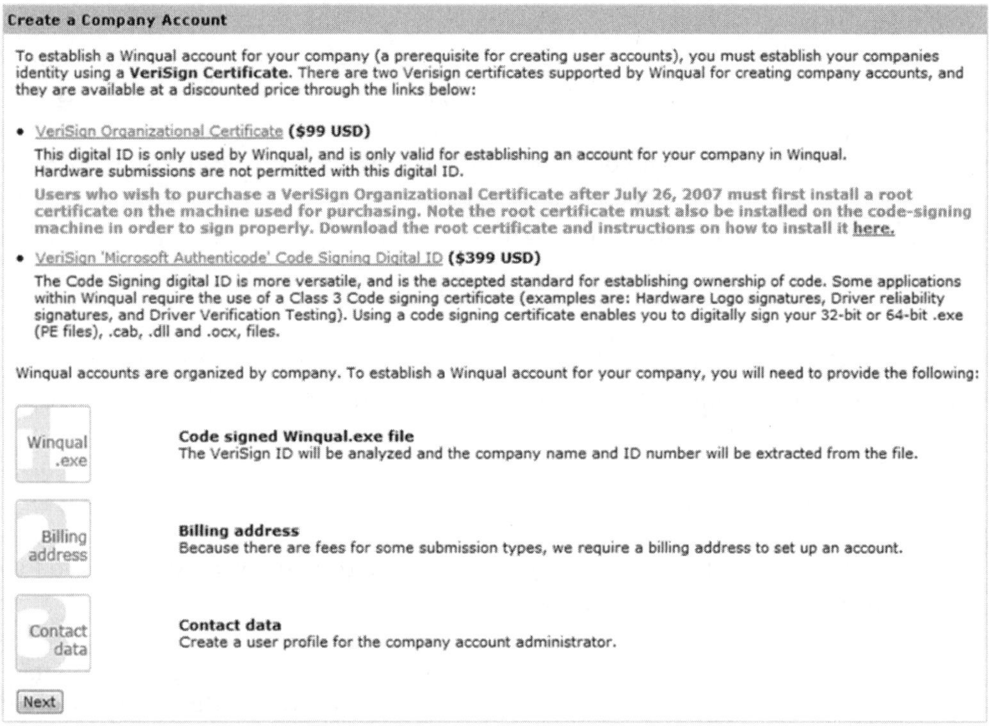

Create a Company Account

To establish a Winqual account for your company (a prerequisite for creating user accounts), you must establish your companies identity using a **VeriSign Certificate**. There are two Verisign certificates supported by Winqual for creating company accounts, and they are available at a discounted price through the links below:

- VeriSign Organizational Certificate **($99 USD)**
  This digital ID is only used by Winqual, and is only valid for establishing an account for your company in Winqual. Hardware submissions are not permitted with this digital ID.

  Users who wish to purchase a VeriSign Organizational Certificate after July 26, 2007 must first install a root certificate on the machine used for purchasing. Note the root certificate must also be installed on the code-signing machine in order to sign properly. Download the root certificate and instructions on how to install it **here.**

- VeriSign 'Microsoft Authenticode' Code Signing Digital ID **($399 USD)**
  The Code Signing digital ID is more versatile, and is the accepted standard for establishing ownership of code. Some applications within Winqual require the use of a Class 3 Code signing certificate (examples are: Hardware Logo signatures, Driver reliability signatures, and Driver Verification Testing). Using a code signing certificate enables you to digitally sign your 32-bit or 64-bit .exe (PE files), .cab, .dll and .ocx, files.

Winqual accounts are organized by company. To establish a Winqual account for your company, you will need to provide the following:

Winqual .exe

Code signed Winqual.exe file
The VeriSign ID will be analyzed and the company name and ID number will be extracted from the file.

Billing address

Billing address
Because there are fees for some submission types, we require a billing address to set up an account.

Contact data

Contact data
Create a user profile for the company account administrator.

Next

Figure 8-5   Creating a company account

There are three steps involved with creating a company account:

1. Generate a code signed `Winqual.exe` file. For a company to participate in WER, Microsoft requires that the company be able to securely and uniquely identify itself. This is accomplished by using a Class 3 digital code signing certificate or an organizational certificate available to purchase from VeriSign www.verisign.com/code-signing/content-signing-certificates/winqual-partners/index.html). After the signing certificate has been received, you need to sign the `Winqual.exe` file with the certificate and upload it to Microsoft for verification.

2. Provide billing information. Although Microsoft does not charge companies for the majority of WER functionality, a few features of WER do cost money; as such, Microsoft requires that you enter your billing information.

3. The last part of the process is to provide contact data by creating a user account that you use to access your company account.

Let's start with step 1 (signing the `Winqual.exe` file). As mentioned, for security reasons, Microsoft requires that all WER company accounts be identified by using a Class 3 digital code signing certificate or an organizational certificate. The rest of the sections on WER assume that you have acquired a signing certificate from VeriSign. The first step is to download the binary we need to sign from Microsoft. Use the following URL to start the download of `Winqual.exe`:

https://winqual.microsoft.com/signup/winqual.exe

Save this file to your hard drive in `C:\Sign`. Next, we need to get the code signing tools that are required to sign binaries. The URL used to download the code signing tools is

https://winqual.microsoft.com/signup/signcode.zip

Save this file and extract the signcode.zip to `C:\Sign`. You should now have two files as a result of extracting the zip file:

- `Readme.rtf`. This file contains instructions on how to code sign a binary using the code signing tools. It also contains a password that must be used when extracting the `signcode.exe` file (password protected) also located in the zip file.
- `Signcode.exe`. This is the application that we will use to code sign the `Winqual.exe` file.

Extract the `signcode.exe` file (remember to enter the password found in the readme file when extracting) to the same location as the `winqual.exe` file (`C:\Sign`). Also, make sure to copy the code signing certificate file (`.spc` extension) and the private key (`.pvk` extension) to the same location. Use the following command line to sign the `winqual.exe` file:

```
C:\Sign>signcode.exe /spc myCert.spc /v myKey.pvk -t
 http://timestamp.verisign.com/scripts/timstamp.dll winqual.exe
Succeeded
```

You need to replace the `mycert.spc` and `mykey.pvk` with the names of your certificate and private key files. During the signing process, you are asked to enter a private key password. Enter the password provided to you by VeriSign during the certificate purchase process. If the signing succeeds, a Succeeded message is shown. If an error occurs, make sure you have typed the name of the certificate and private key files properly and that they are located in the same directory as the `signcode.exe` binary.

The next step in the enrollment process is to take the newly signed `winqual.exe` file and upload it to Microsoft for verification purposes. Continuing from the page illustrated in Figure 8-5, click the Next button. The next page enables you to upload your signed `Winqual.exe` file, shown in Figure 8-6.

Simply enter the path to the signed `winqual.exe` binary and click Next to upload the file. The next page in the process is the Billing information page, shown in Figure 8-7.

As mentioned earlier, most of the WER features are free of charge, but there are some that Microsoft charges for. The billing information is used if a customer utilizes the WER services that cost money.

Please enter the billing information for your company (**bold** fields are required), and click the Next button, which takes you to the account (profile) creation page, shown in Figure 8-8.

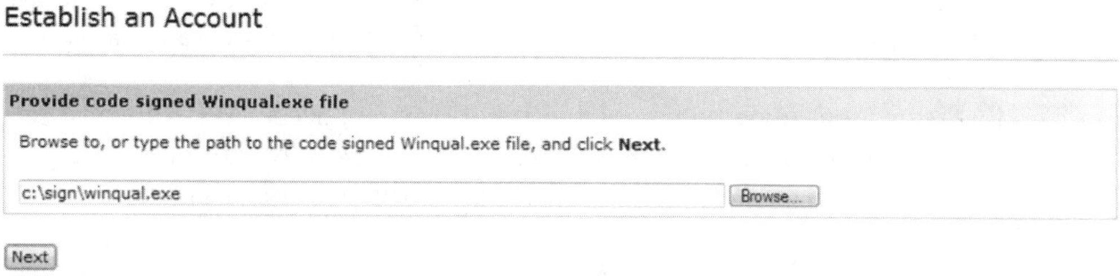

Establish an Account

Provide code signed Winqual.exe file
Browse to, or type the path to the code signed Winqual.exe file, and click **Next**.

c:\sign\winqual.exe	Browse...

`Next`

Figure 8-6   Uploading the signed Winqual.exe binary

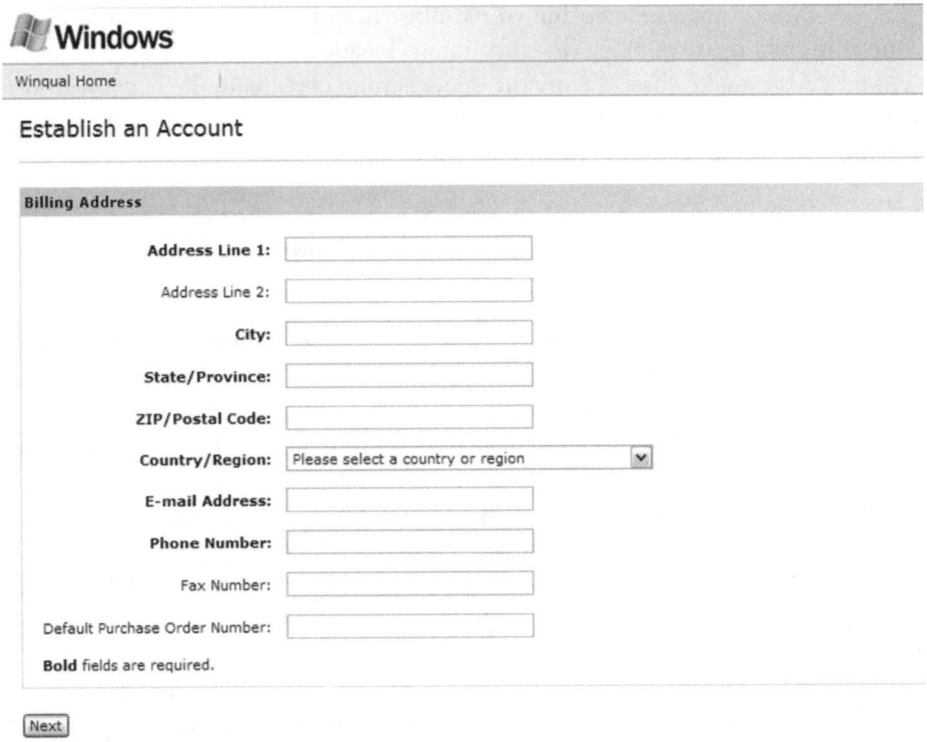

Figure 8-7   Billing information page

The user name and password fields represent the logon information that you use when accessing the WER site. Fill in all of the information and pay particular attention to the strong password requirements listed at the bottom. These password requirements are important to ensuring that your company's error information is kept secure.

After all the information has been filled in, click the Next button, and you are taken to a page that indicates that the account has been successfully created, as shown in Figure 8-9.

The final steps that must be completed before we can access WER involve setting up permissions and signing the legal agreements. Let's start with managing permissions. Click the Manage Permissions link to access the permissions page, shown in Figure 8-10.

Make sure the Sign Master Legal Agreements, View WER Data, and Download WER Data checkboxes are enabled for your account, and click the Update button.

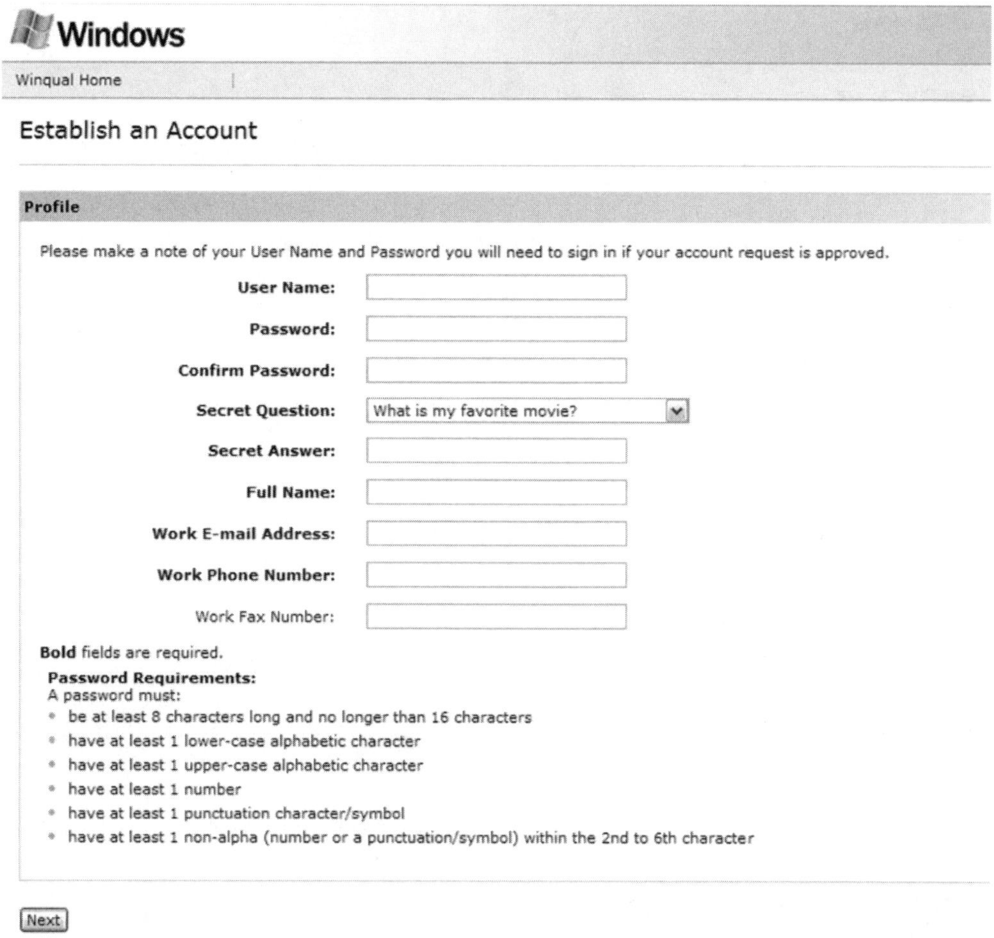

Figure 8-8   Profile information page

Note that it is possible to have multiple accounts associated with a company account in WER. This can be quite useful if you want different users to have different levels of access (as shown in Figure 8-10). For example, one user can be granted access to the error reports, whereas another user can be granted access to sign legal agreements.

Next, we go back to the page shown in Figure 8-9 to complete the process by signing legal agreements as required by Microsoft. Click the Sign Legal Agreements link, which takes you to the Windows Error Reporting legal agreement page.

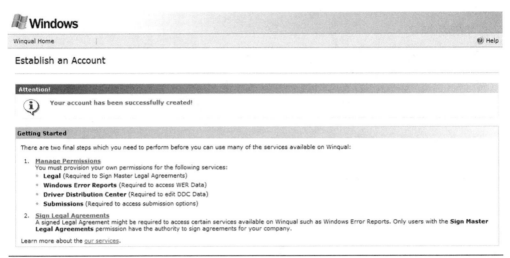

Figure 8-9   Account creation succeeded

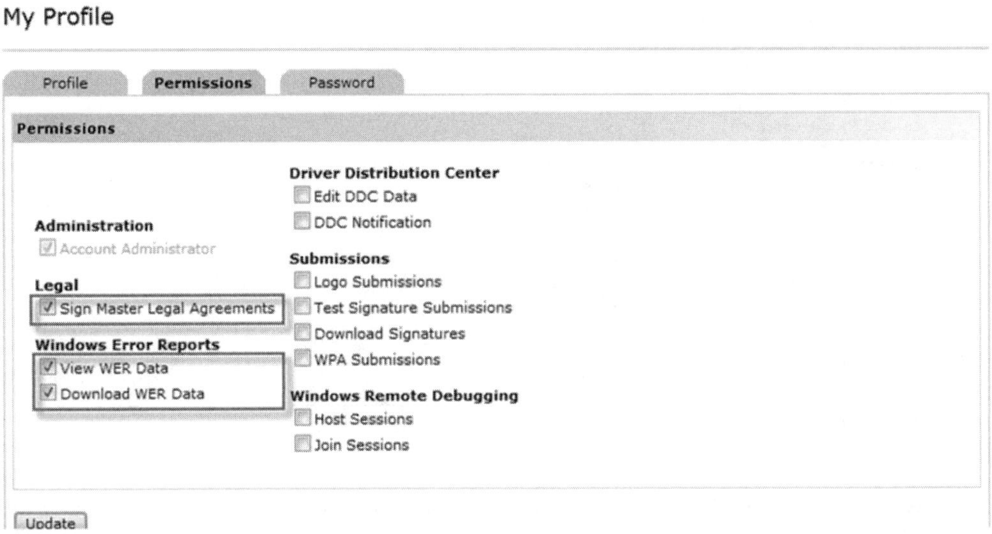

My Profile

Figure 8-10   Manage Permissions

Carefully read through all the information presented, and if you choose to accept, fill in the information at the bottom of the last page to sign the agreement. If you want a copy of the agreement for your records, you can enter your company information in the form and print a copy.

The signup process is now complete, and you can access the full range of WER features by signing in to your account using the following URL:

https://winqual.microsoft.com/default.aspx

Navigating the WER Web Site

When you log onto the WER Web site, you are presented with a page that contains recent Winqual announcements. To the left of the announcements is a pane that allows you to navigate to different parts of the site. The three main sections of the navigation pane are

- Windows Logo Program
- Windows Error Reports
- Driver Distribution Center

In this chapter, we will only cover the Windows Error Reports section of the Web site and, more specifically, the Software portion of WER. Figure 8-11 illustrates the options that are available in the Software menu.

The Product Rollups option under the Event Views category shows a view that organizes the error reports according to product name and version. Figure 8-12 shows an example of the Product Rollup page.

Figure 8-12 shows one product registered: Advanced .NET Debugging. The product has two columns that allow you to dig deeper into any events (crashes or other) that may have been reported for the applications:

- Eventlist. The event list icon takes you to a page that details the complete list of events that have occurred in the application.
- Hotlist. The hot list icon takes you to a page that details the biggest hitters for the application chosen over the last 90 days.

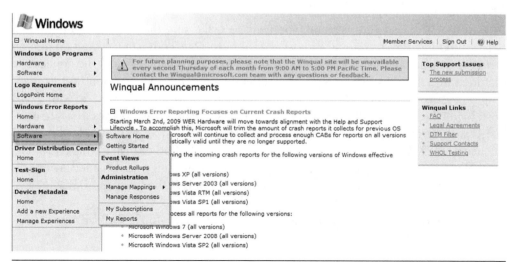

Figure 8-11 WER Software options

Product Rollup

The Product Rollups view organizes your error events by the product name and version (provided in the Mapping file submitted by the Microsoft Product Feedback Mapping to Only Products containing at least one WER report are displayed.

This page includes:
- **Eventlists** that show you all the error events for a product version.
- **Hotlists** for examining the most critical issues on a product version by volume and growth.

Please select the help icon at the top right of this page for more information.

Export as Xml					
Eventlist	Hotlist	Product Name	Product Version	Total Events	Total Responses
		Advanced .NET Debugging	1.0.0.0	2	0

Figure 8-12   Example of the Product Rollup page

The next menu item is the Administration category. It contains the following options:

- Manage Mappings. This option allows you to map binaries with products so that WER knows which binaries go with which product. We will show you how to create a mapping file later in this chapter.
- Manage Responses. This option allows you to define responses to common problems reported by customers and, in essence, create a feedback loop that may contain anything from informative messages to fixes. We will look at how to generate a response later in this chapter.

Now that we have familiarized ourselves with the general layout of the WER site, it is time to map our product's binaries to a particular product so that WER knows which binary belongs to which product.

Mapping Binaries to Products

After you've accessed your account, you need to make sure that any error information that is reported for your applications get routed to your company account. When an error report is sent to the WER service, it needs to know what it is about the application that identifies it as belonging to a particular company. The key ingredient in this mapping process is the name of the application. As such, companies that sign up with WER need to tell the service the name of the applications (including all binaries) that are associated with their companies. The mapping information is then presented to the WER site using an XML file that the WER service understands. Rather than having customers manually compile this mapping XML file, the WER site has a tool named Microsoft Product Feedback Mapping Tool. The tool can be found at the following URL:

www.microsoft.com/downloads/details.aspx?FamilyId=4333E2A2-5EA6-4878-BBE5-60C3DBABC170&displaylang=en

Let's download the tool and give it a shot. When installed, run the tool from Start, Programs, Microsoft Product Feedback Mapping Tool, and you are presented with a wizard that guides you through the mapping process. The first page of the wizard is illustrated in Figure 8-13.

To illustrate the process of setting up a mapping file for WER, we will use the 08SimpleExc.exe application used earlier in the chapter. Make sure Create a New Mapping File is selected and click Next. Figure 8-14 shows the Gathering Product Mapping Information page.

The options shown in Figure 8-14 are explained below. Please make sure you enter the information as shown in the figure.

- Product File(s) Directory Path. Specifies the directory path to the application binaries that you want to map.
- Product Name. Specifies the name of the product that you want the binaries to be associated with. Please note that the product name is simply a friendly name used on the WER site so that users can more efficiently group and search for error information.
- Product Version. Specifies the product version that you want the binaries to be associated with. Please note that the product version is simply a friendly version used on the WER site so that users can more efficiently group and search for error information.

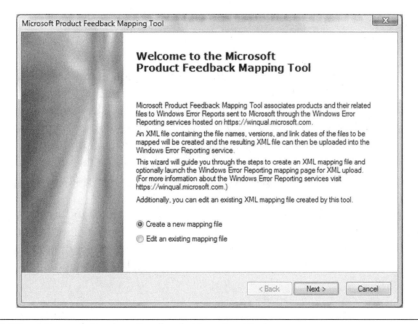

Figure 8-13   Microsoft Product Feedback Mapping Tool

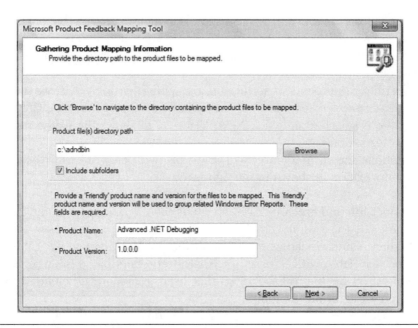

Figure 8-14   Gathering Product Mapping Information

When all information has been entered, click Next, followed by another Next. The wizard now asks you to specify a filename for the mapping file it is about to generate. Enter the following path for the map file and click Next.

```
C:\testmap.xml
```

Figure 8-15 shows the last step of the process, which allows you to upload the mapping file to the WER site.

Make sure the checkbox is checked and click Finish. The wizard now launches your browser and presents the File Upload page, as illustrated in Figure 8-16.

Enter the path to the map file we just created and click Submit. Upon successful upload, the file mapping process and upload are completed. If you have more than one product, you go through the whole mapping process again, once for each product.

Back on the main WER site, you can manage your Product and File mappings by choosing Software, Manage Mappings options in the left navigation pane. You can choose to manage Product and File Mappings as well as upload a mapping file. For example, selecting the File Mapping link after we uploaded the mapping file is shown in Figure 8-17.

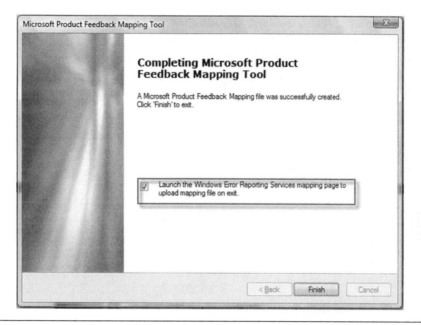

Figure 8-15   Uploading the mapping file to WER

The High-tech Avenue - Site Data Last Updated: 11-Mar-2009

File Upload

File mapping is an integral part of Windows Error Reporting (WER). It is the process of associating Error Reporting data with your applications' files. New mappings are proce and associated with Error Reporting data every 24 hours.

A small client tool is used to create a mapping file containing the required PE file information used for Windows Error Reporting. The tool is called the **Microsoft Product Feedback Mapping Tool** (download now). The File Mapping Process for Software works as follows:

1. Locate your shipping files for a given Product and Version you wish to map.
2. Run the Microsoft Product Feedback Mapping Tool on the folder(s) containing the files. This creates an XML file containing the mapping of your files to your product.
3. Upload the XML file to WER using this Upload File Mapping page.

Please select the help icon at the top right of this page for more information.

■ ■ ■

Please select the file to upload using the Browse button, and then click Submit button to upload.

| c:\workzone\testmap.xml | Browse... |

Submit

Figure 8-16   Mapping file upload page

The High-tech Avenue - Site Data Last Updated: 11-Mar-2009

Manage File Mappings

Windows Error Reporting for Software applications provides two ways to view and manage file mappings: At the file level, and by the products the files are grouped by.

Files are mapped using the XML output of the Microsoft Product Feedback Mapping Tool. The XML mapping files are uploaded to Windows Error Reporting using the Upload File Mappings link under the Manage Mappings left navigational menu selection. When files are unmapped, they will appear disabled in the list until the system processes the change. Deleted files and products can take up to 24 hours to process and update the product rollups.

The Manage Product Mappings and Manage File Mappings pages work together:
- The **Manage Product Mappings** page lists all your company's products that have files related to them.
- The **Manage File Mappings** page displays all the files that are related to your company's products.

Please select the help icon at the top right of this page for more information.

* * *

		Export as Xml					Prev Next Page 1	of 2 G

Product Mappings	File Name	File Version	Link Date	Map Date	Mapped By
	01MDASample.exe	0.0.0.0	06-Feb-09 03:20:07 PM	16-Mar-09 06:00:36 AM +00	marioh
	01sample.exe	1.0.0.0	26-Oct-07 06:23:24 AM	20-Nov-07 01:35:14 PM +00	marioh
	02ExcSample.exe	0.0.0.0	06-Feb-09 03:20:07 PM	16-Mar-09 06:00:36 AM +00	marioh
	02sample.exe	1.0.0.0	26-Oct-07 06:23:24 AM	20-Nov-07 01:35:14 PM +00	marioh
	02Simple.exe	0.0.0.0	06-Feb-09 03:20:07 PM	16-Mar-09 06:00:36 AM +00	marioh
	02TypeSample.exe	0.0.0.0	06-Feb-09 03:20:08 PM	16-Mar-09 06:00:36 AM +00	marioh

Figure 8-17 WER File Mappings

From Figure 8-17, we can see that we have several file mappings, each with specific attributes (such as link date and map date), as well as administrative information, such as who created the mapping and her email address.

Now that we have created a product and file mapping, it is time to look at the report generation aspects of WER. We will look at how we can generate reports of the error information sent by customers as well as delve deeper into each individual error report (such as crash dumps).

Querying the Windows Error Reporting Service

Now that we have created an account and mapped our 08SimpleExc.exe binary to a product, it's time to look at how we can query WER for uploaded error reports. Let's run our 08SimpleExc.exe application several times and when it crashes, tell Dr. Watson to upload the error information to the WER site. Note that there is a time delay between the time that a user uploads a report and when it becomes available to view.

After the error reports have been uploaded and made available to you, you will see a table of products on the Product Rollup page, as illustrated in Figure 8-18. Figure 8-18 shows the product we mapped (Advanced .NET Debugging) as well as the total number of events that have been reported. Additionally, the Eventlist and Hotlist

Product Rollup

The Product Rollups view organizes your error events by the product name and version (provided in the Mapping file submitted by the Microsoft Product Feedback Mapping to Only Products containing at least one WER report are displayed.

This page includes:
- **Eventlists** that show you all the error events for a product version.
- **Hotlists** for examining the most critical issues on a product version by volume and growth.

Please select the help icon at the top right of this page for more information.

Export as Xml

Eventlist	Hotlist	Product Name	Product Version	Total Events	Total Responses
📄	📊	Advanced .NET Debugging	1.0.0.0	2	0

Figure 8-18   Product Rollup with error events

columns contain icons that display all the events that have occurred for that particular product as well as the top error events that have occurred over the last 90 days. The hot list is a convenient way to identify the top issues with the product. Figure 8-19 illustrates the event list page that is displayed when clicking on the event list icon.

The event list page contains a table where each row represents a unique error event. In Figure 8-19, we can see that there is only one event with a total hit count of 2. The table also shows what type of event caused the report; in our case, the event type is CLR20 Managed Crash, which simply means that the event occurred due to a crash in a managed application based on CLR version 2.0. If you click on the event ID, you will see a breakdown of information related to that particular event. The event details page is broken down into three main sections:

- Event Signature. Because one product can have multiple events associated with it, each event must be made unique. The different pieces of information that make an event unique are: Application name and version, module name and version, and the offset into the module that caused the event to occur. As you can see from Figure 8-20, the offset into the 08SimpleExc.exe module that caused the crash was 4734.

- Event Time Trending Details. The graph displayed in the Event Time Trending Details section shows how the event manifested itself over time. In Figure 8-20, we can see that our event spiked on March 16th and gradually decreased in frequency over time.

- Platform details. The last section shows the platform details for the specific event. It shows the operating system breakout as well as language breakout. This section is critical when trying to identify problems that only occur under certain configurations and can yield clues such as the event only occurring on non-English versions of the product.

Event List for product: Advanced .NET Debugging 1.0.0.0

The Event List page displays events for a specified product or search criteria. This page is useful for reviewing the complete list of events for a given product or search cri

Please select the help icon at the top right of this page for more information.

⊞ Show filter

Event ID	Cabs	Responses	Total Hits	Avg. Hits	Growth Percent	Event Type	Application Name	Application Version	Module Name	Module Version
504156229	📁		2	0.02		CLR20 Managed Crash	08SimpleExc.exe	0.0.0.0	08SimpleExc	0.0.0.0

Figure 8-19   Event list for Advanced .NET Debugging

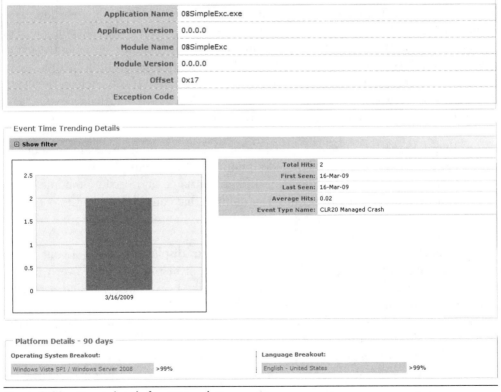

Event Signature

Application Name	08SimpleExc.exe
Application Version	0.0.0.0
Module Name	08SimpleExc
Module Version	0.0.0.0
Offset	0x17
Exception Code	

Event Time Trending Details

⊞ Show filter

Total Hits:	2
First Seen:	16-Mar-09
Last Seen:	16-Mar-09
Average Hits:	0.02
Event Type Name:	CLR20 Managed Crash

Platform Details - 90 days

Operating System Breakout:
Windows Vista SP1 / Windows Server 2008   >99%

Language Breakout:
English - United States   >99%

Figure 8-20   Event details for 08simpleExc.exe

Figure 8-21   Data collection section

Figure 8-20 illustrates the data that is displayed for 08SimpleExc.exe.

The events details page also contains a Cab data collection section, shown in Figure 8-21.

The Data Collection section allows you to either go to the list of available Cabs for the particular event by clicking on the Cab Status icon, or to make changes to the data collection policy for the particular event by clicking on the Data Request icon. Figure 8-22 illustrates the data collection policy window.

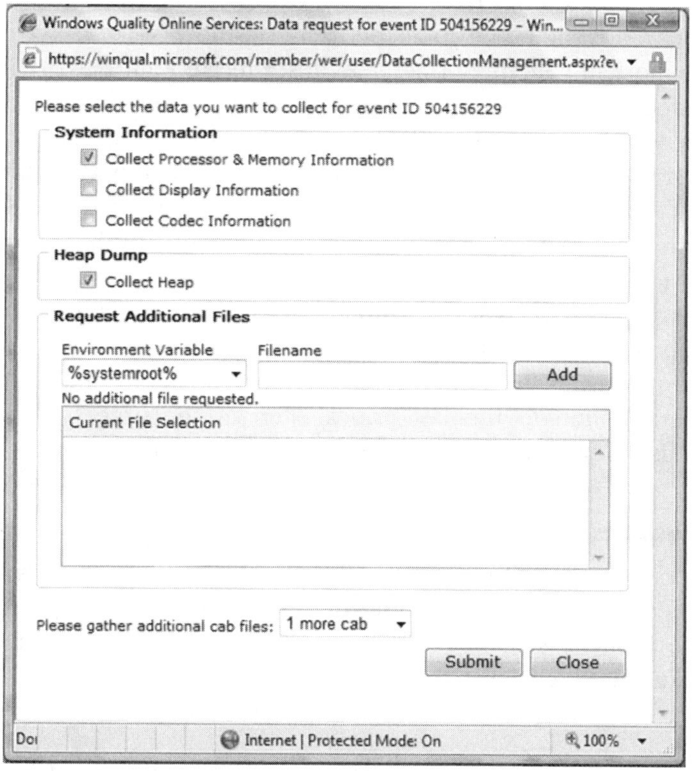

Figure 8-22   Data collection policy

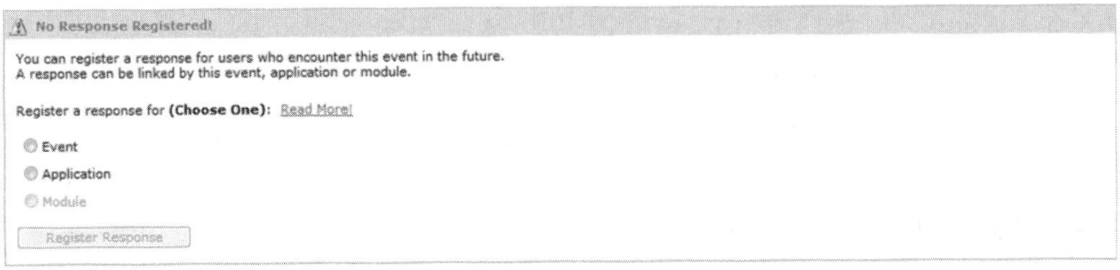

Figure 8-23   Event response options

Remember, when a fault occurs in an application, the machine on which the fault occurred contacts WER to check on the data collection policy. If the policy has changed and requires a new upload, the client machine creates a Cab according to the policy and uploads it to WER. The data collection policy window allows you to specify additional information to be collected in this process. In addition to system information, heap memory can be collected as well as additional files based on a pre-defined set of environment variables. Finally, you also have the ability to specify how many additional Cabs should be collected using this new policy.

The last important column in the table illustrated in Figure 8-19 is the Cabs column. Clicking the icon gives a list of Cabs available for the event. A Cab is nothing more than a conglomerate of files that represent the event information (one Cab per upload) sent by users who choose to upload the information to Microsoft. One of the most critical files in the Cab is the dump file that was generated at the point of failure. This dump file can be used while debugging the problem postmortem as explained previously.

Now that we have looked at the various pieces of information accessible through the WER Web site, everything from a high-level overview of the events to a more detailed drilldown using the information the customer uploaded to Microsoft, we next turn our attention to the last critical step in the process: how to provide responses to customers after the issue has been understood.

Providing Responses

To provide a response to customers about a particular event, you must navigate to the Event Details page for a particular event. If a response has not yet been recorded for the event, the topmost section of the page will contain options for registering a response, as illustrated in Figure 8-23.

Responses can be registered at three different levels:

- Event. Typically used when a fix is very isolated and will not be incorporated into a product update.

- Application. Providing a response at the application level allows you to create a rules-based response that all users with a particular version of your application see. The response can be in the form of an update (such as a new version).
- Module. Providing a response at the module level allows you to create a rules-based response that your users with a particular version of your module see. The response can be in the form of an update (such as a new version).

For our particular scenario, we will choose to use the event-based response registration. Select the Event radio button and click Register Response. The next step is to fill out details about the event response. The following information is required before a response can be registered:

- Products. Enter the name of the product into the Products field.
- URL of Solution/Info. Enter a URL to the response. The URL should point to a page with all the required information for that particular response.
- Response Template. You can choose to use a predefined template for your response or use your own custom template. Examples of predefined templates include: System Does Not Meet Minimum Requirements, Product Upgrade, Upgrade to New Version, and more. Depending on which template is chosen in this drop-down, the preview field changes.
- Response Template Preview: Shows a preview of what information will be included in the response.
- Additional Information: Enter any additional information you want to include with the response.

When all the information is filled out, proceed to register the response and you are redirected to the Response Management page, which lists all the responses that you have registered. Please note that a newly registered response does not go into effect immediately, but rather goes through an approval process that takes a few days to process. The Response Management page also allows you to manage all the responses that have been created. You can view the responses in detail, make changes, and delete individual responses that are no longer applicable.

How will this response be presented to the user? The next time a user experiences a failure that has a response associated with it, she will see the dialog illustrated in Figure 8-24.

If the user clicks the Close Program button, a notification area balloon tip is displayed notifying them that a solution exists for the problem encountered. An example is shown in Figure 8-25.

Furthermore, if the notification area is clicked, Windows brings up the Problem Reports and Solutions dialog with the solution text, as shown in Figure 8-26.

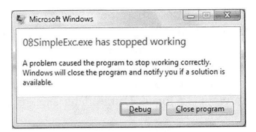

Figure 8-24   User experience with an application failure that has a response

Figure 8-25   Problem solution notification area balloon tip

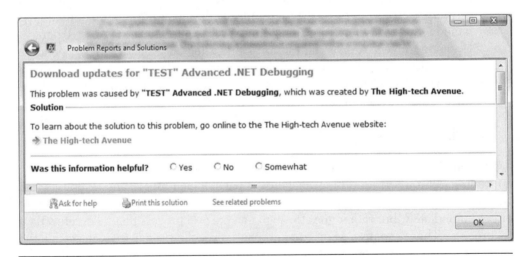

Figure 8-26   User experience with an application failure that has a response

In this particular case, the user can click the link (The High-Tech Avenue), which brings her to a site where the solution is described in detail.

Reporting and Subscribing

Two new features included in the WER service are Reporting and Subscriptions. Subscriptions allow you to register for notifications based on specific criteria and can be accessed from the Software →My Subscriptions menu item. Figure 8-27 illustrates the different criteria available.

The High-tech Avenue - Site Data Last Updated: 11-Mar-2009

My Subscriptions

Report Title	Recurrence		Active Status	Filters	
General Summary	Weekly ▾	Monday ▾	☐ Activate Subscription	N/A	⌄

This report shows an overall summary of important information on the website. This is the best report to subscribe to for overall information on your companies activity on the website.

New Cab Arrival	Weekly	Monday ▾	☐ Activate Subscription	Available	⌄
Security Alerts	Weekly	Monday ▾	☐ Activate Subscription	N/A	⌄
New Escalations	Weekly	Monday ▾	☐ Activate Subscription	N/A	⌄
Hot Lists	Weekly ▾	Monday ▾	☐ Activate Subscription	Available	⌄
Response Integration	Weekly	Monday ▾	☐ Activate Subscription	N/A	⌄
New File Mapping	Weekly	Monday ▾	☐ Activate Subscription	N/A	⌄

Figure 8-27 Available subscriptions

To activate a subscription, please check the box next to the subscription of interest. Each subscription can also be customized to specify the date (and in some cases frequency) when the email notification will be sent.

The Reporting feature contains a set of precreated reports that can be ran over the data stored in WER. At the time of this writing, only one report was available, named the Response Satisfaction report, which shows the overall response quality and the amount of times that customers have viewed and submitted survey results. The reporting feature is a relatively new feature and we can expect the number of reports that are available to grow in the future.

As you can see, WER is an incredibly powerful service that allows you to monitor how well your application behaves in the real world. Allowing customers to send up error information that you can analyze and create a response to is an incredible technology that eases the pain customers go through when encountering software problems.

Programmatic Access to Windows Error Reporting

Windows Error Reporting is a great opportunity for companies to monitor and react to how their applications behave after they are released. Simply by creating an account and registering their products and binaries they can get extensive fault information based on real-world scenarios. One of the caveats about using WER is that it requires a user to log onto the site in regular intervals and see if there are any new events that have occurred. If so, the user looks at the event data and may decide to download the Cab associated with the event and investigate postmortem. A much better approach to monitoring applications is to use the programmatic access that WER offers in the form of Web Service APIs. The Web Service APIs allow companies to create their own automatic fault monitoring systems by downloading all the event data without human intervention. The WER team has published the Web Services access layer to CodePlex (http://wer.codeplex.com/) and includes a number of different sample projects (including a Windows Vista Gadget that pulls WER for information). Additionally, it also includes a client assembly (http://wer.codeplex.com/Release/ProjectReleases.aspx?ReleaseId=12825) that exposes the WER object model, making it very easy for developers to start writing their own monitoring applications. Figure 8-28 illustrates a high-level overview of the WER workflow and client–object model.

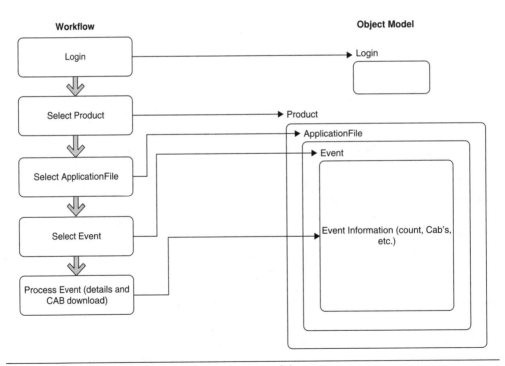

Figure 8-28 WER workflow and client–object model

Each WER workflow begins with the client logging in to the WER system using the `Login` class. The credentials used during the login are the credentials of an authorized user on the account (for example, the primary administrator). Upon success, the login object is typically cached in the client application and subsequently used for all other WER operations. Next, the client application can enumerate the available products in the account (previously mapped using the Product Feedback Mapping Tool) and can select the products of interest. The product is represented by the `Product` class. Each Product instance aggregates a set of applications that correspond to each of the binaries mapped during the mapping process. An application is represented by the `ApplicationFile` class and can be used to get detailed application information. Much in the same way that a product class aggregates a collection of applications, each application in turn aggregates a set of events (represented by the `Event` class) where each event contains detailed information such as event type and associated Cab files. The client application can now use the event information to do further processing (such as store in a DB and/or integrate with an automatic bug tracking system).

To get a better understanding of how to integrate with WER, let's look at an example console-based client that gets the event details of a specified event. The source code for the application is shown in Listing 8-2.

Listing 8-2 Sample application that talks to the WER service

```
using System;
using System.IO;
using System.Text;
using System.Runtime.InteropServices;
using Microsoft.WindowsErrorReporting.Services.Data.API;

namespace Advanced.NET.Debugging.Chapter8
{
    class WerConsole
    {
        static void Main(string[] args)
        {
            WerConsole s = new WerConsole();
            s.Run();
        }
```

(continues)

Listing 8-2 Sample application that talks to the WER service *(continued)*

```csharp
public void Run()
{
    int eventId;
    string product, file, cabLoc, userName, password;
    Login login;

    Console.Write("Enter user name: ");
    userName = Console.ReadLine();

    Console.Write("Enter password: ");
    password = Console.ReadLine();

    Console.WriteLine("Login into WER...");
    login=WerLogin(userName, password);
    Console.WriteLine("Login succeeded");

    Console.Write("Enter Product: ");
    product=Console.ReadLine();

    Console.Write("Enter File: ");
    file=Console.ReadLine();

    Console.Write("Enter Event ID: ");
    eventId=Int32.Parse(Console.ReadLine());

    Console.Write("Enter Location to store CABs: ");
    cabLoc = Console.ReadLine();
    if (Directory.Exists(cabLoc) == false)
    {
        Directory.CreateDirectory(cabLoc);
    }

    Event e=GetEvent(product, file, eventId, ref login);
    Console.WriteLine("Event succesfully retreived");
    Console.WriteLine("Event ID: " + e.ID);
    Console.WriteLine("Event Total Hits: " + e.TotalHits.ToString());
    Console.WriteLine("Storing CABs...");
    foreach (Cab c in e.GetCabs(ref login))
    {
        try
        {
            c.SaveCab(cabLoc, true, ref login);
        }
        catch (Exception)
```

```
            {
            }
        }
        Console.WriteLine("CABs stored to: " + cabLoc);
    }

    public Login WerLogin(string userName, string password)
    {
        Login login = new Login(userName, password);
        login.Validate();
        return login;
    }

    public Event GetEvent(string pr,
                          string fi,
                          int eventId,
                          ref Login login)
    {
        foreach (Product p in Product.GetProducts(ref login))
        {
            if (p.Name == pr)
            {
                ApplicationFileCollection ac =
                        p.GetApplicationFiles(ref login);
                foreach (ApplicationFile file in ac)
                {
                    if (file.Name == fi)
                    {
                        EventPageReader epr=file.GetEvents();
                        while (epr.Read(ref login) == true)
                        {
                            EventReader er = epr.Events;
                            while (er.Read() == true)
                            {
                                Event e = er.Event;
                                return e;
                            }
                        }
                    }
                }
            }
        }
        throw new Exception("Event Not Found");
    }
  }
}
```

The source code and binary for Listing 8-2 can be found in the following folders:

- Source code: `C:\ADND\Chapter8\WerConsole`
- Binary: `C:\ADNDBin\08WerConsole.exe`

For the purpose of this sample, the WER client assembly (`Microsoft.WindowsErrorReporting.Services.Data.API.dll`) is located in the `C:\ADND\Chapter8\WerConsole` folder and automatically gets placed in the `C:\ADNDBin` folder as part of building the project. For the most up-to-date version of the WER client assembly, please go the WER CodePlex site at the following URL:

http://wer.codeplex.com/Release/ProjectReleases.aspx?ReleaseId=12825

As seen in Listing 8-2, the application is a simple command-line application that prompts the user for the following information:

- Username. This is the username to authenticate with WER.
- Password. The password associated with the username. Please note that the password is displayed on the console when input.

After the username and password have been entered, the application uses the `Login` method, passing the entered information in as parameters. Upon success, the `Login` method returns an instance of the Login class representing the newly established WER session. This instance is required for subsequent WER operations. When connected to WER, the application prompts for further information:

- Product. This is the product name of interest.
- File. This is the application file of interest.
- Event ID. This is the event ID of interest.
- Location to store Cabs. This is the location in which all Cabs associated with the event ID will be stored.

After the above information has been specified, the application connects to WER and attempts to find the event. It does so by using the following process:

1. Tries to find the specified product by enumerating all products registered with the company (associated with the specified username).
2. Tries to find the specified application file by enumerating all application files associated with the product found in (1).

3. Tries to find the specified event by enumerating all events associated with the application file found in (2).
4. When the event is found, it downloads all the associated Cab files.

Please note that any of the preceding operations that require a call to WER also require the login instance (i.e., established session) to be passed as a parameter.

Let's take a look at a sample run:

```
C:\ADNDBin>08WerConsole.exe
Enter user name: MarioH
Enter password: <password>
Login into WER...
Login succeeded
Enter Product: Advanced .NET Debugging
Enter File: 08SimpleExc.exe
Enter Event ID: 504156229
Enter Location to store CABs: c:\zone\CAB
Event successfully retrieved
Event ID: 504156229
Event Total Hits: 2
Storing CABs...
CABs stored to: c:\zone\CAB
```

Please note that depending on how many Cabs are being downloaded and the amount of information each Cab contains, it may take a few minutes to download. If we take a look at the Cab location specified, we can now see the following files:

```
C:\ADNDBin>dir /B c:\Zone\cab
504156229-CLR20ManagedCrash-0605004230.cab
504156229-CLR20ManagedCrash-0605004408.cab
504156229-CLR20ManagedCrash-0605004551.cab
504156229-CLR20ManagedCrash-0605004647.cab
504156229-CLR20ManagedCrash-0605004808.cab
504156229-CLR20ManagedCrash-0605004930.cab
504156229-CLR20ManagedCrash-0605005030.cab
504156229-CLR20ManagedCrash-0605005112.cab
504156229-CLR20ManagedCrash-0606022813.cab
504156229-CLR20ManagedCrash-0606025125.cab
```

We can now extract any of the downloaded Cab files, load the associated dump file in the debugger, and do postmortem debugging to find out the root cause of a problem that occurred on a customer's machine.

Programmatic access to WER is an incredibly powerful feature that allows companies to develop their own monitoring applications that can easily integrate with onsite bug tracking systems. One can easily imagine developing a service that periodically pings the WER service to download new application failures into a DB that integrates with an on-premise bug tracking solution, allowing developers quick notifications about failures, thereby enabling them to provide rapid responses to customers.

Summary

Postmortem debugging is a critical aspect of a software engineer's job. After an application is shipped to customers, it is usually difficult to troubleshoot problems. Having the knowledge and capability to respond quickly, accurately, and with as little pain as possible for the customer is key to a company being able to efficiently manage customer complaints.

In this chapter, we discussed the reasons why it's necessary to sometimes debug a problem postmortem. We looked at what type of debug information is required for postmortem debugging to work and what tools we can utilize to collect that information. After the information is in our hands, we also discussed how the debugger can be used to analyze the debug information to arrive at the source of the problem.

A powerful service called Windows Error Reporting was detailed, which gives you the capability to monitor your application's health in the real world and even get access to error information (such as crash dumps) for each particular problem your application may be experiencing, as well as provide a response to the problem. Furthermore, recent enhancements to the WER service were discussed including the capability to programmatically access your WER account, enabling integration scenarios that further make troubleshooting applications much more efficient.

## CHAPTER 9

POWER TOOLS

Plenty of tools exist that make troubleshooting application bugs easier. Throughout this book, we have already seen and made use of a plethora of tools to hone in on the source of application bugs. Most of the tools discussed so far are related to the native debuggers (such as the SOS and SOSEX extensions), but there are other tools out there that can dramatically reduce the time spent on debugging and ease the troubleshooting of difficult bugs. In this chapter, we will take a look at some of these powerful tools including

- PowerDbg
- SOS and Visual Studio 2008 integration
- Visual Studio 2008 and .NET framework source-level debugging
- The upcoming Visual Studio 2010
- The all-powerful CLR Profiler
- WinDbg and the `CmdTree` command

PowerDbg

PowerDbg is a script that allows you to control the execution of the native debuggers through PowerShell. The script allows you to fold the power of the native debuggers into the rich scripting language of PowerShell and thereby leverage both the debuggers' scripting capabilities as well as PowerShell's, creating new commands that can do post processing of the debugger command output and display the results in an easy-to-digest fashion. PowerDbg works on both live debug sessions as well as dump file debugging.

Installing PowerDbg

The latest version of PowerDbg requires PowerShell version 2.0. At the time of this writing, PowerShell 2.0 was in Customer Technology Preview release version 3 (CTP3) and can be downloaded for free from the Microsoft Web site. After PowerShell is installed, the PowerDbg bits have to be downloaded and can be found on Codeplex at the following location:

- www.codeplex.com/powerdbg

The download comes in the form of a ZIP file that contains the following files:

- `Microsoft.PowerShell_profile.ps1`. This file contains all the cmdlets that parse the native debuggers command output and must be placed in the following path:

`%USERPROFILE%\Documents\WindowsPowerShell`

- `WinDbg.psm1`. This file contains all the cmdlets that handle communication with the native debuggers and must be placed in the following path:

`%WINDIR%\System32\WindowsPowerShell\v1.0\Modules\WinDbg`

Before PowerDbg can be used, a couple of configuration steps have to be made. The first step is to instruct PowerShell to allow for execution of script files. This can easily be accomplished by running the following command from the PowerShell window:

```
PS C:\Windows\System32> set-executionpolicy Unrestricted
```

The preceding command sets the script execution policy to allow running any script on the system. If the script was downloaded from the Internet, PowerShell prompts for permission before executing.

Next, you have to perform a one-time import of the `WinDbg.psm1` module by using the following command:

```
Import-module WinDbg
```

Please note that the import is persisted and a one-time configuration step only.

The next step is to configure the debugger for remote debugging. To get a better understanding of why this is required, it is important to understand that the way the PowerDbg cmdlets communicate with the native debuggers is via the built-in remoting capabilities of the native debuggers. In other words, the remote pipe has to first be set up in the debugger for PowerDbg to work. To set up a remote pipe, in the debugger, use

```
.server tcp:port=<port_number>
```

where `port_number` is an available TCP port to be used during communication. For example, if we want to use TCP port `8888`, we would use the following the command:

```
.server tcp:port=8888
```

The next step is making sure that the debug session has the proper symbol path's setup. We can utilize the good old `.symfix` command from within the WinDbg session to set the symbol path to the Microsoft public symbol server.

The final step is to tell PowerDbg to connect to the debug session by using the `Connect-WinDbg` cmdlet. The `Connect-WinDbg` cmdlet takes as an argument the remote connection string established while setting up the remote connection in the WinDbg session and takes on a similar syntax

```
tcp:Port=<port_number>,Server=<server_name>
```

where `port_number` is the TCP port used earlier to create the remote pipe and the `server_name` is the name of the server that the WinDbg session is running on. For example, with a TCP port of `8888` and a server name of `MARIOH-LAPTOP`, we would specify the following command to make the connection:

```
Connect-WinDbg "tcp:Port=8888,Server=MARIOH-LAPTOP"
```

Currently, only one open connection at a time is supported, and if you want to reconnect to a different remote session, you must first use the `Disconnect-WinDbg` command.

DOES IT ONLY SUPPORT WINDBG? Not at all. All of the debuggers in the Debugging Tools for Windows package share the same debugger engine and as such WinDbg, cdb, or ntsd can be used to create the remote connection.

That is all the preparatory work that is required to get started with PowerDbg (launch debugger, create a remote connection, set symbols, and use the `Connect-WinDbg` command to connect). Next, we'll take a look at a few of the cmdlets available in PowerDbg.

Analyze-PowerDbgThreads

The `Analyze-PowerDbgThreads` command enumerates all the existing threads in the process and displays their respective states. The available states are listed in Table 9-1.

The way in which the cmdlet finds the state of a thread is by sending a k (display stack trace) command to the debugger session and mapping the symbols on the stack to the corresponding state. It's extremely easy to change the cmdlet and add your

Table 9-1   Available States in Analyze-PowerDbgThreads cmdlet

State	Description
UNKNOWN_SYMBOL	The state of the thread is unknown.
WAITING_FOR_CRITICAL_SECTION	The thread is waiting for a critical section.
DOING_IO	The thread is doing file manipulations.
WAITING	The thread is waiting on a synchronization primitive.
GC_THREAD	The thread is doing a garbage collection.
WAIT_UNTIL_GC_COMPLETE	The thread is waiting for a garbage collection to complete.
SUSPEND_FOR_GC	The thread is suspended by the garbage collector.
WAIT_FOR_FINALIZE	The thread is waiting for objects to be finalized.
TRYING_MANAGED_LOCK	The thread is trying to acquire a managed lock.
DATA_FROM_WINSOCK	The thread is waiting for data from the Windows sockets layer.

own symbols and states by simply changing the `Classify-PowerDbgThreads` function in

```
%USERPROFILE%\Documents\WindowsPowerShell\Microsoft.PowerShell_profile.ps1
```

Here is an example of the output from the command when run on `05Heap.exe`:

```
Threads sorted by User Time...

Thread Number   User Time      Kernel Time          Activity
    0            0:00:00.031    0:00:00.078     Thread working and
doing unknown activity.
    4            0:00:00.000    0:00:00.000     Thread in wait state.
    3            0:00:00.000    0:00:00.000     Thread working and doing unknown
activity.
```

```
     2               0:00:00.000    0:00:00.000    Thread waiting for the Finalizer
event. The Finalizer thread might be b
locked.
     1               0:00:00.000    0:00:00.000    Thread is the CLR Debugger Thread.
```

As can be seen from the output, in addition to the activity state of each thread, the user and kernel times are also displayed making it easy to detect potential runaway or blocked threads.

Send-PowerDbgCommand

Commands such as Analyze-PowerDbgThreads performs all the steps necessary to display the results of the command. In some cases, however, you may want to send an arbitrary command to the debugger and do your own post processing on the output of the command. In these cases, the Send-PowerDbgCommand can be used. The Send-PowerDbgCommand takes a string as an argument that includes the command you want to execute in the debugger. For example, if we want to run the kb 200 command, we would run the following:

```
PS C:\Windows\System32> Send-PowerDbgCommand "kb 200"
```

The net result of the command execution is a file called POWERDBG-OUTPUT.LOG that contains the results. This file can then be used to do post processing of the command result and display the data in the most appropriate format. Because parsing the file can be cumbersome, PowerDbg also comes with a set of cmdlets called Parse-PowerDbg* where * is replaced by the equivalent debugger command. These commands take the file contents produced by the Send-PowerDbgCommand cmdlet and create a new file (POWERDBG-PARSED.LOG) where the content is nicely formatted and suitable to be used with the Convert-PowerDbgCSVToHashTable cmdlet, which converts it into a hash table for easier scripting. For example, the native debugger command ~* kpn 1000 (displays stack traces of all threads in the process) can be executed using the PowerDbg in the following fashion:

```
PS C:\Windows\System32> Send-PowerDbgCommand "~* kpn 1000"
PS C:\Windows\System32> Parse-PowerDbgK
PS C:\Windows\System32> $ht = @{}
PS C:\Windows\System32> $ht = Convert-PowerDbgCSVToHashTable
```

The first command sends the ~*kpn 1000 command to the debugger, which runs the command and stores the results in the POWERDBG-OUTPUT.LOG. The

Parse-PowerDbgK cmdlet then parses the results stored in that file and creates a new file called POWERDBG-PARSED.LOG, which is subsequently used by the Convert-PowerDbgCSVToHashTable cmdlet to return a hash table with the content of the parsed file. After we have the hash table, we can use it to display the different stack traces by using the write-host command:

```
PS C:\Windows\System32> write-host $ht["0"].Replace($global:g_frameDelimiter, "'n")
ChildEBP RetAddr
00 0017f060 778d8d94 ntdll!KiFastSystemCallRet
01 0017f064 778e9522 ntdll!NtRequestWaitReplyPort+0xc
02 0017f084 77507e05 ntdll!CsrClientCallServer+0xc2
03 0017f170 77507f35 KERNEL32!GetConsoleInput+0xd2
04 0017f190 001ca61c KERNEL32!ReadConsoleInputA+0x1a
Frame IP not in any known module. Following frames may be wrong.
05 0017f218 793e8f28 0x1ca61c
06 0017f280 793e8e33 mscorlib_ni+0x328f28
07 0017f2d0 79e7c6cc mscorlib_ni+0x328e33
08 0017f350 79e7c8e1 mscorwks!CallDescrWorkerWithHandler+0xa3
09 0017f490 79e7c783 mscorwks!MethodDesc::CallDescr+0x19c
0a 0017f4ac 79e7c90d mscorwks!MethodDesc::CallTargetWorker+0x1f
0b 0017f4c0 79eefb9e mscorwks!MethodDescCallSite::Call+0x18
0c 0017f624 79eef830 mscorwks!ClassLoader::RunMain+0x263
0d 0017f88c 79ef01da mscorwks!Assembly::ExecuteMainMethod+0xa6
0e 0017fd5c 79fb9793 mscorwks!SystemDomain::ExecuteMainMethod+0x43f
0f 0017fdac 79fb96df mscorwks!ExecuteEXE+0x59
10 0017fdf4 7900b1b3 mscorwks!_CorExeMain+0x15c
11 0017fe04 774a4911 mscoree!_CorExeMain+0x2c
12 0017fe10 778be4b6 KERNEL32!BaseThreadInitThunk+0xe
13 0017fe50 778be489 ntdll!_RtlUserThreadStart+0x23
14 0017fe68 00000000 ntdll!_RtlUserThreadStart+0x1b

PS C:\Windows\System32> write-host $ht["1"].Replace($global:g_frameDelimiter, "'n")
ChildEBP RetAddr
00 016ff95c 778d9244 ntdll!KiFastSystemCallRet
01 016ff960 774ac3e4 ntdll!ZwWaitForMultipleObjects+0xc
02 016ff9fc 774ac64e KERNEL32!WaitForMultipleObjectsEx+0x11d
03 016ffa18 79f4e8d8 KERNEL32!WaitForMultipleObjects+0x18
04 016ffa78 79f4e831 mscorwks!DebuggerRCThread::MainLoop+0xe9
05 016ffaa8 79f4e765 mscorwks!DebuggerRCThread::ThreadProc+0xe5
06 016ffad8 774a4911 mscorwks!DebuggerRCThread::ThreadProcStatic+0x9c
07 016ffae4 778be4b6 KERNEL32!BaseThreadInitThunk+0xe
08 016ffb24 778be489 ntdll!_RtlUserThreadStart+0x23
09 016ffb3c 00000000 ntdll!_RtlUserThreadStart+0x1b
```

Table 9-2 details the different Parse-PowerDbg* Cmdlets available.

Table 9-2 Parse-PowerDbg* cmdlets

CmdLet	Description
Parse-PowerDbgDT	Parses the output from the `dt` command.
Parse-PowerDbgNAME2EE	Parses the output from the SOS `name2ee` command.
Parse-PowerDbgDUMPMD	Parses the output from the SOS `dumpmd` command.
Parse-PowerDbgDUMPMODULE	Parses the output from the SOS `dumpmodule` command.
Parse-PowerDbgLMI	Parses the output from the `lm1` command.
Parse-PowerDbgVERTARGET	Parses the output from the `vertarget` command.
Parse-PowerDbgRUNAWAY	Parses the output from the `runaway` command.
Parse-PowerDbgK	Parses the output from the `k` command.
Parse-PowerDbgSymbolsFromK	Extracts symbolic information from the `k` command.
Parse-PowerDbgLM1M	Parses the output from the `lm1m` command.
Parse-PowerDbgPRINTEXCEPTION	Extracts exception information.
Parse-PowerDbgDD-L1	Parses the output from the `dd` command.
Parse-PowerDbgGCHANDLELEAKS	Parses the output from the SOS `gchandleleaks` command.
Parse-PowerDbgDUMPOBJ	Parses the output from the SOS `dumpobj` command.

Extending PowerDbg

In addition to the plethora of cmdlets that the PowerDbg tool contains, it is also extremely easy to extend by utilizing the existing cmdlet source. In this part of the chapter, we will take a look at an example of how to extend PowerDbg's functionality by writing a cmdlet that gets the thread execution block (TEB). The first thing we must do is figure out which debugger command gives us the results that we need.

In this case, the `teb` command can be used, which displays all the data contained within the `teb`. Below is an example of the `teb` command:

```
0:004> !teb
TEB at 7ffda000
    ExceptionList:          04a3f9a4
    StackBase:              04a40000
    StackLimit:             04a3c000
    SubSystemTib:           00000000
    FiberData:              00001e00
    ArbitraryUserPointer:   00000000
    Self:                   7ffda000
    EnvironmentPointer:     00000000
    ClientId:               0000196c . 000018ac
    RpcHandle:              00000000
    Tls Storage:            00000000
    PEB Address:            7ffdb000
    LastErrorValue:         0
    LastStatusValue:        0
    Count Owned Locks:      0
    HardErrorMode:          0
```

We can use the `Send-PowerDbg` command to send the `teb` command to the bugger and get the preceding results in the `POWERDBG-OUTPUT.LOG`. The next step is to implement the `Parse-PowerDbgHandle` command, which takes the results in `POWERDBG-OUTPUT.LOG` and massages them into a format suitable for the `Convert-PowerDbgCSVToHashTable` cmdlet and stores that result in `POWERDBG-PARSED.LOG`. We could then use the `Convert-PowerDbgCSVToHashTable` cmdlet to get the data into a hash table and manipulate it using other scripts. The majority of the work required is in implementing the `Parse-PowerDbgHandle` cmdlet, which is shown in Listing 9-1.

Listing 9-1 Parse-PowerDbgHandle cmdlet

```
function Parse-PowerDbgTEB()
{
    set-psdebug -strict
    $ErrorActionPreference = "stop"
    trap {"Error message: $_"}

    # Extract output removing commands.
    $builder = New-Object System.Text.StringBuilder

    # Title for the CSV fields.
    $builder = $builder.AppendLine("key,value")
```

```
    foreach($line in $(get-content $global:g_fileCommandOutput))
    {
      if($line.Contains("TEB at"))
      {
      }
      else
      {
        $fields=$line.Split(":");
        if([String]::IsNullOrEmpty($fields[0]))
        {
        }
        if([String]::IsNullOrEmpty($fields[1]))
        {
        }
        else
        {
          $f1=$fields[0].Trim();
          $f2=$fields[1].Trim();
          $builder = $builder.AppendLine($f1 + $global:g_CSVDelimiter + $f2)
        }
      }
    }


    # Send output to our default file.
    out-file -filepath $global:g_fileParsedOutput -inputobject "$builder"
}
```

The function walks each line in the raw data file and extracts each field's name and value and appends each key value pair to a string. After all fields have been extracted, the string is written to the parsed output file. Subsequently, we can use the Convert-PowerDbgCSVtoHashTable to convert the parsed output file to a hash table as shown:

```
PS C:\> $h={}
PS C:\> $h=Convert-PowerDbgCSVtoHashTable
```

To see the values in the hash table, simply specify the hash table and PowerShell iterates through all the key pair values and displays them:

```
PS C:\> $h

Name                          Value
----                          -----
LastErrorValue                0
ExceptionList                 04a3f9a4
FiberData                     00001e00
```

```
StackLimit                04a3c000
StackBase                 04a40000
Count Owned Locks         0
RpcHandle                 00000000
Self                      7ffda000
LastStatusValue           0
HardErrorMode             0
SubSystemTib              00000000
ClientId                  0000196c . 000018ac
PEB Address               7ffdb000
ArbitraryUserPointer      00000000
Tls Storage               00000000
EnvironmentPointer        00000000
```

The PowerDbg library is quite extensible and cmdlets can easily be created to reduce the time spent debugging certain categories of bugs by doing automatic analysis of debugger command output.

Visual Studio

Visual Studio is an extremely popular integrated developer environment among developers. The power of this IDE coupled with its ease of use makes it the environment of choice for .NET developers today. As part of the Visual Studio integrated experience comes a highly sophisticated debugger that can be used to perform troubleshooting on a myriad of different problems, such as using source-level debugging, script debugging, and SQL debugging. The one area where Visual Studio debugging has lacked functionality is in production-level debugging where we either need to work with post mortem dump files or have access to the internals of the CLR (such as the SOS commands). Fortunately, the Visual Studio team recognized and addressed the latter part of the problem by making Visual Studio compatible with the SOS debugger extension. In this part of the chapter, we will take a look at how to configure Visual Studio 2008 to make full use of the SOS debugger extension as well as how to configure Visual Studio to have access to the .NET framework source code. Finally, we will take a sneak peak at some of the new debugging features available with the upcoming release of Visual Studio 2010.

SOS Integration

To illustrate how the SOS debugger extension can be integrated into Visual Studio, start by creating a simple C# project (command-line application will suffice). After the project has been created, set a breakpoint on the first line of code and start debugging by pressing F5. Figure 9-1 shows the debugger after the breakpoint has been hit.

The next step in the SOS integration process is to bring up the intermediate window. The intermediate window is used to execute various commands (such as variable assignments, expression evaluations, etc.) during a debugging session. Figure 9-2 shows how to enable the Immediate Window.

After the Immediate Window has been enabled, you can begin entering debugging commands. One of the commands available at our disposal is the `load` command, which can be used to load the SOS debugger extension. Figure 9-3 illustrates the result of executing the `load` command.

The net result of using the `load` command is that Visual Studio fails by stating that unmanaged debugging support must be enabled for the project. Figure 9-4 illustrates the process of enabling unmanaged debugging support.

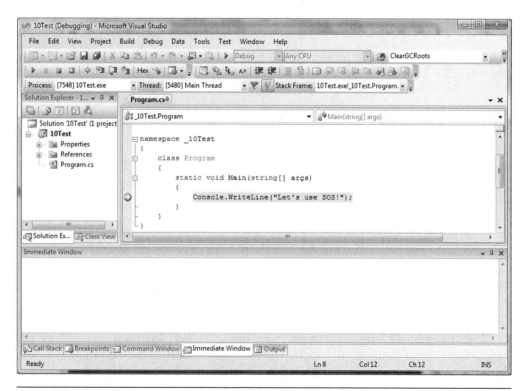

Figure 9-1 Breakpoint hit in Visual Studio

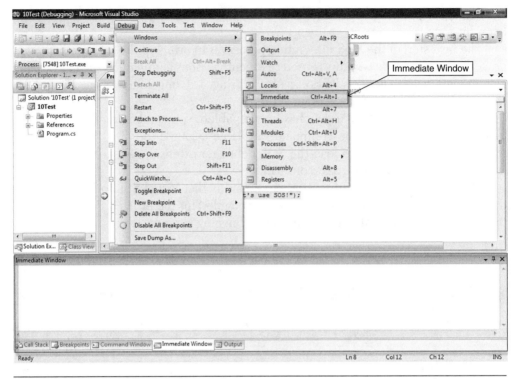

Figure 9-2 Enabling the Immediate Window

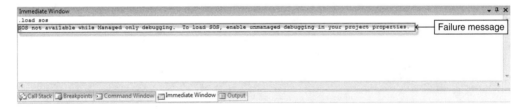

Figure 9-3 Using the load command to load the SOS debugger extension

Start by right-clicking the project in Solution Explorer followed by selecting the Properties context menu item, which brings up the properties page on the right side. In the properties page, select the Debug tab and check the Enable Unmanaged Code Debugging checkbox.

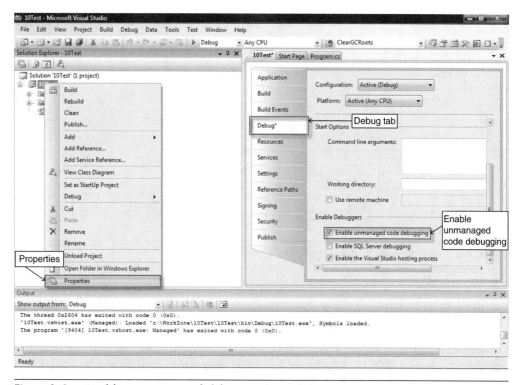

Figure 9-4 Enabling unmanaged debugging support

After unmanaged code debugging has been enabled, you can restart the debugging session, issue the `load SOS` command, and start using the SOS debugger extension commands in the Immediate Window (see Figure 9-5).

In Figure 9-5, we used two SOS commands (`EEVersion` and `DumpHeap`) to illustrate what the output looks like in the Immediate Window.

Combining the power and ease of Visual Studio with the in-depth CLR knowledge of SOS creates a single, integrated experience for complex debugging scenarios.

.NET Framework Source-Level Debugging

Any given .NET application typically utilizes a number of different types defined in the .NET frameworks. Types can range from simple data types to complex Web service bindings, and abstracts much of the underlying complexity associated with using

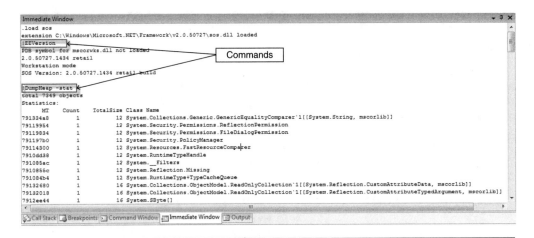

Figure 9-5 Using the SOS debugger extension

the technology directly. As with any abstraction though, the situation gets a little hairy if you get stuck and need to debug a problematic application. Rather than having to attempt to reverse engineer the abstraction to get clues as to why the application may be failing, it is much easier if source code is available to look at or even better if source code is available to debug with! Luckily, Microsoft recognized this need and published the source code for parts of the .NET framework. The really great thing about this is that not only is the source code available, but it can also be integrated into Visual Studio so that the source-level debugging that all developers have come to expect also works with the published .NET framework source code. Here, we will take a look at what it takes to configure Visual Studio for seamless .NET framework source-level debugging.

VISUAL STUDIO HOT FIX To use the integrated .NET framework source code with Visual Studio, the hot fix located at https://connect.microsoft.com/VisualStudio/Downloads/DownloadDetails.aspx?DownloadID=10443&wa=wsignin1.0 must first be installed.

For source-level debugging to work, the Visual Studio debugger must be told where it can find the source code for the module that is being debugged. Where does it get this information from? It gets it from the corresponding symbol files that are also made publicly available. Much in the same way that Microsoft publishes all public symbols for other available products on the public Microsoft symbol server, so is the case for the .NET framework. The biggest difference, however, is how much information is exposed in the symbol files being exposed. The symbols made available on the public symbol server are "stripped," meaning that certain information (including source-level information) has been removed from the symbol file. In contrast, the symbols made available for the .NET framework binaries have full debug information including source-level access, which Visual Studio uses to then find the source code published on the Internet. The first step is to tell Visual Studio that we plan on using a source server to access source code during our debug sessions. This can be enabled by selecting the Tools, Options, Debugging, General menu, which brings up the dialog shown in Figure 9-6.

In the Debugging, General page, please uncheck the `Enable Just My Code` (`Managed only`) checkbox and check the `Enable source server support` checkbox.

Next, we navigate to the Symbols page (in the same Options page) to specify the location of the symbol server we want to use, as shown in Figure 9-7.

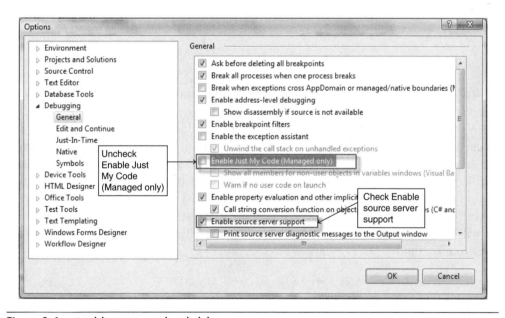

Figure 9-6 Enabling source-level debugging

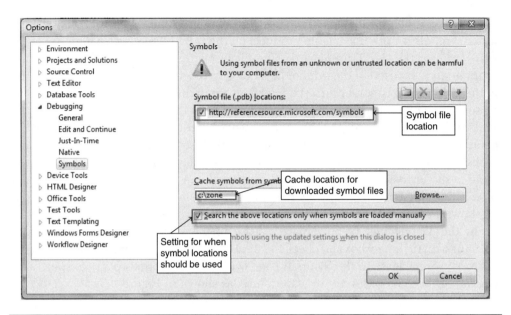

Figure 9-7   Setting the symbol server

In the symbol file locations, we add the following URL, which contains .NET framework symbols: http://referencesource.microsoft.com/symbols. Additionally, we tell Visual Studio that we would like to cache all downloaded symbol files in the folder C:\Zone. The caching mechanism can be a time saver to avoid downloading the same symbol's files each time a debug session is started. Finally, we tell Visual Studio that we want the locations to be used only when the symbols are manually loaded—that is, all the configuration that is needed for Visual Studio to support source-level debugging of the .NET frameworks. Let's give it a shot and see how easy it is. Create a simple C# console application with the following line of code in the `Main` method:

```
Console.WriteLine("Let's use SOS!");
```

Build the project and set a breakpoint on the preceding line of code using F9. Next, press F5 to debug the application; after the breakpoint hits, bring up the Modules window using CTRL-ALT-U. Locate the `mscorlib.dll` module and right-click it followed by Load Symbols. This downloads the symbols for the

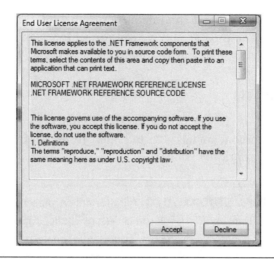

Figure 9-8   .NET Framework source EULA

`mscorlib.dll` module that will enable source-level debugging. When the symbol has finished downloading, the Symbol Status column shows `Symbols Loaded`. Now, we can step into the `Console.WriteLine` code by pressing F11. The first thing you will notice is that an End User License Agreement (EULA) is displayed, as shown in Figure 9-8.

Please take your time reading through the EULA and, if you agree to the terms, click the Accept button. The source code behind the `Console.WriteLine` method is now automatically downloaded and shown in the debugger, allowing you to step through the code just like you would your own code.

Please note that, at the moment, the following symbols are made available on the symbol server:

- `mscorlib.dll`
- `system.dll`
- `system.data.dll`
- `system.drawing.dll`
- `system.web.dll`
- `system.web.extensions.dll`
- `system.windows.forms.dll`
- `system.xml.dll`
- Windows Presentation Foundation DLL's
- `Microsoft.visualbasic.dll`

Microsoft has made sure that the infrastructure behind publishing new symbols and source code is fully automatic, and we can expect to see more and more symbols and source code become available with time.

Visual Studio 2010

With the imminent release of Visual Studio 2010, debug aficionados will be happy to learn that the Visual Studio team has invested many resources in plugging some of the gaps that have existed in prior versions.

CTP RELEASE OF VISUAL STUDIO 2010 All information presented here is based on the Customer Technology Preview (CTP) release of Visual Studio 2010 available as a VHD download from Microsoft (www.microsoft.com/visualstudio/en-us/products/2010/default.mspx). Microsoft reserves the right to rename, change, or remove features/functionality entirely in the final release version.

One of the great new features of Visual Studio 2010 is the ability to debug managed dump files. By taking a snapshot of a problematic process (using any of the techniques described in Chapter 8, "Postmortem Debugging"), the resulting dump file can now be loaded into Visual Studio 2010. Due to some very fundamental changes in the core debugging architecture, managed dump file debugging using Visual Studio 2010 requires that the application from which the dump file was generated is built against version 4.0 of the CLR. If an attempt to debug a prior version is made, Visual Studio displays an error dialog. To perform managed dump file debugging, select the Open Project menu item from the File menu. After the project has been created, you can start debugging by going to the Debug menu and selecting the Start Debugging menu item. Visual Studio then tells you what the latest event was that caused the debugger to break and you can begin inspecting the state of the process. Prior to Visual Studio 2010, all call stacks showed the native code equivalent, now they show the actual managed code frames. All other functionality works as before, and you can double-click a frame to go to the corresponding managed source code. Other functionality such as listing local variables of particular frames also now works on managed code, although some restrictions apply in the sense that if you work with optimized release binaries, local variables may not always be accurate. Figure 9-9 shows an example of debugging a dump file generated on the 05Heap.exe application.

The example in Figure 9-9 shows what the debugger looks like when broken into while in the Console.ReadKey method call. The Call Stack window on the right side shows the entire managed code call stack, and the Locals window on the left side shows the local variables that are part of the selected frame.

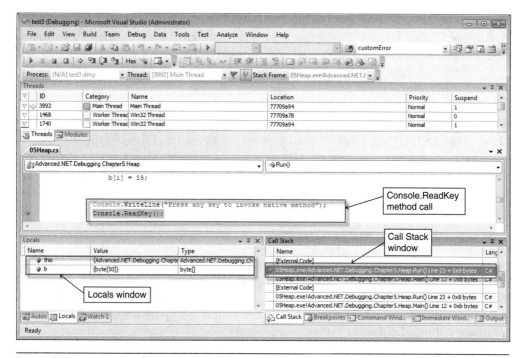

Figure 9-9 Example of Visual Studio 2010 managed code dump debugging

To build an application targeting .NET 4.0, you can use the MSBUILD build system that comes as part of .NET 4.0. Please note that the /toolsversion:4.0 switch must be used. By default, the MSBUILD build system will target version 2.0.

Did Microsoft Skip a CLR Version?

Between major and minor revisions of the CLR and the .NET frameworks, the version numbers started getting out of sync. The last major update to the CLR was version 2.0, whereas the .NET framework has grown to version 3.5. To minimize confusion, Microsoft decided to realign the CLR and .NET framework versions in version 4.0. Both the CLR and the .NET framework are now at version 4.0.

Another great new debugging feature of Visual Studio 2010 is dubbed historical debugging. The historical debugging feature helps greatly reduce the amount of time that developers spend on theorizing and proving how an application got into the state that it is currently in. Rather than having to *manually* backtrack history, the historical debugging feature records important events throughout the execution of an application and allows you to step backward and forward to those events during debug sessions. Because collecting this historic application execution flow data can be an expensive proposition and affect performance adversely, Visual Studio defaults to a relatively low collection level. By default, only significant debug events are recorded. The collection level can be controlled by selecting Options on the Tools menu and clicking the Debugging, History tab. Figure 9-10 shows the History Options page.

The `Enable Historic Debugging` section controls the level of debugging you want to enable. The `Events Only` radio button is the default and sets the collection level to minimum. The `Methods and Parameters` radio button collects method and parameter information and the `Customize Specific Level of Detail` allows you to define your own collection levels. Additionally, you can control the location of the recordings as well as maximum disk space to be used to avoid exhausting the drive. Let's look at a very simple and contrived example of how historic debugging works. First, make sure to set the recording level to `Methods and Parameters` and then load the `History` project located under: `C:\ADNDSRC\Chapter9\History`. The application is very simple and performs a division of two numbers entered by the user. Press `F5` to start debugging the application and enter numbers `12` and `-6` when prompted. As you'll quickly see, a division by zero

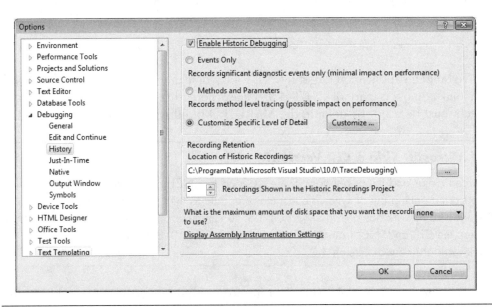

Figure 9-10 History debugging options page

exception is thrown and execution halts in the debugger. Bring up the Debug History window (Debug, Windows, Show Debug History Window) to get the historical information, as shown in Figure 9-11.

The Debug History window consists of three main panes. The topmost pane shows the frames that lead up to the failure. In our case, the thread entry called our `Main` method, which in turn called the `Divide` method. The middle pane shows diagnostic events that occurred in the selected frame as well as any other functions that may have been made. In our example, the only diagnostics event that was recorded was the fact that we called the `Divide` method. The bottommost pane shows the function called (`Divide`) with its associated parameters. Here, we can see that the numbers we entered are being passed to the function. Because the bottommost frame represents the `Divide` method, we can now inspect the local variables used in that method (by using the debugger Locals window) and we can see that the `number1` and `number2` variables are set to `12` and `0`, respectively. Because the second number should be `-6`, we can quickly (by code inspection) see that any negative number gets

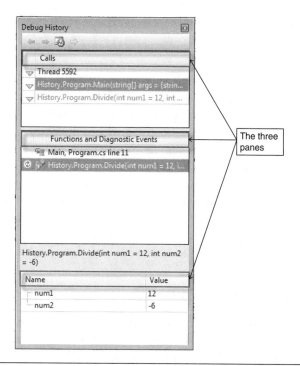

Figure 9-11 Debug History window

set to 0 resulting in a division by zero exception. Although this was an extremely trivial example, it should be easy to see the power of this feature, which allows you to backtrack and see how the application ended up in the state it's in.

In earlier versions of Visual Studio, performing mixed mode debugging (managed and native code) was only available on x86. Because the movement toward 64-bit computing has become more prevalent, the Visual Studio team added support for x64 mixed mode debugging, making life much easier when working with that architecture.

Finally, although not a debugging feature per se, the way in which certain exceptions are treated in the CLR has changed. More specifically, exceptions that you cannot, generally speaking, recover from are no longer converted to CLR exceptions. The primary reason behind this is to avoid those exceptions being mistakenly caught in a catch-all statement. A great example of this is the famous access violation exception. Catching access violation exceptions is typically only going to postpone imminent disaster and letting the exception stop the execution of the application is advisable. By not converting and inadvertently catching the exception, you have a better chance of catching it during testing and fixing the root cause.

This concludes our abbreviated tour of Visual Studio 2010. Great work has gone into enhancing the debugging experience, making it much easier for developers to track down the root cause of bugs in their applications.

CLR Profiler

In Chapter 5, "Managed Heap and Garbage Collection," we took a detailed tour of the managed heap manager and the garbage collector. As part of the tour, we also looked at the various tools available to efficiently track down memory-related issues. One of the tools that was not covered is the CLR Profiler. The CLR Profiler is an extremely powerful tool that allows you to analyze managed heap activity and display the results in a wide array of different formats. In this part of the chapter, we will take a look at the fundamentals of the CLR Profiler by utilizing the 05Fragment.exe sample application (located under C:\ADNDBin folder). Please refer to Chapter 1, "Introduction to the Tools," on CLR Profiler download and installation instructions.

Running the CLR Profiler

The CLR Profiler can be launched from the command line by executing CLRProfiler.exe from the installation folder (in my case, C:\CLRProfiler). Please note that the CLR Profiler supports both x86 and x64 and as such you must ensure to launch the correct flavor from either:

```
C:\CLRProfiler\binaries\x86
```

or

```
C:\CLRProfiler\binaries\x64
```

After the CLR Profiler has been launched, it displays the main window, as shown in Figure 9-12.

The main window has a few buttons as well as checkboxes that can be used to control the profiling session. Let's begin by specifying the `05Fragment.exe` application. Select the `Set Parameters` menu item from the `File` menu. This action brings up another window that allows you to specify, among other parameters, the command line you want to use with your target application. Because `05Fragment.exe` takes two command-line arguments, we specify them in the `Enter Command Line` edit field. The two command-line arguments we choose for this run are `50000` (size of allocation) and `500` (max size). Clicking the OK button brings you back to the main window again. Now we can click the Start Application button, which brings up a dialog that allows you to choose which application to profile. Browse to the `C:\ADNDBin` folder and select the `05Fragment.exe` application. The application now starts running and the two other buttons (Kill Application and Show Heap now) become enabled. At this point, you can either wait for the application to finish entirely (in which case the Summary view is automatically displayed) or, as in our case, the application displays a user prompt and waits until the user presses any key. You can now use the View menu to select any one of the myriad of views that exist to get detailed information on the application run. Please note that some of the views may not be available until the application has finished executing. To that extent, go to the command line from where the CLR Profiler was launched and press any key until the application finishes. In the next few sections, we will look at a few examples of different views available and how to properly interpret the information presented.

Figure 9-12 Main window of CLR Profiler

Where Does the CLR Profiler Store the Profiling Data?

The CLR Profiler stores all the profiling data in a log file located in the `C:\Windows\Temp` folder. The name of the log file can be found when a profiling session begins by looking at the command line where the CLR Profiler was executed from. For example, launching `05Fragment.exe` from the CLR Profiler shows the following on the command line:

```
Log file name transmitted from UI is: pipe_78000.log
```

Please note that collecting profiling data can generate massive log files, which in turn may slow the application down. As such, using the CLR Profiler during performance measuring runs should be avoided.

Summary View

After our application finishes executing, the CLR Profiler automatically displays the Summary view of the profiling session, as shown in Figure 9-13.

The Summary view has five major groupings of information. The first group, Heap Statistics, shows the following general information about the heap throughout the profiling session:

- Allocated bytes show the total size of all objects allocated on the managed heap.
- Relocated bytes shows the total size of objects that have been moved during garbage collections.
- Final heap bytes show the total size of all objects on the managed heap when the application exited. The final heap bytes may include objects with finalizers that are rootless but have not yet been collected.
- Objects finalized show the number of objects that have had their Finalize methods successfully executed.
- Critical objects finalized show the number of objects that had their critical Finalize methods successfully executed. An object in this category has what is known as a critical Finalize method that places stronger guarantees on being executed than normal objects.

If we look at the data presented in the Heap Statistics section in the context of our application run, we can see that about half of the memory consumed has been released by the time the application finished.

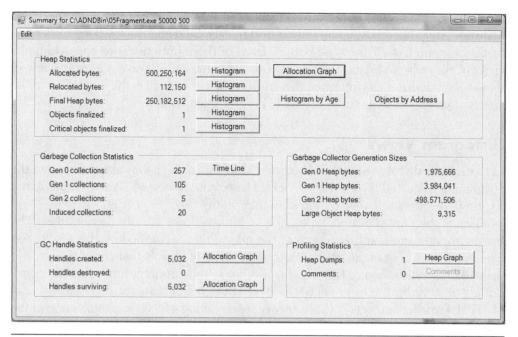

Figure 9-13 Summary view of the CLR Profiler

The next group of information is called Garbage Collection Statistics. This section is pretty straightforward and displays the number of garbage collections that have occurred in each of the generations (0-2) and the Induced collection represents the number of garbage collections that have been explicitly invoked (such as via the GC.Collect method).

The GC Handle Statistics section contains valuable information when tracking down the handle usage in an application. It shows the number of handles that have been created throughout the lifetime of the application, how many handles were destroyed, and finally how many handles survived at the end of the applications run. In our particular case, we can see that all the handles created survived, which may indicate a possible handle leak.

The Garbage Collector Generation Sizes shows the *average* size of each of the generations (including the large object heap) throughout the application run.

Finally, the Profiling Statistics section gives details on the profiling run itself. It includes how many heap dumps were caused as a result of profiling as well as the number of comments added to the log file.

Some of the groups have buttons associated with them. For example, the Heap Statistics group has a Histogram button next to each field and the Garbage Collection Statistics group has a Time Line button. Each of these buttons represents additional views of the collected data. In the next few sections, we will take a look at a few of these views and how to interpret the output. Please note that the views can all be accessed via the View menu in the CLR Profiler main window.

Histogram Views

Let's start our discussion on the Histogram views by taking a look at a view called the Histogram Allocated Types view (View, Histogram Allocated Types menu item). Figure 9-14 shows this view on the sample profiling run.

The Histogram Allocated Types view is broken down into four main areas. The bar graph area shows a breakdown of the allocations performed by the application based on size. For example, there is a total of 39KB of objects that are of size greater than 16KB but less than 32KB. The biggest bar in this profiling run is the bar representing objects that are less than 64KB in size but greater than 32KB. There is a total of 477MB worth of objects in this category representing a 99.98% overall usage of the managed heap. The color of the bar can be used in the righthand pane to correlate what the specific object(s) are. In this case, the bar is red and the righthand pane shows that it represents a `System.Byte []` type. The topmost two panes allow you to control the vertical and horizontal scale of the bar pane.

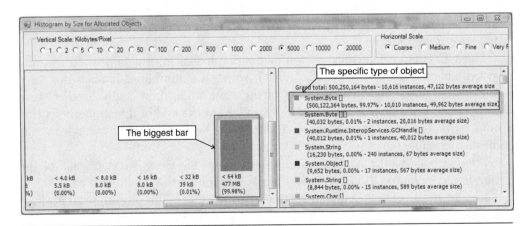

Figure 9-14   Histogram Allocated Types view of 05Fragment.exe

Analyzing the Histogram Allocated Types view in our particular sample run, we can draw the conclusion that the majority of the managed heap is filled with `System.Byte []`. Knowing which type is occupying the most space on the managed heap is very useful information, but it would also be good if we could find out where in the source code the allocations were made. This can easily be accomplished by right-clicking the bar in question and selecting the Show Who Allocated menu item. The net result is an Allocation Graph view, as shown in Figure 9-15.

From Figure 9-15, we can see that the allocation graph shows that the root frame (main entry point) calls the `Main` method of the `Fragment` class, which in turn calls the `Run` method, which finally ends up allocating an instance of `System.Byte []`. Please note that in order to save screen space, the CLR Profiler truncates the full type name.

Another useful histogram is the Histogram by Age view (View, Histogram by Age), which allows you to see how long objects lived. Figure 9-16 shows an example of the Histogram by Age view.

Here, we can see that 239MB worth of `System.Byte []` has an age between 100 and 150 seconds. As with other histogram views, you can right-click the bar and select the Show Who Allocated menu item to get the Allocation Graph.

Graph Views

In addition to histogram views, there are graph views that can be highly useful when analyzing a profile run. We've already seen an example of the allocation graph view but there are also other views that are extremely useful. An example of a graph view is the Heap Graph (View, Heap graph). The Heap Graph view shows all the objects on the managed heap and their associated connections. Figure 9-17 shows an example of the Heap Graph view.

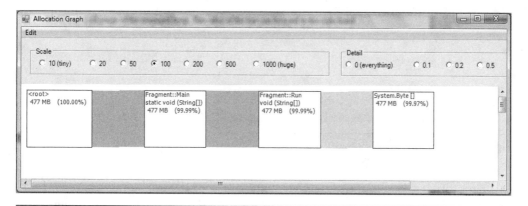

Figure 9-15   Allocation Graph view of the largest managed heap occupier

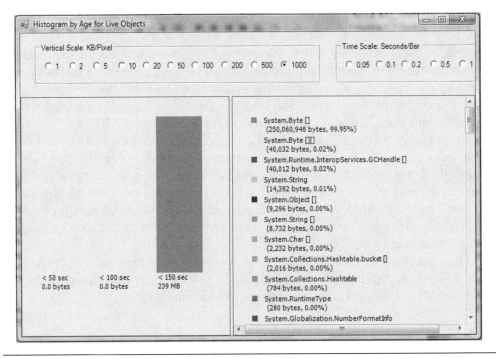

Figure 9-16 Histogram by Age view

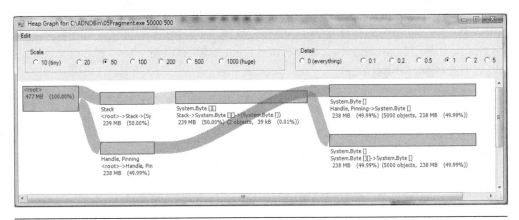

Figure 9-17 Heap Graph view

From Figure 9-17, we can see that there was 239MB worth of System.Byte [] consumed from a stack-based source as well as 238MB due to a handle (pinned).

SOS AND CLR PROFILER The SOS `TraverseHeap` command can be used while debugging to produce a file in a format that the CLR Profiler understands. The file can then be loaded into the CLR Profiler to reap the benefits of the powerful functionality of the CLR Profiler.

Even though the CLR Profiler is a very versatile tool that can provide a slew of information about the managed heap, there are some limitations.

- Slowdown. Anywhere from 10x to 100x slowdown can be expected when running an application under the CLR Profiler.
- Size of log files. The CLR Profiler collects a huge amount of data that is stored on the local drive.
- Applications must be started by the CLR Profiler rather than attaching to an already running application.

WinDbg and the CmdTree Command

Throughout the book, we have used the console-based version of the native debuggers called ntsd and cdb. There is one more flavor of the native debuggers called WinDbg, which is a GUI version of the corresponding console debuggers. The commands we have discussed so far work across all three of the debuggers, but there are also commands that only work in the context of WinDbg. One of these commands is the undocumented `cmdtree` command. This command makes it very easy to automate a lot of the typing that you otherwise have to do with the various debugger commands. The `cmdtree` command works on the basis of displaying a window that contains a hierarchical view of commands that the user can double-click on and execute. Typically, commands are grouped by area functionality such as threads, processes, modules, and so on. The commands that are displayed in the window can be customized by writing a simple text file that adheres to the syntax laid out by the `cmdtree` command. After the text file has been written, it can be loaded by using the `cmdtree <filename>` command. For example, loading the `sample.txt` cmdtree data file using the `cmdtree` command is shown below.

```
windbg> .cmdtree c:\adndbin\sample.txt
```

Figure 9-18 shows the `cmdtree` window displayed as a result of the preceding command.

Figure 9-18   Example of a cmdtree window

The window shown in Figure 9-18 contains three commands listed under the Sample Commands node. Double-clicking on any of these commands will run the corresponding command listed in the cmdtree file and output the results in the WinDbg command window.

The cmdtree file `sample.txt` is shown in Listing 9-2.

Listing 9-2   Sample cmdtree file

```
windbg ANSI Command Tree 1.0
title {"Sample Command tree"}
body
{"Sample Commands"}
 {"Critical Sections"} {"!cs"}
 {"Loader lock"} {"X ntdll!LdrpLoaderLock"}
 {"Fix symbols"} {".symfix"}
```

The first line represents the header of the file and simply specifies that the file adheres to the Command Tree version 1.0 command. The `title` command specifies the title of the command window, and then finally, the `body` command represents the content that will be displayed in the actual window. Each of the lines in the body section corresponds to either a tree node, in which case no associated commands are specified, or an actual leaf node, in which case the name of the command is followed by the commands that the debugger will execute after the node has been double-clicked. For example, the `Loader lock` line in Listing 9-2 executes the `X ntdll! LdrpLoaderLock` command in the command window of the debugger.

It's easy to see how this cmdtree file can grow to include a large number of very useful commands that can save a ton of time while debugging. Rather than having to constantly type the commands in the command window, double-clicking yields the results in a fast and efficient matter.

Summary

Although the native debuggers pack an incredibly powerful punch, they do not preclude you from using other debugging tools/aids available. In some cases, using an entirely different tool or simply augmenting the usage of the native debuggers with a complementary tool can yield a more successful debug session. In this chapter, we looked at some powerful auxiliary tools that can be used during the debugging process. We took a look at the PowerDbg library, which allows you to control the native debuggers via PowerShell by combining the scriptability of PowerShell with the native debugger engine. We looked at how SOS can be used within Visual Studio 2008 as well as how to access the .NET framework source server to do source-level debugging of the code behind the .NET frameworks. Additionally, we took a sneak peak at the upcoming Visual Studio 2010 and some of the amazing enhancements made in the debugging area (managed dump debugging, historical debugging, and more). We also discussed the all-powerful CLR Profiler that can be used to gain insights into the managed heap and garbage collector. Finally, we detailed an extremely useful command in the WinDbg debugger called cmdtree that can be used to define short cuts to commonly executed debugger commands.

## CHAPTER 10

CLR 4.0

The .NET framework version 1.0 was first released in early 2002; Microsoft has since released several new versions (.NET 1.1, 2.0, 3.0, and 3.5) with exciting enhancements. Most of the changes lay in making framework enhancements, while the CLR experienced smaller and more surgical changes as part of each release (with the exception of 2.0). The latest upcoming version of .NET is version 4.0, and as part of this release the CLR has undergone major changes in the area of reliability, performance, and feature enhancements. In this chapter, we will take a guided tour of the new and exciting capabilities that CLR 4.0 has to offer. Each section in this chapter covers CLR components discussed in previous chapters of the book and the most critical differences between CLR 2.0 and CLR 4.0.

CLR 4.0 BETA Please note that at the time of this writing, Beta 1 of .NET 4.0 was available and all information presented in this chapter is based on that release. Microsoft reserves the right to change, modify, add, and remove any features that are part of Beta 1 before the product releases.

Tools

For the most part, the tool set we have used throughout the book remains the same with the exception of enhanced feature sets within the tools themselves.

Debugging Tools for Windows

To use the native debuggers with CLR 4.0, the latest debuggers must be downloaded from the following location. The samples in this chapter were run using Debugging Tools for Windows version 6.11.0001.404.

```
http://www.microsoft.com/whdc/devtools/debugging/default.mspx
```

.NET 4.0 Redistributable

The .NET 4.0 Beta 1 redistributable package is available at the following location:

```
http://www.microsoft.com/visualstudio/en-us/try/default.mspx
```

Please note that if you are using MSBUILD (console-based build system) to build your .NET 4.0 applications, you must use the /toolsversion switch and specify 4.0 as the target version. For example, to build 0500M.exe using the 4.0 build system, the following command can be used:

```
MSBuild.exe /toolsversion:4.0 build.xml
```

SOS

As we've shown throughout the book, the SOS debugger extension is an invaluable resource when debugging tough .NET application problems that requires a great deal of insight into the runtime itself. Each version of the SOS debugger extension is tied to a specific version of the CLR and ships as part of the redistributable package. Because the loadby debugger command finds the correct version of SOS (based on specified dll), typically there is no need to know the exact location of SOS (or even which CLR version is being used). The one caveat with CLR 4.0 is that the mscrowks.dll has been replaced with the clr.dll module. Thus, to load the SOS debugger extension for a CLR 4.0 application, the following command should be used:

```
0:006> .loadby sos clr
```

The new SOS debugger extension contains a bunch of new and exiting commands, as shown in Table 10-1.

Each of the new commands will be covered in the respective sections later in the chapter.

Managed Heap and Garbage Collection

The garbage collector in CLR 4.0 has undergone some really exciting changes/additions primarily in the area of exposing additional diagnostics and the addition of a new garbage collection mode called background garbage collection. In this part of the chapter, we will take a look at the additional diagnostics information followed by the background garbage collection mode.

Table 10-1 New SOS 4.0 Commands

Name	Description
ThreadState	Translates a thread state to a textual representation.
COMState	Outputs the apartment model for each thread in the process.
DumpSigElem	Outputs a single element in a signature object.
VerifyObj	Checks the object passed in for signs of corruption.
FindRoots	Sets a breakpoint that causes the debugger to stop the next time a garbage collection occurs (in any generation or specified generation).
HeapStat	Outputs a detailed breakdown of each generation including the sizes of each heap, total, and free space.
GCWhere	Shows the location of the specified object on the managed heap (including which generation the object lives in).
ListNearObj (lno)	Outputs the object preceding and succeeding the specified object.
FindAppDomain	Finds the application domain of the specified object.
AnalyzeOOM (ao)	Outputs information on the last out-of-memory exception that occurred as a result of an allocation request.

Extended Diagnostics

In Chapter 5, "Managed Heap and Garbage Collection," we took a close look at the internals of the managed heap and garbage collector (GC). We extensively utilized the SOS debugger commands to gain insight into how the GC works and what information we can use to troubleshoot difficult application problems. With CLR 4.0, the SOS debugger extension has been extended to include a new set of commands that further aid in troubleshooting application problems related to the GC. In this section, we will take a look at these new commands and how they can be used.

VerifyObj

The first command of interest is the `VerifyObj` command, which has the following syntax:

```
!VerifyObj <object address>
```

The command takes an object address and checks the object for possible signs of corruption. The algorithm used to detect corruption is primarily in the area of making sure that the method table is intact both with the actual object and any contained objects. If you suspect that a heap corruption is rearing its head, the output of this command can serve as a quick indicator. Here is an example of a corrupt object and the output of the `VerifyObj` command:

```
0:000> !VerifyObj 0x02126804
object 0x2126804 does not have valid method table
```

FindRoots

Finding the reason why an object has not yet been collected can be a tedious process. Objects that have "simple" roots are relatively straightforward, but at times, an object's root can be less than straightforward to spot. For example, if an object has a cross-generational reference to it and the referencing generation has not yet been collected, the object will still appear to be live and well. To make life easier when detecting these cross-generational references, the `FindRoots` command can be used:

```
!FindRoots -gen <N> | -gen any | <object address>
```

The `FindRoots` command instructs the runtime to set a breakpoint the next time a garbage collection occurs in the specified generation (using the gen `<N>` switch) or anytime a garbage collection occurs regardless of the generation (using the gen `any` switch). After the breakpoint hits, the `FindRoots` command can be fed an object's address to display the roots for the object.

The first step in the process is typically finding the generation that the object belongs to by using the `GCWhere` command:

```
0:003> !GCWhere 00b08580
Address   Gen   Heap   segment    begin      allocated    size
00b0b400  0     0      00b00000   00b01000   00b0c010     0xc(12)
```

The output shows that the object at address `0x00b08580` belongs to generation 0.

Next, we use the `FindRoots` command to break on the next garbage collection that occurs in the generation and resume execution:

```
0:003> !FindRoots -gen any
0:003> g
(710.970): CLR notification exception - code e0444143 (first chance)
CLR notification: GC - Performing a gen 2 collection. Determined surviving
```

objects...
First chance exceptions are reported before any exception handling.
This exception may be expected and handled.
eax=0013f118 ebx=00000000 ecx=00000000 edx=00000006 esi=0013f1dc edi=00000003
eip=7c812afb esp=0013f114 ebp=0013f168 iopl=0   nv up ei pl nz na pe nc
cs=001b ss=0023 ds=0023 es=0023 fs=003b gs=0000   efl=00000206
KERNEL32!RaiseException+0x53:
7c812afb 5e   pop   esi

After the breakpoint is hit, we can use the `FindRoots` command with the object's address to find out the roots of the object:

```
0:000> !FindRoots 00b0b400
Scan Thread 0 OSTHread 970
ESP:13fac8:Root:  01b01010(System.Object[])->
  00b0ab38(System.Collections.Hashtable)->
  00b0ab70(System.Collections.Hashtable+bucket[])->
  00b0b400(System.Int32)
Scan Thread 2 OSTHread acc
DOMAIN(0016CB98):HANDLE(Pinned):9713fc:Root:  01b01010(System.Object[])->
  00b0ab38(System.Collections.Hashtable)->
  00b0ab70(System.Collections.Hashtable+bucket[])->
  00b0b400(System.Int32)
```

HeapStat

The `HeapStat` command shows a nice and detailed breakdown of the used and free bytes for each generation on each managed heap. Additionally, it provides a summary view showing free versus used memory (as a percentage) on the small object heap (SOH) and large object heap (LOH). The syntax of the command is

```
!HeapStat [-inclUnrooted | -iu]
```

The default output shows all rooted objects. The `inclUnrooted` (or `iu` shortcut) switch can be used to include all rooted as well as unrooted objects. Here is an example of running the `HeapStat` command on the `0500M.exe` application:

```
0:004> !HeapStat
Heap     Gen0    Gen1    Gen2    LOH
Heap0  2166844 134200  159064  33328

Free space                        Percentage
Heap0  1865804    12      36     96   SOH: 75% LOH:  0%
```

The output shows both how much memory is in use: 2.1MB in Gen 0, 134KB in Gen 1, 159KB in Gen 2, and finally 33KB in the LOH. The free space indicates that there is 1.8MB available in Gen 0, and 12 and 36 in Gen 1 and Gen 2, respectively.

GCWhere

In Chapter 5, we described the process of finding out to which generation a particular object belonged. The process involved dumping out the managed heap segments (using the eeheap command) and then matching the address of the object to one of the segments listed in the output (output specifies which generation each segment corresponds to). This process may work fine if you're only trying to find the generation of one or two objects, but any more than that and it becomes rather tedious. Fortunately, SOS 4.0 introduces a command called GCWhere that displays information about the object passed in as an argument. The syntax of the command is

```
!GCWhere <object address>
```

Here is an example of the output when ran against a FileStream object:

```
0:000> !GCWhere 0x01efd3f8
Address   Gen   Heap   segment    begin     allocated        size
01efd3f8   0     0      01ea0000   01ea1000   020f99cc       0x50(80)
```

The output shows the address of the object in question (0x01efd3f8), the generation to which the object belongs (Gen 0), the managed heap (0), the segment pointer (0x01ea0000), the starting address of the segment (0x01ea1000), number of bytes allocated on the segment (0x020f99c), and finally the size of the object (0x50). Please note that the size is not the recursive size (i.e., does not include the size of child objects).

ListNearObj

The ListNearObj command can be used to validate the consistency of the heap. The command takes an object address as an argument and attempts to validate both the object before and after the specified object. The syntax of the command is shown here:

```
!ListNearObj <object address>
```

For example, running the ListNearObj against an object that is valid and is surrounded by valid objects yields the following output:

```
0:000> !ListNearObj 0x01efd3f8
Before:  01efd3c8   48 (0x30)   System.Collections.Hashtable+bucket[]
Current: 01efd3f8   80 (0x50)   System.IO.FileStream
After:   01efd448   28 (0x1c)   System.String
Heap local consistency confirmed.
```

The output is broken down into the `before`, `current`, and `after` followed by the result of the validation. The before, current, and after sections specify the object's address, size, and type. In the preceding example, all three objects were considered valid and therefore the command considers the heap local consistency to be intact. If, on the other hand, we run the command against an object that is corrupted (where the size of the object has been overwritten), we see the following output:

```
0:000> !ListNearObj 0x01efd3f8
Before:  01efd3c8            48 (0x30)   System.Collections.Hashtable+bucket[]
After:   01efd448            28 (0x1c)   System.String
Heap local consistency not confirmed.
```

AnalyzeOOM

In Chapter 5, we took a look at a few sample applications that were developed in such a way to cause an out-of-memory exception to be thrown. We also showed how we can analyze the managed heap to get more information as to the source of the out-of-memory exception. SOS 4.0 introduces a new command called `AnalyzeOOM` that helps in the out-of-memory diagnosis process. The syntax for the command is shown here:

```
!AnalyzeOOM
```

Let's use a small application called `100OM.exe` to illustrate how the command can be used. The `100OM.exe` application simply sits in a tight loop and allocates large amounts of memory until the memory is exhausted. Run the application under the debugger until the out-of-memory exception is thrown:

```
(2b14.281c): C++ EH exception - code e06d7363 (first chance)
(2b14.281c): CLR exception - code e0434352 (first chance)
ModLoad: 75370000 75378000   C:\Windows\system32\VERSION.dll

Unhandled Exception: OutOfMemoryException.
(2b14.281c): CLR exception - code e0434352 (!!! second chance !!!)
eax=0030edc0 ebx=00000005 ecx=00000005 edx=00000000 esi=0030ee6c edi=003fa160
```

```
eip=75e242eb esp=0030edc0 ebp=0030ee10 iopl=0         nv up ei pl nz ac pe nc
cs=001b  ss=0023  ds=0023  es=0023  fs=003b  gs=0000             efl=00000216
KERNEL32!RaiseException+0x58:
75e242eb c9              leave
```

Next, we execute the `AnalyzeOOM` command:

```
0:000> !AnalyzeOOM
Managed OOM occured after GC #247 (Requested to allocate 1048576 bytes)
Reason: Low on memory during GC
Detail: SOH: Failed to reserve memory (16777216 bytes)
```

The output tells us that an out-of-memory condition occurred after the 247th garbage collection and that the requested amount of memory was `1048576`. It also gives us the reason behind the condition (low on memory during garbage collection). Lastly, the details section tells us that it failed to reserve `16777216` bytes of memory, which corresponds to the smallest segment size on the small object heap.

In our example, it's quite clear why the out-of-memory condition occurred, but there may be other reasons such as the CLR attempting to allocate internal data structures or other components throwing out-of-memory exceptions.

Background Garbage Collection

Prior to CLR 4.0, the garbage collector could work in two different modes. The first mode is known as the workstation mode (or concurrent GC) and targets applications running on workstations such as UI applications. The second mode, known as server mode (or blocking GC), targets server-side applications that typically do not require any UI. The reason behind having two modes lies primarily in the response time while a garbage collection occurs. As we discussed in Chapter 5, after a garbage collection is underway, the execution engine and associated managed threads must be periodically suspended to avoid triggering another garbage collection. This suspension of managed threads can obviously create a short pause that can manifest itself to users of the application. In the case of workstation type of applications with a UI, this can result in the UI flashing or other subtle nuances such as lag times between a user click and the action associated with the click. In these cases, it is crucial that the amount of time that threads stay in a suspended mode be as small as possible. The concurrent (or workstation) GC accomplishes this by only suspending all the managed threads twice during a GC rather than throughout the entire duration, as is the case with the server GC. During the time that the managed threads are not suspended, they are allowed to keep allocating memory up until the end of the ephemeral segment. If the ephemeral segment is exhausted while a concurrent GC is underway, the managed threads are suspended until the concurrent GC completes (turning the concurrent GC into a blocking GC). In essence, this means that as long as the ephemeral segment is not exhausted, lag times can be avoided.

On the other hand, the server GC doesn't have to worry about immediate response times as much as the workstation GC, because most server applications don't have the need for immediate response times (such as in the case of UI applications). Instead of allowing allocations to occur while the GC is working, the server mode GC keeps all managed threads suspended throughout the duration of a GC. Although this may result in a nonvisible lag time while a GC is underway, the benefit of a server GC is higher throughput primarily due to not having to worry about other managed threads working at the same time. Additionally, in a server GC, each processor has a dedicated GC thread which, in turn, means that we can have X GCs happen at the same time (where X is number of processors° number of cores).

One of the primary drawbacks with the existing concurrent GC is that it works really well with applications that have relatively small-sized managed heaps (remember that as long as the ephemeral segment is not exhausted, managed threads can keep allocating memory). In today's world, it is not uncommon to have applications whose managed heaps are in the gigabytes. In these cases, lag times can still be experienced since the concurrent GC becomes a blocking GC when the ephemeral segment limit has been reached. To address this deficiency, CLR 4.0 replaces the concurrent GC with what is known as the background GC. The biggest difference between a concurrent GC and a background GC is that the background GC allows for a full GC and allocations to happen at the same time as well as allowing a collection of generation 0 and 1. The background GC periodically checks to see if a concurrent allocation resulted in a GC in an ephemeral segment and if so, suspends itself and allows the ephemeral GC to take place (foreground GC). This means that although a full GC is taking place, we still have the capability to get rid of dead short-lived objects. Because the background GC allows for collections in generation 0 and 1, what happens if the threshold of the ephemeral segment is reached? In this case, the foreground GC grows the ephemeral segment as needed.

To summarize, server GCs always block throughout the duration of a GC. To avoid lag times during this suspension, the workstation GC was introduced, which minimizes the time threads spend in the suspended state during a GC. Although this approach works well with applications that have a relatively small managed heap foot print, lag times can still be observed if the ephemeral segment is exhausted. This deficiency led to an evolution of the workstation GC called the background GC, which allows for true concurrent allocations and ephemeral collections (and segment expansion if needed).

Please note that in CLR 4.0, the background GC is only available in workstation mode.

Synchronization

In Chapter 6, "Synchronization," we took a look at the most commonly used synchronization primitives in .NET 2.0 as well as the internals of synchronization in the CLR. In .NET 4.0, a lot of great additions have been made in the form of enhancing existing synchronization primitives as well as adding new ones. In this part of the chapter, we will take a look at some of the additions and enhancements made in .NET 4.0.

Thread Pool and Tasks

The thread pool that is available in CLR 2.0 provides a nice mechanism of queuing up work and having that work eventually be executed by one of the threads in the thread pool. The great thing about the thread pool is that you can leave the decision of which thread gets to execute which work item up to the underlying runtime. This approach works well because the thread pool has the most knowledge about what is being executed and which threads are the most appropriate to serve other requests. Having said that, at the end of the day, the runtime really only knows that it has a queue of "work items" and a bunch of threads to service those requests. This can lead to less than optimal performance because work items that, for example, are related can't be ordered properly for optimal performance (after all, the thread pool picks up new requests in a FIFO fashion). Furthermore, although an implementation detail, the data structures associated with the queue itself, as well as the cost of locking that queue every time a work item is enqueued and dequeued, adds to the overall cost. To address the locking inefficiency, .NET 4.0 switched to a lock-free data structure to avoid the performance cost of constantly locking and unlocking. Additionally, it changed the data structure by making it more GC friendly, thereby speeding up the collection of these data structures. Although these two improvements will yield gains in performance, it still doesn't address the fact that the thread pool knows nothing about the work items themselves. They are simply treated as opaque items in a FIFO order. If we could somehow tell the thread pool more about the work items, the order in which they were serviced could be optimally organized. It turns out that .NET 4.0 addresses this problem also by introducing what is known as the Task Parallel library (TPL). Although we won't go into the details of the TPL (`System.Threading.Tasks`), suffice to say that it exposes a much richer API set that allows the details of work items to be more clearly defined, thereby allowing more efficient scheduling and execution of the tasks.

10. CLR 4.0

Monitor

In Chapter 6, we looked at an application that utilized the `Abort` API to terminate a thread. We also discussed the internal workings of aborting a thread and how it can cause problems when it comes to threads that have taken a lock (using the `lock` statement). The fundamental problem was in the IL that was generated by the compiler. More specifically, a `nop` instruction was inserted before the try block. The net result is that if the `ThreadAbortException` was thrown while executing the `nop` instruction, the `finally` clause would never execute and hence the lock would never be released. To solve this problem, .NET 4.0 introduces an overloaded version of the `Monitor.Enter` method:

```
public static void Enter(Object obj, ref bool lockTaken)
```

The `lockTaken` argument is `true` if the lock was in fact acquired; otherwise, it is `false`. This new overloaded method allows the following pattern:

```
bool acquired=false;

try
{
    Monitor.Enter(objToLock, ref acquired);

    // Do work while holding the lock
}
Finally
{
    if(acquired)
    {
        Monitor.Exit(objToLock);
    }
}
```

The IL that the compiler now generates for a `lock` statement has also been updated to follow the same pattern and always takes the lock inside of the try statement, thereby guaranteeing that the lock is released in the finally clause even in the presence of `ThreadAbortExceptions`.

Barrier

A Barrier (`System.Threading.Barrier`) can best be thought of as a way of sequencing a series of operations by using one or more explicit checkpoints that have to be reached before the operation is complete. For example, let's say that we have a task that requires a number of buffers to be populated followed by using the data across the buffers in various calculations. Before the second phase (performing calculations) can start, all the buffers need to be filled in. By creating a Barrier that contains X number of participants, each participant can't execute each of the phases (write, read) and use the barrier after each phase to wait for all the other participants before resuming.

CountdownEvent

The `CountdownEvent` class (`System.Threading.CountdownEvent`) is a counting event that is only signaled when its count reaches 0.

ManualResetEventSlim

The `ManualResetEventSlim` class (`System.Threading.ManualReset EventSlim`) is similar to the already existing `ManualResetEvent`. The key difference is that the newly introduced `ManualResetEventSlim` primitive will utilize spinning first in order to acquire a lock that has already been acquired. If, within a given spin threshold, the lock still can't be acquired, it enters a wait state (such as the case with `ManualResetEvent`). Because entering a wait state is not required by default, the data structures that are required for this wait state need not be allocated, which is why the name includes the word `Slim`. Please note that in contrast to the `ManualResetEvent` class, the Slim version can only be used intraprocess.

SemaphoreSlim

Much like the `ManualResetEventSlim` discussed, the `Semaphore` class also contains an efficient and Slim (spinning) version called `SemaphoreSlim` (`System.Threading.SemaphoreSlim`). Please note that in contrast to the `Semaphore` class, the Slim version can only be used intraprocess.

SpinWait and SpinLock

In cases where the amount of time that any given lock is held is small, spinning may be a more resource-efficient way of waiting for a lock to be released. The primary reason is that rather than allocate the resource needed (such as an event) to enter a wait state, the thread can simply spin and check to see if the lock has become available. The cost of spinning, in short-lived lock scenarios, is far smaller than the equivalent resources required for an efficient wait. The `SpinLock` class (`System.Threading`) can be used when you want to utilize only the spinning aspects of a lock, whereas the

SpinWait (`System.Threading`) class can be used if you want to spin for a little bit before entering a wait state.

Interoperability

Just as other areas of CLR 4.0 have undergone some dramatic improvements, so has interoperability. One of the major headaches with doing COM interoperability is the use of the primary interop assembly (PIA). We already discussed the PIA in Chapter 7, "Interoperability," in great length; to recap, the PIA is a separate assembly that acts as a managed code "proxy" to the underlying COM object. The biggest drawback with a PIA is that it is in fact a separate assembly that has to accompany the application using it, which causes problems in the area of deployment such as versioning and size. For example, to use a PIA, the entire PIA has to be deployed with the application even if only small portions of the PIA are actually being used. To address this problem, CLR 4.0 introduces what is known as COM interop via NoPIA (No Primary Interop Assembly). This can be achieved by embedding all the necessary information that is required to call the COM object into the application itself, thereby eliminating the need for separate deployment of the PIA as well as taking the size hit if only portions of it are being used. In Chapter 7, "Interoperability," we looked at a simple example (`07ComInterop.exe`) of COM interop using a PIA. The example required a separate PIA assembly to function. To use the new NoPIA with the same example, we can use the exact same code with the minor exception of how the application is built. Rather than referencing the PIA assembly as part of the build, we now can use the `/link` compiler switch (new in CLR 4.0) to specify a PIA assembly and tell the compiler to embed the metadata into our application. Please note that it will only embed the metadata that is being used in the application, hence reducing the size requirements drastically if only small portions are being utilized.

Another major enhancement is around making it easier to write P/Invoke signatures. A new tool was created called the P/Invoke Interop Assistant and is available on CodePlex:

```
http://www.codeplex.com/clrinterop
```

The P/Invoke Interop Assistant tool generates the signatures and wrappers by reading the information in the `windows.h` header file, which contains a lot of the function exposed by Windows. In addition, it also understands the SAL annotations that have now become standard practice for functions available in Windows, thus making it easier for the tool to generate accurate signatures and wrappers. Figure 10-1 shows an example of the tool and the generated code for the `CreateFileW` API.

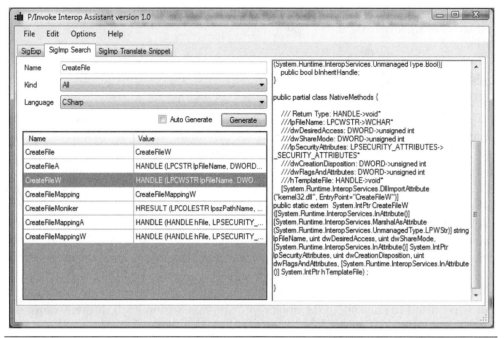

Figure 10-1   Example of P/Invoke Interop Assistant

Lastly, the `RCWCleanupList` command was available but undocumented in SOS 2.0 and is now fully documented and functional in SOS 4.0. The command displays the global list of runtime callable wrappers that are no longer in use and are in the queue to be cleaned up:

```
0:000> !RCWCleanupList
MTA Interfaces to be released: 0
STA Interfaces to be released: 1
```

Postmortem Debugging

There have been some exciting changes in the area of postmortem debugging for CLR 4.0. In Chapter 8, "Postmortem Debugging," we discussed various options of enabling a JIT debugger for managed code. We showed how the `AeDebug` registry key can be used to enable JIT debugging capabilities for native code and the equivalent `DbgManagedDebugger` registry key for managed code. In CLR 4.0, these two keys have been unified and only looks at the `AeDebug` key to determine when to launch a JIT debugger (native or managed code). This greatly simplifies the process of automating the JIT debugging experience.

Summary

.NET 4.0 represents the latest update to the .NET framework and contains an incredible wealth of new features, ranging from exciting new framework additions to serious enhancements in the runtime in areas such as performance, reliability, and security.

Throughout the book, we have discussed specific debugging scenarios, and in this chapter, we detailed some of the scenarios and the differences encountered when using .NET 4.0. The discussion started with the new tool requirements and then showed the specific debugging scenarios related to a specific technology, such as the managed heap and garbage collector, synchronization, interoperability, and more.

INDEX

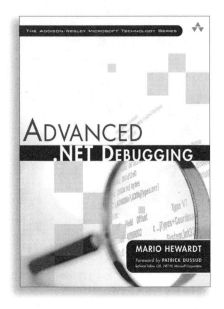

FREE Online Edition

Your purchase of **Advanced .NET Debugging** includes access to a free online edition for 45 days through the Safari Books Online subscription service. Nearly every Addison-Wesley Professional book is available online through Safari Books Online, along with more than 5,000 other technical books and videos from publishers such as Cisco Press, Exam Cram, IBM Press, O'Reilly, Prentice Hall, Que, and Sams.

SAFARI BOOKS ONLINE allows you to search for a specific answer, cut and paste code, download chapters, and stay current with emerging technologies.

Activate your FREE Online Edition at
www.informit.com/safarifree

> **STEP 1:** Enter the coupon code: VHFJAZG.

> **STEP 2:** New Safari users, complete the brief registration form.
> Safari subscribers, just log in.

If you have difficulty registering on Safari or accessing the online edition,
please e-mail customer-service@safaribooksonline.com